GERMAN RAILWAYS

PART 1. LOCOMOTIVES & MULTIPLE UNITS OF DEUTSCHE BAHN

SIXTH EDITION

The complete guide to all Locomotives and Multiple Units of Deutsche Bahn

Brian Garvin

Published by Platform 5 Publishing Ltd., 52 Broadfield Road, Sheffield S8 0XJ, England.

Printed in England by The Lavenham Press, Lavenham, Suffolk.

ISBN 978 1 909431 53 9

Above: One of the last locomotive classes procured by DR, Class 114 is likely to see its work taken over by new Classes 147, 445 and 446 in the future. Still looking in good condition, 114 031 is seen passing Weiterstadt on 23 June 2016. **Keith Fender**

Front cover: Diesel Vectron 247 903 is leased by DB Cargo and nominally allocated to Halle, but is seen stabled on Seelze depot on 5 May 2018. **Brian Garvin**

Back cover, top: DB has leased a number of hybrid locomotives from Alstom for assessment. 1002 008 stands at Nürnberg Hbf on 24 February 2017, carrying a special livery to emphasise its green credentials. **Brian Garvin**

Back cover, bottom: 423 044 and 423 040 (nearest the camera) leave Neuss Hbf with an S-Bahn route S11 service to Düsseldorf Flughafen Terminal on 2 April 2015. **Robert Pritchard**

CONTENTS

Foreword 4

Acknowledgements 4

Historical Background 4

Getting there from Great Britain 5

DB Fares.. 5

Organisation of German Railways 6

Locomotive & Multiple Unit Numbering System.................................... 7

Layout of Information 9

Foreign Motive Power in Germany 11

Maps of the German Railway Network 13

1. Electric Locomotives 23

2. Main Line Diesel Locomotives.. 51

3. Diesel Shunting Locomotives 68

    3.1 Standard Gauge... 68

    3.2 Narrow Gauge 76

    3.3 Hybrid Locomotives 76

4. Inter-City Express (ICE) 77

5. Electric Multiple Units... 97

6. Diesel Multiple Units... 150

7. Self-Propelled Departmental Vehicles 180

8. Internal User Locomotives.. 190

9. Preserved Locomotives & Railcars 192

    9.1. Steam Locomotives 192

    9.2. Electric Locomotives... 203

    9.3. Diesel Locomotives 206

    9.4. Electric Multiple Units 215

    9.5. Diesel Multiple Units 217

Appendix I. Builders.. 220

Appendix II. Vehicle Type Codes for Railcars & Multiple Units 221

Appendix III. Common Terms in German and English 221

Appendix IV. DB Depot Codes 222

Appendix V. Abbreviations 223

FOREWORD

In the five years since the previous edition of this book the DB organisation has been fairly stable with privatisation well on the back burner. But there have been changes. DB Fernverkehr is concentrating on its core business of ICE and IC services with new trains being delivered and services expanded. The future is ICE4 trains being constructed each year until circa 2030 with double-deck IC trains to replace some existing services and indeed to allow new IC routes to be introduced. On the negative side Fernverkehr gave up running overnight sleeping car trains (which have mostly been taken up by Austrian Federal Railways) and has absorbed the Westerland car train shuttles into the main business so DB Auto Zug no longer exists. DB Regio continues with varying success with new contracts and has been held up with its plans by the extremely slow certification of its new double-deck EMUs. During 2017/18 approval was eventually given with over 100 new power cars entering service quite rapidly.

On the freight side the wheel has gone full circle as DB Schenker Rail has reverted to being called DB Cargo. As a company it now has subsidiaries in many countries and now wants its locomotives to work through on international services. To a certain extent this was already happening with the 185s and 189s but now it has ordered Siemens Vectron locomotives with a view to them working throughout on trains from Italy to North Sea ports and similar services from elsewhere. The active locomotives of Classes 151 and 155 have all been sold and leased back. This is obviously a financial arrangement presumably to release finance to purchase the new locomotives. Several shunting locomotives that were in departmental use have been reinstated as full traffic locomotives but others remain confined to depot shunting. Both Fernverkehr and Regio have new shunting locomotives on trial but interestingly Cargo has not!

The infrastructure companies have received some new stock whilst a revised version of the Tunnel Rescue Trains has seen Class 212s and 714s rebuilt with new cabs and other improvements. Older departmental units are being withdrawn and replaced by new rail vehicles or even road-rail vehicles.

Details of new, withdrawn and transferred locomotives etc regularly appear in the Platform 5 magazine *Today's Railways Europe.*

This new edition is updated to September 2018.

Brian Garvin

ACKNOWLEDGEMENTS

Data for this book has been collected from many sources including magazines, books, internet sites and individuals. The following magazines should be particularly mentioned: Bahn Report, Drehscheibe, Eisenbahn Revue International, Eisenbahn Kurier, Locomotive Club of Great Britain *BULLETIN,* LOK-Report and the Platform 5 Publishing magazine *Today's Railways Europe.* On the internet the websites of LOK-Report, Elektrolok, Drehscheibe-online and Revisionsdaten have been particularly useful. Thanks to all those people that submitted photographs including Matthias Müller and Keith Fender and others who are individually credited. Thanks must also go to Peter Grosse who keeps us all up to date providing DB statistical data for *Today's Railways Europe* magazine.

GERMANY

HISTORICAL BACKGROUND

After World War II Germany (*Deutschland* in German) was split up by the allies. The Soviets took part of eastern Poland with that country shifting westwards to the "Oder-Neisse Line". The remainder of Germany was divided up with the Soviets getting the eastern part and eastern Berlin and the three Western Allies getting western Berlin and the western part of the country. Eventually the allies grouped their parts together to form the *Bundesrepublik Deutschland* (BRD) which had Bonn as its capital and the eastern zone (Soviet) becoming the *Deutsche Demokratische Republik* (DDR) with East Berlin as its capital. At the end of the 1980s the communist countries started to collapse allowing the unification of the two Germanys which was achieved on 3 October 1990. In effect the DDR applied to join the BRD. The locomotive fleets were merged but passenger and freight traffic in the former East Germany was decimated and consequently many former DR types have been scrapped.

LANGUAGE

The standard language in Germany is, of course, German. However many people can speak very good English, but older people in the former DDR often cannot speak English, as the main foreign language which used to be taught in schools was Russian. The situation is changing rapidly and English speakers should not find too many problems.

GETTING THERE FROM GREAT BRITAIN

By Rail

Eurostar services run daily from London St. Pancras to Brussels Midi taking around 2h30. There are onward connections to Köln (Cologne) by Thalys and DB ICEs calling at Aachen Hbf. If you want to avoid supplements take an IC to Liège or Welkenraedt from where there is an hourly local to Aachen. Eupen has frequent buses which stop outside Aachen Hbf.

By Sea

Stena Line offers a Harwich–Hoek van Holland overnight service, but Hoek van Holland to Rotterdam is in the process of being converted to be part of Rotterdam Metro. Onward connections are available on the NS from Rotterdam via Arnhem/Emmerich or via Hengelo/Bad Bentheim; going via Venlo means a change of train into a stopping service into Germany.

By Air

There are flights from all London airports and many regional airports direct to many German Airports. Berlin, Dresden, Düsseldorf, Frankfurt/Main, Hamburg, Stuttgart and München (Munich) airports are all rail-connected (Bremen is even tram connected!), as are the London airports of Gatwick, Heathrow, Luton and Stansted and the British regional airports at Birmingham and Manchester. Newcastle Airport is served by the Tyne & Wear Metro. The low cost carriers are also useful often serving areas different to the main players.

DB FARES

DB has set fares but there are many discounts available that can be obtained either by purchasing a "Bahncard" or by booking in advance on specific trains with many offers available on the DB website.

There are three Bahncards available, Bahncard 25 costing €100 first class or €50 second class per annum and giving a 25% discount on fares, Bahncard 50 costing €400 first class or €200 second class and giving a 50% discount and Bahncard 100 costing €5000 first class or €3000 second class which is an all-line pass for the year. The Bahncard 50 is available at half-price to children aged 6–17, students aged 18–25 and seniors (over 60).

Sparpreis tickets are quota-controlled and only valid on the trains stated. *Sparpreis 25* gives a 25% discount and requires a 3-day advance purchase. *Sparpreis 50* gives a 50% discount and requires a 3-day advance purchase but is valid only at the weekend, or for a journey involving a Saturday night away.

PASSES (ROVER TICKETS)

Without doubt the Lander tickets and the Schoneswochenende tickets represent good value especially now that some of the former are valid for 1–5 persons and also available at weekends as well. Valid only on Regio services after 09.00. Many are valid also on in town trams and buses in "Verbund" areas. Another useful ticket for a long journey is the Quer durch Deutschland ticket valid after 09.00 on Regio services. It pays to shop around. The DB website and www.diebefoerderer.de contain lots of information on validity.

The Platform 5 magazine *Today's Railways Europe* has, each spring, articles giving the latest information on rail passes in Europe.

ORGANISATION OF GERMAN RAILWAYS

EISENBAHNBUNDESAMT (EBA)

This company has a great influence on current events. The Eisenbahn Bundesamt (German Federal Railway Authority) or EBA was set up to cover areas thought not to be part of the new railway companies' remits. It is responsible amongst other things for: the certification of locomotives and rolling stock; the overall supervision of the railways, and is in effect a government department.

DEUTSCHE BAHN AG (DB AG = DB)

The major railways of Germany were nationalised after World War I becoming the *Deutsche Reichsbahn*. After the Second World War the *Bundesrepublik* called its railway system the *Deutsche Bundesbahn* (DB) and the railway of the *Deutsche Demokratische Republik* retained the pre-war name. In this book the pre-war Reichsbahn is referred to as DRG (*Deutsche Reichsbahn Gesellschaft*) whilst the post-war Reichsbahn is referred to as simply DR.

Although split into two systems by the aftermath of the second world war, the DB and DR worked closely together and numbered their loco fleets so that numbers did not clash, so that once Germany was reunited there would be no problem in combining the railways. For example the DB numbered its new electric locos as E10 whilst the DR had E11. Similarly the DB had E40, E41 and the DR E42. Then in the 1960s came the Berlin Wall and all cooperation came to a halt as the eastern part of the country was sealed off. The real break then came with computerisation when DR adopted a completely different system to the DB. It was no doubt done deliberately just to show that DR was in charge of its own house and was probably ordered from on high.

The combined West German *Deutsche Bundesbahn* (DB) and East German *Deutsche Reichsbahn* (DR) were merged into a new public limited company in 1994 known as *Deutsche Bahn AG*. This company adopted the DB numbering system with most DR stock having been renumbered from 01/01/92 in anticipation or the merger.

DBAG is a holding company for the various "sectors" which are now self-standing subsidiaries, the principal ones being as follows:

DB Fernverkehr AG: This is the long distance operator but also operates car train shuttles from Niebüll to Westerland and the narrow gauge line on Wangerooge.
DB Regio AG: This is the company responsible for local and regional passenger trains once the "Nahverkehr" sector. DB Regio has many subsidiaries for particular areas e.g. DB Regionalbahn Rhein-Ruhr GmbH Essen, DB Zug Bus Regionalverkehr Alb Bodensee GmbH, Ulm etc.
S-Bahn Berlin GmbH: A separate company for the Berlin S-Bahn.
S-Bahn Hamburg GmbH: A separate company for the Hamburg S-Bahn.
S-Bahn München GmbH: A separate company for the München S-Bahn.
Userdomer Bäderbahn GmbH: DB Regio formed a separate company to cover the lines on the Island of Usedom which may now revert to being part of the main business.
DB Cargo AG: The freight train operator formerly known as DB Schenker Rail, Railion and before that DB Cargo!
DB Netze: This is the infrastructure company, the "Network Rail" of Germany but with differing responsibilities to its British counterpart.
DB Stations & Service: This company manages the stations, terminals and land.
DB Bahnbau GmbH: A general engineering company for track, bridges, embankments etc.
DB Gleisbau GmbH: A track renewal company.
DB Systemtechnik: The former research and test centres of Halle, Minden and München.

ROLLING STOCK OF DBAG SUBSIDIARIES

DB Fernverkehr. The intercity operator is in charge of the ICE, IC and EC networks. Its main depots are at Hamburg (Eidelstedt), Berlin (Rummelsburg), Frankfurt/M (Griesheim), München Hbf, Leipzig and Köln.

DB Regio. This sector has been going through a rough patch. Not so long ago it took years to get its Class 442s into service and more recently this scenario has been repeated with the 445s. But they started entering service in December 2017 and during 2018 there will be a big knock-on effect. Electrification plans will cause more changes in the years ahead.

DB Cargo. The last ten years have seen the electric fleet renewed with new Classes 185, 189 and 193, but the diesel fleet has been stable for some time. However, DB Cargo is now assessing the diesel version of the Vectron so there may be some movement there soon. No new shunting locomotives have been ordered.

ELECTRIFICATION

Much of the German network is electrified on the overhead system at 15 kV AC 16.7 Hz. This system is also used in Switzerland and Austria, permitting through running of locos. Thus DB locos are commonplace in Austria running right over the Brenner Pass to the Italian border. Austrian locos also work deep into Germany. All electric locos and multiple units are assumed to work on the 15 kV AC system unless stated otherwise. Much time and effort has gone into the new high speed line from Erfurt to Nürnberg which opened in December 2017. Now attention can be given to other areas with München to Lindau work starting early in 2018 with other schemes gathering momentum e.g. Ulm–Friedrichshafen–Lindau, Nürnberg–Hof, Regensburg–Marktredwitz, the Breisgau S-Bahn area and Herzogenrath to the Dutch border.

DB TRAIN SERVICES

These are classified as follows:

IC   Intercity. An interconnecting network between major centres offering a high standard of accommodation.
EC   Eurocity. Similar to IC, but running between different countries.
ECE   Eurocity Express
ICE   Intercity Express. The high-speed Intercity train offering a very high standard of accommodation in new trains.
IRE   Inter Regio Express. The same as RE but between *Länder*.
D   Express train (Schnellzug).
RE   Regional Express (semi-fast).
RB   Regionalbahn (local train).
S   S-Bahn (train on suburban network).
NJ   Night Jet overnight trains operated by ÖBB.

Supplements are payable for travel on ICE, IC, EC, ECE; overnight trains often feature "Global Pricing".

For freight trains DB Cargo has many different classifications, far too many to list individually.

LOCOMOTIVE & MULTIPLE UNIT NUMBERING SYSTEM

The present day DB numbering system can be traced back to that introduced in 1923 when the German railways were nationalised and became the Deutsche Reichsbahn. The system was one that we are now quite used to as it involved having a class number followed by the running number e.g. 01 001. The Reichsbahn grouped its locomotives into definite series. Express passenger locomotives were 01–19, freight locomotives were 50–59 etc. This system was also used for electric locomotives with the addition of an "E" prefix e.g. E04 02. However when it came to diesel locos the class number used was an indication of the horse power and the prefix used was "V" (Verbrennungsmotoren = internal combustion engine). EMUs were "ET" (T = Triebwagen = railcar) whilst DMUs were "VT".

This system remained in use until 1968 when the DB was one of the first railways in Europe to computerise its locomotive numbers. In the new system the locomotive numbers are divided into three parts, all of which are numeric. The first part is the class number, usually the existing number with an additional digit to denote the type of traction being inserted in front of the former class number. The running number follows which is limited to three digits. This does not cause any problems as far as diesels and electrics are concerned but some steam classes had over 1000 locomotives and new numbers had to be given in some cases. Finally a computer check digit is added at the end of the number.

Examples:

E 10 001	became	110 001-5
V 60 150	"	260 150-8
VT24 624	"	624 624-3

The full breakdown of the traction type digits is:

0	Steam locomotive	5	Battery electric railcar (none now remain in service)
1	Electric locomotive	6	Diesel railcar
2	Diesel locomotive	7	Diesel railbus & departmental
3	Shunting tractors	8	Electric railcar trailers
4	Electric railcars	9	Diesel railcar/railbus trailers

After the running number there is a computer check digit which double checks that all the preceding digits are correct. It is arrived at by multiplying the class and running number digits alternately by 1 and 2. The resulting digits are added together and the sum deducted from the next whole ten gives the check number.

Example 624 624-3

$$
\begin{array}{rl}
 & 6+2+4 + 6 \ \ +2+4 \\
\times & \underline{1+2+1 + 2 \ \ +1+2} \\
= & 6+4+4 +1+2+2+8 = 27. \\
 & 30-27 = 3.
\end{array}
$$

EUROPEAN VEHICLE NUMBER & VEHICLE KEEPER MARKING

A new development is the European Vehicle Number (EVN). This is a refinement of the former UIC full identification number. Because of open access in Europe it is essential that all traction (and indeed all rolling stock) has a European number. The Vehicle Keeper Marking (VKM) has been deemed necessary because of the large number of railway operators in a country following open access and follows the country code. This has helped to simplify matters in Germany as many private operators had duplicate numbers. Now they have a unique EVN as well!

Taking electric loco 120 151 as an example its full EVN is 91 80 6120 151-6 D-DB which breaks down as follows:

The first digit is a code for a traction unit with the second digit giving the type of traction. In Germany the types are
90. Miscellaneous traction – mostly used for steam locomotives e.g. 90 80 0001 509-3 D-PRESS but also hybrid locomotives.
91. Electric Locomotives faster than 99 km/h e.g. 91 80 6186 336-4 D-DB
92. Diesel locomotives faster than 99 km/h e.g. 92 80 1261 036-8 D-DB
93. High speed EMU e.g. 93 80 5403 027-6 D-DB
94. EMUs e.g. 94 80 0440 106-3 D-AGIL
95. DMUs e.g. 95 80 0650 067-1 D-ODEG
96. Loose trailers (Not used in Germany)
97. Electric shunting locomotives or electric locomotives with maximum speed less than 100 km/h e.g. 97 80 8194 052-7 D-LEG
98. Diesel shunting locomotives or diesel locomotive with maximum speed less than 100 km/h e.g. 98 80 3363 622-2 D-DB
99. Departmental self powered vehicles – includes tamping machines etc. Because of this several DB departmental locomotives have regained their original numbers.

Note that the old UIC railway number (in this case 80 for DB) now stands for the country and not the railway. The railway concerned is indicated at the end as the vehicle keeper. In some cases this might not be a railway such a leasing company.

It will be seen that the old classification, e.g. 120, forms part of the new number. But in years to come there could be a 5120, 7120 etc. (This is already happening with the new Class 442 EMUs which have appeared as 442, 1442 and 2442!) DB in fact chose the extra digit in the classification to keep existing computer check digits the same but this does not apply to all types, in particular DMU and EMU. The running number and check digit are next followed by a country code and the VKM.

The full EVN/VKM is shown on the sides of locomotives and vehicles and can be very small as it is a rather long piece of information. For this same reason numbers on the front of locomotives and units only show the basic number without a check digit. With this development check digits have not been shown in the main lists.

Of the VKMs shown above, DB is self explanatory, AGIL is AGILIS one of the new private operators whilst ODEG is Ostdeutsche Eisenbahn Gesellschaft. These codes are used in Part 2 of this book to identify the various private operators.

LAYOUT OF INFORMATION

For each class of vehicle general data and dimensions in metric units are provided. Vehicle lengths are lengths over couplers. The following standard abbreviations are used:

km/h	kilometres per hour		m	metres
kN	kilonewtons		mm	millimetres
kW	kilowatts		TE	tractive effort

Builder codes are shown in Appendix I on page 220. For explanation of codes used for accommodation in hauled coaching stock and multiple units see Appendix II is on page 221.

For each vehicle the number is given in the first column. Where a vehicle has been renumbered the former number is generally shown in parentheses after the current number. Further columns show, respectively, the livery (in bold condensed type), any detail differences, the depot allocation and name where appropriate.

Important note: In multiple unit trains, references to number of engines, traction motors etc. should be understood to be per power car, except for articulated units where the total number in the unit is stated. Weights are in full working order, i.e. with a full tank of fuel etc.

DEPOTS

The changing railway structure has had an effect on depots. Many depots have closed since unification especially in the east where the organisation was in a steam era time warp allocating electric locomotives to numerous little depots etc. Traction fleets are concentrated at fewer and fewer depots with some sectorisation of depots taking place. Baden Württemberg is a good example where Mannheim, an obvious freight depot, had many passenger locos allocated. These have now been moved away to depots reopened by DB Regio in Freiburg and Ludwigshafen. Frankfurt/M S-Bahn units are now based in a new depot adjacent to the main station in what was previously the main postal depot.

The use of the depot abbreviations has declined with the new businesses using the full name (in some cases an amended name) of the depot e.g. NN1 formerly Nürnberg Hbf is now Nürnberg West or even Nürnberg Göstenhof. For the depot code we will continue to use NN1. The depots, once known as a Bahnbetriebswerk (Bw) then became a Betriebeshof (Bh) and are in some cases now a Werk. Most people still refer to the depots as a Bw! One change to the branding of locomotives is that instead of just "Nürnberg West" the business concerned is also shown, as two businesses could be at the same depot.

Some new depots have been built in the first instance for Fernverkehr to house new ICE trains, but DB Cargo is also into new depots. These are "Kombi" depots – combined depots for locomotives and rolling stock (wagons). Both depots in Nürnberg have been rebuilt. In Köln the existing depots are to be supplemented by three new ones; there are now two in the Nippes area (ICE and S-Bahn) and the third at the Deutzerfeld site (DMUs). DB Cargo had closed its maintenance facility in Bremen, subcontracting the work to the locomotive works at Bremen-Sebaldsbrück but this works is now closing and the locomotives will probably have to go to Osnabrück or Seelze for maintenance. There is of course "the man in the van" to attend to failures.

A list of depot codes and depots is shown in Appendix IV on page 222.

MAIN WORKS

The workshops after several years in limbo in the run up to anticipated privatisation are now rather firmly based. There have been some closures but Nürnberg once slated for closure is busy refurbishing ICEs and having had workshops modernised now has a secure future with EMU overhauls. Those remaining are:

Works	Code	Workload
Berlin Schöneweide	BSWSX	Berlin S-Bahn units
Bremen	HBX	218,225, 290–295. (In the process of closing, work transferring to Cottbus).
Chemnitz	DCX	Hydraulic transmissions. Part of the works has replaced the old DC depot.
Cottbus	BCSX	232, 233, 234, 290–298, 361–365, 7xx. (also overhauls electric locomotives as required).
Dessau	LDX	Electric locomotives.
Fulda	FFU	Brake-gear (future uncertain).
Kassel	FKX	Diesel multiple units and carriages.
Krefeld-Oppum	KKROX	Electric multiple units – all types including ICEs.
Meiningen	UMX	Steam locomotives and special work.
Neumünster	ANX	Carriages.
Nürnberg	NNX	ICEs being refurbished currently but is also overhauling EMUs of Classes 420, 423, 440, 442.
Paderborn	EPX	Wagons.
Wittenberge	WWX	Carriages and 708.

Having modernised many of the depots these are now able to perform complete overhauls so the workload at the main workshops remains steady. The depots and works belong to a separate maintenance organisation and as such they often take in private operators' locomotives for repairs and overhauls.

▲ 101 056 arrives at Hamburg Harburg with an IC train on 7 May 2018.   **Brian Garvin**

LIVERIES

The standard livery for all DB locomotives and multiple units is red (verkehrsrot – traffic red). However, the Berlin S-Bahn units remain in their traditional colours at the request of Berliners. All ICE trains are white with a red band .

A   Advertising livery.
N   Non-standard livery.
Y   Yellow.

ABBREVIATIONS

The following codes are used in the lists of locomotives which are common to all classes:

a	automatic coupling.		m	multiple working fitted.
c	CIR ELKE.		p	push-pull (KWS).
l	LZB.		r	push-pull (ZWS/ZDS).

A detailed list of abbreviations used in this book can be found in Appendix V on page 223.

FOREIGN MOTIVE POWER IN GERMANY

Germany has important ports at Hamburg, Bremen and Bremerhaven which attract export/import traffic from/to many parts of Europe as well as for Germany itself. There are also big ports in the adjoining countries especially Belgium (Antwerpen) and The Netherlands (Rotterdam and Amsterdam) which produce lots of traffic going to/from and through Germany. Whilst DB Cargo shares in this traffic there are many private operators involved working through from one country to another. Germany-based private operators will be found in German Railways Part 2. Obviously foreign motive power reaches the various border points but the following state operators work well into Germany. Under open access arrangement many foreign private companies also work into Germany.

AUSTRIA

Locomotives of Classes 1016, 1116 and 1144 operate well into the southern area of Germany mostly to München but have workings on freights to Ingolstadt, Nürnberg and also Bremen/Bremerhaven as well as Hamburg. 1116s also turn up now on the overnight sleeping car trains working through to Hamburg. Austrian owned 411s (ÖBB 4011) share work with DB units on the Wien–Frankfurt/M route. New Vectron locomoives of Class 1293 will no doubt be working into Germany and get to the North Sea ports.

BELGIUM

Lineas TRAXX electric locomotives work through from Belgium via Aachen West to Köln (Gremberg), Mannheim and Duisburg (Rheinhausen) and elsewhere in the Ruhr area. These locomotives are gradually being replaced by Railpool 186s which can also work to other countries.

CZECH REPUBLIC

CD and CD Cargo electric locos of Class 371/372 have workings into Germany getting to Dresden and Leipzig, but they are gradually being replaced. New in 2018 are Czech 193s working through from Praha to Berlin and Hamburg and perhaps Kiel.

DENMARK

DB Cargo Class 3100s work through from Sweden and Denmark to Hamburg (Maschen). Passenger services from Denmark are mostly formed of DSB IC3 DMUs.

FRANCE

Thalys TGVs work via Aachen to Köln and the Ruhr area whilst TGV Euroduplex sets work to Frankfurt/M, Stuttgart and München. SNCF (Akiem) 37000s and 37500s work deep into Germany on freight trains having been seen as far east as Frankfurt/O on the Polish border!

ITALY

FS class ETR 610 alternates with SBB Class 503 on the new Milano–Basel–Frankfurt/M service.

LUXEMBOURG

CFL electric locomotives of Class 4000 work into Germany on selected freight trains. EMUs of Class 2300 work through to Koblenz with one pair of trains going through to the Ruhr.

NETHERLANDS

NS ICE3s share the work with DB units on Amsterdam to Frankfurt/M trains.

POLAND

PKP electric locomotives work international passenger trains through to Berlin. PKP hired-in multi-voltage locos work through to many areas in Germany with one coal train having PKP motive power through to Ulm! Passenger trains from Wrocław bring PKP diesel locos to Cottbus and railcars to Görlitz.

SWITZERLAND

SBB Class 503 alternates with FS class ETR 610 on the new Milano–Basel–Frankfurt/M service. Swiss Cargo electric locomotives of Classes 423 and 482 can be seen over large areas of Germany, many being on hire to private operators. 423s also work into Lindau from Switzerland via Austria. SBB EMUs now operate local services over German lines near Basel and from Konstanz.

MAPS OF THE GERMAN RAILWAY NETWORK

KEY TO MAPS

Notes:

The maps on pages 14–22 are not to scale and are a guide both to railways of DB Netz and those of private operators whose stock is detailed in the second part of this book. They should not be used to determine the exact location of any particular line or station.

Whilst we hope these maps will prove very useful to readers of this book, we would refer readers looking for more detailed maps to the comprehensive atlases produced by Schweers and Wall, details of which are below.

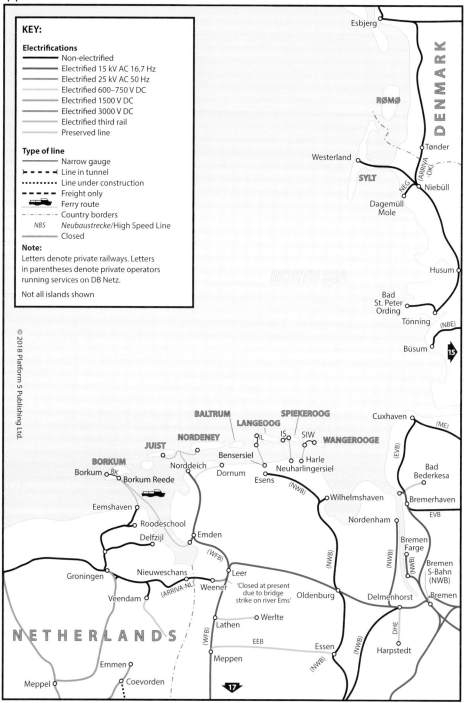

KEY:

Electrifications
- Non-electrified
- Electrified 15 kV AC 16.7 Hz
- Electrified 25 kV AC 50 Hz
- Electrified 600–750 V DC
- Electrified 1500 V DC
- Electrified 3000 V DC
- Electrified third rail
- Preserved line

Type of line
- Narrow gauge
- Line in tunnel
- Line under construction
- Freight only
- Ferry route
- Country borders
- *NBS* *Neubaustrecke*/High Speed Line
- Closed

Note:
Letters denote private railways. Letters in parentheses denote private operators running services on DB Netz.

Not all islands shown

© 2018 Platform 5 Publishing Ltd.

DENMARK

Esbjerg

RØMØ

Tønder

Westerland

SYLT

(ARRIVA -DK)

NEG

Niebüll

Dagemüll Mole

Husum

Bad St. Peter Ording

Tönning

(NBE)

Büsum

15

NORTH SEA

BALTRUM

LANGEOOG

SPIEKEROOG

Cuxhaven

(ME)

NORDENEY

IL

IS

SIW

WANGEROOGE

(EVB)

JUIST

Bensersiel

Harle

Bad Bederkesa

BORKUM

Noddeich

Dornum

Neuharlingersiel

Borkum

BK

Borkum Reede

Esens

(NWB)

Wilhelmshaven

Bremerhaven

EVB

Eemshaven

Nordenham

Roodeschool

Emden

Bremen Farge

Delfzijl

(WFB)

(NWB)

(NWB)

Bremen S-Bahn (NWB)

Groningen

Nieuweschans

Leer

(NWB)

Bremen

Veendam

(ARRIVA-NL)

Weener

'Closed at present due to bridge strike on river Ems'

Oldenburg

Delmenhorst

NETHERLANDS

(WFB)

Werlte

Lathen

EEB

Essen

(NWB)

DHE

Harpstedt

Emmen

Meppen

(NWB)

Meppel

Coevorden

17

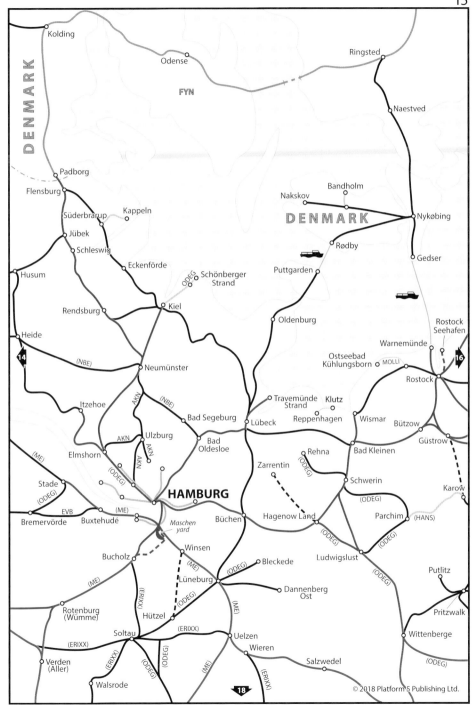

Kolding

Odense

FYN

Ringsted

Naestved

DENMARK

Padborg

Flensburg

Süderbrarup

Kappeln

Jübek

Schleswig

Eckenförde

Husum

Bandholm

Nakskov

DENMARK

Nykøbing

Rødby

Gedser

Puttgarden

ODEG

Schönberger
Strand

Rendsburg

Kiel

Oldenburg

Rostock
Seehafen

Warnemünde

Heide

14

(NBE)

Neumünster

Ostseebad
Kühlungsborn

MOLLI

Rostock

16

Itzehoe

(NBE)

Travemünde
Strand

Klutz

Reppenhagen

Wismar

Bützow

Güstrow

AKN

Bad Segeburg

Lübeck

AKN

Ulzburg

AKN

Bad
Oldesloe

Rehna

(ODEG)

Bad Kleinen

Karow

Elmshorn

AKN

Zarrentin

Schwerin

(ME)

Stade

(ODEG)

(ODEG)

HAMBURG

(ME)

Büchen

Hagenow Land

(ODEG)

Parchim

(HANS)

Bremervörde

EVB

Buxtehude

Maschen
yard

(ODEG)

Ludwigslust

Putlitz

Bucholz

Winsen

(ME)

(ODEG)

Bleckede

(ODEG)

Rotenburg
(Wümme)

(ME)

(ERIXX)

Lüneburg

(ODEG)

Dannenberg
Ost

Pritzwalk

Hützel

(ME)

Wittenberge

Soltau

(ERIXX)

Uelzen

(ERIXX)

Verden
(Aller)

(ERIXX)

(ODEG)

(ODEG)

(ME)

Wieren

Salzwedel

(ERIXX)

(ODEG)

Walsrode

18

© 2018 Platform 5 Publishing Ltd.

Malmö
Simrishamn
Ystad
Trelleborg

BALTIC SEA

© 2018 Platform 5 Publishing Ltd.

Sassnitz
RÜGEN
Sassnitz
Mukran
Bergen
Ostseebad Binz
Barth
Graal-
Müritz
Pütbus
RüBB
Stralsund
Lauterbach
Mole
Göhren
Rövershagen
Velgast
15
Lubmin
Peenemünde
Greifswald
USEDOM
Tessin
Demmin
Züssow
Wolgast
Seebad Heringsdorf
Swinoujście Centrum
Swinoujście
Lalendorf
Ueckermünde
Stadthafen
Friedland
Trzebież
Szczecińskie
Jatznick
Police
Waren
(Müritz)
Neubrandenburg
Pasewalk
POLAND
(HANS)
Malchow
(ODEG)
Prenzlau
Szczecin
Meyenburg
Neustrelitz
(HANS)
Mirow
Passow
Poznan
(HANS)
Wittstock
Rheinsberg
(Mark)
Fürstenberg
Templin
Schwedt
(Oder)
Angermünde
(NEB)
Joachimsthal
(NEB)
Gross
Schönebeck
(HANS)
(ODEG)
Neuruppin
Löwenberg
(Mark)
Eberswalde
(NEB)
Neustadt-
(Dosse)
(ODEG)
19
Kostrzyn

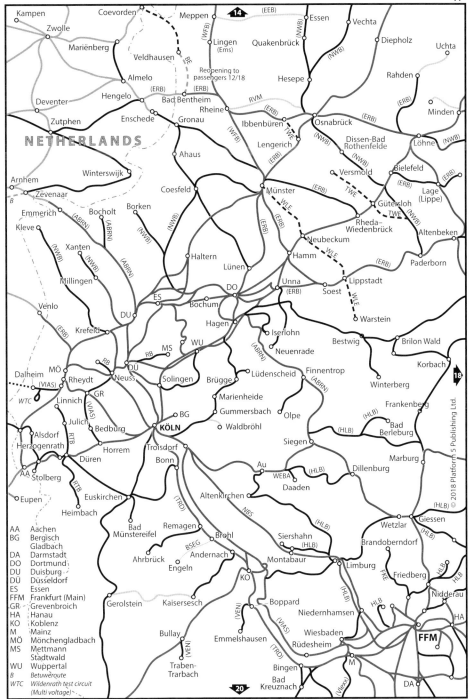

Kampen
Zwolle
Mariënberg
Coevorden
Veldhausen
Almelo
Hengelo
Deventer
Enschede
Zutphen
NETHERLANDS
Winterswijk
Arnhem
B
Zevenaar
Emmerich
Bocholt
Kleve
Xanten
Millingen
Venlo
Krefeld
MÖ
Dalheim
Rheydt
WTC
Linnich
Julich
Alsdorf
Herzogenrath
AA
Stolberg
Eupen
Heimbach

Meppen
14
(EEB)
Essen
Vechta
Lingen (Ems)
Quakenbrück
Diepholz
Uchta
(WFB)
(NWB)
BE
Reopening to passengers 12/18
Hesepe
Rahden
(ERB)
(ERB)
Bad Bentheim
Rheine
Gronau
Ibbenbüren
Osnabrück
Minden
RVM
(ERB)
(ERB)
(ERB)
Ahaus
Lengerich
Dissen-Bad Rothenfelde
Löhne
(NWB)
Coesfeld
Münster
Versmold
Bielefeld
(WFB)
(NWB)
(ERB)
Lage (Lippe)
Borken
Gütersloh
TWE
Altenbeken
Rheda–Wiedenbrück
(NWB)
(NWB)
(ABRN)
(NWB)
(ERB)
Haltern
Neubeckum
Hamm
Paderborn
(ABRN)
Lünen
WLE
(ERB)
DO
Unna
Soest
Lippstadt
ES
Bochum
(ERB)
WLE
DU
Hagen
Iserlohn
Warstein
Krefeld
Bestwig
Brilon Wald
(ERB)
MS
WU
Korbach
RB
RB
Neuenrade
18
DÜ
(ABRN)
Neuss
Solingen
Lüdenscheid
Finnentrop
Winterberg
RB
Brügge
GR
Marienheide
Frankenberg
Bedburg
BG
Gummersbach
Olpe
(HLB)
Bad Berleburg
KÖLN
Waldbröhl
(HLB)
Horrem
Siegen
Marburg
Düren
Troisdorf
Bonn
Au
Dillenburg
WEBA
(HLB)
Euskirchen
Altenkirchen
Daaden
(TRD)
NBS
Wetzlar
Giessen
Bad Münstereifel
Remagen
(HLB)
(HLB)
Brohl
Siershahn
Brandoberndorf
BSEG
(HLB)
Ahrbrück
Andernach
Montabaur
Limburg
Friedberg
Engeln
FKE
Nidderau
KO
HA
Gerolstein
Kaisersesch
Boppard
Niedernhamsen
(HLB)
(VEN)
(HLB)
FFM
Bullay
Emmelshausen
Wiesbaden
(VIAS)
Rüdesheim
(VEN)
(TRD)
M
Traben-Trarbach
Bingen
DA
20
Bad Kreuznach
(Vlexx)

AA   Aachen
BG   Bergisch Gladbach
DA   Darmstadt
DO   Dortmund
DU   Duisburg
DÜ   Düsseldorf
ES   Essen
FFM   Frankfurt (Main)
GR   Grevenbroich
HA   Hanau
KO   Koblenz
M   Mainz
MÖ   Mönchengladbach
MS   Mettmann Stadtwald
WU   Wuppertal
B   Betuweroute
WTC   Wildenrath test circuit (Multi voltage)

© 2018 Platform 5 Publishing Ltd.

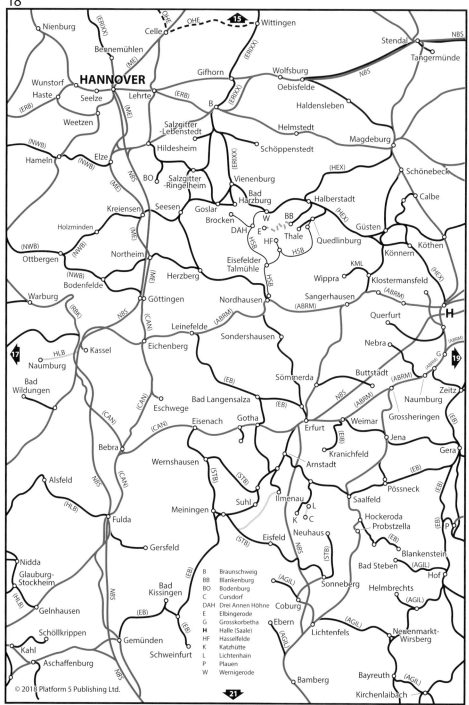

Nienburg

Celle

OHE

OHE

15

Wittingen

(ERIXX)

Bennemühlen

(ME)

Stendal

NBS

Tangermünde

Gifhorn

Wolfsburg

NBS

HANNOVER

Wunstorf

Haste

Seelze

Lehrte

(ERB)

Oebisfelde

(ERIXX)

B

Haldensleben

(ERB)

Weetzen

(ME)

Salzgitter
-Lebenstedt

Helmstedt

Magdeburg

Helmstedt

(NWB)

Hildesheim

Schöppenstedt

Hameln

Elze

(NWB)

BO

Salzgitter
-Ringelheim

Vienenburg

(HEX)

Schönebeck

Calbe

Kreiensen

Seesen

Goslar

Bad
Harzburg

Halberstadt

(HEX)

Güsten

Holzminden

Brocken

W

DAH

BB

E

Thale

Quedlinburg

Könnern

Köthen

(NWB)

(NWB)

Northeim

HF

HSB

HSB

Ottbergen

(ME)

Herzberg

Eisefelder
Talmühle

Wippra

KML

Klostermansfeld

(HEX)

Warburg

Bodenfelde

(NWB)

(ME)

Göttingen

Nordhausen

HSB

Sangerhausen

(ABRM)

(ABRM)

H

(RBK)

NBS

(CAN)

Leinefelde

(ABRM)

Querfurt

17

HLB

Kassel

Eichenberg

Sondershausen

Nebra

(ABRM)

19

Naumburg

G

Bad
Wildungen

(EB)

Sömmerda

Buttstädt

(ABRM)

Zeitz

(CAN)

Eschwege

Bad Langensalza

(EB)

NBS

(ABRM)

Naumburg

Grossheringen

(EB)

Eisenach

Gotha

Erfurt

Weimar

(CAN)

Bebra

(EIB)

Jena

Gera

(CAN)

Wernshausen

Kranichfeld

(EB)

Alsfeld

(STB)

(STB)

Arnstadt

Pössneck

(EB)

(HLB)

(CAN)

Meiningen

Suhl

Ilmenau

L

Saalfeld

K

C

Hockeroda

Probstzella

P

Fulda

(STB)

Neuhaus

NBS

Eisfeld

Blankenstein

(AGIL)

Gersfeld

Bad Steben

Hof

Nidda

Glauburg-
Stockheim

B   Braunschweig

BB   Blankenburg

BO   Bodenburg

(AGIL)

Sonneberg

Helmbrechts

(AGIL)

(HLB)

Bad
Kissingen

(EB)

C   Cursdorf

DAH Drei Annen Höhne

E   Elbingerode

Coburg

Gelnhausen

(EB)

G   Grosskorbetha

H   Halle (Saale)

Ebern

Lichtenfels

Neuenmarkt-
Wirsberg

Schöllkrippen

Gemünden

Schweinfurt

HF   Hasselfelde

K   Katzhütte

L   Lichtenhain

(AGIL)

Kahl

Aschaffenburg

NBS

P   Plauen

W   Wernigerode

Bayreuth

(AGIL)

© 2018 Platform 5 Publishing Ltd.

21

Bamberg

Kirchenlaibach

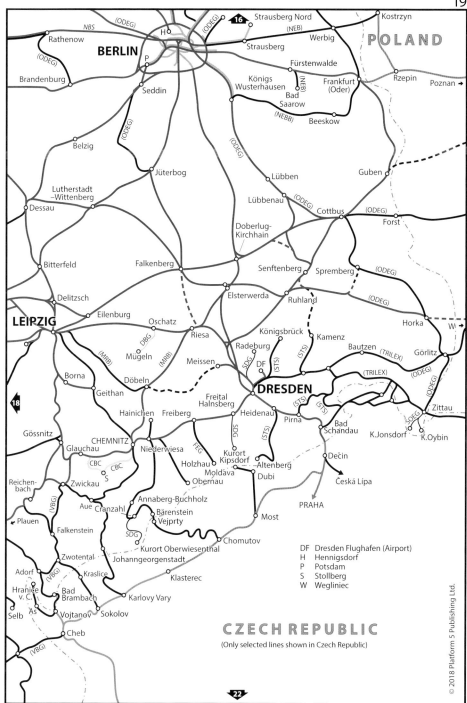

Wasserbillig

Trier
To reopen to
passengers soon -
see S+W atlas

LUXEMBOURG

Neubrücke

Apach

Thionville

Bouzonville

Metz

Réding

Lebach

Dillingen

Forbach

Illingen

Saarbrücken

Sarreguemines

Kusel

Homburg

Pirmasens

(17)

Lauterecken-
Grumbach

Kaiserslautern

Kl

Landau

Bad Bergzabern

Wissembourg

Lauterbourg

Bad
Münster

Alzey

Worms

Ramsen-
Eiswoog

NW

Wörth

Rastatt

(Vlexx)

(Vlexx)

L

M

K

(VIAS)

Gross-
Umstadt

Bensheim

Fürth

Weinheim

H

Neckargemünd

(AVG)

(AVG)

NBS

Pforzheim

(AVG)

(AVG)

Weissach

Weil
der
Stadt

H   Heidelberg
K   Karlsruhe
Kl   Kirchheimboladen
L   Ludwigshafen
M   Mannheim
NW Neustadt (Weinstrasse)
TS   Trossingen Stadt

Mommenheim

Strasbourg

Offenburg

Achern

Kehl

(OSB)

(OSB)

SWEG

SWEG

(AVG)

Ottenhöfen

Bad Griesbach

(AVG)

Freudenstadt

Horb

(21)

FRANCE

(OSB)

(OSB)

Hausach

Riegel

Colmar   Breisach

Neuf Breisach

Mulhouse

Müllheim

Haltingen

Basel

(SBB)

Kandern
Zell

SWEG

SWEG

SWEG

(BSB)

(BSB)

Elzach

Freiburg
(Breisgau)

Münstertal

Seebrugg

Villingen

Donaueschingen

Neustadt

Waldshut

Koblenz

Brugg

Zürich

Rottweil

(HzL)

TS

Tuttlingen

(HzL)

(HzL)

Immendingen

Schaffhausen

Singen

SWITZERLAND

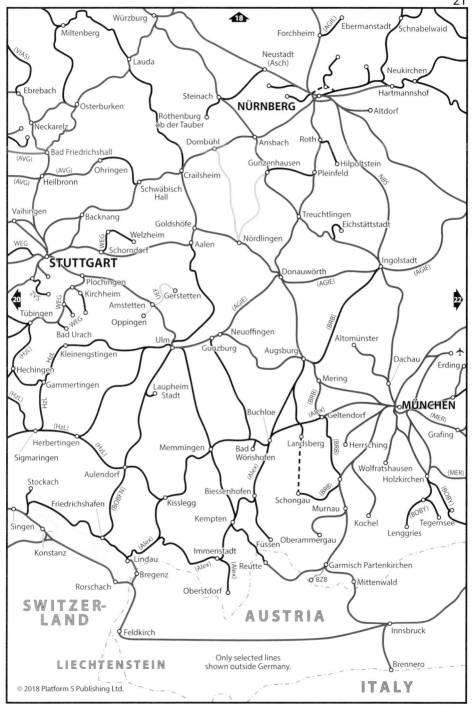

Only selected lines
shown outside Germany.

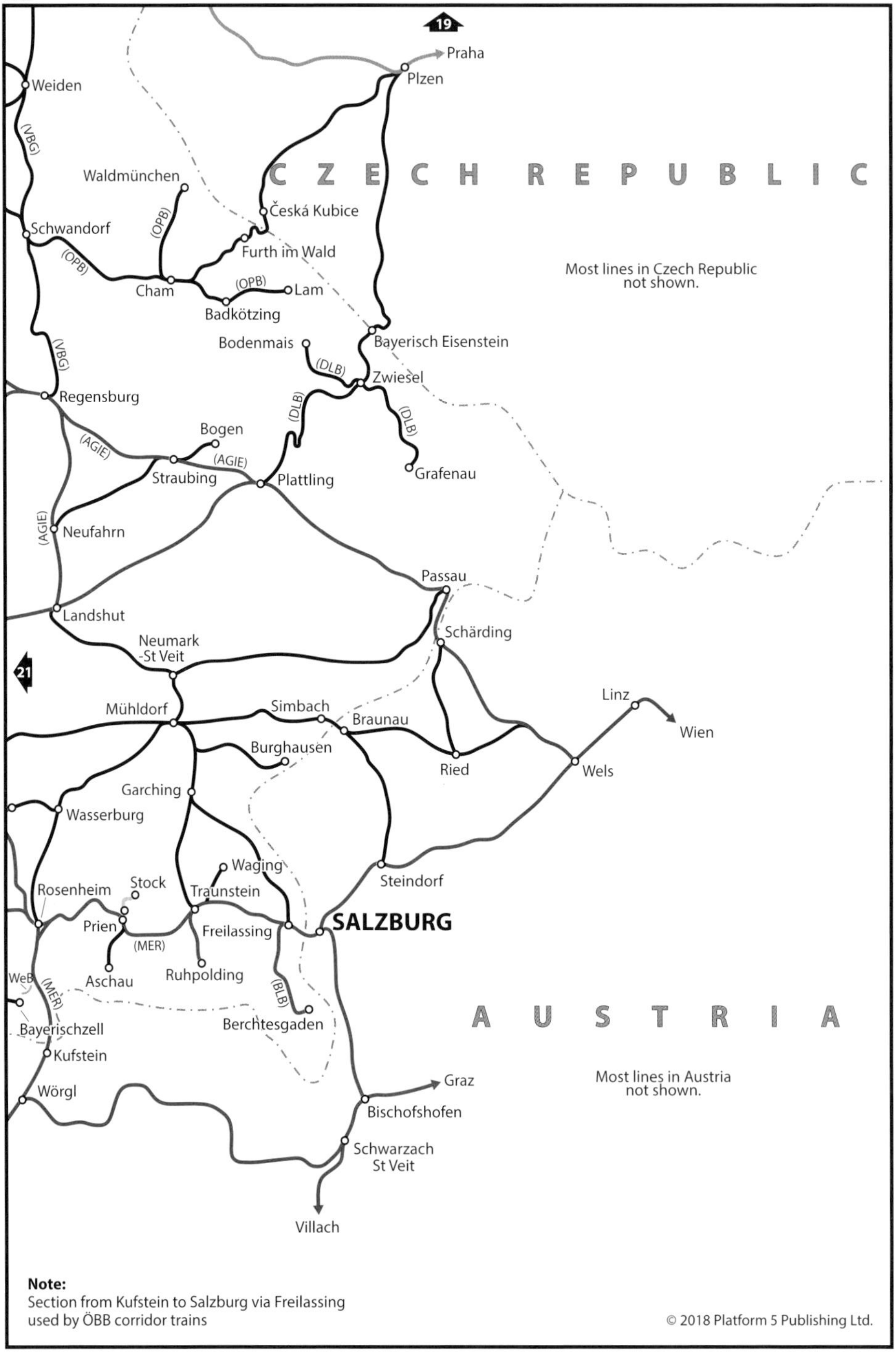

CZECH REPUBLIC

Most lines in Czech Republic
not shown.

Weiden

(VBG)

Waldmünchen

Schwandorf

(OPB)

(OPB)

Cham

(OPB) Lam

Badkötzing

Česká Kubice

Furth im Wald

Bodenmais

Bayerisch Eisenstein

(DLB) Zwiesel

Regensburg

(VBG)

(DLB)

(DLB)

(AGIE)

Bogen

(AGIE)

Straubing

Plattling

Grafenau

(AGIE)

Neufahrn

Landshut

Passau

Neumark
-St Veit

Schärding

21

Mühldorf

Simbach

Braunau

Linz

Wien

Burghausen

Ried

Wels

Garching

Wasserburg

Waging

Steindorf

Rosenheim

Stock

Traunstein

SALZBURG

Prien

(MER)

Freilassing

WeB

(MER)

Aschau

Ruhpolding

(DLB)

AUSTRIA

Bayerischzell

Berchtesgaden

Kufstein

Most lines in Austria
not shown.

Wörgl

Graz

Bischofshofen

Schwarzach
St Veit

Villach

Praha

Plzen

19

Note:
Section from Kufstein to Salzburg via Freilassing
used by ÖBB corridor trains

© 2018 Platform 5 Publishing Ltd.

1. ELECTRIC LOCOMOTIVES

Note: All electric locomotives operate only on the 15 kV 16.7 Hz overhead system unless otherwise stated.

DB INVITATION TO TENDER

On 28/02/2017 DB invited tenders for a framework contract for locomotive-hauled single-deck trains to enter service at a rate of 20 trains per year from 2021. No further announcements have since been made.

CLASS 101   Bo-Bo

Class 101 remains DB Fernverkehr's heavy duty Inter City locomotive working all over Germany and reaching Graz, Villach, Klagenfurt and Innsbruck in Austria. At one time the locos were used on overnight fast freights but this has ceased as passenger duties have increased. Many of the IC trains are push-pull operated. There are 129 diagrams which includes the Regio RE services over the High Speed Line Nürnberg–München. These locos will be released soon by the new Class 102s. Several Class 101s have all over advertising but many more carry DB slogans about tickets and punctuality

Built: 1996–99.
Builder: ABB Henschel, later Adtranz, Kassel.
One Hour Rating: 6600 kW.   **Weight:** 84 tonnes.
Continuous Rating: 6400 kW.   **Length over Buffers:** 19.10 m.
Maximum Tractive Effort: 300 kN.   **Maximum Speed:** 220 km/h.
Wheel Diameter: 1250 mm.   **Electric Brake:** Rheostatic.
Advertising Liveries: 101 042 Ecophant; 101 071 Gold; 101 112 Rheingold; 101 144 Hertha BSC Berlin/Die Zukunft Ist Am Zug (Blue).

101 001	AH1	101 035	AH1	101 069		AH1
101 002	AH1	101 036	AH1	101 070		AH1
101 003	AH1	101 037	AH1	101 071	A	AH1
101 004	AH1	101 038	AH1	101 072		AH1
101 005	AH1	101 039	AH1	101 073		AH1
101 006	AH1	101 040	AH1	101 074		AH1
101 007	AH1	101 041	AH1	101 075		AH1
101 008	AH1	101 042	A AH1	101 076		AH1
101 009	AH1	101 043	AH1	101 077		AH1
101 010	AH1	101 044	AH1	101 078		AH1
101 011	AH1	101 045	AH1	101 079		AH1
101 012	AH1	101 046	AH1	101 080		AH1
101 013	AH1	101 047	AH1	101 081		AH1
101 014	AH1	101 048	AH1	101 082		AH1
101 015	AH1	101 049	AH1	101 083		AH1
101 016	AH1	101 050	AH1	101 084		AH1
101 017	AH1	101 051	AH1	101 085		AH1
101 018	AH1	101 052	AH1	101 086		AH1
101 019	AH1	101 053	AH1	101 087		AH1
101 020	AH1	101 054	AH1	101 088		AH1
101 021	AH1	101 055	AH1	101 089		AH1
101 022	AH1	101 056	AH1	101 090		AH1
101 023	AH1	101 057	AH1	101 091		AH1
101 024	AH1	101 058	AH1	101 092		AH1
101 025	AH1	101 059	AH1	101 093		AH1
101 026	AH1	101 060	AH1	101 094		AH1
101 027	AH1	101 061	AH1	101 095		AH1
101 028	AH1	101 062	AH1	101 096		AH1
101 029	AH1	101 063	AH1	101 097		AH1
101 030	AH1	101 064	AH1	101 098		AH1
101 031	AH1	101 065	AH1	101 099		AH1
101 032	AH1	101 066	AH1	101 100		AH1
101 033	AH1	101 067	AH1	101 101		AH1
101 034	AH1	101 068	AH1	101 102		AH1

101 103		AH1	101 118		AH1	101 132		AH1
101 104		AH1	101 119		AH1	101 133		AH1
101 105		AH1	101 120		AH1	101 134		AH1
101 106		AH1	101 121		AH1	101 135		AH1
101 107		AH1	101 122		AH1	101 136		AH1
101 108		AH1	101 123		AH1	101 137		AH1
101 109		AH1	101 124		AH1	101 138		AH1
101 110		AH1	101 125		AH1	101 139		AH1
101 111		AH1	101 126		AH1	101 140		AH1
101 112	A	AH1	101 127		AH1	101 141		AH1
101 113		AH1	101 128		AH1	101 142		AH1
101 114		AH1	101 129		AH1	101 143		AH1
101 115		AH1	101 130		AH1	101 144	A	AH1
101 116		AH1	101 131		AH1	101 145		AH1
101 117		AH1						

CLASS 102   SKODA TYPE 109E3   Bo-Bo

For some time DB Regio has been running RE trains München–Ingolstadt–Nürnberg over the high speed line Ingolstadt to Nürnberg with locos and stock hired from DB Fernverkehr. DB Regio then tendered for locos and stock for this service and when the contract was announced there were gasps in high places as the contract went to Skoda for the locos and double deck stock! Class 102 is a modification of the Skoda Class 380 built for Czech Railways and called the 109E3 by Skoda the version for Germany being German voltage only. After a prolonged acceptance period the trains were expected to enter service in 2018.

Built: 2015–16.
Builder: Skoda Transportation, Plzen.
One Hour Rating: 6400 kW.
Continuous Rating:
Maximum Tractive Effort: 275 kN.
Wheel Diameter: 1250 mm.

Weight: 88 tonnes.
Length over Buffers: 18.00 m.
Maximum Speed: 200 km/h.
Electric Brake:

102 001		102 003	MH1	102 006	MH1
102 002		102 005			

▲ Class 102 has been the source of much controversy, it being the first type of Skoda locomotive to be ordered by DB. 102 001 is seen undergoing trials at the Velim test circuit in the Czech Republic on 22 January 2017. **Quintus Vosman**

CLASS 103 — Co-Co

DB seems to be reluctant to get rid of the last 103s. During 2014–16 the class dwindled to just one locomotive and then that was withdrawn but amazingly reinstated as it was in such good condition having been well looked after by MH1 depot. It now belongs to DB Museum but currently has an IC turn between München and Ulm.

Built: 1969–74 for DB.
Builder–Mech. Parts: Henschel/Krauss-Maffei/Krupp.
Builder–Elec. Parts: Siemens/AEG-Telefunken/Brown-Boveri.
One Hour Rating: 7780 kW.
Continuous Rating: 7440 kW.
Maximum Tractive Effort: 314 kN.
Wheel Diameter: 1250 mm.
Weight: 114 tonnes.
Length over Buffers: 20.20 m.
Maximum Speed 200 km/h.
Electric Brake: Rheostatic.
Class Specific Livery: E Old Trans-Europe Express/Intercity livery, red & beige.

103 245	E	MH1

CLASS 111 — Bo-Bo

Once used on IC and IR services this class has been demoted to Regio work, whether that be S-Bahn or RB/RE trains, but the recent influx of new EMUs is seeing many placed into store pending sale or scrapping. Even the youngest locos are now over 30 years old.

Built: 1974–1984 for DB.
Builder–Mech. Parts: Krupp/Krauss-Maffei/Henschel.
Builder–Elec. Parts: Siemens/AEG/Brown Boveri.
One Hour Rating: 3700 kW.
Continuous Rating: 3620 kW.
Maximum Tractive Effort: 295 kN.
Wheel Diameter: 1250 mm.
Weight: 83 tonnes.
Length over Buffers: 16.75 m.
Maximum Speed: 160 km/h.
Electric Brake: Rheostatic.

Loco	Depot	Loco			Depot	Loco	Depot
111 008	EHM (Z)	111 044			MH1	111 079	TU (Z)
111 009	EHM (Z)	111 046			TS	111 080	TU
111 010	EDO	111 047			TU	111 081	EHM (Z)
111 011	EDO	111 048		l	TS	111 082	TU
111 012	EDO (Z)	111 049		l	TS	111 083	EHM (Z)
111 013	EHM (Z)	111 050		l	TS	111 084	EDO (Z)
111 014	EDO (Z)	111 051		cl	TS	111 086	FGM
111 016	EDO (Z)	111 052		cl	MH1	111 087	TU
111 017	MH1	111 053		cl	MH1	111 088	TS (Z)
111 018	RL	111 054		l	EDO	111 089	EHM (Z)
111 019	TS	111 055		cl	MH1	111 091	TU
111 020	EDO (Z)	111 056		cl	EHM (Z)	111 092	TU
111 021	TS	111 057		c	EHM (Z)	111 093	KA
111 022	MH1	111 058		c	TU	111 094	FGM
111 023	MH1	111 059	Y	l	DBN	111 095	EDO
111 024	KK2	111 060		c	TS	111 096	KA
111 025	TU	111 061		l	EDO	111 097	EHM (Z)
111 026	RL	111 062		l	EDO	111 098	KD (Z)
111 027	MH1	111 063		l	KD (Z)	111 100	EDO
111 028	EDO (Z)	111 064		l	EHM (Z)	111 101	EDO (Z)
111 029	TU	111 065		l	MH1	111 103	NN1
111 031	MH1	111 066		l	MH1	111 104	EHM (Z)
111 032	EDO (Z)	111 067		l	TS	111 105	KD (Z)
111 035	MH1	111 069			EHM (Z)	111 106	MTL (Z)
111 036	MH1	111 070			EHM (Z)	111 107	MTL (Z)
111 037	EDO	111 071			MH1	111 108	FGM
111 038	KD (Z)	111 073			TU (Z)	111 110	TU
111 039	MH1	111 074			TU	111 111	EDO
111 040	KD (Z)	111 075			TU	111 112	EDO
111 041	EHM (Z)	111 076			TU	111 113	EDO
111 042	RL	111 077			TU	111 114	EDO
111 043	TS	111 078			TU	111 115	EDO

▲ The last Class 103 in service – 103 245 – is now owned by DB Museum, but still sees some passenger use between München and Ulm. On 12 January 2014 it is seen leaving München Hbf with the then booked afternoon train IC2206, 15.40 to Nürnberg. **Keith Fender**

▼ A common sight, soon to become exceptionally rare: Two Class 111s side-by-side at München Hbf. Seen on 13 February 2018 are 111 183 and 111 187 with the 14.34 RB service to Pfaffenhofen and the 14.25 RB service to Treuchtlingen respectively. **Keith Fender**

111 116	EDO (Z)	111 150	KK2	111 186	MTL (Z)		
111 118	KA	111 151	EHM (Z)	111 187	NN1		
111 119	EDO	111 155	EDO	111 188	MH1		
111 120	TU	111 156	EDO (Z)	111 189	HBS		
111 121	EDO	111 157	EHM (Z)	111 190	NN1		
111 122	EDO	111 158	EDO	111 191	KA		
111 123	NN1	111 159	NN1	111 193	NN1 (Z)		
111 124	KK2 (Z)	111 160	EHM (Z)	111 194	FGM		
111 125	EDO	111 161	TS	111 197	KA		
111 126	EDO	111 162	TU (Z)	111 198	TS (Z)		
111 127	EDO	111 163	TU	111 200	EHM (Z)		
111 128	KK2	111 164	TS (Z)	111 201	MH1		
111 129	KK2	111 165	TU	111 202	EHM (Z)		
111 130	NN1	111 166	TS (Z)	111 203	TS (Z)		
111 131	TU	111 167	TS (Z)	111 204	EHM (Z)		
111 132	TU	111 168	TS	111 206	EHM (Z)		
111 133	HB (Z)	111 169	EDO (Z)	111 207	NN1		
111 134	RL	111 171	EHM (Z)	111 208	EHM (Z)		
111 135	TU	111 172	EHM (Z)	111 209	HB		
111 136	EHM (Z)	111 173	EHM (Z)	111 211	TS (Z)		
111 137	TU	111 174	TS	111 212	TS (Z)		
111 138	TS (Z)	111 175	EHM (Z)	111 213	EHM (Z)		
111 139	TU	111 176	TS (Z)	111 214	MTL (Z)		
111 140	TS (Z)	111 177	MH1	111 216	MTL (Z)		
111 141	HB (Z)	111 178	MH1 (Z)	111 217	NN1		
111 142	EHM (Z)	111 179	EHM (Z)	111 219	EHM (Z)		
111 143	EDO (Z)	111 180	EHM (Z)	111 221	MH1		
111 144	EHM (Z)	111 181	MH1	111 223	EHM (Z)		
111 145	EHM (Z)	111 182	EHM (Z)	111 224	EHM (Z)		
111 146	EHM (Z)	111 183	MH1	111 225	EHM (Z)		
111 147	KD (Z)	111 184	NN1	111 226	MTL (Z)		
111 148	NN1	111 185	EHM (Z)	111 227	NN1		
111 149	EDO						

Names:

111 060	1000 Jahre Gundelfingen		111 062	Neuenburg am Rhein

CLASS 112   Bo-Bo

Class 112 is the express passenger version of Class 143 built after unification. This is another class going through a period of change thanks to the arrival of the new double-deck EMUs of Classes 445/446 and in the case of Stuttgart, the new Class 147s.

Built: 1992–93 for DR and DB.
Builder: LEW.
One Hour Rating: 4200 kW.
Continuous Rating: 4020 kW.
Maximum Tractive Effort: 248 kN.
Wheel Diameter: 1250 mm.

Weight: 82 tonnes.
Length over Buffers: 16.64 m.
Maximum Speed 160 km/h.
Electric Brake: Rheostatic.

112 101		WR	112 110	WR	112 119	BLO	
112 102		BCS	112 111	BCS	112 120	BCS	
112 103		BLO	112 112	BCS	112 121	BLO	
112 104		BCS	112 113	BCS	112 122	BCS	
112 105		TS	112 114	BCS	112 123	WR	
112 106		TS	112 115	WR	112 124	BCS	
112 107		WR	112 116	BLO	112 125	LMB	
112 108	A	TS	112 117	BCS	112 126	EHM (Z)	
112 109		WR	112 118	BLO	112 127	EHM (Z)	

112 128	EHM (Z)	112 150	BCS	112 171	AK
112 129	UKF (Z)	112 151	AK	112 172	EHM (Z)
112 130	EHM (Z)	112 152	WR	112 173	AK (Z)
112 131	LMB	112 153	AK	112 174	TS
112 132	UKF (Z)	112 154	AK	112 175	AK
112 133	BLO	112 155	BCS	112 176	AK
112 134	TS (Z)	112 156	AK	112 177	AK
112 136	EHM (Z)	112 157	LMB	112 178	AK
112 137	EHM (Z)	112 158	EHM (Z)	112 179	AK
112 138	TS	112 159	AK	112 180	AK
112 139	TS	112 160	AK	112 181	AK
112 140	AK	112 161	TS (Z)	112 182	BLO
112 141	AK	112 162	EHM (Z)	112 183	BLO
112 142	AK	112 163	AK	112 184	BLO
112 143	AK	112 164	LMB	112 185	BLO
112 144	AK	112 165	BLO	112 186	BLO
112 145	AK	112 166	LMB	112 187	WR
112 146	BCS	112 167	AK	112 188	WR
112 147	AK	112 168	AK	112 189	BLO
112 148	BCS	112 169	TS	112 190	BLO
112 149	AK (Z)	112 170	TS		

CLASS 114   Bo-Bo

This former DR local passenger train locomotive is under threat with the recent arrival of Classes 147, 445, 446 and the ever present threat of local trains being taken over by private operators.

Built: 1990–92 for DR.
Builder: LEW.
One Hour Rating: 4200 kW.
Continuous Rating: 4020 kW.
Maximum Tractive Effort: 248 kN.
Wheel Diameter: 1250 mm.

Weight: 82 tonnes.
Length over Buffers: 16.64 m.
Maximum Speed 160 km/h.
Electric Brake: Rheostatic.

114 002		TS	114 022		FGM
114 003		UKF (Z)	114 023		FGM
114 004		TS	114 024		TS
114 005		WR	114 026		EHM (Z)
114 006		TS	114 027		TS
114 007		FGM	114 028		TS
114 008		FGM	114 029		FGM
114 009ⁱⁱ	(143 873)	BCS	114 030		FGM
114 010		FGM	114 031		FGM
114 011		FGM	114 032		TS
114 012		FGM	114 033		FGM
114 013		FGM	114 034		FGM
114 014		FGM	114 035		TS
114 015		TS	114 036		FGM
114 016		FGM	114 037		FGM
114 017		TS	114 038		FGM
114 018		FGM	114 039		TS
114 020		FGM	114 040		WR
114 021		FGM	114 501		STMI (Z)

▲ One of the few remaining Class 115 locomotives still in traffic, 115 350 leads a most unusual empty coaching stock movement from Frankfurt/Main to München, near Uhingen in the Filstal on 23 September 2017. As well as empty coaching stock the train includes locomotives of Classes 143, 111 and 120. **Matthias Müller**

▼ 120 123 is seen arriving at Hannover Hbf at the head of IC2002 to Hamburg on 5 May 2018.
Brian Garvin

CLASS 115 Bo-Bo

Originally Class 110, various modifications etc led to reclassifications to 112, 113 and 115. The last of these 1960s express locomotives are mainly used on ecs trips, whether short distance or long distance. In the latter case there are trains travelling the length of the country serving the main carriage depots and connecting them with the main works at Neumünster.

Built: 1956–68 for DB.
Builder–Mech. Parts: Henschel/Krauss-Maffei/Krupp.
Builder–Elec. Parts: AEG/Brown Boveri/Siemens.
One Hour Rating: 3700 kW.   **Weight:** 86 (*86.4) tonnes.
Continuous Rating: 3620 kW.   **Length over Buffers:** 16.44 (*16.49) m.
Maximum Tractive Effort: 275 kN.   **Maximum Speed:** 150 km/h.
Wheel Diameter: 1250 mm.   **Electric Brake:** Rheostatic.

*   Denotes early body style.

115 114	*	BRG	115 293		BRG	115 459		clp	BRG
115 198	*	BRG	115 350	cl	BRG	115 509	A	clp	BRG
115 261	*	BRG							

CLASS 120 Bo-Bo

Once likely to take over from the 103s to become the main long distance locomotive, in fact construction reached only 60 locomotives, being surpassed by ICEs and later Class 101s. The class is still used on IC/EC duties throughout Germany but a good number stand spare each day as reserve locomotives. The 120.2 version has been re-equipped for Regio work on the Rostock–Hamburg and Aachen–Siegen routes but with a certain amount of unreliability certainly on the latter route. One of the main IC routes that sees this class is Karlsruhe–Stuttgart–Nürnberg but with new Class 147.5 expected to be in service soon, together with Czech locomotives working through to Berlin from Praha several Class 101s will become spare and replace the 120s.

Built: 1987–88 for DB.
Builder–Mech. Parts: Krupp/Henschel/Krauss-Maffei.
Builder–Elec. Parts: Brown Boveri.
One Hour Rating: 6300 kW.   **Weight:** 84 tonnes.
Continuous Rating: 5600 kW.   **Length over Buffers:** 19.40 m.
Maximum Tractive Effort: 347 kN.   **Maximum Speed:** 200 km/h.
Wheel Diameter: 1250 mm.   **Electric Brake:** Rheostatic.

120 101	MH1	120 144			MH1
120 102	MH1	120 145			EHM (Z)
120 103	EHM (Z)	120 146			MH1
120 104	MH1	120 147			MH1
120 105	MH1	120 148			EHM (Z)
120 108	MH1	120 149			MH1
120 111	MH1	120 150			MH1
120 113	MH1	120 151			MH1
120 114	EHM (Z)	120 152			MH1
120 115	MH1	120 154			EHM (Z)
120 118	STMI	120 155			EHM (Z)
120 119	EHM (Z)	120 157			MH1
120 120	MH1	120 159			MH1
120 122	EHM (Z)	120 201	(120 116)		WR (Z)
120 123	MH1	120 202	(120 129)		WR
120 125	MH1	120 203	(120 107)		WR
120 126	MH1	120 204	(120 128)		WR
120 127	EHM (Z)	120 205	(120 121)		WR
120 132	MH1	120 206	(120 117)		KA (Z)
120 133	MH1	120 207	(120 136)		KA
120 134	EHM (Z)	120 208	(120 139)		KA (Z)
120 137	EHM (Z)	120 501	(120 153)	A	STMI
120 141	EHM (Z)	120 502	(120 160)	Y	STMI
120 143	MH1				

CLASS 139   Bo-Bo

The previous edition of this book showed most of this class in store; well, they still are! Just why DB Cargo has not written them off is unclear. The class is basically a Class 140 fitted with rheostatic brakes and given a new class number. Many examples are in use with private operators.

Details as Class 140 below except:

Weight: 86 tonnes.   **Electric Brake:** Rheostatic.

p   Push-pull and multiple-working fitted.

139 132		WRS (Z)	139 313		p	WM (Z)	139 557	WM (Z)
139 222		WM (Z)	139 314		p	WM (Z)	139 562	WM (Z)
139 309	p	WRS (Z)	139 554			WM (Z)		

CLASS 140   Bo-Bo

The standard freight loco of the 1960s; its time is up. Although notionally still allocated to three depots, all the remaining locos are stored, mostly at Mukran. Some have been sold to private operators.

Built: 1957–73 for DB.
Builder–Mech. Parts: Krauss-Maffei.
Builder–Elec. Parts: Siemens.
One Hour Rating: 3700 kW.
Continuous Rating: 3620 kW.   **Weight:** 83 tonnes.
Maximum Tractive Effort: 170 kN.   **Length over Buffers:** 16.49 m.
Wheel Diameter: 1250 mm.   **Maximum Speed:** 110 km/h.

140 018	WM (Z)	140 491		WM (Z)	140 637	c	WRS (Z)
140 169	AM (Z)	140 495		WM (Z)	140 677		AM (Z)
140 172	WM (Z)	140 501		WM (Z)	140 680		WM (Z)
140 218	WM (Z)	140 506		HS (Z)	140 716		WM (Z)
140 261	WM (Z)	140 528		WM (Z)	140 799	m	WM (Z)
140 291	WM (Z)	140 535		HS (Z)	140 805	m	WM (Z)
140 327	WM (Z)	140 537		WRS (Z)	140 808	m	FWD
140 353	WM (Z)	140 539		WM (Z)	140 821	m	WM (Z)
140 354	WM (Z)	140 544		WM (Z)	140 843	m	WM (Z)
140 368	WM (Z)	140 569		WM (Z)	140 855	m	FWD
140 401	WRS (Z)	140 590		WM (Z)	140 858	m	WM (Z)
140 459	WM (Z)	140 600	c	WM (Z)			

CLASS 143   Bo-Bo

This class was the standard mixed traffic locomotive of East Germany. German unification saw the class spread far and wide, being handed over to DB Regio in recent times. But the loss of local services to private operators and the large number of EMUs introduced in recent years has seen Class 143 numbers decimated. In 2017 a large batch was transferred to DB Cargo for the autumn peak but once the peak was passed many of the locos were stored and even handed back to Regio which had no need for them. A good number are now in use with private operators. New EMU orders mean there will be less need for Class 143s resulting in the class being withdrawn in the near future.

143 002–368 built 1984–88 and push-pull fitted.
143 802–967 built 1988–89 push-pull and multiple-working fitted.
143 551–661 built 1989–90 and push-pull fitted.
143 970 + 973 are rebuilds of accident damaged locos from the first series, push-pull and multiple-working fitted.

Built: 1982–90 for DR.
Builder: LEW.
One Hour Rating: 3720 kW.
Continuous Rating: 3540 kW.   **Weight:** 82 tonnes.
Maximum Tractive Effort: 248 kN.   **Length over Buffers:** 16.64 m.
Wheel Diameter: 1250 mm.   **Maximum Speed** 120 km/h.
                                            Electric Brake: Rheostatic.

143 660 + 661 were renumbered from 243 322/096.
143 970 + 973 were renumbered from 243 051/172.

Class 143.0. Standard Design.

No.	c	Code	No.	c	Code	No.	c	Code
143 009		STR	143 177			143 332	c	DNDR (Z)
143 012		AM (Z)	143 178		UKF (Z)	143 333		BSE
143 017		DNDR (Z)	143 181		FGM	143 336		NN1
143 018		STR (Z)	143 189		FGM	143 337		DNDR (Z)
143 019		BSE	143 190		DNDR (Z)	143 338		DNDR (Z)
143 030		WRS (Z)	143 192		DNDR (Z)	143 339		DNDR (Z)
143 034		LH2 (Z)	143 193		BCS	143 346		FGM
143 038		DNDR (Z)	143 194		STR	143 347		DNDR (Z)
143 042	c	TS (Z)	143 195		AM (Z)	143 348		AM (Z)
143 043		WRS (Z)	143 201		DNDR (Z)	143 350	c	WRS (Z)
143 045		NN1	143 205		LH2 (Z)	143 354	c	WRS (Z)
143 047		DNDR (Z)	143 215		NN1	143 355		UKF (Z)
143 050	c	LMR	143 216		UKF (Z)	143 358		NN1
143 055	c	WRS (Z)	143 225		WRS (Z)	143 359		DA (Z)
143 062		DNDR (Z)	143 227		FGM	143 360		DA
143 064		FGM	143 238		FGM	143 361		LL (Z)
143 065		BCS (Z)	143 239		DNDR (Z)	143 364	c	DNDR (Z)
143 071		AM (Z)	143 241		KD	143 365		UKF (Z)
143 073		UKF (Z)	143 243		DA	143 366		DNDR (Z)
143 074		DNDR (Z)	143 244		DA (Z)	143 368		UKF (Z)
143 076		FGM	143 247		NN1	143 555		STR
143 091		AM (Z)	143 248		FGM	143 558		LH2 (Z)
143 092		TU (Z)	143 250		BSE	143 562		UE (Z)
143 098		UKF (Z)	143 259		NN1	143 566		DNDR (Z)
143 106		DNDR (Z)	143 263		STR	143 568		STR
143 107		FGM	143 265		DNDR (Z)	143 575		EHM (Z)
143 109		UKF (Z)	143 267		FGM	143 580		AM (Z)
143 112		TS (Z)	143 270		FGM	143 583		DNDR (Z)
143 114		STR	143 283		BSE	143 591		DA
143 116		DNDR (Z)	143 285		DNDR (Z)	143 597		LH2 (Z)
143 119		NN1	143 288		WRS (Z)	143 621		EHM (Z)
143 120		DA (Z)	143 292		WRS (Z)	143 625		NN1 (Z)
143 123		EHM (Z)	143 293		UKF (Z)	143 628		NN1
143 129		UKF (Z)	143 295		LMB (Z)	143 630		WM (Z)
143 130		DNDR (Z)	143 298		NN1	143 632		NN1 (Z)
143 137		LH2 (Z)	143 308	c	DNDR (Z)	143 637		FGM
143 138		FGM	143 311		AH3 (Z)	143 640	c	DNDR (Z)
143 140		DNDR (Z)	143 312	c	DNDR (Z)	143 642		EHM (Z)
143 141		FGM	143 313	c	DNDR (Z)	143 644		WRS (Z)
143 152		DNDR (Z)	143 314		EHM (Z)	143 645		DNDR (Z)
143 162		EHM (Z)	143 315		DNDR (Z)	143 647		BCS (Z)
143 163		WM (Z)	143 316	c	WRS (Z)	143 651		BSE
143 166		FGM	143 319		AM (Z)	143 653		DNDR (Z)
143 168		DA	143 321		DNDR (Z)	143 655		TS (Z)
143 169		DNDR (Z)	143 324		LMR	143 658		DNDR (Z)
143 170		FGM	143 326		WRS (Z)	143 660		KD
143 176		WRS (Z)	143 327		BSE	143 661		STR

Class 143.8. Multiple Working Fitted.

No.	c	Code	No.	c	Code	No.	c	Code
143 802		UKF (Z)	143 829		UKF (Z)	143 853		KD
143 803		FGM	143 831		DNDR (Z)	143 854		KD (Z)
143 804		DNDR (Z)	143 832		UKF (Z)	143 855		NN1
143 807		AM (Z)	143 837		WRS (Z)	143 856	c	LMB
143 810	c	DA (Z)	143 839		AK	143 857		DNDR (Z)
143 816		DNDR (Z)	143 840		WRS (Z)	143 858		UKF (Z)
143 821		DA	143 841		WRS (Z)	143 859		AM (Z)
143 823		KD (Z)	143 844		BSE	143 860		WRS (Z)
143 825		BSE	143 845		DNDR (Z)	143 864		BCS
143 827		LH2 (Z)	143 848		BCS	143 867		TS (Z)
143 828		DA	143 850		LH2 (Z)	143 870		NN1

143 871	LH2 (Z)	143 905		NN1	143 934	DNDR (Z)
143 875	DA	143 906	c	UKF (Z)	143 935	WM (Z)
143 880	DNDR (Z)	143 909		DA	143 944	LL (Z)
143 881	DNDR (Z)	143 910		DA	143 949	KD
143 882	DNDR (Z)	143 914		NN1	143 952	DNDR (Z)
143 883	DA	143 919		DA	143 957	DA
143 884	DA	143 920		EHM (Z)	143 959	LMR
143 885	DA	143 922		DNDR (Z)	143 962	EHM (Z)
143 891	BSN (Z)	143 924		AM (Z)	143 963	LH2
143 893	BCS	143 925		STR	143 965	UKF (Z)
143 896	BSN (Z)	143 926		WRS (Z)	143 966	EHM (Z)
143 899	DNDR (Z)	143 928		UKF (Z)	143 967	DA
143 900	DNDR (Z)	143 930		DNDR (Z)	143 970	NN1 (Z)
143 903	LH2 (Z)	143 932		DA	143 973	DA
143 904	DNDR (Z)	143 933		DA		

▲ Class 143 is another former DR class of locomotive now struggling to find work. In happier times 143 339 is seen approaching Meissen Alstadt with a rake of double-deck stock on 16 June 2015.
Antony Guppy

CLASS 145   TRAXX F140 AC   Bo-Bo

Class 145 is an early version of the Bombardier TRAXX family but originated prior to the Bombardier takeover of ADtranz. Some locomotives were turned out with a "passenger package" with a higher maximum speed, in effect preparing the way for Class 146; it is unclear whether these locomotives have reverted to standard. During summer 2018 several locomotives were placed on loan with DB subsidiaries MEG and RBH, replacing Class 143s.

Built: 1996–99.
Builders: ADtranz (Hennigsdorf) 001–010; ADtranz Kassel (remainder).
Continuous Rating: 4200 kW.
Maximum Tractive Effort: 300 kN.   **Weight:** 84 tonnes.
Wheel Diameter: 1250 mm.   **Length over Buffers:** 18.90 m.
Electric Brake: Regenerative.   **Maximum Speed** 140 km/h (*160 km/h).

No.		Depot	No.		Depot	No.	Depot
145 001		BSE	145 029		BSE	145 055	BSE
145 002		BSE	145 030		BSE	145 056	MEG
145 003		BSE	145 031	*	BSE	145 057	BSE
145 004		MEG	145 032	*	BSE	145 058	BSE
145 005		BSE	145 033	*	BSE	145 059	RBH
145 007		RBH	145 034	*	RBH	145 060	BSE
145 008		BSE	145 035	*	BSE	145 061	BSE
145 009		RBH	145 036	*	BSE	145 062	BSE
145 010		RBH	145 037	*	BSE	145 063	RBH
145 011		RBH	145 038	*	BSE	145 064	RBH
145 012		MEG	145 039	*	BSE	145 065	BSE
145 013ᴵᴵ		RBH	145 040	*	BSE	145 066	BSE
145 014		BSE	145 041	*	RBH	145 067	BSE
145 015		RBH	145 042	*	BSE	145 068	BSE
145 016		BSE	145 043	*	MEG	145 069	BSE
145 017		MEG	145 044	*	BSE	145 070	BSE
145 018	*	BSE	145 045	*	BSE	145 071	BSE
145 019	*	RBH	145 046	*	BSE	145 072	RBH
145 020		RBH	145 047	*	BSE	145 073	BSE
145 021		BSE	145 048	*	BSE	145 074	BSE
145 022		BSE	145 049	*	BSE	145 075	BSE
145 023		BSE	145 050	*	RBH	145 076	BSE
145 024		BSE	145 051		BSE	145 077	BSE
145 025		BSE	145 052		BSE	145 078	BSE
145 026		RBH	145 053		BSE	145 079	BSE
145 027		RBH	145 054		BSE	145 080	BSE
145 028		RBH					

CLASS 146   TRAXX P160 AC 2   Bo-Bo

This is the Bombardier TRAXX P160 AC 2 based on the Class 145. Several batches have been built reflecting improvements in design over the years from TRAXX, TRAXX 2 but now the latest version, TRAXX 3, is Class 147.

Class 146 will normally be found working RE trains formed of double-deck carriages. All the 146.0 were at Dortmund but have moved on to other depots, having been replaced by later versions. Stuttgart has lost most of its locos to other depots in the area as part of the plans for Stuttgart 21, which will see the existing depot site cleared upon completion of the new through main station.

The 146.5 locomotives are Fernverkehr locomotives. In effect they carry out the same work as the other locos but the locomotive and double deck train are painted white for Inter City (carriage interiors will vary). They came as a surprise as Fernverkehr had already indicated that the future network was to be ICEs of varying lengths. Just why they are numbered in the 146 5xx series is unclear. These locomotives and trains are based at the new Leipzig West ICE depot. Locomotives are beginning to carry set numbers to reflect that they will normally be working with the same set. (eg. 146 551 carries 2853 but 146 560 carries 2870).

Built: 2001–02 (146.0), 2003–05 (146.1), 2005–07/2013 onwards (146.2), 2012 onwards (146.5).
Builder: Bombardier Kassel.
Continuous Rating: 4200 kW (146.0) 5600 kW others.
Maximum Tractive Effort: 300 kN.   **Weight:** 84 tonnes.
Wheel Diameter: 1250 mm.   **Length over Buffers:** 18.90 m.
Electric Brake: Regenerative.   **Maximum Speed** 160 km/h.
Class Specific Livery: I Intercity, white with red band.

Class 146.0.

146 001	KA	146 012		DA	146 022		LMB
146 002	KA	146 013	A	LMB	146 023		LMB
146 003	KA	146 014		DA	146 024		LMB
146 004	KA	146 015		LMB	146 025		DA
146 005	KA	146 016		DA	146 026		LMB
146 006	KA	146 017	A	DA	146 027		LMB
146 007	FGM	146 018		LMB	146 028		LMB
146 008	A LMB	146 019		LMB	146 029		LMB
146 009	LMB	146 020		LMB	146 030		LMB
146 010	A DA	146 021		DA	146 031		LMB
146 011	DA						

Name:

146 006   Stuart

Class 146.1.

146 101	HB	146 112	A	RF	146 123		HB
146 102	HB	146 113	A	RF	146 124		HB
146 103	HB	146 114	A	RF	146 125		HB
146 104	HB	146 115	A	RF	146 126		HB
146 105	HB	146 116	A	RF	146 127	A	HB
146 106	HB	146 117		EMST	146 128		HB
146 107	HB	146 118		EMST	146 129		HB
146 108	HB	146 119		EMST	146 130		HB
146 109	A RF	146 120		EMST	146 131		HB
146 110	A RF	146 121		EMST	146 132		HB
146 111	A RF	146 122		EDO			

Names:

146 109	Lahr/Schwarzwald	146 114	Landkreis Emmendingen
146 110	Müllheim	146 115	Breisgau-Hochschwarzwald
146 113	Ortenaukreis	146 116	Lörrach

▲ Inter City-liveried 146 575 is seen with a matching rake of empty coaching stock near Bornheim, on its way from Koblenz Hbf to Köln on 5 October 2016. The locomotive is a Bombardier TRAXX P160 AC 2, operated by DB Fernverkehr.   **Matthias Müller**

Class 146.2.

146 201		TU	146 228		RF	146 257		EDO
146 202	A	TU	146 229	A	RF	146 258		EDO
146 203		TU	146 230	A	RF	146 259		EDO
146 204		TU	146 231		RF	146 260		EDO
146 205		RF	146 232		RF	146 261		EDO
146 206		RF	146 233		RF	146 262		EDO
146 207		TU	146 234		TU	146 263		EDO
146 208	A	TU	146 235		RF	146 264		EDO
146 209	A	TS	146 236	A	RF	146 265		EDO
146 210		TU	146 237		RF	146 266		EDO
146 211		TU	146 238		RF	146 267		EDO
146 212		TU	146 239	A	RF	146 268		EDO
146 213		RF	146 240		NN1	146 269		EDO
146 214		RF	146 241		NN1	146 270		EDO
146 215		RF	146 242		NN1	146 271		EDO
146 216		RF	146 243		NN1	146 272		EDO
146 217		RF	146 244		NN1	146 273		EDO
146 218		RF	146 245		NN1	146 274		EDO
146 219		RF	146 246	A	NN1	146 275		EDO
146 220	A	TU	146 247	A	NN1	146 276		EDO
146 221	A	RF	146 251		FGM	146 277		EDO
146 222	A	RF	146 252		FGM	146 278		EDO
146 223	A	TS	146 253		FGM	146 279		EDO
146 224	A	TU	146 254		FGM	146 280		EDO
146 225	A	RF	146 255		FGM	146 281		EDO
146 226	A	RF	146 256		FGM	146 282		EDO
146 227	A	RF						

Names:

146 228	St. Georgen		146 236	Triberg
146 233	Donauschingen		146 237	Karlsruhe

Class 146.5. Some locos also carry a carriage set number; these are shown in brackets.

146 551	(2853)	I	LL2		146 565	(2865)	I	LL2
146 552		I	LL2		146 566		I	LL2
146 553	(2868)	I	LL2		146 567		I	LL2
146 554	(2850)	I	LL2		146 568		I	LL2
146 555		I	LL2		146 569	(2856)	I	LL2
146 556		I	LL2		146 570		I	LL2
146 557		I	LL2		146 571	(2874)	I	LL2
146 558	(2860)	I	LL2		146 572	(2873)	I	LL2
146 559	(2869)	I	LL2		146 573		I	LL2
146 560	(2870)	I	LL2		146 574	(2852)	I	LL2
146 561	(2863)	I	LL2		146 575		I	LL2
146 562		I	LL2		146 576		I	LL2
146 563		I	LL2		146 577	(2858)	I	LL2
146 564		I	LL2					

CLASS 147   TRAXX P160 AC 3   Bo-Bo

The Bombardier TRAXX locomotive has been around since the beginning of the 21st Century with the Class 147 being the latest passenger version, hence TRAXXP160AC3. The first to be delivered were to DB Regio for use with TWINNDEXX carriages on routes from Stuttgart. The fact that the first locomotives have been allocated to Stuttgart is a surprise as this depot is to be closed under the Stuttgart 21 plans.

DB Fernverkehr has also ordered two batches of 17 and 25 locos which will be numbered in the 147 5xx series for use on IC services also with TWINDEXX carriages. As the Stuttgart to Zürich route is to be covered the 147.5s will need clearance for running in Switzerland.

As ever with modern building techniques, although shown as built at Kassel the bodies come from Poland, the bogies from Siegen and electrical equipment from various in-house suppliers, all being put together at Kassel.

The locomotives come with all the latest fittings: PZB, LZB, NBU, EPB, FIS, push-pull, multiple working, door opening and side selection. Bombardier states they can be used for 18 hours a day with a life expectancy of 32 years.

Built: 2016 onwards.
Builder: Bombardier, Kassel.
One Hour Rating: 5600 kW.
Weight: 84 tonnes.
Wheel Diameter: 1250 mm.
Maximum Tractive Effort: 300 kN.
Class Specific Livery: I Intercity, white with red band.

Continuous Rating:
Length over Buffers: 18.90 m.
Maximum Speed: 160 km/h.
Electric Brake: Regenerative.

Class 147.0.

147 001	TS	147 008	TS	147 015	TS
147 002	TS	147 009	TS	147 016	TS
147 003	TS	147 010	TS	147 017	TS
147 004	TS	147 011	TS	147 018	TS
147 005	TS	147 012	TS	147 019	TS
147 006	TS	147 013	TS	147 020	TS
147 007	TS	147 014	TS		

Class 147.5.

147 551	I	147 565	I	147 579	I
147 552	I	147 566	I	147 580	I
147 553	I	147 567	I	147 581	I
147 554	I	147 568	I	147 582	I
147 555	I	147 569	I	147 583	I
147 556	I	147 570	I	147 584	I
147 557	I	147 571	I	147 585	I
147 558	I	147 572	I	147 586	I
147 559	I	147 573	I	147 587	I
147 560	I	147 574	I	147 588	I
147 561	I	147 575	I	147 589	I
147 562	I	147 576	I	147 590	I
147 563	I	147 577	I	147 591	I
147 564	I	147 578	I	147 592	I

CLASS 151   Co-Co

All the active Class 151s were sold by DB Cargo recently to Railpool and immediately leased back! This was probably to release finance to pay for the 187s and 193s (q.v.). The 151s are Co-Co locomotives and were the heavy duty freight locomotives of the 1970s introducing thyristor control to the freight sector. Many 151s had already been sold by DB Cargo to other operators before the sale to Railpool. DB still owns the stored locomotives

Built: 1973–77 for DB.
Builder–Mech. Parts: Krupp.
Builder–Elec. Parts: AEG.
One Hour Rating: 6000 kW.   **Weight:** 126 tonnes.
Continuous Rating: 6470 kW.   **Length over Buffers:** 19.49 m.
Maximum Tractive Effort: 459 kN.   **Maximum Speed:** 120 km/h.
Wheel Diameter: 1250 mm.   **Electric Brake:** Rheostatic.
Non-Standard Livery: N Raspberry red.

All multiple working/push-pull fitted.

a   Fitted with automatic coupler at one end for use on heavy iron ore trains.
a2   Automatic coupler at both ends.
s   Fitted with Swiss safety equipment (Integra).

151 001	NN2	151 022	NN2	151 040	NN2
151 002	NN2	151 023	NN2	151 041	NN2
151 005	EHM (Z)	151 026	NN2	151 043	NN2
151 006	NN2	151 028	NN2	151 045	NN2
151 008	NN2	151 029	NN2	151 046	NN2
151 009	NN2	151 031	NN2	151 048	NN2
151 011	WM (Z)	151 032	NN2	151 049	NN2
151 012	NN2	151 034	NN2	151 053	NN2
151 015	NN2	151 035	NN2	151 055	NN2
151 016	NN2	151 036	NN2	151 059	NN2
151 020	NN2	151 037	NN2	151 061	NN2

▲ 151 094 and 151 113 hurry through Celle with a Hamburg to Beddingen heavy freight on 3 August 2015.   **Brian Garvin**

Number		Code	Number		Code	Number		Code
151 062		NN2	151 102	a	NN2	151 141		NN2
151 063		NN2	151 103		NN2	151 142		WM (Z)
151 064		NN2	151 104	a2	NN2	151 146	s	NN2
151 065		WM (Z)	151 106	a2	NN2	151 148		NN2
151 068		NN2	151 108	a	NN2 (Z)	151 149		NN2
151 069		NN2	151 109		NN2	151 150		NN2
151 073		NN2	151 110	a2	NN2	151 153		NN2
151 075		NN2	151 112	a2	NN2	151 155		NN2
151 076		NN2	151 113	a2	NN2	151 157		NN2
151 077		NN2	151 115	a	WM (Z)	151 159		WM (Z)
151 082		NN2	151 116	a	NN2	151 160		NN2
151 085		NN2	151 126		NN2	151 161		NN2
151 086	N	NN2	151 129		NN2	151 163		NN2
151 087		NN2	151 130		NN2	151 164		NN2
151 088		NN2	151 132		NN2	151 165		NN2
151 094	a2	NN2	151 134	N	NN2	151 166		NN2
151 095	a2	NN2	151 135		NN2	151 167		NN2
151 098	a2	NN2	151 136		NN2	151 168		NN2
151 099		NN2	151 140		NN2	151 169	a	NN2
151 101		NN2						

CLASS 152   Bo-Bo

Class 152 is part of the Siemens Eurosprinter family predating the change to the Taurus styling. 152 032 became 152 190, being fitted with Insulated Gate Bipolar Transistors as part of the development programme. Based at one depot, the class works all over Germany.

Built: 1997–2001.
Builder–Mech. Parts: Krauss Maffei, Siemens/Duewag.
Builder–Elec. Parts: Siemens.

One Hour Rating: 6600 kW.	**Weight:** 86 tonnes.	
Continuous Rating: 6400 kW.	**Length over Buffers:** 19.58 m.	
Maximum Tractive Effort: 300 kN.	**Maximum Speed:** 140 km/h.	
Wheel Diameter: 1250 mm.	**Electric Brake:** Regenerative.	

Number	Code	Number	Code	Number	Code
152 001	NN2	152 029	NN2	152 058	NN2
152 002	NN2	152 030	NN2	152 059	NN2
152 003	NN2	152 031	NN2	152 060	NN2
152 004	NN2	152 033	NN2	152 061	NN2
152 005	NN2	152 034	NN2	152 062	NN2
152 006	NN2	152 035	NN2	152 063	NN2
152 007	NN2	152 036	NN2	152 064	NN2
152 008	NN2	152 037	NN2	152 065	NN2
152 009	NN2	152 038	NN2	152 066	NN2
152 010	NN2	152 039	NN2	152 067	NN2
152 011	NN2	152 040[II]	NN2	152 068	NN2
152 012	NN2	152 041	NN2	152 069	NN2
152 013	NN2	152 042	NN2	152 070	NN2
152 014	NN2	152 043	NN2	152 071	NN2
152 015	NN2	152 044	NN2	152 072	NN2
152 016	NN2	152 045	NN2	152 073	NN2
152 017	NN2	152 046	NN2	152 074	NN2
152 018	NN2	152 047	NN2	152 075[II]	NN2
152 019	NN2	152 048	NN2	152 076	NN2
152 020	NN2	152 049	NN2	152 077	NN2
152 021	NN2	152 050	NN2	152 078	NN2
152 022	NN2	152 051	NN2	152 079	NN2
152 023	NN2	152 052	NN2	152 080	NN2
152 024	NN2	152 053	NN2	152 081	NN2
152 025	NN2	152 054	NN2	152 082	NN2
152 026	NN2	152 055	NN2	152 083	NN2
152 027[II]	NN2	152 056	NN2	152 084	NN2
152 028	NN2	152 057	NN2	152 085	NN2

152 086	NN2	152 115	NN2	152 144	NN2
152 087	NN2	152 116	NN2	152 145	NN2
152 088	NN2	152 117	NN2	152 146	NN2
152 089	NN2	152 118	NN2	152 147	NN2
152 090	NN2	152 119	NN2	152 148	NN2
152 091	NN2	152 120	NN2	152 149	NN2
152 092	NN2	152 121	NN2	152 150	NN2
152 093	NN2	152 122	NN2	152 151	NN2
152 094	NN2	152 123	NN2	152 152	NN2
152 095	NN2	152 124	NN2	152 153	NN2
152 096	NN2	152 125	NN2	152 154	NN2
152 097	NN2	152 126	NN2	152 155	NN2
152 098	NN2	152 127	NN2	152 156	NN2
152 099	NN2	152 128	NN2	152 157	NN2
152 100	NN2	152 129	NN2	152 158	NN2
152 101	NN2	152 130	NN2	152 159	NN2
152 102	NN2	152 131	NN2	152 160	NN2
152 103	NN2	152 132	NN2	152 161	NN2
152 104	NN2	152 133	NN2	152 162	NN2
152 105	NN2	152 134 A	NN2	152 163	NN2
152 106	NN2	152 135 A	NN2	152 164	NN2
152 107	NN2	152 136 A	NN2	152 165	NN2
152 108	NN2	152 137 A	NN2	152 166	NN2
152 109	NN2	152 138 A	NN2	152 167	NN2
152 110	NN2	152 139	NN2	152 168	NN2
152 111	NN2	152 140	NN2	152 169	NN2
152 112	NN2	152 141	NN2	152 170	NN2
152 113	NN2	152 142	NN2	152 190	NN2
152 114	NN2	152 143	NN2		

▲ On 24 February 2018, 152 052 hauls a southbound mixed freight between Bad Honnef and Unkel on the right bank of the Rhein. In the background can be seen the famous Drachenfels rock with its ruined castle at the summit.   **Matthias Müller**

CLASS 155   Co-Co

This class was the DR heavy duty electric locomotive featuring thyristor control, all being based in Seddin. In recent years there have been many withdrawals but a surprise development in 2017 was the sale of all the active locomotives to leasing company Railpool with DB Cargo leasing them back. Locos in store at the time of the sale remain with DB Cargo. This is seen as a good move as with new 187s and 193s due to arrive, DB Cargo will gradually hand back 155s to the leasing company.

Built: 1974–84 for DR.
Builder: LEW.
One Hour Rating: 5400 kW.
Maximum Tractive Effort: 465 kN.   **Weight:** 123 tonnes.
Wheel Diameter: 1250 mm.   **Length over Buffers:** 19.60 m.
Electric Brake: Rheostatic.   **Maximum Speed:** 125 km/h.
Non-Standard Livery: N Raspberry red.

Note: 155 212 and 245 were previously 155 225 and 166 respectively.

155 004	BSE	155 038	WM (Z)	155 086	BSE
155 006	BSE	155 039	BSE	155 087	BSE
155 009	WM (Z)	155 040	WM (Z)	155 091	WM (Z)
155 010	BSE	155 043	BSE	155 095	BSE
155 011	WM (Z)	155 048	WM (Z)	155 097	BSE
155 013	BSE	155 055	BSE	155 099	BSE
155 015	BSE	155 056	BSE	155 101	BSE
155 019	BSE	155 060	BSE	155 107	BSE
155 020	WM (Z)	155 061	BSE	155 108	BSE
155 023	BSE	155 063	WM (Z)	155 109	WM (Z)
155 024	WM (Z)	155 065	BSE	155 111	BSE
155 028	WM (Z)	155 066	WM (Z)	155 112	BSE
155 030	BSE	155 068	WM (Z)	155 113	BSE
155 031	BSE	155 073	WM (Z)	155 114	WM (Z)
155 032	WM (Z)	155 075	BSE	155 115	BSE
155 033	BSE	155 077	BSE	155 117	WM (Z)
155 035	WM (Z)	155 082	BSE	155 118	WM (Z)
155 036	WM (Z)	155 084	BSE	155 121	BSE
155 037	WM (Z)	155 085	BSE	155 122	BSE

▲ 155 222 with a Mega-Kombi trailer train to Dillingen is seen near Bornheim on a sunny 6 July 2017.   **Matthias Müller**

155 123	BSE	155 171	BSE	155 219	N	BSE
155 126	BSE	155 175	WM (Z)	155 222		BSE
155 127	WRS (Z)	155 178	BSE	155 224		WM (Z)
155 128	BSE	155 180	BSE	155 229		BSE
155 130	BSE	155 181	BSE	155 232		BSE
155 132	WM (Z)	155 182	BSE	155 236		BSE
155 133	WM (Z)	155 191	BSE	155 239		BSE
155 134	BSE	155 192	WM (Z)	155 243		BSE
155 135	WM (Z)	155 197	WM (Z)	155 245[II]		BSE
155 138	WM (Z)	155 201	BSE	155 251		BSE
155 141	BSE	155 204	BSE	155 253		BSE
155 147	BSE	155 206	BSE	155 260		BSE
155 148	BSE	155 207	BSE	155 261		BSE
155 151	BSE	155 211	BSE	155 265		WM (Z)
155 152	BSE	155 212[II]	BSE	155 269		BSE
155 157	BSE	155 218	BSE	155 273		BSE
155 168	WM (Z)					

CLASS 181 — Bo-Bo

Just a few locomotives remain in stock for working to Strasbourg in France. One locomotive is used on empty stock movements from Basel to Dortmund, a job that can be covered by an ordinary locomotive if there is a shortage of fit locomotives to work into France.

Built: 1974–75 for DB.
Builder–Mech. Parts: Krupp.
Builder–Elec. Parts: AEG.
One Hour Rating: 3300 kW.
Continuous Rating: 3200 kW.
Maximum Tractive Effort: 285 kN.
Wheel Diameter: 1250 mm.

Systems: 15 kV AC 16.7 Hz/25 kV AC 50 Hz.
Weight: 83 tonnes.
Length over Buffers: 17.94 m.
Maximum Speed: 160 km/h.
Electric Brake: Rheostatic.

All multiple working/push-pull fitted.

181 204	FGM	181 211	FGM	181 215	FGM
181 205	FGM	181 213	FGM	181 218	FGM

Names:

181 211	LORRAINE	181 213	SAAR

CLASS 182 — Bo-Bo

This small batch of Eurosprinter (Taurus) locomotives was ordered because the Class 152s were refused permission to operate in Austria. Later the 182s were handed over to DB Regio, which now uses them on RE services. With a 230 km/h top speed one wonders why they are not with DB Fernverkehr which could have then withdrawn more Class 120s! 182 506 is a former MRCE hire loco taken over by the research department at Minden.

Built: 2001.
Builder–Mech. Parts: Krauss Maffei, Duewag.
Builder–Elec. Parts: Siemens.
One Hour Rating: 6600 kW.
Continuous Rating: 6400 kW.
Maximum Tractive Effort: 300 kN.
Wheel Diameter: 1250 mm.

Systems: 15 kV AC 16.7 Hz/25 kV AC 50 Hz.
Weight: 86 tonnes.
Length over Buffers: 19.58 m.
Maximum Speed: 230 km/h.
Electric Brake: Rheostatic.

182 001		BCS	182 010	BCS	182 019	WR
182 002	A	BCS	182 011	BCS	182 020	BCS
182 003		BCS	182 012	BCS	182 021	BCS
182 004		BCS	182 013	BCS	182 022	BCS
182 005		BCS	182 014	BCS	182 023	WR
182 006		BCS	182 015	WR	182 024	BCS
182 007		BCS	182 016	BCS	182 025	WR
182 008		BCS	182 017	WR	182 506	STMI
182 009		BCS	182 018	BCS		

▲ 182 024 is in charge of propelling the double-deck stock of train RE 1 – 3118 Frankfurt/Oder to Magdeburg Hbf on 31 March 2018, seen here at Berlin-Ostbahnhof. **Matthias Müller**

▼ Dual-voltage capability enables Class 185 locomotives to work into France, Austria and Switzerland. Here 185 125 and 185 091 are seen at Wassen on 25 May 2016, taking the Gotthard route though Switzerland. **Keith Fender**

CLASS 185 TRAXX F140 AC Bo-Bo

To replace the 1960s standard freight locomotive (Class 140), DB chose the Bombardier dual voltage TRAXX locomotive. Although to be mainly used on the German voltage, the provision of 25 kV AC with modern electronics caused Bombardier to concentrate on providing a dual-voltage locomotive as standard, the extra cost being marginal. DB ordered the 185s and was able to replace some 800 Class 140s with 400 185s. The locomotives work into France, Austria and Switzerland. The previously joint arrangement with Green Cargo in Sweden has ended but the locomotives continue on the same work with 185 401–403 coming into DB stock. 185 400 does not exist, having been turned out as 146 228 in a demonstration to customers of how quickly the conversion can be done.

Built: 2000–10.
Builder: Bombardier Transportation (Kassel).
Continuous Rating: 5600 kW.
Maximum Tractive Effort: 300 kN.
Wheel Diameter: 1250 mm.

Systems: 15 kV AC 16.7 Hz/25 kV AC 50 Hz.
Weight: 84 tonnes.
Length over Buffers: 18.90 m.
Maximum Speed: 140 km/h.
Electric Brake: Regenerative.

185 020–039 Fitted for working into France.
185 085–094 Fitted for working into Switzerland and Austria (Kornwestheim–Konstanz–Wolfurt).
185 095–128 Fitted for working into Switzerland (Gotthard route primarily)
185 321–337 DB Cargo Scandinavia locomotives for Hamburg–Denmark–Sweden.
185 338–399 Fitted for working into Austria. (Agreement changed 01/08/12 which excluded earlier locomotives).

185 001	RM	185 042	RM	185 083	RM
185 002	RM	185 043	RM	185 084	RM
185 003	RM	185 044	RM	185 085	RM
185 004	RM	185 045	RM	185 086	RM
185 005	RM	185 046	RM	185 087	RM
185 006	RM	185 047	RM	185 088	RM
185 007	RM	185 048	RM	185 089	RM
185 008	RM	185 049	RM	185 090 A	RM
185 009	RM	185 050	RM	185 091	RM
185 010	RM	185 051	RM	185 092	RM
185 011	RM	185 052	RM	185 093	RM
185 012	RM	185 053	RM	185 094	RM
185 013	RM	185 054	RM	185 095	RM
185 014	RM	185 055	RM	185 096	RM
185 015	RM	185 056	RM	185 097	RM
185 016	RM	185 057	RM	185 098	RM
185 017	RM	185 058	RM	185 099	RM
185 018	RM	185 059	RM	185 100	RM
185 019	RM	185 060	RM	185 101	RM
185 020	RM	185 061	RM	185 102	RM
185 021	RM	185 062	RM	185 103	RM
185 022	RM	185 063	RM	185 104	RM
185 023	RM	185 064	RM	185 105	RM
185 024	RM	185 065	RM	185 106	RM
185 025	RM	185 066	RM	185 107	RM
185 026	RM	185 067	RM	185 108	RM
185 027	RM	185 068	RM	185 109	RM
185 028	RM	185 069	RM	185 110	RM
185 029	RM	185 070	RM	185 111	RM
185 030	RM	185 071	RM	185 112	RM
185 031	RM	185 072	RM	185 113	RM
185 032	RM	185 073	RM	185 114	RM
185 033	RM	185 074	RM	185 115	RM
185 034	RM	185 075	RM	185 116	RM
185 035	RM	185 076	RM	185 117	RM
185 036	RM	185 077	RM	185 118	RM
185 037	RM	185 078	RM	185 119	RM
185 038	RM	185 079	RM	185 120	RM
185 039	RM	185 080	RM	185 121	RM
185 040	RM	185 081	RM	185 122	RM
185 041	RM	185 082	RM	185 123	RM

185 124		RM	185 188		RM	185 252		RM
185 125		RM	185 189		RM	185 253		RM
185 126		RM	185 190		RM	185 254		RM
185 127		RM	185 191		RM	185 255		RM
185 128		RM	185 192		RM	185 256		RM
185 129		RM	185 193		RM	185 257		RM
185 130		RM	185 194		RM	185 258		RM
185 131		RM	185 195		RM	185 259		RM
185 132		RM	185 196		RM	185 260		RM
185 133		RM	185 197		RM	185 261		RM
185 134		RM	185 198		RM	185 262		RM
185 135		RM	185 199		RM	185 263		RM
185 136		RM	185 200		RM	185 264		RM
185 137		RM	185 201		RM	185 265		RM
185 138		RM	185 202		RM	185 266		RM
185 139		RM	185 203		RM	185 267		RM
185 140		RM	185 204		RM	185 268		RM
185 141		RM	185 205		RM	185 269		RM
185 142	A	RM	185 206		RM	185 270		RM
185 143		RM	185 207		RM	185 271		RM
185 144		RM	185 208		RM	185 272		RM
185 145		RM	185 209		RM	185 273	A	RM
185 146		RM	185 210		RM	185 274		RM
185 147		RM	185 211		RM	185 275		RM
185 148		RM	185 212		RM	185 276		RM
185 149		RM	185 213		RM	185 277		RM
185 150		RM	185 214		RM	185 278		RM
185 151		RM	185 215		RM	185 279		RM
185 152	A	RM	185 216		RM	185 280		RM
185 153		RM	185 217		RM	185 281		RM
185 154		RM	185 218		RM	185 282		RM
185 155		RM	185 219		RM	185 283		RM
185 156		RM	185 220		RM	185 284		RM
185 157		RM	185 221		RM	185 285		RM
185 158		RM	185 222		RM	185 286		RM
185 159		RM	185 223		RM	185 287		RM
185 160		RM	185 224		RM	185 288		RM
185 161		RM	185 225		RM	185 289		RM
185 162		RM	185 226		RM	185 290		RM
185 163		RM	185 227		RM	185 291		RM
185 164		RM	185 228		RM	185 292		RM
185 165		RM	185 229		RM	185 293		RM
185 166		RM	185 230		RM	185 294		RM
185 167		RM	185 231		RM	185 295		RM
185 168		RM	185 232		RM	185 296		RM
185 169		RM	185 233		RM	185 297		RM
185 170		RM	185 234		RM	185 298		RM
185 171		RM	185 235		RM	185 299		RM
185 172		RM	185 236		RM	185 300		RM
185 173		RM	185 237		RM	185 301		RM
185 174		RM	185 238		RM	185 302		RM
185 175		RM	185 239		RM	185 303		RM
185 176		RM	185 240		RM	185 304		RM
185 177		RM	185 241		RM	185 305		RM
185 178		RM	185 242		RM	185 306		RM
185 179		RM	185 243		RM	185 307		RM
185 180		RM	185 244		RM	185 308		RM
185 181		RM	185 245		RM	185 309		RM
185 182		RM	185 246		RM	185 310		RM
185 183		RM	185 247		RM	185 311		RM
185 184		RM	185 248		RM	185 312		RM
185 185		RM	185 249		RM	185 313		RM
185 186		RM	185 250		RM	185 314		RM
185 187		RM	185 251		RM	185 315		RM

185 316	RM	185 345	RM	185 374	RM
185 317	RM	185 346	RM	185 375	RM
185 318	RM	185 347	RM	185 376	RM
185 319	RM	185 348	RM	185 377	RM
185 320	RM	185 349	RM	185 378	RM
185 321	RM	185 350	RM	185 379	RM
185 322	RM	185 351	RM	185 380	RM
185 323	RM	185 352	RM	185 381	RM
185 324	RM	185 353	RM	185 382	RM
185 325	RM	185 354	RM	185 383	RM
185 326	RM	185 355	RM	185 384	RM
185 327	RM	185 356	RM	185 385	RM
185 328	RM	185 357	RM	185 386	RM
185 329	RM	185 358	RM	185 387	RM
185 330	RM	185 359	RM	185 388	RM
185 331	RM	185 360	RM	185 389 A	RM
185 332	RM	185 361	RM	185 390	RM
185 333	RM	185 362	RM	185 391	RM
185 334	RM	185 363	RM	185 392	RM
185 335	RM	185 364	RM	185 393	RM
185 336	RM	185 365	RM	185 394	RM
185 337	RM	185 366	RM	185 395	RM
185 338	RM	185 367	RM	185 396	RM
185 339	RM	185 368	RM	185 397	RM
185 340	RM	185 369	RM	185 398	RM
185 341	RM	185 370	RM	185 399 A	RM
185 342	RM	185 371	RM	185 401	RM
185 343	RM	185 372	RM	185 402	RM
185 344	RM	185 373	RM	185 403	RM

▲ TRAXX 187 126 is seen with a mixed freight train from Mannheim to Köln Gremberg yard, passing Bonn-Beuel on 5 July 2017.   **Matthias Müller**

CLASS 186   TRAXX F140 MS   Bo-Bo

The previous edition of this book showed DB as having 186 321–340. These have all been sold to its French subsidiary Euro Cargo Rail and thus no longer count as DB Cargo locomotives. However they continue to be leased back when traffic levels are high.

CLASS 187   TRAXX F160 AC 3   Bo-Bo

This class is the updated version of Class 185 with Bombardier continuing with the TRAXX name, this being the Mark 3 version. The first deliveries were to private operators and were fitted with last mile diesel engine modules, but DB Cargo went for a straight electric locomotive. When first delivered DB Cargo put the locos into use on Mannheim to Köln Gremberg workings but as more locos arrived their workings spread over the network. 187 080–084 were acquired in 2017 as Bombardier had not been able to sell them to private operators who all wanted the last mile version. DB needed more locos so was glad to have them no doubt at a good price! Deliveries continue.

Built: 2016–
Builder: Bombardier, Kassel.
One Hour Rating:
Continuous Rating: 5600 kW.
Wheel Diameter: 1250 mm.
Maximum Tractive Effort: 300kN.
Weight: 86 tonnes.
Length over Buffers: 18.90 m.
Maximum Speed: 140 km/h.
Electric Brake: Regenerative.

187 080	RM	187 134	RM	187 173 RM
187 081	RM	187 135	RM	187 174 RM
187 082	RM	187 136	RM	187 175 RM
187 083	RM	187 137	RM	187 176 RM
187 084	RM	187 138	RM	187 177 RM
187 100	RM	187 139	RM	187 178 RM
187 101	RM	187 140	RM	187 179 RM
187 102	RM	187 141	RM	187 180 RM
187 103	RM	187 142	RM	187 181 RM
187 104	RM	187 143	RM	187 182 RM
187 105	RM	187 144	RM	187 183 RM
187 106	RM	187 145	RM	187 184 RM
187 107	RM	187 146	RM	187 185 RM
187 108	RM	187 147	RM	187 186 RM
187 109	RM	187 148	RM	187 187 RM
187 110	RM	187 149	RM	187 188 RM
187 111	RM	187 150	RM	187 189 RM
187 112	RM	187 151	RM	187 190 RM
187 113	RM	187 152	RM	187 191 RM
187 114	RM	187 153	RM	187 192 RM
187 115	RM	187 154	RM	187 193 RM
187 116	RM	187 155	RM	187 194 RM
187 117	RM	187 156	RM	187 195 RM
187 118	RM	187 157	RM	187 196 RM
187 119	RM	187 158	RM	187 197 RM
187 120	RM	187 159	RM	187 198 RM
187 121	RM	187 160	RM	187 199 RM
187 122	RM	187 161		187 200
187 123	RM	187 162		187 201
187 124	RM	187 163		187 202
187 125	RM	187 164		187 203
187 126	RM	187 165		187 204
187 127	RM	187 166		187 205
187 128	RM	187 167		187 206
187 129	RM	187 168		187 207
187 130	RM	187 169		187 208
187 131	RM	187 170		187 209
187 132	RM	187 171		187 210
187 133	RM	187 172		

CLASS 189   Bo-Bo

This class is the multi-system version of the Eurosprinter family but is of a different appearance to the Taurus family. 189 001–003 were prototypes and were replaced by three standard locomotives in 2003. It took a long time to get the class approved for working into neighbouring countries with the idea of running into Belgium abandoned. There are now regular workings into Poland, Czech Republic and the Netherlands with two batches of locos involved working to Rotterdam and Amsterdam, some having automatic couplings fitted for the heavy coal and ore trains. 189 090–099 have been sold to MRCE. In 2017 DB acquired 189 822/823 from Siemens as no buyers were forthcoming as everyone now wanted Vectrons of Class 193 (q.v.) Another good buy for DB? 189 822 was subsequently sold to DB Cargo Italia.

Built: 2002–05.
Builder: Siemens.
One Hour Rating: 6600 kW.
Continuous Rating: 6400 kW.
Maximum Tractive Effort: 300 kN.
Wheel Diameter: 1250 mm.

Systems: 15 kV AC 16.7 Hz; 25 kV AC 50 Hz; 1500 V DC; 3000 V DC.
Weight: 86 tonnes.
Length over Buffers: 19.58 m.
Maximum Speed: 140 km/h.
Electric Brake: Regenerative.

cz   Authorized to operate in the Czech Republic.
n   Authorized to operate in the Netherlands and has white warning panel at each end.
E   Capable of operating in Germany, Austria, Switzerland, Italy, the Netherlands, Slovenia, Hungary and Romania.

189 001[II]	cz	NN2	189 032	a n	NN2	189 063	cz	NN2
189 002[II]	cz	NN2	189 033	a n	NN2	189 064	cz	NN2
189 003[II]	cz	NN2	189 034	a n	NN2	189 065	n	NN2
189 004	cz	NN2	189 035	a n	NN2	189 066	n	NN2
189 005	cz	NN2	189 036	a n	NN2	189 067	n	NN2
189 006	cz	NN2	189 037	a n	NN2	189 068	n	NN2
189 007	cz	NN2	189 038	a n	NN2	189 069	n	NN2
189 008	cz	NN2	189 039	a n	NN2	189 070	n	NN2
189 009	cz	NN2	189 040	a n	NN2	189 071	n	NN2
189 010	cz	NN2	189 041	a n	NN2	189 072	n	NN2
189 011	cz	NN2	189 042	a n	NN2	189 073	n	NN2
189 012	cz	NN2	189 043	a n	NN2	189 074	n	NN2
189 013	cz	NN2	189 044	a n	NN2	189 075	n	NN2
189 014	cz	NN2	189 045	a n	NN2	189 076	n	NN2
189 015	cz	NN2	189 046	a n	NN2	189 077	n	NN2
189 016	cz	NN2	189 047	a n	NN2	189 078	n	NN2
189 017	cz	NN2	189 048	n	NN2	189 079	n	NN2
189 018	cz	NN2	189 049	n	NN2	189 080	n	NN2
189 019	cz	NN2	189 050	n	NN2	189 081	n	NN2
189 020	cz	NN2	189 051	n	NN2	189 082	n	NN2
189 021	cz	NN2	189 052	n	NN2	189 083	n	NN2
189 022	cz	NN2	189 053	n	NN2	189 084	n	NN2
189 023	n	NN2	189 054	n	NN2	189 085	n	NN2
189 024	n	NN2	189 055	cz	NN2	189 086	n	NN2
189 025	n	NN2	189 056	cz	NN2	189 087	n	NN2
189 026	n	NN2	189 057	cz	NN2	189 088	n	NN2
189 027	n	NN2	189 058	cz	NN2	189 089	n	NN2
189 028	n	NN2	189 059	cz	NN2	189 100	n	NN2
189 029	n	NN2	189 060	cz	NN2	189 502		STMI
189 030	a n	NN2	189 061	cz	NN2			
189 031	a n	NN2	189 062	cz	NN2	189 823	E	NN2

▲ Class 189 is Siemens' early 21st century design of multi-system locomotive, capable of operating in many countries. 189 043 and 189 049 are seen near Giessenburg on the Betuweroute freight-only line in the Netherlands on 26 March 2016. The train is a 42-car loaded coal train from the port of Rotterdam, heading for Duisburg. **Quintus Vosman**

▼ Vectron 193 300 leads six other members of the class from Regensburg to Köln Gremberg yard on 1 July 2018, seen near Porz-Wahn towards the end of their journey. The lead locomotive carries a special livery promoting the green credentials of Siemens latest electric locomotive. **Matthias Müller**

CLASS 193   SIEMENS VECTRON   Bo-Bo

The Siemens Vectron is a very successful locomotive being the follow-on and updated locomotive after the Eurosprinter series. Many private operators went after the type as soon as Siemens put it on the market. Just like its predecessor, locos have country specific packages allowing them to be used in various European countries. DB Cargo just had to get in on the act and acquire some for its increasing cross-border traffic. It in fact hired some for a while and was obviously satisfied with the type. Siemens with the Vectron has done good preparatory work getting the type accepted all across Europe in very good time. The first DB locomotives have been allocated to Nürnberg Rbf depot with some going straight into the Netherlands for driver training there. Locos are fitted out with the D A CH I NL package so it is obvious the locos will see use on traffic flowing out of Europort and Amsterdam through Germany and Switzerland to Italy. The Class 193 can also be fitted with a last mile diesel module and be fitted out for use in any country on the European mainland. DB has an option for 100 193s but has only confirmed 60 locos so far.There was talk of the locos working into Belgium but so far none have appeared with a "Belgian Package", indeed early locos have appeared only cleared for Germany and Austria. The higher numbered locomotives are with DB Regio working Nürnberg Hbf–Sonneberg services over the high speed line for which locos fitted with ETCS are required. They are used in top and tail mode as there are no driving trailers fitted with ETCS.

Built: 2017–
Builder: Siemens, München-Allach.
One Hour Rating: 6400 kW.
Continuous Rating: 6400 kW.
Wheel Diameter: 1250 mm.
Maximum Tractive Effort: 300 kN.
Non-Standard Livery: N MRCE livery.

Weight: 88–96 tonnes.
Length over Buffers: 18.98 m.
Maximum Speed: 200km/h.
Electric Brake:

Class 193.3.

193 300	A	NN2	193 320		NN2	193 340	NN2
193 301		NN2	193 321		NN2	193 341	NN2
193 302		NN2	193 322		NN2	193 342	NN2
193 303		NN2	193 323		NN2	193 343	NN2
193 304		NN2	193 324		NN2	193 344	NN2
193 305		NN2	193 325		NN2	193 345	
193 306		NN2	193 326		NN2	193 346	
193 307		NN2	193 327		NN2	193 347	
193 308		NN2	193 328		NN2	193 348	
193 309		NN2	193 329		NN2	193 349	
193 310		NN2	193 330		NN2	193 350	
193 311		NN2	193 331		NN2	193 351	
193 312		NN2	193 332		NN2	193 352	
193 313		NN2	193 333		NN2	193 353	
193 314		NN2	193 334		NN2	193 354	NN2
193 315		NN2	193 335		NN2	193 355	NN2
193 316		NN2	193 336		NN2	193 356	NN2
193 317		NN2	193 337		NN2	193 357	NN2
193 318		NN2	193 338		NN2	193 358	NN2
193 319		NN2	193 339			193 359	NN2

Class 193.6.

193 600	N	NN2	193 608	N	NN2	193 609	N	NN2
193 607	N	NN2						

Class 193.8.

193 801	N	NN1	193 805	N	NN1	193 859	N	NN2
193 802	N	NN1	193 806	N	NN1	193 860	N	NN2
193 804	N	NN1						

2. MAIN-LINE DIESEL LOCOMOTIVES

CLASS 077   "CLASS 66"   Co-Co

Locomotives numbered in this series can be found under Class 247.

CLASS 202   B-B

At one time there were nearly 900 Class 201/2/4 locomotives but now few are left in DB service. Class 202 belonged to DB Regio with the last examples withdrawn in 2002. Two survive with 202 563 at Meiningen works being a rescue locomotive for overhauled locomotives when out on test and is in a light blue livery. 202 646 belongs to DB Regio Erzgebirgbahn being used to rescue failed DMUs but also used on ballast trains and snowplough duties and retains the old DR Bordeaux red livery. Many withdrawn Class 202s have been modernised at Stendal works and sold to private operators - see German Railways Part 2.

Built: 1964–78 for DR.
Builder: LEW.
Engine: 853 kW.
Transmission: Hydraulic.
Maximum Tractive Effort: 222 kN.
Wheel Diameter: 1000 mm.
Train Heating: Steam.

Weight: 64 tonnes.
Length over Buffers: 14.24 m.
Maximum Speed: 100 km/h.

| 202 563 | N | UMX | 202 646 | N | DC (Z) |

CLASS 203   B-B

The former DB Regio workshops at Stendal ended up with over 200 Class 201/202/204 stored there. Realising that the demise of the classes would leave it with no work, the works began to modernise these classes as a local initiative and soon found buyers in the emerging private sector. Such has been the success of these conversions that some DB subsidiaries have now purchased some of these locomotives. First the München S-Bahn hired a locomotive and then bought it. Later DB Bahnbau (DBB) and DB Gleisbau (DGB) purchased some of the 203.3 version; these locomotives now come under DB Netz. Centrally controlled by DB Netz (DBN) maintenance is undertaken at any convenient depot.

Built: 1964–78 for DR.
Builder: LEW.
Rebuilt: 2001–2003 by Alstom Locomotive Service, Stendal.
Engine: MTU 12V4000 R10 of 1380 kW (203.0); CAT 3512B DI-TA of 1305 kW (203.3).
Tansmission: Hydraulic.
Maximum Tractive Effort: 206 kN.
Wheel Diameter: 1000 mm.
Train Heating: None.

Weight: 72 tonnes.
Length over buffers: 14.24 m.
Maximum Speed: 100 km/h.

Class Specific Livery: Y Some Class 203.3 are in a variation of departmental yellow livery with a blue band around the base of the body and a large blue triangle on the front ends.

Class 203/3. Caterpillar engine.

203 301	Y	DBN	203 307	Y	DBN	203 312	Y	DBN
203 302	Y	DBN	203 308	Y	DBN	203 313	Y	DBN
203 303	Y	DBN	203 309	Y	DBN	203 314	Y	DBN
203 304	Y	DBN	203 310	Y	DBN	203 315	Y	DBN
203 305	Y	DBN	203 311	Y	DBN	203 316	Y	DBN
203 306	Y	DBN						

CLASS 212 B-B

This class was in effect totally withdrawn by DB Schenker (now DB Cargo) but sectorisation saw other sectors wanting their own locomotives rather than hiring in. Consequently some 212s have been reinstated after overhaul at Cottbus where new MTU engines were fitted and the steam heating boiler was removed. Other 212s have been rebuilt at Stendal in a manner similar to the 202s and have been snapped up by private operators. A larger modernisation has also taken place with some emerging from Stendal as Class 214. Some locomotives were converted to Class 714 in the old system and have now been given EVNs that show the old 212 number. All of the Class 212s remaining with DB are in use with DB Netz. Where given, the allocations are nominal as locomotives needing attention often get sent to the nearest depot available. More locomotives are expected to change to a yellow livery in due course. Locos with new engines are with Fahrwegdienste the other two are with DB Bahnbau Gruppe.

Built: 1962–65 for DB.
Builder: MaK/Jung/Deutz/Henschel.
Engine: MTU MB 12V652 TA/MAN V6 V 18/21 TL. * MTU 8V4000 R41.
Power: 1005 kW (1350 hp).
Transmission: Hydraulic. Voith L216 rs.
Maximum Tractive Effort: 183 kN.   **Weight:** 62 tonnes.
Wheel Diameter: 950 mm.   **Length over Buffers:** 12.30 m.
Train Heating: None.   **Maximum Speed:** 100 km/h.
Non-Standard Livery: N 212 093 is in old DB purple red livery.
           212 329 is in old DB turquoise & beige livery.

All multiple working fitted.

212 034		*	TK	212 265		*	TK	212 317		*	TK
212 036		*	TK	212 274		*	TK	212 323		*	TK
212 093	N	*	TK	212 298		*	TK	212 329	N	*	TK
212 094		*	TK	212 306	Y		EDEF	212 347		*	TK
212 097	Y		EDEF	212 310		*	TK			

▲ DB Netz 203 315, in distinctive yellow livery, waits for work at Fulda on 2 March 2017. **Brian Garvin**

CLASS 215 B-B

DB Autozug acquired these locomotives for working its trains between Niebüll and Westerland (Sylt). They were stored circa 2008 and put up for sale but there were no takers. In October 2017 the first few locos were sent off for scrap and it cannot be long before the remainder follow.

Built: 1968–69 for DB.
Builder: Krupp/MaK/Henschel/Krauss-Maffei.
Engine: MTU MB 16V 652 TB (MAN 12 V 956 TB*).
Power: 1400 kW (1900 h.p.); 1840 kW (2400 h.p.*).
Transmission: Hydraulic. Voith L820 rs or MTU K252 SU.
Maximum Tractive Effort: 245 kN.   **Weight:** 79–80 tonnes
Wheel Diameter: 1000 mm.   **Length over Buffers:** 16.40 m.
Train Heating: Steam.   **Maximum Speed:** 140 km/h

All multiple working fitted.

215 901	DCX (Z)	215 904	DCX (Z)	215 909	DCX (Z)
215 902	DCX (Z)	215 907	DCX (Z)	215 910	DCX (Z)

CLASS 218 B-B

Most of this class is used by DB Regio and its subsidiaries on push-pull services but some are hired in by DB Fernverkehr and used on EC/IC trains in some areas (eg. München–Lindau). Those allocated to Niebüll are used on Itzehoe–Westerland IC trains and the car shuttles to Westerland when a 245 is not available. The 218.8 series are DB Fernverkehr rescue locos with numbers allocated according to their original construction batch number. Continuing deliveries of new DMUs and loss of services to private operators as well as more electrification (München–Lindau) will mean further reallocations or indeed withdrawals. Locomotives 218 329 and 330 have been fitted with Caterpillar 3516B HD engines for assessment. Overhauls of 218 002–218 298 have now ceased. A large number of locomotives are stored at Bremen works and Hamm pending sale. 218 002-218 011 were recently running as Class 225 but the authorities insisted that as they had not been rebuilt they should revert to their original numbers! These locomotives belong to DB Cargo for freight use. During 2011 DB placed a framework contract with Bombardier for a new class of diesel locomotive (Class 245). These locos were likely to replace all the remaining 218s within a few years, but continuing teething problems with the Class 245s may cause a rethink.

Built: 1968–79 for DB.
Builder: Krupp/MaK/Henschel/Krauss-Maffei.
Engine: MTU MA 12V 956 TB 10 (*12V 956 TB 11; §Pielstick 16 PA 4V 200; †MTU MA 12V956 TBG11; ‡MTU 16V 4000R40 of 2000 kW).
Power: 1840 kW (2500 hp) (*§2061 kW (3000 hp)).
Transmission: Hydraulic. Voith L820 rs.
Maximum Tractive Effort: 245 kN.   **Weight:** 76.5–78.5 tonnes.
Wheel Diameter: 1000 mm.   **Length over Buffers:** 16.40 m.
Train Heating: Electric.   **Maximum Speed:** 140 km/h.
Non-Standard Livery: N 218 387 Old DB purple red livery (Purpurrot).

All multiple working fitted.

Class 218.0.

218 005	‡	DCX (Z)	218 009		DCX (Z)	218 011	DCX (Z)

Class 218.1.

218 153		EHM (Z)	218 223	*		EHM (Z)	218 321	‡	ANB
218 156		EHM (Z)	218 224	‡		EHM (Z)	218 322	‡	ANB
218 161		EHM (Z)	218 249			FWD	218 326	§	TU
218 163		EHM (Z)	218 261	Y		EDEF	218 329	§	AK
218 164		EHM (Z)	218 272			FWD	218 330	§	AK
218 201	*	EHM (Z)	218 287	Y		EDEF (Z)	218 333	‡	AK
218 202	*	EHM (Z)	218 304	Y	*	EDEF	218 340	*	ANB
218 205	*	EHM (Z)	218 307		‡	ANB	218 341	*	ANB
218 208		FWD	218 311		*	ANB	218 342	*	EHM (Z)
218 219	*	MKP (Z)	218 313		*	ANB	218 343	*	TU
218 220	*	DCX (Z)	218 314		*	ANB	218 345	‡	ANB

218 359		*	ANB	218 417	*	TU	218 458	‡	EHM (Z)
218 362		*	EHM (Z)	218 418		MMF	218 460	‡	FSK
218 363		*	ANB	218 419	‡	MMF	218 461	‡	EHM (Z)
218 364		*	ANB	218 420	*	MKP	218 462	‡	MMF (Z)
218 366		*	ANB	218 421	‡	MMF	218 463	‡	MMF
218 369		*	ANB	218 422	t	MMF	218 464	*	TU (Z)
218 371		*	EHM (Z)	218 423	‡	MMF	218 465	‡	MMF
218 372		*	EHM (Z)	218 424	*	MKP	218 466	‡	EHM (Z)
218 376		*	ANB	218 425	*	MKP	218 468	‡	DCX (Z)
218 379		*	ANB	218 426	*	MMF	218 470	*	AK
218 380		*	ANB	218 427	§	TU	218 471	Y ‡	DBN
218 381		*	ANB	218 428	‡	MMF	218 473	*	ANB
218 385		*	ANB	218 429	§	MKP	218 474	*	AOP
218 386		*	ANB	218 430	§	MMF	218 476	*	TU
218 387	N	*	FK	218 431	‡	TS	218 477	Y *	DBN
218 389		*	ANB	218 432	‡	TU	218 481	*	TU
218 391	Y	*	EDEF	218 433	‡	MMF	218 483	*	RK
218 392	Y		BSE	218 434	‡	TU	218 484	*	RK
218 397		*	ANB	218 435	‡	TU	218 485	‡	EHM (Z)
218 401		‡	MMF	218 436	‡	TU	218 486	§	TP
218 403		‡	MMF	218 438	‡	TU	218 487	‡	AL
218 404		*	MMF	218 439	*	TU	218 488	‡	EHM (Z)
218 406			TU	218 440	*	EHM (Z)	218 489	‡	EHM (Z)
218 407		*	AK	218 442	*	EHM (Z)	218 491	‡	TU
218 408		*	TU	218 443	*	TU	218 492	‡	EHM (Z)
218 409		*	TU	218 445	*	EHM (Z)	218 493	‡	TU
218 410		*	MKP	218 446	*	MKP	218 494	‡	TU
218 411		*	MKP	218 449	*	EDEF	218 495	‡	TU
218 412		*	TU	218 452	*	MMF	218 496	†	MKP
218 413		*	HBX (Z)	218 453	*	AK	218 497	†	MKP
218 414		*	MKP	218 454	*	MMF (Z)	218 498	§	MMF
218 415		*	MKP	218 456	‡	TU	218 499	§	TU
218 416		‡	MMF	218 457	‡	EHM (Z)			

Class 218.8.

218 810	FGM	218 830	FGM	218 835	BRG
218 812	FGM	218 831	BRG	218 836	BRG
218 813	FGM	218 832	BRG	218 837	BRG
218 824	FGM	218 833	BRG	218 838	FGM
218 825	FGM	218 834	BRG	218 839	FGM

CLASS 225   B-B

Previously Class 215, the classification of those locomotives in the freight sector was changed to denote their different use. As can be seen several are in store.

Built: 1968–69 for DB.
Builder: Krupp/MaK/Henschel/Krauss-Maffei.
Engine: MTU MB 16V 652 TB (*MAN 12 V 956 TB).
Power: 1400 kW (1900 hp) (*1840 kW (2400 hp).
Transmission: Hydraulic. Voith L820 rs or MTU K252 SU.
Maximum Tractive Effort: 245 kN.   **Weight:** 79–80 tonnes.
Wheel Diameter: 1000 mm.   **Length over Buffers:** 16.40 m.
Train Heating: None.   **Maximum Speed:** 140 km/h.

All multiple working fitted.

b   Fitted with Belgian safety equipment.
e   Fitted with electric train heating.

225 003	*	DCX (Z)	225 010	Y *	EDEF	225 031	DCX (Z)
225 009	*	DCX (Z)					

55

▲ Class 218s have long been the staple power for IC services to and from the island of Sylt. Here, 218 389 and 218 380 are at the head of IC2375 from Westerland (Sylt) to Karlsruhe, seen on the island near Morsum on 25 September 2016. **Matthias Müller**

▼ In DB Bahnbau yellow livery, 225 010 takes a train of empty rail-carrying wagons to Duisburg on 1 August 2015. It is seen near Hammerstein on the right bank of the Rhein between Koblenz and Bonn. **Matthias Müller**

CLASS 232   "LUDMILLA"   Co-Co

Once there were over 1100 Soviet built diesels on the DR but fewer than half this number survive and they are Classes 232 and 233 (Classes 220, 230, 231, 234, 241 and 242 having gone). Class 232 was built specifically for the eastern bloc countries and featured an electric train supply. As inherited, Class 232 was a mixed traffic locomotive but now the class is dedicated to freight work. Built like a Soviet tank these locomotives are quite powerful and DB found them quite useful resulting in many being moved to the west part of the country at Oberhausen where one 232 could replace two Class 216s in multiple. Because of the recession and loss of freight traffic, many locomotives are in store at places such as Mukran, Rostock and Chemitz. The 232.9s are fitted out for working into the Netherlands and have a white warning panel on the front. Several locomotives have been sold to DB Cargo subsidiaries in other countries such as Poland (East West Railways) only to be hired back for work in Germany!

Built: 1973–82 for DR.
Builder: October Revolution Locomotive Works, Voroshilovgrad, USSR.
Engine: Kolomna 16-cylinder 5D49.
Power: 2200 kW (2950 hp).
Transmission: Electric.
Maximum Tractive Effort: 340 kN.   **Weight:** 123 tonnes.
Wheel Diameter: 1050 mm.   **Length over Buffers:** 20.62 m.
Train Heating: Electric.   **Maximum Speed:** 140 km/h.
Non-Standard Livery: N These locomotives are hired from East West Railways (EWR – a DB Polish subsidiary) and are in a red and white livery.

All locomotives now fitted for multiple working.

No.	N	Code	No.	N	Code	No.	N	Code
232 005	N	BSE	232 262		NN2	232 502		BCSX (Z)
232 045	N	BSE	232 280		BSE	232 512	N	BSE
232 079	N	BSE	232 294	N	BSE	232 528		NN2
232 092	N	BSE	232 303	N	BSE	232 531	N	BSE
232 093		NN2	232 309	N	BSE	232 567	N	BSE
232 105	N	BSE	232 347		LH1	232 569		NN2
232 117		EOB	232 358		WRS (Z)	232 571		TK
232 128	N	BSE	232 359		DCX (Z)	232 583		NN2
232 131		EOB	232 388		EHM (Z)	232 587		EOB
232 137		WRS (Z)	232 401	N	WRS	232 589		EOB
232 189	N	BSE	232 409	N	BSE	232 609		NN2
232 201		HS	232 413		DCX (Z)	232 618		NN2
232 209		NN2	232 426		DCX (Z)	232 635		EOB
232 230		EOB	232 428		EOB	232 654		LH1
232 240		LH1 (Z)	232 448		DCX (Z)	232 668	N	EOB
232 241		NN2	232 469		BSE	232 669		NN2
232 254		NN2	232 472		NN2 (Z)	232 693		WM (Z)
232 255		EOB	232 484	N	BSE	232 703		LH1
232 259		TK	232 498		HS	232 704		DCX (Z)

No.		Code	No.		Code
232 903	(232 170)	HO (Z)	232 908"	(232 699)	FMB
232 905	(232 423)	BSE	232 909	(232 657)	NN2
232 906	(232 504)	BSE			

CLASS 233   "LUDMILLA"   Co-Co

In the middle 1990s several Class 232 locomotives were experimentally fitted with new engines built by MaK, Caterpillar, Kolomna and Krupp, with Kolomna winning as 64 locos were modified with this new engine by Cottbus works and reclassified as Class 233. These are an updated version of the previous engine with higher efficiency and cleaner exhaust etc. Some locomotives are stored at Hamm, Mukran and Chemnitz. Details as Class 232 except:

Engine: Kolomna 16-cylinder 12D49.

233 040	HS	233 306	BSE	233 547	DCX (Z)
233 043	DCX (Z)	233 314	LH1	233 562	DCX (Z)
233 076	DCX (Z)	233 321	NN2	233 572	HS
233 112	NN2	233 322	BSE	233 586	DCX (Z)
233 118	DCX (Z)	233 326	DCX (Z)	233 588	DCX (Z)
233 127	HS	233 373	MMF	233 596	DCX (Z)
233 151	DCX (Z)	233 450	DCX (Z)	233 616	DCX (Z)
233 176	HS	233 451	DCX (Z)	233 622	DCX (Z)
233 179	LH1 (Z)	233 452	LH1	232 625	DCX (Z)
233 206	DCX (Z)	233 458	DCX (Z)	233 636	NN2
233 219	MMF	233 478	HS	233 643	DCX (Z)
233 232	HS	233 486	EHM (Z)	233 652	LH1 (Z)
233 233	LH1	233 493 Y	BSE (Z)	233 662	NN2
233 264	DCX (Z)	233 510	MMF	233 683	DCX (Z)
233 281	DCX (Z)	233 511	BSE	233 689	DCX (Z)
233 285	LH1	233 515	DCX (Z)	233 698	NN2
233 288	LH1	233 521	FMB	233 705	DCX (Z)
233 289	DCX (Z)	233 525	NN2	233 709	HS
233 295	DCX (Z)				

▲ An unusual visitor to Bremen Hbf is "Ludmilla" **232 209**, seen running through the station light engine heading for the docks on 7 May 2018.   **Brian Garvin**

▲ The latest diesel version of the TRAXX family, 245 009 and 245 010 stand at München Hbf on 28 June 2016. Both locomotives are at the head of DB Regio-operated services to Mühldorf.

Keith Fender

▼ Class 247, instantly recongisable in the UK as Class 66, was acquired by DB when it purchased UK freight operator EWS and its French subsidiary Euro Cargo Rail. Although DB has designated these locos Class 247 (EVNs use 266!), recent transfers from France have received numbers in the 077 series to match their French 77000 classification. 247 053 is seen passing München Ost on 20 March 2014 with a westbound oil train.

Keith Fender

CLASS 245   TRAXX DE   Bo-Bo

This is the new diesel version of the TRAXX family (P160 DE ME) featuring four "industrial" type engines as found in road vehicles etc. The idea being that when maximum power is needed all four engines will be used but as the going gets easier engines will shut down with possibly only one in use sometimes. Computers control the engines in use and help to even out engine hours. There are obvious fuel savings involved. A framework contract for 200 locos is involved with DB Regio coming in first with an order for 20 locos which have replaced some Class 218s on passenger work. Erected at Kassel the bodies come from Wrocław in Poland, bogies are from Siegen, whilst Hennigsdorf and Mannheim are involved in the electrical components all being other Bombardier plants. DB Fernverkehr ordered 245 021–027 for the car shuttles from Niebüll to Westerland and 028–034 for use as rescue locos for the Erfurt–Nürnberg NBS line but these locomotives have not yet appeared although 245 035–037 have appeared for DB Regio!

Built: 2012–
Builder: Bombardier Kassel.
Engine: 4 x Caterpillar C18 564 kW.
Power: 564–2256 kW.
Transmission: Electric.
Maximum Tractive Effort: 300 kN.
Wheel Diameter: 1250 mm.
Train Heating: Electric.

Weight: 83 tonnes.
Length over Buffers: 18.90 m.
Maximum Speed: 160 km/h.
Braking: Electric 150 kN, dynamic 1600 kW.

245 001	MKP	245 014	MMF	245 026	ANB
245 002	MKP	245 015	MMF	245 027	ANB
245 003	MKP	245 016	FGM	245 028	I
245 004	MKP	245 017	FGM	245 029	I
245 005	MKP	245 018	FGM	245 030	I
245 006	AN	245 019	FGM	245 031	I
245 007	TU	245 020	FGM	245 032	I
245 008	MMF	245 021	ANB	245 033	I
245 009	MMF	245 022	ANB	245 034	I
245 010	MMF	245 023	ANB	245 035	TU
245 011	MMF	245 024	ANB	245 036	TU
245 012	MMF	245 025	ANB	245 037	TU
245 013	MMF				

CLASS 247   "CLASS 66"   Co-Co

Class 247 or 266 that is the question! When DB Schenker (now DB Cargo) bought English Welsh and Scottish Railway it also inherited Euro Cargo Rail and with it a batch of EMD JT42CWRM - a modernised EWS Class 66 which was given the French classification 77000. As Class 186s were replacing diesels in France, DB Schenker transferred some 247s to its operations in Germany. The main visual difference to the earlier Class 66s is the air conditioning pod on the cab roof. The former Railion had some 66s which were classified as 266 but surprisingly DB gave the ECR locomotives Class 247 only for the EBA to allocate Class 266! DB Schenker officially renumbered the locomotives as 266.4xx but all locomotives still carry Class 247 DB numbers and 266 EVNs!

Later transfers from France have retained their French 77000 numbers and now DB Cargo refers to them as 077 xxx but the EVNs are French!

There are two main centres of operation - Mühldorf where pairs of 217/218s have been released and the Ruhr area where 225s and 232s have been replaced.

Built: 2007–08.
Builder: EMD London, Ontario, Canada (Model JT42CWRM).
Engine: General Motors 12N-710G3B-EC two stroke.
Power: 2385 kW at 904 rpm.
Transmission: Electric.
Maximum Tractive Effort: 260 kN.
Wheel Diameter: 1120 mm.
Train Heating: None.
Non-Standard Livery: N All Class 247s retain their Euro Cargo Rail grey livery with front end yellow warning panels.

Weight: 127 tonnes.
Length over Buffers: 21.35 m.
Maximum Speed: 120 km/h.

077 001	N	EOB		077 027	N	MMF		247 045	N	MMF
077 002	N	EOB		077 028	N	SSR		247 046	N	MMF
077 004	N	HS		247 429	N	EOB		247 047	N	MMF
247 407	N	MMF		077 030	N	EOB		247 048	N	MMF
077 008	N	EOB		247 431	N	MMF		247 049	N	NN2
077 010	N	SSR		077 032	N	MMF		247 050	N	EOB
247 411	N	HBX		077 033	N	NN2		247 051	N	MMF
077 012	N	RM		247 434	N	EOB		247 052	N	MMF
077 014	N	MMF		247 435	N	EOB		247 053	N	MMF
247 416	N	EOB		077 036	N	MMF		247 054	N	MMF
077 018	N	MMF		247 438	N	NN2		247 055	N	MMF
077 020	N	EOB		247 039	N	NN2		247 056	N	MMF
077 021	N	SSR		077 040	N	MMF		247 057	N	MMF
077 022	N	EOB		247 041	N	MMF		247 058	N	MMF
077 024	N	HS		247 042	N	EOB		247 059	N	MMF
077 025	N	EOB		247 043	N	MMF		247 060	N	MMF
247 426	N	MMF		077 044	N	MMF				

CLASS 247.9   VECTRON DE   Bo-Bo

As the name suggests this type is a diesel electric version of the Vectron electric locomotive. Siemens seems to have built a small number of locomotives for assessment but has not found many takers. So a deal seems to have been done for DB Cargo to take the surplus locomotives and see how they perform bearing in mind that eventually the 232s and 233s will need to be replaced.

Built: 2010–16.
Builder: Siemens, München Allach.
Engine: MTU 16V4000R84 o 2400 kW.
Transmission: Electric.
Maximum Tractive Effort: 275 kN.
Wheel Diameter: 1100 mm.
Train Heating: ?.

Weight: 81–88 tonnes.
Length over Buffers: 19.98 m.
Maximum Speed: 160 km/h.

247 902	LH1	247 904	NN2	247 906	LH1
247 903	LH1				

▲ Voith's lower-powered version of the Gravita locomotive is Class 261. Here, 261 011 is seen shunting at Grosskorbetha on 26 February 2015.   **Quintus Vosman**

CLASS 261   GRAVITA 10   B-B

This new class was ordered to replace non-modernised locomotives of Classes 290 291, 295 and 298. DB surprisingly ordered 130 of these locomotives from Voith, the firm only having started locomotive production in 2008. The type is known as "Gravita 10BB". The first ten locomotives were numbered as Class 260 as they lacked particle filters and after being used for driver training were returned to Voith. Consequently Class 261 starts at 261 011. The locomotives work over wide areas often far from their allocated base.

Built: 2010–13.
Builder: Voith Turbo Lokomotivtechnik GmbH & Co KG, Kiel.
Engine: MTU 8V 4000 R3.
Power: 1000 kW.
Transmission: Hydraulic, L4r4zseU2.
Maximum Tractive Effort: 337 kN.
Wheel Diameter: 1000 mm.
Train Heating: None.

Weight: 80 tonnes.
Length over Buffers: 15.72 m.
Maximum Speed: 100 km/h.

261 011	LH1	261 044	LH1	261 077	AM
261 012	LMR	261 045	LH1	261 078	FMB
261 013	LMR	261 046	LH1	261 079	FMB
261 014	LMR	261 047	LH1	261 080	FMB
261 015	LH1	261 048	LH1	261 081	LH1
261 016	KG	261 049	AM	261 082	LH1
261 017	AM	261 050	AM	261 083	HS
261 018	LH1	261 051	FMB	261 084	HS
261 019	LH1	261 052	FMB	261 085	KG
261 020	LH1	261 053	FMB	261 086	EHGV
261 021	LH1	261 054	FMB	261 087	LH1
261 022	HS	261 055	AM	261 088	LH1
261 023	LH1	261 056	FMB	261 089	LH1
261 024	LH1	261 057	FMB	261 090	LH1
261 025	EOB	261 058	FMB	261 091	AM
261 026	LH1	261 059	FMB	261 092	AM
261 027	AM	261 060	LH1	261 093	LH1
261 028	AM	261 061	LH1	261 094	LH1
261 029	AM	261 062	LH1	261 095	LH1
261 030	AM	261 063	LH1	261 096	AM
261 031	FMB	261 064	LH1	261 097	AM
261 032	HS	261 065	LH1	261 098	AM
261 033	AM	261 066	LH1	261 099	AM
261 034	AM	261 067	AM	261 100	AM
261 035	AM	261 068	HS	261 101	KG
261 036	AM	261 069	AM	261 102	EHGV
261 037	AM	261 070	HS	261 103	AM
261 038	AM	261 071	HS	261 104	AM
261 039	FMB	261 072	HS	261 105	EOB
261 040	AM	261 073	HS	261 106	KG
261 041	LH1	261 074	HS	261 107	EOB
261 042	LH1	261 075	HS	261 108	EHGV
261 043	LH1	261 076	HS	261 109	EOB

CLASS 265   GRAVITA 15   B-B

Yet another new class for DB Cargo. This is the more powerful Gravita locomotive - the Gravita 15BB. Being more powerful than Class 261 they are found in areas with heavy freight traffic.

Built: 2012–13.
Builder: Voith Turbo Lokomotivtechnik GmbH & Co KG, Kiel.
Engine: MTU 12V4000R43.
Power: 1500 kW.
Transmission: Hydraulic, L5r4zseU2.
Maximum Tractive Effort: 317–330 kN.   **Weight:** 84–90 tonnes.
Wheel Diameter: 1000 mm.   **Length over Buffers:** 16.90 m.
Train Heating: None.   **Maximum Speed:** 100 km/h.

265 001	FMB	265 012	FMB	265 022	EHGV
265 002	LH1	265 013	LH1	265 023	KG
265 003	HS	265 014	LH1	265 024	KG
265 004	KG	265 015	EOB	265 025	HS
265 005	FMB	265 016	EHGV	265 026	HS
265 006	FMB	265 017	HS	265 027	EHGV
265 007	HS	265 018	HS	265 028	EHGV
265 008	LH1	265 019	LH1	265 029	KG
265 009	FMB	265 020	LH1	265 030	EHGV
265 010	HS	265 021	LH1	265 031	EHGV
265 011	EHGV				

CLASS 290   B-B

This is the heavy duty shunting and trip locomotive of the old DB. Since 1996 many have been converted to operate under remote radio control (Class 294) and thus can be driverless allowing the duties of shunter and driver to be combined. Some Class 290s are fitted with hump shunting radio control. This allows the hump tower to take control of the loco when hump shunting to allow better co-ordination between point setting and train movement. 290 626/77/90 at München Nord are such locos and these have been given altered liveries to denote this, being fitted with yellow/black chevrons and flashing lights. However a further renumbering saw locomotives fitted with an MTU 8V 4000 R1 engine which is more efficient and meets modern emission standards etc. At the same time other improvements were made to enable these locomotives to last another 10–15 years. Upon completion the running number was increased by 500. Conversions from Class 290 to 294 stopped with the arrival of Class 261. Many early locomotives that have not been modernised have been sold to private operators.

Built: 1964–74 for DB.
Builder: MaK/Jung/Deutz/Henschel.
Engine: MTU MB 16V 652 TA 10 (290.0); MTU 8V 4000 R1 (290.5).
Power: 820 kW (1100 hp).
Transmission: Hydraulic. Voith L206 rs.   **Weight:** 78.8 tonnes.
Maximum Tractive Effort: 241 kN.   **Length over Buffers:** 14.32 m.
Wheel Diameter: 1100 mm.   **Maximum Speed:** 80 km/h.
Non-Standard Livery: N 290 371 is a designated museum locomotive and is in original purple red livery.

f   funk = radio control for hump shunting.

290 371	N	LH1	290 561		BSE	290 636		BSE
290 504		LH1	290 565		BSE	290 639		TK
290 505		LH1	290 569		AM	290 641		NN2
290 520		TK	290 591		BSE	290 677	f	MIH
290 521		SSR (Z)	290 621		NN2	290 678		NN2
290 524		WRS (Z)	290 626	f	MIH	290 679		NN2
290 527		BSE	290 632		AM	290 688		MIH
290 532		WRS	290 633		TK	290 690	f	MIH
290 557		MIH					

▲ Heavy duty Gravita shunter 265 019 is seen stabled at Nordhausen station on 28 February 2017. **Brian Garvin**

▼ 294 791 takes a local freight train past Duisburg Lotharstrasse en route to Oberhausen West yard on 26 May 2018. **Matthias Müller**

CLASS 291 B-B

Slightly more powerful than the Class 290, most 291s operate at North Sea ports such as Bremen, Bremerhaven and Hamburg on freight tripping and shunting associated with the ports. Those rebuilt with remote radio controls are now Class 295. Most early locomotives that have not been modernised are now in store or have been sold to private operators.

Built: 1965–78 for DB.
Builder: MaK/Jung/Deutz/Henschel.
Engine: MTU MB 16V 652 TA 10.
Power: 820 kW (1100 hp).
Transmission: Hydraulic. Voith L26 rsb. **Weight:** 78 tonnes.
Maximum Tractive Effort: 245 kN. **Length over Buffers:** 14.00 m.
Wheel Diameter: 1100 mm. **Maximum Speed:** 90 km/h.

291 036	DCX (Z)	291 038	AM (Z)	291 901	WRS (Z)

CLASS 294 B-B

These locomotives are Class 290 fitted with remote radio controls. Many locomotives have been further modified with new MTU engines with 500 being added to the running number. All locos fitted with the radio controls have new automatic couplings. In 2000 ten locomotives were modified for multiple working at either end of a train via radio transmission. These locomotives became Class 294.90x later being renumbered to 294.95x. For technical details see Class 290. Recently two class 294s have been taken to Cottbus works to be rebuilt into hybrid locomotives; if this experiment is successful it could mean another lease of life for the class. Some German sources show the MIH locomotives as allocated to München Nord but as there is no locomotive maintenance facility there this book continues to show them as at MIH. The same applies to Saarbrücken which now comes under Mannheim for administration but retains full maintenance facilities.

Class 294.0 Standard design.

294 571	HS	294 607	FB	294 656	RM
294 572	HS	294 609	RM	294 657	KG
294 573	SSR	294 610	TK	294 658	RM
294 574	NN2	294 612	NN2	294 659	SSR
294 575	MIH	294 613	FMB	294 661	MIH
294 576	LH1	294 614	LH1	294 662	LH1
294 577	FB	294 616	RM	294 663	LH1
294 578	FB	294 617	TK	294 664	RM
294 579	FB	294 618	KG	294 665	FMB
294 580	NN2	294 619	LH1	294 667	KG
294 581	HS	294 620	RM	294 668	LH1
294 582	EOB	294 622	SSR	294 669	EOB
294 583	FMB	294 624	MMF	294 670	AM
294 584	EHGV	294 628	FB	294 671	EHGV
294 585	AM	294 629	TK	294 672	HBX
294 586	TK	294 630	EOB	294 673	FMB
294 587	HS	294 631	SSR	294 674	AM
294 588	TK	294 634	LH1	294 675	MIH
294 589	TK	294 635	NN2	294 676	FMB
294 590	EHGV	294 638	FMB	294 680	AM
294 593	TK	294 640	RM	294 681	TK
294 594	MMF	294 642	HBX	294 682	KG
294 595	FMB	294 643	FMB	294 683	FMB
294 597	HS	294 644	FB	294 684	LH1
294 598	NN2	294 645	MIH	294 685	NN2
294 599	NN2	294 646	FMB	294 686	FMB
294 600	EHGV	294 647	NN2	294 687	NN2
294 601	NN2	294 648	RM	294 691	HBX
294 602	LMR	294 649	EOB	294 692	KG
294 603	HBX	294 650	RM	294 693	EOB
294 604	HBX	294 651	FMB	294 694	EOB
294 605	HS	294 653	LH1	294 695	RM
294 606	MIH	294 655	HBX	294 696	KG

294 698	HB	294 765	NN2	294 833	TK
294 700	EOB	294 766	MIH	294 834	MIH
294 701	MIH	294 767	MMF	294 835	RM
294 702	LH1	294 768	MIH	294 836	MIH
294 703	KG	294 769	HS	294 837	FMB
294 704	SSR	294 770	HB	294 838	TK
294 705	RM	294 771	FMB	294 839	HBX
294 706	LH1	294 772	MIH	294 840	RM
294 707	EOB	294 773	EOB	294 841	HBX
294 708	MIH	294 774	HS	294 842	RM
294 710	MIH	294 775	RM	294 843	TK
294 711	FMB	294 776	RM	294 844	TK
294 712	MIH	294 777	TK	294 845	KG
294 713	HBX	294 778	MIH	294 846	HS
294 714	EOB	294 779	LH1	294 847	EHGV
294 715	KG	294 780	EHGV	294 848	EOB
294 716	TK	294 781	RM	294 849	MIH
294 717	NN2	294 782	KG	294 850	EHGV
294 718	EHGV	294 783	KG	294 851	NN2
294 719	RM	294 785	EHGV	294 852	KG
294 720	KG	294 786	TK	294 853	EOB
294 721	MIH	294 787	NN2	294 854	TK
294 722	KG	294 788	NN2	294 855	TK
294 723	EHGV	294 789	EOB	294 856	HBX
294 724	RM	294 790	RM	294 857	FMB
294 725	KG	294 791	EOB	294 858	SSR
294 727	AM	294 792	EOB	294 859	FMB
294 728	SSR	294 794	EHGV	294 860	EOB
294 729	NN2	294 795	RM	294 861	RM
294 730	SSR	294 797	MIH	294 862	FMB
294 731	HBX	294 798	EOB	294 863	TK
294 732	RM	294 799	NN2	294 864	RM
294 733	FMB	294 800	FMB	294 865	EHGV
294 734	MIH	294 801	EOB	294 866	EHGV
294 735	SSR	294 802	FMB	294 867	NN2
294 736	TK	294 803	RM	294 868	RO
294 737	FMB	294 804	MIH	294 869	SSR
294 738	LH1	294 805	SSR	294 870	HS
294 739	FMB	294 806	HBS	294 872	FMB
294 740	RM	294 807	EHGV	294 873	FMB
294 741	RM	294 808	KG	294 874	EHGV
294 742	EHGV	294 809	NN2	294 875	TK
294 743	EHGV	294 810	NN2	294 876	SSR
294 744	SSR	294 811	SSR	294 877	FMB
294 745	NN2	294 812	SSR	294 878	HO
294 746	RM	294 813	EHGV	294 879	HBX
294 747	NN2	294 814	MIH	294 880	KG
294 748	TK	294 816	NN2	294 881	EOB
294 749	TK	294 817	EHGV	294 882	EHGV
294 750	NN2	294 818	FMB	294 883	SSR
294 751	HS	294 819	FB	294 885	TK
294 752	TK	294 820	LMR	294 886	AM
294 753	NN2	294 821	SSR	294 887	TK
294 754	US	294 822	FMB	294 888	LH1
294 755	HS	294 823	SSR	294 889	LH1
294 756	RM	294 824	TK	294 890	EOB
294 757	TK	294 825	HS	294 891	HBX
294 758	KG	294 826	NN2	294 892	EOB
294 759	MIH	294 827	LH1	294 893	KG
294 760	NN2	294 828	FMB	294 895	LH1
294 761	HS	294 829	HS	294 896	EOB
294 762	NN2	294 830	EOB	294 897	BSE
294 763	TK	294 831	EOB	294 898	NN2
294 764	RM	294 832	KG	294 899	FMB

294 901[II]	RM	294 904[II]	RM	294 907[II]	LH1
294 902[II]	NN2	294 905[II]	LH1	294 908[II]	MIH
294 903[II]	AM	294 906[II]	EOB		

Class 294.9 Fitted with radio-controlled multiple working.

294 951	KG	294 955	HS	294 958	HS
294 952	HS	294 956	HS	294 959	HS
294 953	TK	294 957	HS	294 960	HS
294 954	HS				

CLASS 295   B-B

These are Class 291s fitted with remote radio controls and automatic couplers. Many have now been sold to private operators. For technical details see Class 291.

295 003	DCX (Z)	295 021	AM	295 054	AM
295 006	EHM (Z)	295 022	HBX	295 056	DCX (Z)
295 007	HE (Z)	295 040	HBX	295 058	HS
295 012	AM	295 041	DCX (Z)	295 059	HBX
295 016	AM	295 043	AM	295 071	DCX (Z)
295 018	AM	295 051	HBX	295 089	DCX (Z)
295 019	AM	295 052	HBX	295 094	HBX

▲ 298 336 stands in the Messe Berlin exhibition complex on 19 September 2016. The loco had been in use delivering trains to the bi-annual Innotrans exhibition. **Keith Fender**

CLASS 296   B-B

These locomotives are former Class 290s fitted with remote control, not only from staff nearby but full remote control from a hump tower in a manner similar to the 290s at München. The 296s have new MTU 8V 4000 RI engines but were given a new class number rather than being in the 290.5 series.

296 023	HS	296 042	KG	296 052	KG
296 028	AM	296 043	RM	296 053	KG
296 029	HS	296 044	HS	296 054	HS
296 030	AM	296 045	LH1	296 055	HS
296 034	RM	296 046	LH1	296 056	RM
296 037	AM	296 047	AM	296 058	HS
296 038	RM	296 048	AM	296 059	KG
296 039	RM	296 049	HS	296 060	HS
296 040	KG	296 050	KG	296 063	RM
296 041	AM	296 051	KG	296 068	RM

CLASS 298   B-B

This is the old DR equivalent of Classes 290/1. Built as heavy duty shunters (298.3 or V100.4). All have now been fitted with remote radio controls. Automatic couplers were fitted when converted. All have been rebuilt with a Caterpillar engine.

Rebuilt: 1978 RAW Stendal.
Engine: 773 kW Caterpillar AT DI –TA 3508.
Transmission: Hydraulic.
Maximum Tractive Effort: **Weight:** 63.7 tonnes.
Wheel Diameter: 1000 mm.   **Length over Buffers:** 14.24 m.
Train Heating: None.   **Maximum Speed:** 60 km/h.

298 303	BSE	298 317	BSE	298 326	BSE
298 306	BSE (Z)	298 318	WRS	298 327	BSE
298 307	BSE	298 319	BSE	298 328	BSE
298 308	BSE	298 320	BSE	298 329	BSE
298 309	BSE (Z)	298 321	BSE	298 330	BSE
298 310	BSE	298 322	BSE	298 331	BSE
298 312	WRS	298 323	BSE	298 334	BSE
298 313	BSE	298 324	BSE	298 336	BSE
298 316	BSE	298 325	BSE	298 337	BSE

3. DIESEL SHUNTING LOCOMOTIVES

3.1. STANDARD GAUGE

In this section the code 'D' denotes a locomotive in departmental use. (depot and wagon shop pilots, DB Netz depot pilots etc.)

CLASS 0650   G6   C

Both DB Fernverkehr and DB Regio have leased some Vossloh G6 shunting locos since shortly after the locomotives were built. It is thought this is a deal with Vossloh to let DB have experience of the type with a view to replacing the Class 362/363 series. However, what was thought to be just a temporary situation has now become somewhat permanent hence the inclusion in this edition of the book. DB has had some of them since 2010/11!

Built: 2011–14.
Builder: Vossloh.
Engine: Cummins QSK23-L, 671kW 1800 rpm (* MTU 12V1600R50, 690 kW 1900 rpm).
Weight: 60–67.5 tonnes.
Transmission: Hydraulic, Voith L3r4zeU2 or L3r4zseU2.
Maximum Tractive Effort:
Non-Standard Livery: N Grey body, green cab (Vossloh livery).
Wheel Diameter: 1000 mm.
Length over Buffers: 10.35 or 10.79 m.
Maximum Speed: 35–80 km/h.

0650 107	N	BCS	0650 114	N		WR	0650 301	N	BLO
0650 108	N	BCS	0650 123	N	*	MH2	0650 303	N	* BCS

CLASS 310   B

These are the only survivors of the former DR Köf series, having been retained as departmental shunters.

Built: 1933–34 for DR.
Builder: Orenstein & Koppel & BMAG.
Engine: 6KVD 145.
Power: 192 kW.
Transmission: Mechanical.
Non-Standard Livery: N 310 279 light blue, remainder black.

310 279	N	D	UMX	310 631	N	D	BRG	310 734	N	UE

CLASS 311   B

This class was the post-war small shunting locomotive in East Germany. Just one locomotive of this class remains in departmental use at Meiningen works.

Built: 1962 for DR.
Builder: LKM.
Engine: 6KVD 18/15-1 SRW.
Power: 132 kW.
Transmission: Hydraulic.
Non-Standard Livery: N Light blue.

311 632   N   D   UMX

CLASS 312   B

Another former DR class with a slightly more powerful engine than Class 311. All those that remain are now in departmental use.

Built: 1967–71 for DR.
Builder: LKM.
Engine: 6KVD 18/15-1 SRW.
Power: 162 kW.
Transmission: Hydraulic.

Class 312/0.

Maximum Tractive Effort: 80 kN.
Wheel Diameter: 1000 mm.   **Weight:** 24 tonnes.
Length over Buffers: 6.94 m.   **Maximum Speed:** 55 km/h.
Non-Standard Livery: N 312 021 blue; 312 039 red and white.

312 021   **N**   D   BCSX | 312 039   **N**   D   LL

Class 312/1.

Maximum Tractive Effort: 71 kN.
Wheel Diameter: 1000 mm.   **Weight:** 24.3 tonnes.
Length over Buffers: 8.00 m.   **Maximum Speed:** 40 km/h.
Non-Standard Livery: N 312 139 light blue.

312 139   **N**   D   WWX

▲ For some years DB Regio has been leasing G6 shunting locomotives from Vossloh. Here, 0650 301 shunts at Berlin Lichtenberg on 2 August 2015. Note it does have a DB logo!   **Brian Garvin**

CLASS 323 B

These are former DB Köf type shunters retained for departmental use.

Built: 1953–60 for DB.
Builder: Gmeinder/Jung.
Engine: Kaeble GN 130s / KHD A6M 517/617.
Power: 95 kW (128 hp).
Transmission: Hydraulic.   **Weight:** 16 tonnes.
Maximum Tractive Effort: 47 kN.   **Length over Buffers:** 6.45 m.
Wheel Diameter: 850 mm.   **Maximum Speed:** 45 km/h.
Non-Standard Livery: N All locomotives retain original DB red livery.

323 260	**N**		HHL		323 729	**N**	D	TK (Z)		323 818	**N**	D	FMB

Name:

323 818   Tuffel

CLASS 332 B

This class is the West German 1950s updated version of the pre-war Köf. Once totalling over 300 locos, those that remain are in departmental use whilst others have found further use with private operators.

Built: 1959–66 for DB.
Builder: Gmeinder/Jung/Orenstein & Koppel.
Engine: MWM RHS 518Ä/Kaeble MD 140.
Power: 179 kW (240 hp).
Transmission: Hydraulic.   **Weight:** 20 tonnes.
Maximum Tractive Effort: 55 kN.   **Length over Buffers:** 7.83 m.
Wheel Diameter: 950 mm.   **Maximum Speed:** 45 km/h.

332 013	**Y**		MAOB	332 220	D	NN1	332 263	D	NN1
332 022		D	TU	332 221	D	MKP	332 281	D	EDO
332 062			MAOB	332 255	D	TS	332 294	D	EHGV
332 064		D	ANX	332 260	D	STR			

CLASSES 333 & 335 B

This is the West German 1960s version of the Köf. Class 335 are 333s converted to remote radio control and fitted with automatic couplers. With changing freight needs the radio control has been removed from some locos and these are now 333.5.

Built: 1967–78 for DB.
Builder: Gmeinder/Jung/Orenstein & Koppel.
Engine: MWM RHS 518Ä/Kaeble MD 140.
Power: 179 kW (240 hp).
Transmission: Hydraulic.   **Weight:** 24 tonnes.
Maximum Tractive Effort: 80 kN.   **Length over Buffers:** 7.83 m.
Wheel Diameter: 950 mm.   **Maximum Speed:** 45 km/h.
Non-Standard Livery: N 335 124/125/200/214 raspberry red and white; 335 128 turquoise and beige.

*   Modified front end appearance with circular fan visible.

333 104		D	AOP	335 054	D	MIH (Z)	335 112		*	LMR
333 117		D	MAOB	335 066	D	MH1	335 113		D	MMF
333 145	**Y**	D	EDEF	335 070	D	NN2	335 114		D	EHGV
335 006			BSE (Z)	335 072	D	BCSX	335 116		*	MKP
335 011			NN2 (Z)	335 082	D	EOB	335 118		*	STR (Z)
335 024		D	DCX	335 103	*	FK	335 120		*	MIH
335 027			KG (Z)	333 104	D	AOP	335 121		*	EOB
333 028		D	AOP	335 107	*	TK	335 122		*	STR
335 029		D	RB	335 109	*	AM	335 124	**N**	*	EOB
335 047		D	WRS (Z)	335 111		ANX	335 126		D	HBR

335 128	N	*	RM (Z)	335 160		*	AM	335 232		D	HBS
335 129		*	RM	335 161		D	LDX	335 234		D	AM
335 131		*	RO	335 163			KG	335 236		D	KG
335 133		*	LMR	335 164		*	RO	335 238		D	Lohnde
335 134		D	SSR	335 175		D	WRS (Z)	335 244		D	HO
335 135		*D	TK	335 177		*	RO	335 248		D	HS
335 136		*	AM	335 185		D	KG (Z)	335 249		D	LH1
335 137		*	EOB (Z)	335 186		D	HBR	335 251		D	HBS
335 138		*	TK	335 200	N	*D	FGM	333 525		D	LOHNDE
335 141		*	NN2	335 207		D	WRS	333 570		D	NN2
335 142		*	RM (Z)	335 210		D	AM	333 647		D	RM
335 144		*	KG	335 213		D	HS	333 649		*	KG
335 150		*	NN2	335 214	Y	D	BRG	333 651		D	RO
335 151			RO	335 217		D	KG (Z)	333 668		D	RO
335 152		*	STR	335 220			EDEF	333 669		D	BCS
335 153		*	TK (Z)	335 221		D	MKP	333 670		D	WR
335 154		*	STR	335 224		D	FMB (Z)	333 671		D	BCSX
335 155		*	NN2	335 227		D	HS	333 673		D	BCS
335 156		*	NN2	335 228		D	AM (Z)	333 676		D	NNX (Z
335 157		*	LDX								

Name:

335 047   Werklok II

CLASS 345   D

This class was the continuation of Class 346 which once exceeded 1000 examples. The loco is now the last in use with DB but many more are in use with private operators.

Built: 1959–82 for DR.
Builder: LKM.
Engine: 12KVD21SVW of 478 kW.
Transmission: Hydraulic.
Maximum Tractive Effort: 175 kN.
Wheel Diameter: 1100 mm.

Weight: 55 tonnes.
Length over Buffers: 10.88 m.
Maximum Speed: 60 km/h.

345 021   Y   EDEF

CLASS 352   G400   B

DB Fernverkehr has leased these locomotives from Northrail and is trialing them at Berlin Rummelsburg depot. Interestingly DB Regio has leased another type of shunting engine for trials. When one looks at the age of Classes 362–365 it can be seen that they must be replaced soon.

Built: 2003 .
Builder: SFT/Vossloh.
Engine: MTU 8V183TD13 of 390 kW.
Transmission: Hydraulic, Voith L2r4zseU2.
Maximum Tractive Effort:
Wheel Diameter: 1000 mm.
Non-Standard Livery: N Northrail orange.

Weight: 40 tonnes.
Length over Buffers: 9.40 m.
Maximum Speed: 70 km/h.

352 101	N	BRG		352 103	N	BRG		352 105	N	BRG
352 102	N	BRG							

▲ 335 152 has little to do at Trier station during the 2018 Plandampf event on 28 April 2018. It was perhaps stabled there in case of an emergency. **Brian Garvin**

▼ A big surprise in 2018 was the appearance of 363 810 painted in Inter City livery, pictured here at Maschen wagon shops on 6 May 2018. It would be more at home at AH1 depot! **Brian Garvin**

CLASSES 362 & 364   C

Formerly Class 260, Class 360 was adopted when the locomotives were downgraded to shunting tractors. Along came radio controls so another new class number 364 was allocated. Class 362 is the last reclassification when the locomotives were fitted with Caterpillar engines.

Built: 1956–61 for DB.
Builder: Krupp/MaK/Jung/Krauss-Maffei/Deutz/Henschel/Esslingen/Gmeinder.
Engine: MTU GTO6/GTO6A/MB 12V 493 AZ (Class 364); Caterpillar 3412 E D1-TTA (Class 362).
Power: 485 kW (650 hp).   **Weight:** 48–49.5 tonnes.
Transmission: Hydraulic. Voith L27z Ub/L37z Ub/L217.
Maximum Tractive Effort: 122 kN.   **Length over Buffers:** 10.45 m.
Wheel Diameter: 1250 mm.   **Maximum Speed:** 60 km/h.
Non-Standard Livery: N 364 533/858 purple red; 364 776 turquoise and beige.

No.		Depot	No.		Depot	No.		Depot
362 362		LH1	362 568		MIH	362 849		HB
363 378		MIH	362 571		AM	362 852		AM (Z)
362 382		MN (Z)	362 574		AM (Z)	362 853		LH1
362 388		RM	362 582		KG	362 855		LH1
362 389		AM	362 587		HS	362 856		BSE
362 390	D	NN2	362 589		TK	364 858	N	TU (Z)
362 391		FMB	362 592		TK	362 873		MN (Z)
362 400		MN (Z)	362 594		MIH	362 875		MN (Z)
362 406		AM	362 596		BSE	362 878		RM
362 419		HS (Z)	362 597		AM	362 892		AM (Z)
362 423		BSE	362 598		NN2	362 896		MIH
362 427		MN (Z)	362 600		LH1	362 900		WRS
362 502	D	SSR	362 612		LH1	362 903		AM
362 509		AM	362 614		KG	362 904		MIH
362 510		TK	362 754		KG (Z)	364 906		FB (Z)
362 517		LH1	362 756		HB	362 916	D	BSE
362 526		DCX (Z)	362 761	D	NN2	362 919		HE (Z)
364 533	N	TU	364 767	D	RM	362 921		KG
362 538		TK	362 768		MMF	362 926		LH1
362 540		KG	362 769		AM (Z)	362 939		KG
362 547		RM	364 776	N D	MMF (Z)	362 940		WRS (Z)
362 551		LH1	362 791		AM (Z)	362 941		SSR
362 559		AM(Z)	362 797		AM (Z)	362 942		EOB
362 560		LH1 (Z)	362 805		AM (Z)	362 943		MIH
362 564		LH1	362 845		MIH			

CLASSES 363 & 365   C

A modified Class 360 for use in areas where heavy trains are found (steel, coal etc). These locos are ballasted to give greater adhesion for shunting these heavy trains. Reclassified 365 when radio controls were fitted and another class number (363) was given when Caterpillar engines were fitted.

Built: 1955–64 for DB.
Builder: Krupp/MaK/Henschel/Krauss-Maffei/Esslingen.
Engine: MTU GTO6/GTO6A (Class 365); Caterpillar 3412 E D1-TTA (Class 363).
Power: 485 kW (650 hp).   **Weight:** 53 tonnes.
Transmission: Hydraulic. Volith L27z Ub/L37z Ub/L217.
Maximum Tractive Effort: 138 kN.   **Length over Buffers:** 10.45 m.
Wheel Diameter: 1250 mm.   **Maximum Speed:** 60 km/h.
Non-Standard Livery: N 365 143 Turquoise and beige, 363 810 Inter City, white with red band.

No.		Depot	No.		Depot	No.		Depot
363 042		DCX (Z)	363 112		TK	363 124		DCX (Z)
363 044		AM (Z)	363 113		KG	363 128		MIH
363 103		TK	363 114		LH1 (Z)	363 132		BSE
365 104		MIH	363 115		FMB	363 136		WRS (Z)
363 106		MIH	363 116		FMB	363 139		RM
363 107		MN (Z)	363 117		KG	363 141		TK
363 110		MIH	363 118		TU	365 143	N	TU
363 111		AM	363 122		RM	363 146		EHM (Z)

No		Code	No		Code	No		Code
363 147		HBX	363 211		RM	363 680		SSR
363 149		LH1	363 212	D	NN2	363 681		TK
363 150		RM	363 218		FMB	363 682		HBX (Z)
363 153		RM	363 219		HS	365 683		TU
363 154		TK	363 220		TK (Z)	363 686		FMB
363 155		MN (Z)	363 223		KG	363 691		MIH
363 156		LH1	363 224		EHGV	363 692		RM
363 160		HB	363 231		MIH	363 696		LH1
363 163	D	BSE	363 235		AM	363 699		FMB (Z)
363 165		BSN	363 238		LH1	363 701		FMB (Z)
363 166		FK	363 240		SSR	363 702		EHGV
363 167		SSR	363 241		MIH	363 703		LH1
363 169		RM	363 424		RM	363 704		MIH
363 172		TK	363 425		AM (Z)	363 706		MIH
363 176		MN (Z)	363 436		TK	363 708		HS
363 177		NN2 (Z)	363 437		MIH	363 710		NN2 (Z)
363 178		EHGV	363 438		HBX (Z)	363 711	D	MMF
363 179		MIH	363 439		MIH	363 713		MN (Z)
363 182		EOB	363 440		LH1	363 719		MIH (Z)
363 185		HBX (Z)	363 441		KG (Z)	363 724		LH1 (Z)
363 187		TK	363 444		NN2 (Z)	363 736		AM (Z)
363 188		BSE	363 446		BSE (Z)	363 737		LH1
363 189		MN (Z)	363 622		AM	363 739		EHGV
363 190		MIH	363 625		TK	363 809		AM (Z)
363 191		EHGV	363 626		AM (Z)	363 810	N D	AM
363 192		MIH	363 628		FMB	363 811		BSE
363 193		TK	363 649		RM	363 814		MIH
363 194		RM	363 650		AM (Z)	363 816		AM (Z)
363 195		NN2	363 651		AM	363 819		MN (Z)
363 199		MIH	363 652		KG	363 821		DCX (Z)
363 201		BSE (Z)	363 655		AM	363 824		EHGV
363 205		RM	363 658		TK	363 827		DCX (Z)
363 206		EOB	363 660		KG (Z)	363 830		AM
363 207		TU	363 664	D	MIH	363 832		FMB
363 209		RM	363 669		MIH	363 836	D	MKP
363 210		EOB	363 676		AM (Z)	363 840		MN (Z)

CLASS 381   Bo

These battery electric shunting locomotives were all withdrawn from capital stock but remain in departmental use.

Built: 1936–38.
Builder Mechanical Parts: Windhoff.
Builder Electrical Parts: AEG/Siemens.   **Length over Buffers:** 6.45 m.

381 005	D	KK2	381 018	D	LDX	381 020	D	FMB

CLASS 382   Bo

This battery electric shunting engine is used on the Hamburg S-Bahn as a depot shunter.

Built: 1953 for DB.   **Length over Buffers:** 6.43 m.
Builder Mechanical Parts: Gmeinder.   **Weight:** 21 tonnes.
Builder Electrical Parts: Kiepe.   **Maximum Speed:** 30km/h.

382 001	D	AOP

▲ 365 143 is the only member of the class to retain the once commonplace turquoise and beige livery. It is seen at Ulm Hbf on 17 May. 2015 **Keith Fender**

▼ DB Fernverkehr's most bizarre operation is surely the metre gauge railway on the North Sea island of Wangerooge. One of the line's most modern locomotives, 399 108 is seen at Westanlege (Wangerooge) on 16 September 2014. **Keith Fender**

3.2. NARROW GAUGE

The island of Wangerooge has a narrow gauge railway which was part of the old DB and surprisingly has never been privatised as were lines in the East after unification. It now comes under DB Fernverkehr!

399 105/6   C

Since unification, many industries in the former DDR have closed down and consequently many former industrial locomotives have come on the market. DB acquired these two from a steelworks in Helbra. They were built in Romania and are the manufacturer's type L18H.

Built: 1989.
Builder: U23A.
Engine: D2156HMN8 (MAN design built under licence).
Power: 132 kW (180 hp).   **Gauge:** 1000 mm.
Transmission: Hydraulic.   **Weight:** 16.5 tonnes.
Maximum Tractive Effort: 50 kN.   **Length over Buffers:** 5.40 m.
Wheel Diameter: **Maximum Speed:** 28 km/h.

399 105	HWG	399 106	HWG

399 107/8   C

These two new locomotives for the DB metre gauge line allowed older locos 399 101–104 to be withdrawn.

Built: 1999.
Builder: Schöma (Type CFL 150 DCL).
Engine: KHD BF6M1013CP.
Power: 166 kW.   **Gauge:** 1000 mm.
Transmission: Hydraulic.   **Weight:** 16 tonnes.
Maximum Tractive Effort: 50 kN   **Length over Buffers:** 6.597 m.
Wheel Diameter: **Maximum Speed:** 20 km/h.

399 107	HWG	399 108	HWG

3.3. HYBRID LOCOMOTIVES

CLASS 1002   ALSTOM HYBRID H3   Co

After its success with the Class 1001 hybrid locomotive, Alstom at Stendal then went on to build a brand new three-axle version. DB decided to acquire five locomotives for an eight year trial with Bayern Land giving a large grant towards the development. Consequently the locomotives are all based in Nürnberg for carriage pilot duties in Nürnberg and Würzburg. They remain the property of Alstom.

Built: 2014–15.
Builder: Alstom, Stendal.   **Batteries:** 350 kW NiCd.
Engine: Deutz, TCD12.0 V6 Euro IIIB of 390 kW.   **Weight:** 67.5 tonnes.
Transmission: Electric. Three TSA 253 kW nose suspended asynchronous traction motors.
Maximum Tractive Effort: 240 kN   **Length over Buffers:** 12.80 m.
Wheel Diameter: 1000 mm.   **Maximum Speed:** 100 km/h.
Non-Standard Livery: N Half red, half green.

| 1002 004 | N | NN1 | 1002 007 | N | NN1 | 1002 009 | N | NN1 |
| 1002 005 | N | NN1 | 1002 008 | N | NN1 | | | |

4. INTER-CITY EXPRESS (ICE)

The Inter-City Express was introduced in 1989 when the first ICE1 sets were built following some years of running a prototype train. These followed high speed train practice in Europe by have powerful locomotives either end of a rake of carriages. ICE2 was different, being a half-set with a driving trailer at one end. The next version was supposed to be ICE2-2 but in fact came out as a completely different train, ICE3, which had powered-axles throughout the train and was a true EMU. It was produced in various versions – 403, 406, 411 and 415 (q.v.). Class 407 is a complete redesign by Siemens, building the class on its own instead of part of a consortium. These sets are the Siemens Velaro model exported to other countries and used by Eurostar in lengthened form. Years ago DB announced a new generation of ICEs which would be an ICE platform with many different train formations. Subsequently this development became ICE4 and there are now only two formations – 12-car and 7-car trains.

The Principal ICE Routes are shown below, together with the usual type used on that route. In each case only the core route is shown. Route 20 trains from Hamburg may start back from Kiel whilst at the other end of the route at Basel some may run through to Interlaken etc.

ICE 10	Berlin Gesundbrunnen–Hannover–Hamm–Düsseldorf/Köln	ICE 2
ICE 11	Hamburg Altona–Berlin–Leipzig–Frankfurt/M–Stuttgart–München	ICE 1
ICE 12	Berlin Ostbahnhof–Braunschweig–Kassel–Frankfurt/M–Basel	ICE 1
ICE 13	Berlin Ostbahnhof–Braunschweig–Kassel–Frankfurt/M–Ffm Flughafen–Stuttgart	ICE 1
ICE 15	Stralsund–Berlin–Erfurt–Frankfurt/M–Heidelberg–Stuttgart	ICE T
ICE 18	Hamburg Altona–Berlin–Erfurt–Bamberg–Nürnberg–München	ICE T
ICE 20	Hamburg Altona–Kassel–Frankfurt/M–Basel	ICE 1 & 4
ICE 22	Hamburg Altona–Kassel–Frankfurt/M–Stuttgart	ICE 1
ICE 25	Hamburg Altona/Bremen–Hannover–Würzburg–Nürnberg–München	ICE 1, 2 & 4
ICE 28	Hamburg Altona–Berlin–Leipzig–Nürnberg–München	ICE T
ICE 31	Hamburg Altona–Ruhr–Köln–Koblenz–Frankfurt/M–Regensburg/Basel	ICE 1
ICE 41	Essen–Köln–Frankfurt/M–Würzburg–Nürnberg–München	ICE 3
ICE 42	Dortmund–Köln–Frankfurt/M–Stuttgart–München	ICE 3
ICE 43	Hannover/Dortmund–Köln–Frankfurt/M–Basel	ICE 3
ICE 45	Köln–Wiesbaden–Mannheim–Stuttgart	ICE 3
ICE 47	Dortmund–Köln– Frankfurt/M–Mannheim–Stuttgart	ICE 3
ICE 49	Köln–Frankfurt/M	ICE 3
ICE 50	Dresden–Leipzig–Frankfurt/M–Wiesbaden/Mannheim–Saarbrücken	ICE T
ICE 78	Frankfurt/M–Köln–Oberhausen–Amsterdam	ICE 3M
ICE 79	Frankfurt/M–Köln–Brussels	ICE 3M
ICE 82	Frankfurt/M–Saarbrücken–Paris	ICE Velaro & TGV
ICE 84	Frankfurt/M–Strasbourg–Marseille	TGV
ICE 89	München–Innsbrück	ÖBB RJ
ICE 90	München–Salzburg–Wien–Budapest	ÖBB RJ
ICE 91	Frankfurt/M–Nürnberg–Wien	ICE T

CLASS 401   ICE1

Originally each train had a power car on each end with a variable number of trailers in between. With the introduction of the other types of ICEs the trailers on Class 401 sets have now been standardised with 12 trailers being the norm. In 2005 the mid-life refurbishment started or as DB calls it "Redesign". Each set was internally stripped of seats and fittings at the Hamburg base. The trains were then sent to Nürnberg works for their "redesign". Apart from new fittings the major change has seen a first class carriage altered to second class (Class 802.7); the second class seats in the service car have been altered to first class and the carriage relocated in the train. All vehicles have had their generous seat pitch reduced so that five extra seats have been added to first class vehicles and eight to the second class ones. Electrical equipment on the power cars has been improved and new bogie frames provided. Braking and air conditioning have been thoroughly overhauled. Laptop points have been provided. The telephone compartments have been removed in this age of the mobile telephone. After the reformations caused by all this work it was thought the sets would be stable, but there continue to be alterations albeit surprisingly not with the sets that work into Switzerland. The formations shown were as reported towards the end of 2017 when no doubt the end of year peak needed as many trains in service as possible. During the re-design project more than 100 vehicles changed sets including vehicles that carry the names. Unfortunately some were not re-named causing the same name to appear on two different trains! Hopefully this has all been sorted out since.

The terrible accident at Eschede saw set 51 mostly destroyed. 401 020 was written off after fire damage and was replaced by 401 019, which in turn was later replaced by the spare power car from set 51 (401 051). 401 573 is in effect now a new vehicle; having been damaged it received parts from withdrawn vehicles including 401 551. The aftermath of the Eschede accident saw all sets have their set numbers stencilled above all the bogies.

The use of ICE1 sets has changed little since introduction. Their base remains at Hamburg and their main route is still over the North–South high speed line. Sets 72–90 are cleared for working in Switzerland. The class is not allowed on the Köln–Frankfurt/M high speed line. The introduction of the new Class 412 sets will eventually affect Class 401.

As this edition was being prepared it was discovered that a 401 set had already been reduced to a 7-car formation to take over some former IC services. New brake tests will be required.

Power Cars

Built: 1989–93.
Builder–Mech. Parts: Krauss-Maffei, Krupp, Thyssen-Henschel.
Builder–Elec. Parts: ABB, AEG, Siemens.
Wheel Arrangement: Bo-Bo.
Control System: Thyristor with oil-cooled rectifiers (sets 1–20); GTO thyristor (sets 52–90).
Maximum Rating: 4800 kW (6400 hp).
Weight: 80 tonnes (sets 1–20); 77 tonnes (sets 52–90).
Traction Motors: Three-phase asynchronous motors as on Class 120.
Length over Couplers: 20.56 m.
Maximum Speed: 280 km/h.
Livery: White with red stripe.

▲ The first production series of ICE, 401 006 leads ICE1 set 06 through Buggingen, south of Freiburg on 6 September 2016. **Keith Fender**

Trailer Cars

Length over Couplers: 26.40 m.

Class 801.0. A (TFso).

Builders: Duewag, Waggon-Union, ABB/Henschel.
Weight: 52 tonnes.   **Accommodation:** 56/– 1T.

Class 801.4. A (TFso).

Builders: Duewag, Waggon-Union, ABB/Henschel.
Weight: 52 tonnes.   **Accommodation:** 56/– 1T.

Class 801.8. A (TFso).

Builders: Waggon-Union, ABB/Henschel.
Weight: 52 tonnes.   **Accommodation:** 56/– 1T.

Class 802.0. B (TSso).

Builders: Duewag, LHB.
Weight: 53 tonnes.   **Accommodation:** –/71 2T.

Class 802.3. B (TSso).

Builders: Duewag, LHB, MBB, MAN.
Weight: 53 tonnes.   **Accommodation:** –/71 2T.

Class 802.6. B (TSso).

Builders: MBB, MAN.
Weight: 53 tonnes.   **Accommodation:** –/71 2T.

Class 802.7. B (TSso).

Rebuilt from Class 801.4 carriages.

Builders: Duewag, Waggon-Union, ABB/Henschel. Rebuilt at Nürnberg works.
Weight: 53 tonnes.   **Accommodation:** –/71 2T.

Class 802.8. B (TSso).

Builders: MBB, MAN.
Weight: 53 tonnes.   **Accommodation:** –/71 2T.

Class 802.9. B (TSso).

26 extra vehicles built as part of ICE2 order as there were insufficient second class carriages.

Built: 1996–97.
Builders:
Weight: 53 tonnes.   **Accommodation:** –/74 2T.

Class 803.1. AB (TCso). With special facilities (Service car).

Builders: Duewag.
Weight: 53 tonnes.
Accommodation: 29/6 1TD, conference room and conductor's compartment, 3W.

Class 804. Bord Restaurant.

These cars have a restaurant, a kitchen, a bar and bar seating. They are noticeable by their raised roofs, a design feature which has not been perpetuated in future builds.

Builders: Waggon-Union, ABB/Henschel.
Weight: 56 tonnes.   **Accommodation:** 24 restaurant + 16 bar.

For formations, see pages TBA.

Names:

These are carried on the side of the trailer car nearest to the locomotive; consequently the names are shown against the set numbers.

01	401 001	802 031	802 631	802 411	802 053	802 058	802 703	802 393	804 027
02	401 002	802 829	802 653	802 096	802 413	802 093	802 714	802 008	804 044
03	401 003	802 860	802 627	802 372	802 027	802 063	802 901	802 057	804 046
04	401 004	802 856	802 658	802 440	802 622	802 441	802 705	802 059	804 055
05	401 005	802 842	802 642	802 361	802 368	802 087	802 902	802 040	804 041
06	401 006	802 806	802 602	802 329	802 309	802 036	802 718	802 807	804 039
07	401 007	802 816	802 610	802 327	802 326	802 383	802 701	802 098	804 023
08	401 568	802 813	802 618	802 344	802 380	802 081	802 906	802 071	804 028
09	Disbanded								
10	401 010	802 328	802 624	802 047	802 055	802 046	802 922	802 333	802 042
11	401 011	802 837	802 639	802 448	802 419	802 417	802 907	802 308	804 045
12	401 012	802 846	802 606	802 301	802 304	802 026	802 909	802 365	804 018
13	401 013	802 804	802 605	802 371	802 322	802 430	802 343	802 384	804 014
14	401 014	802 859	802 634	802 369	802 360	802 074	802 029	802 024	804 036
15	401 015	802 654	802 647	802 434	802 454	802 437	802 709	802 050	804 032
16	401 016	802 382	802 370	802 064	802 325	802 394	802 914	802 408	804 011
17	401 017	802 835	802 635	802 351	802 010	802 420	802 921	802 042	804 017
18	401 018	802 833	802 611	802 307	802 354	802 035	802 313	802 324	804 012
19	401 509	802 819	802 601	802 314	802 363	802 332	802 312	802 321	804 031
20	401 019	802 811	-	802 366	802 396	802 023	802 908	802 016	804 026
51	Disbanded - Eschede accident								
52	401 052	802 852	802 620	802 390	802 337	802 336	802 704	802 855	804 038
53	401 053	802 818	802 623	802 075	802 407	802 401	802 070	802 073	804 029
54	401 054	802 824	802 613	802 319	802 305	802 302	802 367	802 406	804 009
55	401 055	802 830	802 632	802 303	802 335	802 320	802 926	802 066	804 033
56	401 056	802 826	802 607	802 364	802 652	802 414	802 025	802 049	804 052
57	401 057	802 854	802 616	802 378	802 451	802 415	802 005	802 402	806 043
58	401 058	802 814	802 619	802 381	802 608	802 458	802 919	802 827	804 007
59	401 059	802 838	802 640	802 395	802 018	802 445	802 903	802 072	804 035
60	401 060	802 821	802 604	802 334	802 065	802 004	802 911	802 387	804 005
61	401 061	802 815	802 612	802 398	802 399	802 375	802 002	802 001	804 049
62	401 062	802 850	802 628	802 339	802 338	802 094	802 915	802 015	804 047
63	401 063	802 801	802 625	802 389	802 388	802 056	802 904	802 062	804 024
64	401 064	802 831	802 643	802 349	802 385	802 006	802 913	802 347	804 030
65	401 065	802 802	802 621	802 085	802 077	802 078	802 910	802 020	804 025
66	401 066	802 051	802 637	802 449	802 356	802 355	802 916	802 052	804 022
67	401 067	802 840	802 633	802 400	802 082	802 080	802 920	802 021	804 040
68	401 068	802 841	802 638	802 410	802 409	802 083	802 925	802 084	804 019
69	401 069	802 832	802 630	802 391	802 392	802 003	802 924	802 033	804 016
70	401 070	802 809	802 019	802 433	802 067	802 038	802 924	802 033	804 016
71	401 071	802 823	802 641	802 359	802 079	802 017	802 345	802 028	804 003
72	401 072	802 825	802 644	802 386	802 330	802 060	802 416	802 331	804 021
73	401 073	802 820	802 645	802 447	802 455	802 358	802 712	802 353	804 057
74	401 075	802 847	802 646	802 425	802 310	802 421	802 923	802 405	804 020
75	401 074	802 845	802 614	802 315	802 306	802 422	802 708	802 044	804 008
76	401 076	802 839	802 650	802 428	802 423	802 424	802 707	802 048	804 050
77	401 077	802 828	802 626	802 011	802 089	802 429	802 706	802 076	804 037
78	401 078	802 812	802 649	802 432	802 431	802 426	802 715	802 857	804 013
79	401 079	802 848	802 659	802 379	802 443	802 444	802 710	802 316	804 058
80	401 080	802 810	802 636	802 009	802 442	802 097	802 711	802 069	804 059
81	401 081	802 834	802 629	802 350	802 007	802 012	802 917	802 817	804 034
82	401 082	802 362	802 377	802 091	802 323	802 041	802 716	802 446	804 006
83	401 083	802 853	802 651	802 453	802 318	802 090	802 702	802 843	804 004
84	401 084	802 022	802 657	802 348	802 352	802 438	802 032	802 404	804 002
85	401 085	802 851	802 655	802 095	802 376	802 397	802 043	802 452	804 056
86	401 086	802 822	802 656	802 346	802 439	802 061	802 912	802 013	804 054
87	401 087	802 805	802 617	802 317	802 456	802 341	802 918	802 030	804 051
88	401 088	802 858	802 660	802 435	802 436	802 457	802 717	802 054	804 060
89	401 089	802 844	802 092	802 412	802 088	802 427	802 713	802 045	804 053
90	401 090	802 849	802 648	802 418	802 357	802 014	802 450	802 403	804 048

803 101	801 096	801 434	801 834	401 501	I	AH1	Mühldorf am Inn
803 153	801 427	801 081	801 852	401 502	I	AH1	Jever
803 121	801 410	801 012	801 817	401 503	I	AH1	
803 147	801 045	801 039	801 822	401 504	I	AH1	Fulda
803 109	801 019	801 433	801 842	401 505	I	AH1	Offenbach am Main
803 117	801 027	801 436	801 843	401 506	I	AH1	Itzehoe
803 128	801 049	801 050	801 805	401 507	I	AH1	Plattling
803 129	801 052	801 079	801 841	401 508	I	AH1	Lichtenfels
803 123	801 002	801 037	801 824	401 510	I	AH1	Gelsenkirchen
803 127	801 084	801 083	801 859	401 511	I	AH1	Nürnberg ?
803 119	801 030	801 036	801 821	401 512	I	AH1	Memmingen
803 120	801 035	801 034	801 819	401 513	I	AH1	Frankenthal (Pfalz)
803 106	801 011	801 005	801 816	401 514	I	AH1	Friedrichshafen
803 150	801 093	801 429	801 846	401 515	I	AH1	Regensburg
803 102	801 013	801 409	801 815	401 516	I	AH1	Pforzheim
803 105	801 061	801 087	801 801	401 517	I	AH1	Hof
803 110	801 010	801 041	801 823	401 518	I	AH1	
803 113	801 023	801 058	801 839	401 519	I	AH1	Osnabrück
803 107	801 004	801 033	801 811	401 520	I	AH1	Lüneburg
803 116	801 026	801 417	801 850	401 552	I	AH1	Hanau
803 134	801 072	801 059	801 832	401 553	I	AH1	Neumünster
803 114	801 025	801 016	801 808	401 554	I	AH1	Flensburg
803 133	801 069	801 403	801 833	401 555	I	AH1	Rosenheim
803 103	801 003	801 091	801 851	401 556	I	AH1	Heppenheim an der Bergstrasse
803 143	801 435	801 032	801 818	401 557	I	AH1	Landshut
803 125	801 047	801 046	801 826	401 558	I	AH1	Gütersloh
803 137	801 031	801 029	801 814	401 559	I	AH1	Bad Oldesloe
803 124	801 044	801 048	801 827	401 560	I	AH1	Worms
803 135	801 063	801 017	801 820	401 561	I	AH1	Bebra
803 148	801 065	801 007	801 804	401 562	I	AH1	Geisenheim/Rheingau
803 136	801 073	801 043	801 825	401 563	I	AH1	
803 130	801 068	801 423	801 857	401 564	I	AH1	
803 131	801 066	801 028	801 831	401 565	I	AH1	
803 122	801 040	801 051	801 803	401 566	I	AH1	Gelthausen ?
803 141	801 080	801 076	801 838	401 567	I	AH1	Garmisch Partenkirchen
803 132	801 062	801 082	801 828	401 571	I	AH1	Crailsheim
803 126	801 042	801 064	801 830	401 569	I	AH1	
803 142	801 095	801 055	801 807	401 570	I	AH1	
803 140	801 078	801 077	801 835	?	I	AH1	Heusenstamm
803 118	801 038	801 022	801 837	401 572	I	AH1	Aschaffenburg
803 144	801 071	801 094	801 844	401 573	I	AH1	Basel
803 145	801 438	801 416	801 845	401 574	I	AH1	Zürich
803 146	801 098	801 001	801 809	401 575	I	AH1	
803 151	801 425	801 024	801 847	401 576	I	AH1	Bremen
803 139	801 070	801 086	801 849	401 577	I	AH1	Rendsburg
803 154	801 092	801 089	801 853	401 578	I	AH1	Bremerhaven
803 112	801 067	801 407	801 858	401 579	I	AH1	
803 155	801 085	801 411	801 810	401 580	I	AH1	Castrop-Rauxel ?
803 138	801 405	801 414	801 836	401 581	I	AH1	Interlaken
803 160	801 053	801 401	801 813	401 582	I	AH1	Rüdesheim
803 152	801 090	801 412	801 812	401 583	I	AH1	Trimmendorfer Strand
803 156	801 057	801 006	801 856	401 584	I	AH1	Bruchsal
803 111	801 020	801 430	801 854	401 585	I	AH1	Freilassing
803 159	801 060	801 056	801 855	401 586	I	AH1	Chur
803 115	801 018	801 015	801 829	401 587	I	AH1	Giessen
803 158	801 431	801 054	801 860	401 588	I	AH1	Hildesheim
803 157	801 428	801 088	801 848	401 589	I	AH1	
803 149	801 075	801 408	801 840	401 590	I	AH1	Ludwigshafen am Rhein

82

Spare Cars:

401 008	401 009	401 020	401 051	802 615	802 631
801 008	801 032	801 074	801 805	802 803	802 836
802 039	802 086			803 104	

CLASS 402   ICE2

As already stated these trains are formed as half-sets with a power car at one end being matched by a driving trailer at the other end. Two units in multiple form a "full-train". To ease coupling arrangements at stations the trains are fitted with Scharfenberg couplers. They work from Berlin to the Ruhr area and Köln, splitting at Hamm with a portion going via Essen to Düsseldorf and another going via Wuppertal to Köln and Bonn. Trains from Hamburg and Bremen combine in Hannover and then go on to Kassel, Würzburg and München.

After the refurbishment of ICE1 trains, the ICE2 trains were taken in to Nürnberg works for similar treatment. The train formations remain the same. The children's play area has been reduced and a cloakroom area replaced by seating, allowing an extra 13 second class seats per set.

Power Cars
Built: 1996–97.
Builder–Mech. Parts: Krauss Maffei, SFT Krupp.
Builder–Elec. Parts: Siemens.
Wheel Arrangement: Bo-Bo.
Continuous Rating: 4800 kW.
Maximum Tractive Effort: 300 kN.
Wheel Diameter: 1250 mm.
Weight: 78 tonnes.
Length over Couplers: 20.56 m.
Maximum Speed: 300 km/h.

Trailer Cars
Length over Couplers: 26.40 m.

Class 805.0. A (FO).
Builders: DWA, LHB.
Weight: 45 tonnes.
Accommodation: 53/– 1T, lockers, quiet area.

Class 805.3. A (FO).
Builder: MAN.
Weight: 45 tonnes.
Accommodation: 53/– 2T, lockers.

Class 806.0. B (TSO).
Builder: Duewag.
Weight: 46 tonnes.
Accommodation: –/63 2T 1TD + children's area.

Class 806.3. B (TSO).
Builder: Duewag.
Weight: 46 tonnes.
Accommodation: –/74 2T.

Class 806.6. B (TSO).
Builders: Duewag/LHB.
Weight: 46 tonnes.
Accommodation: –/74 2T.

Class 807. WR (RU). Restaurant car with conductor's compartment.
Builder: LHB.
Weight: 51 tonnes.
Accommodation: 23 chairs, conductor's office 1TD.

Class 808. B (DTSO). Driving trailer second.
Builders: MAN/Adtranz.
Weight: 53 tonnes.
Accommodation: –/52 1T.

201	402 001	805 306	805 004	807 020	806 024	806 310	806 620	808 001	I	BRG
202	402 002	805 314	805 001	807 016	806 028	806 303	806 635	808 002	I	BRG
203	402 003	805 304	805 006	807 025	806 026	806 306	806 639	808 003	I	BRG
204	402 004	805 340	805 032	807 004	806 038	806 307	806 638	808 004	I	BRG
205	402 005	805 331	805 033	807 033	806 029	806 333	806 602	808 005	I	BRG
206	402 046	805 311	805 011	807 017	806 013	806 319	806 604	808 006	I	BRG
207	402 007	805 302	805 041	807 018	806 018	806 318	806 644	808 007	I	BRG

208	402 008	805 308	805 008	807 005	806 011	806 311	806 641	808 008	I	BRG
209	402 009	805 313	805 013	807 031	806 017	806 314	806 603	808 009	I	BRG
210	402 010		805 014	807 032	806 021	806 312	806 605	808 010	I	BRG
211	402 011	805 312	805 010	807 029	806 010	806 324	806 643	808 011	I	BRG
212	402 012	805 309	805 009	807 027	806 001	806 313	806 642	808 012	I	BRG
213	402 013	805 318	805 017	807 041	806 002	806 328	806 601	808 013	I	BRG
214	402 014	805 341	805 037	807 030	806 035	806 335	806 625	808 014	I	BRG
215	402 015	805 342	805 012	807 044	806 041	806 341	806 630	808 045	I	BRG
216	402 016	805 339	805 042	807 043	806 042	806 342	806 637	808 016	I	BRG
217	402 017	805 336	805 026	807 003	806 037	806 337	806 627	808 017	I	BRG
218	402 018	805 303	805 040	807 015	806 015	806 338	806 626	808 018	I	BRG
219	402 019	805 319	805 019	807 023	806 005	806 301	806 614	808 019	I	BRG
220	402 020	805 320	805 020	807 012	806 004	806 302	806 608	808 020	I	BRG
221	402 021	805 321	805 021	807 013	806 006	806 329	806 611	808 021	I	BRG
222	402 022	805 322	805 022	807 014	806 007	806 320	806 610	808 022	I	BRG
223	402 023	805 337	805 003	807 011	806 027	806 327	806 619	808 023	I	BRG
224	402 024	805 328	805 030	807 028	806 040	806 340	806 618	808 024	I	BRG
225	402 025	805 330	805 031	807 038	806 025	806 332	806 609	808 025	I	BRG
226	402 026	805 329	805 027	807 037	806 030	806 317	806 636	808 026	I	BRG
227	402 027	805 333	805 036	807 039	806 034	806 330	806 623	808 027	I	BRG
228	402 006	805 334	805 035	807 040	806 032	806 334	806 621	808 028	I	BRG
229	402 029	805 325	805 028	807 026	806 039	806 339	806 629	808 029	I	BRG
230	402 030	805 305	805 007	807 007	806 008	806 309	806 640	808 030	I	BRG
231	402 031	805 307	805 024	807 021	806 012	806 308	806 612	808 031	I	BRG
232	402 032	805 335	805 038	807 001	806 036	806 336	806 624	808 032	I	BRG
233	402 033	805 327	805 005	807 002	806 020	806 305	806 615	808 033	I	BRG
234	402 034	805 324	805 023	807 035	806 019	806 322	806 616	808 034	I	BRG
235	402 035	805 332	805 034	807 034	806 031	806 331	806 622	808 035	I	BRG
236	402 036	805 316	805 018	807 042	806 003	806 321	806 631	808 036	I	BRG
237	402 037	805 343	805 043	807 009	806 043	806 343	806 632	808 037	I	BRG
238	402 038	805 323	805 025	807 008	806 014	806 316	806 613	808 038	I	BRG
239	402 039	805 317	805 016	807 006	806 023	806 325	806 607	808 039	I	BRG
240	402 040	805 315	805 015	807 036	806 033	806 326	806 606	808 040	I	BRG
241	402 041	805 301	805 002	807 022	806 009	806 304	806 634	808 041	I	BRG
242	402 042	805 326	805 039	807 019	806 016	806 323	806 617	808 042	I	BRG
243	402 043	805 344	805 044	807 010	806 044	806 344	806 633	808 043	I	BRG
244	402 044	805 338	805 029	807 024	806 022	806 315	806 628	808 044	I	BRG
Spare	402 028	805 310						808 015	I	BRG

Names:

201	Rheinsberg		223	Schwerin
202	Wuppertal		224	Bielefeld
203	Cottbus/Chósebuz		225	Oldenburg (Oldb)
204	Bielefeld		226	Lutherstadt Wittenberg
205	Zwickau		227	Ludwiglust
206	Magdeburg		228	Altenburg
207	Stendal		229	Templin
208	Bonn		230	Delitzsch
209	Riesa		231	Brandenburg an der Havel
210	Fontanestadt		232	Frankfurt (Oder)
211	Uelzen		233	Ulm
212	Potsdam		234	Minden (Westfalen)
213	Nauen		235	Görlitz
214	Hamm (Westfalen)		236	Jüterbog
215	Bitterfeld		237	Neustrelitz
216	Dessau		238	Saarbrücken
217	Bergen auf Rügen		239	Essen
218	Braunschweig		240	Bochum
219	Hagen		241	Bad Hersfeld
220	Meiningen		242	Quedlinburg
221	Lubbenau/Spreewald		243	Bautzen
222	Eberswalde		244	Koblenz

CLASS 403 ICE3

The ICE3 sets marked a new generation of ICE trains where the power was spread throughout the train. The trains feature three-phase asynchronous motors for traction. The passenger accommodation features: electronic seat reservation details shown above each seat; electronic destination indicators at carriage doorways; video and audio facilities, etc. With power spread through the train the classification of vehicles was altered and all are now Class 403; technically some vehicles which are not powered should be 8xx, but as they carry vital electrical equipment for the rest of the train they are counted as power cars. In this series of ICE trains the first class cars are always 0xx, 1xx, 2xx; the service car/bar-car is 3xx and the second class cars are 5xx, 6xx, 7xx, and 8xx. The 0xx and 5xx are always the driving cars. ICE3s cover workings over the Köln–Frankfurt/M high speed line. The trains also have set numbers in the 3xx series shown on the body sides above the bogies. From about 2002 seat pitch has been reduced allowing more seats per vehicle to be provided but at the expense of some seats not being alongside a window. Details for individual vehicles are outstanding but the first series has 21 extra seats overall (3/18) whilst the second series has 8 extra seats (3/5).

A + A + A + R + BD + B + B + B (DMFO–TFO–MFO–TRUB–TSO–MSO–TSO–DMSO).

Built: 1998–2002; 2004–05 (403 051–063).
Builder–Elec. Parts: Siemens.
Wheel Arrangement: Bo-Bo + 2-2 + Bo-Bo + 2-2 + 2-2 + Bo-Bo + 2-2 + Bo-Bo.
Continuous Rating: 8000 kW.
Maximum Tractive Effort: 300 kN.
Wheel Diameter: 1250 mm.
Train Weight: 409 tonnes.
Length over Couplers: 200 m (driving car 25.675 m; intermediate cars 24.775 m).
Maximum Speed: 330 km/h.

Class 403.0. A (DMFO).

Builder–Mech. Parts: Adtranz (Nürnberg).
Weight: 51 tonnes.   **Accommodation:** 50/–.

Class 403.1. A (TFO). With transformer.

Builder–Mech. Parts: Siemens.
Weight: 55 tonnes.   **Accommodation:** 48/– 2T.

Class 403.2. A (MFO).

Builder–Mech. Parts: Siemens.
Weight: 50 tonnes.   **Accommodation:** 74/– 2T.

Class 403.3. R (TRUB).

Builders–Mech. Parts: Alstom/LHB.
Weight: 51 tonnes.   **Accommodation:** 24 chairs + service point.

Class 403.8. B (TSO).

Builders–Mech. Parts: Bombardier/DWA Ammendorf.
Weight: 47 tonnes.   **Accommodation:** –/56 1TD.

Class 403.7. B (MSO).

Builder–Mech. Parts: Siemens.
Weight: 50 tonnes.   **Accommodation:** –/74 2T.

Class 403.6. B (TSO). With transformer.

Builders–Mech. Parts: Bombardier/DWA Ammendorf.
Weight: 54 tonnes.   **Accommodation:** –/74 2T

Class 403.5. B (DMSO).

Builder–Mech. Parts: Adtranz (Nürnberg).
Weight: 51 tonnes.   **Accommodation:** –/68.

301	403 001	403 101	403 201	403 301	403 801	403 701	403 601	403 501	I	MH1
302	403 002	403 102	403 202	403 302	403 802	403 702	403 602	403 502	I	MH1
303	403 003	403 103	403 203	403 303	403 803	403 703	403 603	403 503	I	MH1
304	403 022	403 104	403 204	403 304	403 804	403 704	403 604	403 504	I	MH1

305	403 005	403 105	403 205	403 305	403 805	403 705	403 605	403 505	I	MH1
306	403 006	403 106	403 206	403 306	403 806	403 706	403 606	403 506	I	MH1
307	403 007	403 107	403 207	403 307	403 807	403 707	403 607	403 507	I	MH1
308	403 008	403 108	403 208	403 308	403 808	403 708	403 608	403 508	I	MH1
309	403 009	403 109	403 209	403 309	403 809	403 709	403 609	403 509	I	MH1
310	403 010	403 110	403 221	403 310	403 810	403 710	403 610	403 510	I	MH1
311	403 011	403 111	403 211	403 311	403 811	403 711	403 611	403 511	I	MH1
312	403 012	403 112	403 212	403 312	403 821	403 712	403 612	403 512	I	MH1
313	403 013	403 113	403 213	403 313	403 813	403 713	403 613	403 513	I	MH1
314	403 019	403 119	403 225	403 325	403 823	403 714	403 614	403 514	I	MH1
315	403 015	403 115	403 215	403 315	403 815	403 715	403 615	403 515	I	MH1
316	403 016	403 116	403 210	403 316	403 816	403 716	403 616	403 516	I	MH1
317	403 017	403 117	403 217	403 317	403 817	403 717	403 617	403 517	I	MH1
318	403 018	403 118	403 218	403 318	403 818	403 718	403 618	403 518	I	MH1
319	403 014	403 131	403 219	403 319	403 819	403 719	403 619	403 519	I	MH1
320	403 020	403 121	403 220	403 320	403 820	403 720	403 621	403 520	I	MH1
321	403 021	403 120	403 216	403 331	403 812	403 721	403 620	403 521	I	MH1
322	403 004	403 122	403 222	403 322	403 822	403 722	403 622	403 522	I	MH1
323	403 023	403 123	403 223	403 314	403 814	403 723	403 623	403 523	I	MH1
324	403 024	403 124	403 224	403 324	403 824	403 724	403 624	403 524	I	MH1
325	403 025	403 125	403 214	403 321	403 825	403 725	403 625	403 525	I	MH1
326	403 026	403 126	403 226	403 323	403 826	403 726	403 626	403 526	I	MH1
327	403 027	403 127	403 227	403 327	403 827	403 727	403 627	403 527	I	MH1
328	403 028	403 128	403 228	403 328	403 828	403 728	403 628	403 528	I	MH1
329	403 029	403 129	403 229	403 329	403 829	403 729	403 629	403 529	I	MH1
330	403 030	403 130	403 230	403 330	403 830	403 730	403 630	403 530	I	MH1
331	403 031	403 114	403 231	403 326	403 812	403 731	403 631	403 531	I	MH1
332	403 032	403 132	403 232	403 332	403 832	403 732	403 632	403 532	I	MH1
333	403 033	403 133	403 233	403 333	403 833	403 733	403 633	403 533	I	MH1
334	403 034	403 134	403 234	403 334	403 834	403 734	403 634	403 534	I	MH1
335	403 035	403 135	403 235	403 335	403 835	403 735	403 635	403 535	I	MH1
336	403 036	403 136	403 236	403 336	403 836	403 736	403 636	403 536	I	MH1
337	403 037	403 137	403 237	403 337	403 837	403 737	403 637	403 537	I	MH1
351	403 051	403 151	403 251	403 351	403 851	403 751	403 651	403 551	I	MH1
352	403 052	403 152	403 252	403 352	403 852	403 752	403 652	403 552	I	MH1
353	403 053	403 153	403 253	403 353	403 853	403 753	403 653	403 553	I	MH1
354	403 054	403 154	403 254	403 354	403 854	403 754	403 654	403 554	I	MH1
355	403 055	403 155	403 255	403 355	403 855	403 755	403 655	403 555	I	MH1
356	403 056	403 156	403 256	403 356	403 856	403 756	403 656	403 556	I	MH1
357	403 057	403 157	403 257	403 357	403 857	403 757	403 657	403 557	I	MH1
358	403 058	403 158	403 258	403 358	403 858	403 758	403 658	403 558	I	MH1
359	403 059	403 159	403 259	403 359	403 859	403 759	403 659	403 559	I	MH1
360	403 060	403 160	403 260	403 360	403 860	403 760	403 660	403 560	I	MH1
361	403 061	403 161	403 261	403 361	403 861	403 761	403 661	403 561	I	MH1
362	403 062	403 162	403 262	403 362	403 862	403 762	403 662	403 562	I	MH1
363	403 063	403 163	403 263	403 363	403 863	403 763	403 663	403 563	I	MH1

Names:

301	Freiburg im Breisgau		318	Münster Westf.
302	Hansestadt Lübeck		319	Duisburg
303	Dortmund		320	Weil am Rhein
304	München		321	Krefeld
305	Baden-Baden		322	Solingen
307	Oberhausen		323	Schaffhausen
308	Murnau		324	Fürth
309	Aalen		325	Ravensburg
310	Wolfsburg		326	Neunkirchen
311	Wiesbaden		327	Siegen
312	Montabaur		328	Aachen
313	Treuchtlingen		330	Göttingen
314	Bergisch Gladbach		331	Westerland/Sylt
315	Singen (Hohentwiel)		332	Augsburg
316	Siegburg		333	Goslar
317	Recklinghausen		334	Offenburg

335	Konstanz		357	Esslingen am Neckar
336	Ingolstadt		358	St. Ingbert
337	Stuttgart		359	Leverkusen
351	Herford		360	Linz am Rhein
352	Mönchengladbach		361	Celle
353	Neu Ulm		362	Schwerte (Ruhr)
355	Tuttlingen		363	Weilheim

CLASS 406   ICE3M

These multi-voltage sets were built to enable through services to operate off the Frankfurt/M–Köln high speed line into The Netherlands, Belgium and even Frankfurt/M to France with a new ICE depot being built at Frankfurt-Griesheim to service them. DB pantographs are fitted to the 406.1 and 406.6 vehicles, DC pantographs (for NS, SNCB/NMBS and SNCF) are fitted to the 406.2 and 406.7 vehicles whilst AC pantographs (for SBB, SNCB and SNCF) are fitted to the 406.3 and 406.8 vehicles. A mid life refurbishment has started increasing capacity by 25 extra seats (6/19).

A + A + B + R + BD + B + B + B (DMFO–TFO–MSO–TRUB–TSO–MSO–TSO–DMSO).

Built: 1998–2001.
Systems: 15 kV AC 16.7 Hz, 25 kV AC 50 Hz, 1500 V DC.
Wheel Arrangement: Bo-Bo + 2-2 + Bo-Bo + 2-2 + 2-2 + Bo-Bo + 2-2 + Bo-Bo.
Continuous Rating: 8000 kW.
Maximum Tractive Effort: 300 kN.
Wheel Diameter: 1250 mm.
Train Weight: 409 tonnes.
Length over Couplers: 200 m (driving car 25.675 m; intermediate cars 24.775 m).
Maximum Speed: 330 km/h (AC); 220 km/h (DC).

Class 406.0. A (DMFO).

Builder–Mech. Parts: Adtranz (Nürnberg).
Weight: 51 tonnes.   **Accommodation:** 49/–

Class 406.1. A (TFO). With transformer.

Builder–Mech. Parts: Siemens.
Weight: 55 tonnes.   **Accommodation:** 46/– 2T.

Class 406.2. B (MSO).

Builder–Mech. Parts: Siemens.
Weight: 50 tonnes.   **Accommodation:** –/61 2T.

Class 406.3. R (TRUB).

Builders–Mech. Parts: Alstom/LHB.
Weight: 51 tonnes.   **Accommodation:** 24 chairs + service point.

Class 406.8. B (TSO).

Builders–Mech. Parts: Bombardier/DWA Ammendorf.
Weight: 47 tonnes.   **Accommodation:** –/54 1TD.

Class 406.7. B (MSO).

Builder–Mech. Parts: Siemens.
Weight: 50 tonnes.   **Accommodation:** –/74 2T.

Class 406.6. B (TSO). With transformer.

Builders–Mech. Parts: Bombardier/DWA Ammendorf.
Weight: 54 tonnes.   **Accommodation:** –/72 2T

Class 406.5. B (DMSO).

Builder–Mech. Parts: Adtranz (Nürnberg).
Weight: 51 tonnes.   **Accommodation:** –/64.

4601	406 001	406 101	406 201	406 301	406 801	406 701	406 601	406 501	I	FGM
4602	406 002	406 102	406 202	406 302	406 802	406 702	406 602	406 502	I	FGM
4603	406 003	406 103	406 203	406 303	406 803	406 703	406 603	406 503	I	FGM

4604	406 004	406 104	406 204	406 304	406 804	406 704	406 604	406 504	I	FGM
4607	406 007	406 107	406 207	406 307	406 807	406 707	406 607	406 507	I	FGM
4610	406 010	406 110	406 210	406 310	406 810	406 710	406 610	406 510	I	FGM
4611	406 011	406 111	406 211	406 311	406 811	406 711	406 611	406 511	I	FGM
4651	406 051	406 151	406 251	406 351	406 851	406 751	406 651	406 551	I	LD
4652	406 052	406 152	406 252	406 352	406 852	406 752	406 652	406 552	I	LD
4653	406 053	406 153	406 253	406 353	406 853	406 753	406 653	406 553	I	LD
4654	406 054	406 154	406 254	406 354	406 854	406 754	406 681	406 581	I	FGM
4680	406 080	406 180	406 280	406 380	406 880	406 780	406 680	406 580	I	FGM
4681			406 281	406 381	406 881	406 781			I	FGM (Z)
4682	406 082	406 182	406 282	406 382	406 882	406 782	406 682	406 582	I	FGM
4683	406 083	406 183	406 283	406 383	406 883	406 783	406 683	406 583	I	FGM
4684	406 084	406 184	406 284	406 384	406 884	406 784	406 684	406 584	I	FGM
4685	406 085	406 185	406 285	406 385	406 885	406 785	406 685	406 585	I	FGM

Damaged   406 554   406 654

Names:

4603	Mannheim		4653	Utrecht
4604	Brussel/Bruxelles		4680	Würzburg
4607	Hannover		4682	Köln
4610	Frankfurt (Main)		4683	Limburg an der Lahn
4611	Düsseldorf		4684	Forbach-Lorraine
4651	Amsterdam		4685	Schwäbisch Hall
4652	Arnhem			

▲ 406 051 is owned by NS, hence the logo on the front. It has arrived 100 minutes late at Frankfurt/M Hbf with ICE 123 from Amsterdam and is being turned around quickly to form ICE 122 back to Amsterdam. TGV 4702 on the left, waits to leave with TGV 9552 to Paris Est on 10 August 2015.
Brian Garvin

CLASS 407 ICE M/VELARO D

15 more multi-voltage ICE3 (406) were ordered from Siemens in November 2007 for service from December 2011. Just like previous orders the run on order has turned into a new type – Class 407! The trains are based on the Siemens Velaro model which has been exported (Spain, China, Russia) and thus this type is Velaro – D (D= Deutschland). Although only 15 sets were initially ordered there are in fact 17 as an extra one was later ordered to make up for an accident-damaged 406, whilst another extra one was provided by Siemens as compensation for late delivery. Like the 406s the units are intended to work into France, Belgium but with pressure on ICE units the 407s are being kept on internal services until the new 412s have settled in. 407s are expected to be able to work in multiple with Classes 403 and 406 but no reports of this happening have been received. A change to previous ICEs is that the 407 is a Siemens product whereas all previous sets have been constructed by consortia. Certain equipment is now located on the roof (e.g. air conditioning). Each train has four independent converters with one converter feeding four traction motors. Any failure of one converter will not affect the other three thus a train could continue with 75% traction power. Low level three-phase asynchronous motors with cage rotors are provided but it is understood that set 17 has synchronous motors and in effect is another test bed unit. Set numbers are 7xx not 47xx as originally planned. Note that 407 001 is the second set to be allocated this number, the first set going to Turkey as a demonstrator and eventually being taken into stock there.

A + A + AR + B + B + B + B + B (DMFO–TFO–MRFO–TSO–TSO–MSO–TSO–DMSO).

Built: 2009–12.
Builder: Siemens.
Systems: 15 kV AC 16.7 Hz; 25 kV AC 50 Hz; 1500 V DC; 3000V DC.
Wheel Arrangement: Bo-Bo + 2-2 + Bo-Bo + 2-2 + 2-2 + Bo-Bo + 2-2 + Bo-Bo.
Continuous Rating: 8000 kW (AC); 4200kW (DC).
Maximum Tractive Effort: 300 kN.
Wheel Diameter: 1250 mm.
Train Weight: 454 tonnes.
Length over Couplers: 200.72 m (Driving cars 25.735 m, intermediate cars 24.175 m).
Maximum Speed: 320 km/h (AC), 220 km/h (DC).
Width: 2.924 m.
Total Accommodation: 460 (111F, 333S, 16 in Bistro).

Class 407.0. A (DMFO).

Weight: 57.5 tonnes
One door per side.

Accommodation: 42/–

Class 407.1. A (TFO). With transformer.

Weight: 58.8 tonnes
One door per side, 24 quiet seats. DC Pantograph.

Accommodation: 51/– 2T (24 seats quiet area).

Class 407.2. AR (MRFO).

Weight: 59.5 tonnes
Two doors per side.

Accommodation: 18/– 2T (+ 16 seats in Bistro).

Class 407.3. B (TSO).

Weight: 53.9 tonnes
One door per side, staff offices, AC Pantograph.

Accommodation: –/45 2T (1 disabled, 1 staff).

Class 407.8. B (TSO).

Weight: 53.9 tonnes
One door per side, AC Pantograph.

Accommodation: –/76 2T.

Class 407.7. B (MSO). With rectifier.

Weight: 55.3 tonnes
Two doors per side.

Accommodation: –/76 2T.

Class 407.6. B (TSO). With transformer.

Weight: 59 tonnes
One door per side, quiet coach, DC pantograph.

Accommodation: –/72 2T.

Class 407.5. B (DMSO).

Weight: 57.7 tonnes
One door per side.

Accommodation: –/64.

701[II]	407 001	407 101	407 201	407 301	407 801	407 701	407 601	407 501	I	FGM
702	407 002	407 102	407 202	407 302	407 802	407 702	407 602	407 502	I	FGM
703	407 003	407 103	407 203	407 303	407 803	407 703	407 603	407 503	I	FGM
704	407 004	407 104	407 204	407 304	407 804	407 704	407 604	407 504	I	FGM
705	407 005	407 105	407 205	407 305	407 805	407 705	407 605	407 505	I	FGM
706	407 006	407 106	407 206	407 306	407 806	407 706	407 606	407 506	I	FGM
707	407 007	407 107	407 207	407 307	407 807	407 707	407 607	407 507	I	FGM
708	407 008	407 108	407 208	407 308	407 808	407 708	407 608	407 508	I	FGM
709	407 009	407 109	407 209	407 309	407 809	407 709	407 609	407 509	I	FGM
710	407 010	407 110	407 210	407 310	407 810	407 710	407 610	407 510	I	FGM
711	407 011	407 111	407 211	407 311	407 811	407 711	407 611	407 511	I	FGM
712	407 012	407 112	407 212	407 312	407 812	407 712	407 612	407 512	I	FGM
713	407 013	407 113	407 213	407 313	407 813	407 713	407 613	407 513	I	FGM
714	407 014	407 114	407 214	407 314	407 814	407 714	407 614	407 514	I	FGM
715	407 015	407 115	407 215	407 315	407 815	407 715	407 615	407 515	I	FGM
716	407 016	407 116	407 216	407 316	407 816	407 716	407 616	407 516	I	FGM
717	407 017	407 117	407 217	407 317	407 817	407 717	407 617	407 517	I	FGM

CLASS 410 ICE-S

Class 410 is an ICE experimental set, ICE-S where the "S" is understood to stand for Schnellfahrstreckendienst. The two power cars were part of the Class 402 production run built in 1997 but intended for experimental use. Originally based at the München Technical Centre and maintained by MH1 the set is now based in Minden and maintained in Berlin.

Class 410.1. Power cars built by Krauss Maffei/Siemens.

Class 810. 101 built by MAN, 102 built by Duewag.

    410 101   810 101   810 102   410 102   I   BRG

▲ Multi-voltage Velaro D 407 016 waits to leave Mannheim Hbf on 2 May 2018. **Brian Garvin**

CLASS 411 ICE-T

These tilting ICE-3 sets come in two versions. Class 411 is a seven-car set and Class 415 is a five-car set. The 411s feature a restaurant car whereas the 415s have a bistro. The units are intended for running not only over the newly-built high speed lines but also over old lines with curves, hence the decision to fit tilt. In January 2004 vehicles 411 706 and 411 806 were burnt out in the sidings at Leipzig. In the winter of 2006/07 some 411s had their intermediate carriages swapped with Class 415 so that 7-car trains could run into Switzerland (q.v.). About the same time three 411s were sold to Austrian Federal Railways (1190–92) for their share of the revised services into Austria which were to be 411s working Frankfurt/M to Wien. For completeness they are included here.

The driving coaches are interesting in that the driver's position is centrally located and immediately behind is a lounge with a full view through the driving cab. Set numbers are carried above the bogies – 11xx.

A + AB + R (BR*) + BD + B + B + B (DTFO–MCO–MRUB (MRSB*)–TSO–MSO–MSO–DTSO).

Built: 1998–2000, 2004–05 (*1151 onwards ICE-T2 with extra seating).
Builders–Mech. Parts: Bombardier/DWA (Ammendorf and Görlitz) (trailers), Siemens (power cars).
Builder–Elec. Parts: Siemens.
Wheel Arrangement: 2-2 + 1A-A1 + 1A-A1 + 2-2 + 1A-A1 + 1A-A1 + 2-2.
Traction Motors: 2 x 500 kW.
Continuous Rating: 1000 kW.
Length over Couplers: 185 m (driving car 27.45 m, intermediate cars 25.90 m).
Wheel Diameter: 890 mm.
Maximum Speed: 230 km/h.
Tilt: FIAT, hydraulic.

Class 411.0. A (DTFO). With transformer.

Weight: 56 tonnes.　　　　　　　**Accommodation:** 41/– (*43/–).

Class 411.1. AB (MCO).

Weight: 53 tonnes.　　　　　　　**Accommodation:** 12/47 2T.

Class 411.2. R (MRUB).

Weight: 55 tonnes.　　　　　　　**Accommodation:** 24 restaurant with bar and children's compartment including –/6.

Class 411.2*. BR (MRSB).

Weight: 59 tonnes.　　　　　　　**Accommodation:** –/14 with children's compartment and bistro with 14 bar seats.

Class 411.8. B (TSO).

Weight: 47 tonnes.　　　　　　　**Accommodation:** –/64(3) 2T (*–/68(3) 2T).

Class 411.7. B (MSO).

Weight: 53 (*55)tonnes.　　　　　**Accommodation:** –/62 2T (*–/68 2T) with service point.

Class 411.6. B (MSO).

Weight: 52 (*53) tonnes.　　　　　**Accommodation:** –/62 1W 1TD 1T (*–/67 1W 1TD 1T).

Class 411.5. B (DTSO). With transformer.

Weight: 56 tonnes.　　　　　　　**Accommodation:** –/63 (*–/66).

1101–1132. ICE-T.

1101	411 001	411 101	411 201	411 801	411 701	411 601	411 501	I	MH1
1102	411 002	411 102	411 206	411 802	411 702	411 602	411 502	I	MH1
1103	411 003	411 104	411 203	411 803	411 703	411 603	411 503	I	MH1
1104	411 006	411 103	411 204	411 804	411 704	411 604	411 504	I	MH1
1105	411 005	411 105	411 205	411 805	411 705	411 605	411 505	I	MH1
1107	411 007	411 107	411 207	411 807	411 707	411 607	411 507	I	MH1
1108	411 008	411 108	411 208	411 808	411 708	411 608	411 508	I	MH1
1109	411 009	411 109	411 209	411 820	411 709	411 609	411 509	I	MH1
1110	411 010	411 110	411 210	411 810	411 710	411 610	411 510	I	MH1
1111	411 011	411 111	411 211	411 811	411 711	411 611	411 511	I	MH1

1112	411 012	411 112	411 212	411 812	411 712	411 612	411 512	I	MH1
1113	411 013	411 113	411 213	411 813	411 713	411 613	411 513	I	MH1
1117	411 017	411 117	411 217	411 817	411 717	411 617	411 517	I	MH1
1118	411 018	411 118	411 218	411 818	411 718	411 618	411 518	I	MH1
1119	411 019	411 119	411 219	411 819	411 719	411 619	411 519	I	MH1
1125	411 004	411 125	411 225	411 825	411 725	411 625	411 525	I	MH1
1126	411 026	411 126	411 202	411 826	411 726	411 626	411 526	I	MH1
1127	411 027	411 127	411 227	411 827	411 727	411 627	411 527	I	MH1
1128	411 028	411 128	411 228	411 828	411 728	411 628	411 528	I	MH1
1129	411 029	411 129	411 226	411 829	411 729	411 629	411 529	I	MH1
1130	411 030	411 130	411 230	411 830	411 730	411 630	411 530	I	MH1
1131	411 031	411 131	411 231	411 831	411 731	411 631	411 531	I	MH1
1132	411 032	411 132	411 232	411 832	411 732	411 632	411 532	I	MH1

Names:

1101	Neustadt/Weinstrasse	1117	Erlangen
1102	Neubrandenburg	1118	Plauen (Vogtland)
1103	Paderborn	1119	Meissen
1104	Erfurt	1125	Arnstadt
1105	Dresden	1126	Leipzig
1107	Pirna	1127	Weimar
1108	Berlin	1128	Reutlingen
1109	Güstrow	1129	Kiel
1110	Naumburg/Saale	1130	Jena
1111	Hansestadt Wismar	1131	Trier
1112	Freie und Hansestadt Hamburg	1132	Wittenberge
1113	Hansestadt Stralsund		

▲ 411 063 dashes through Uelzen station 0n 13 August 2015 with ICE 1189, the 12.47 Hamburg Altona to München Hbf.   **Brian Garvin**

92

1151–1184. ICE-T2.

1151	411 051	411 151	411 251	411 851	411 751	411 651	411 551	I	MH1
1152	411 052	411 152	411 252	411 852	411 752	411 652	411 552	I	MH1
1153	411 053	411 153	411 253	411 853	411 753	411 653	411 553	I	MH1
1154	411 054	411 154	411 254	411 854	411 754	411 654	411 554	I	MH1
1155	411 071	411 155	411 255	411 855	411 755	411 655	411 555	I	MH1
1156	411 056	411 156	411 256	411 856	411 756	411 656	411 556	I	MH1
1157	411 057	411 157	411 257	411 857	411 757	411 657	411 557	I	MH1
1158	411 058	411 158	411 258	411 858	411 758	411 658	411 558	I	MH1
1159	411 059	411 159	411 259	411 859	411 759	411 659	411 559	I	MH1
1160	411 060	411 160	411 260	411 860	411 760	411 660	411 560	I	MH1
1161	411 061	411 161	411 261	411 861	411 761	411 661	411 561	I	MH1
1162	411 062	411 162	411 262	411 862	411 762	411 662	411 562	I	MH1
1163	411 063	411 163	411 263	411 863	411 763	411 663	411 563	I	MH1
1164	411 064	411 164	411 264	411 864	411 764	411 664	411 564	I	MH1
1165	411 065	411 165	411 265	411 865	411 765	411 665	411 565	I	MH1
1166	411 066	411 166	411 266	411 866	411 766	411 666	411 566	I	MH1
1167	411 067	411 167	411 267	411 867	411 767	411 667	411 567	I	MH1
1168	411 068	411 168	411 268	411 868	411 768	411 668	411 568	I	MH1
1169	411 069	411 169	411 269	411 869	411 769	411 669	411 569	I	MH1
1170	411 070	411 170	411 270	411 870	411 770	411 670	411 570	I	MH1
1171	411 055	411 171	411 271	411 871	411 771	411 671	411 571	I	MH1
1172	411 072	411 172	411 272	411 872	411 772	411 672	411 592	I	MH1
1173	411 073	411 173	411 273	411 873	411 773	411 673	411 573	I	MH1
1174	411 074	411 174	411 274	411 874	411 774	411 674	411 574	I	MH1
1175	411 075	411 175	411 275	411 875	411 775	411 675	411 575	I	MH1
1176	411 076	411 176	411 276	411 876	411 776	411 676	411 576	I	MH1
1177	411 077	411 177	411 277	411 877	411 777	411 677	411 577	I	MH1
1178	411 078	411 178	411 278	411 878	411 778	411 678	411 578	I	MH1
1180	411 080	411 120	411 220	411 821	411 720	411 620	411 580	I	MH1
1181	411 081	411 121	411 221	411 809	411 721	411 621	411 581	I	MH1
1182	411 082	411 122	411 229	411 822	411 722	411 622	411 582	I	MH1
1183	411 083	411 123	411 223	411 823	411 723	411 623	411 583	I	MH1
1184	411 084	411 124	411 224	411 824	411 724	411 624	411 584	I	MH1

1190–1192. ICE-T. Units owned by Austrian Federal Railways.

1190	411 090	411 190	411 290	411 890	411 790	411 690	411 590	I	MH1
1191	411 091	411 191	411 291	411 891	411 791	411 691	411 591	I	MH1
1192	411 092	411 192	411 292	411 892	411 792	411 606	411 506	I	MH1
	Spare	411 025	411 106	411 222	411 592	411 692			

Names:

1151	Elsterwerda	1169	Tutzing
1152	Travemünde	1170	Prenzlau
1153	Ilmenau	1171	Oschatz
1154	Sonneberg	1172	Bamberg
1155	Mühlhausen/Thuringen	1173	Halle (Saale)
1156	Waren (Müritz)	1174	Hansestadt Warburg
1157	Innsbruck	1175	Villingen - Schwenningen
1158	Falkenberg/Elster	1176	Coburg
1159	Passau	1177	Rathenow
1160	Markt Holzkirchen	1178	Ostseebad Warnemünde
1161	Andernach	1180	Darmstadt
1162	Vaihingen an der Enz	1181	Horb am Neckar
1163	Ostseebad Binz	1182	Mainz
1164	Rödental	1183	Oberursel (Taunus)
1165	Bad Oeynhausen	1184	Kaiserslautern
1166	Bingen am Rhein	1190	Wien
1167	Traunstein	1191	Salzburg
1168	Ellwangen	1192	Linz

CLASS 412   ICE4

It was in 2011 that DB and Siemens agreed to build 300 new long-distance trains with production running through to 2030; the project being known as ICEx. The initial order was for 130 sets with talk of 24 different train formations varying between 5 and 14 carriages.

Eventually ICEx became ICE4 and now there are only to be two formations of 7- or 12-car trains. Siemens is the main contractor but with such a large order Bombardier was appointed a sub-contractor with one third of the work. The Siemens plant at Krefeld is building two thirds of the carriages including all the powered vehicles; powered bogies are made in Graz. Bombardier fabricates bodies in Wroclaw or Görlitz whilst its plant in Siegen does all the unpowered bogies. Bombardier is building all the driving trailers. Fitting out and final assembly of the Bombardier vehicles is done at Hennigsdorf. These are then taken to Krefeld or Wildenrath to be formed up with the Siemens production; testing also takes place at Wildenrath. It will be noted that these trains are one voltage only and thus are predominately for use in Germany but workings into Switzerland and Austria will follow. In this connection some of the early units are still used for testing and driver training in Switzerland and Austria. The pantograph carriages have a Germany/Austria pantograph and another for use in Switzerland. Besides the usual German safety systems, ETCS is installed as it is used on the new Erfurt–Nürnberg NBS line.

The first trains entered service in October 2017, replacing ICE1 units on Hamburg–München trains, then from December 2017 some Hamburg to Stuttgart ICE1 trains became 412s. The units will gradually enter service on other routes. In time DB intends to increase the total number of ICE trains and routes; some routes will go half-hourly. Eventually ICE1 sets will be withdrawn but consideration is being given to reducing the length of trains and using them to cover IC services.

It should be noted that the trains have distributed power and that the driving carriages are "trailers". The extra length of the carriages means that each power car is self-contained, whereas in other ICEs transformers etc can be found on non-powered vehicles. There are an equal number of powered and unpowered vehicles. With such a large order and long trains the new European numbering system comes into its own. Set numbers are allocated with the 12-car trains being 9001 onwards whilst the 7-car trains, to be built from 2020, will be 9201 onwards; thus there are 200 set numbers available for 12-car trains. Note that there are no coaches 8 and 13.

Built: 2015–
Builders–Mech. Parts: Siemens, Bombardier.
Builder–Elec. Parts: Siemens.
Wheel Arrangement: 2-2 + Bo-Bo + Bo-Bo + 2-2 + Bo-Bo + Bo-Bo + 2-2 + Bo-Bo + 2-2 + Bo-Bo + 2-2 + 2-2.
Continuous Rating: 9900 kW.
Maximum Tractive Effort:
Wheel Diameter: 920mm (powered), 825mm (trailers).
Train Weight: 670 tonnes.
Length over Couplers: 346.00 m (driving trailers 29.11 m, intermediate vehicles 28.75 m).
Maximum Speed: 250 km/h.
Width: 2.852 m.
Total Accommodation: 830 (184/625, 21 in restaurant).

Class 0812.0. A (DTFO). Coach 14.

Weight: 53 tonnes.   **Accommodation:** 50/– 1T. With quiet area.

Class 1812.0. A (TFO). Coach 12.

Weight: 43 tonnes.   **Accommodation:** 67/– 2T.

Class 1412.0. A (MFO). Coach 11.

Weight: 60 tonnes.   **Accommodation:** 67/– 2T.

Class 8812.0. AR (TRUO). Coach 10.

Weight: 45 tonnes.   **Accommodation:** 21 unclassified, 2T.

Class 6412.0. B (PMGSO). Coach 9.

Weight: 60 tonnes.   **Accommodation:** –/38 1TD, 1TS With conductor's office, children's area, four wheelchair spaces. Two pantographs.

Class 9812.0. B (TSO). Coach 7.

Weight: 49 tonnes.   **Accommodation:** –/88 2T.

Class 2412.0. B (MSO). Coach 6.

Weight: 60 tonnes.   **Accommodation:** –/88 2T.

Class 2412.3 B (MSO). Coach 5.

Weight: 60 tonnes.   **Accommodation:** –/88 2T.

Class 4812.0 B (PTSO). Coach 4

Weight: 49 tonnes   **Accommodation:** –/88 2T. Two pantographs.

Class 2412.5 B (MSO). Coach 3.

Weight: 60 tonnes.   **Accommodation:** –/88 2T. With quiet area.

Class 2412.8. B (MSO). Coach 2.

Weight: 60 tonnes.   **Accommodation:** –/88 2T. With quiet area.

Class 5812.0. BD (DTBSO). Coach 1.

Weight: 53 tonnes.   **Accommodation:** –/59 1T. 8 bicycles.

9001	I	AH1	0812 001	1812 001	1412 001	8812 001	6412 001	9812 001	2412 001
			2412 301	4812 001	2412 501	2412 801	5812 001		
9002	I	AH1	0812 002	1812 002	1412 002	8812 002	6412 002	9812 002	2412 002
			2412 302	4812 002	2412 502	2412 802	5812 002		
9003	I	AH1	0812 003	1812 003	1412 003	8812 003	6412 003	9812 003	2412 003
			2412 303	4812 003	2412 503	2412 803	5812 003		
9004	I	AH1	0812 004	1812 004	1412 004	8812 004	6412 004	9812 004	2412 004
			2412 304	4812 004	2412 504	2412 804	5812 004		
9005	I	AH1	0812 005	1812 005	1412 005	8812 005	6412 005	9812 005	2412 005
			2412 305	4812 005	2412 505	2412 805	5812 005		
9006	I	AH1	0812 006	1812 006	1412 006	8812 006	6412 006	9812 006	2412 006
			2412 306	4812 006	2412 506	2412 806	5812 006		
9007	I		0812 007	1812 007	1412 007	8812 007	6412 007	9812 007	2412 007
			2412 307	4812 007	2412 507	2412 807	5812 007		
9008	I	AH1	0812 008	1812 008	1412 008	8812 008	6412 008	9812 008	2412 008
			2412 308	4812 008	2412 508	2412 808	5812 008		
9009	I		0812 009	1812 009	1412 009	8812 009	6412 009	9812 009	2412 009
			2412 309	4812 009	2412 509	2412 809	5812 009		
9010	I	AH1	0812 010	1812 010	1412 010	8812 010	6412 010	9812 010	2412 010
			2412 310	4812 010	2412 510	2412 810	5812 010		
9011	I	AH1	0812 011	1812 011	1412 011	8812 011	6412 011	9812 011	2412 011
			2412 311	4812 011	2412 511	2412 811	5812 011		
9012	I	AH1	0812 012	1812 012	1412 012	8812 012	6412 012	9812 012	2412 012
			2412 312	4812 012	2412 512	2412 812	5812 012		
9013	I	AH1	0812 013	1812 013	1412 013	8812 013	6412 013	9812 013	2412 013
			2412 313	4812 013	2412 513	2412 813	5812 013		
9014	I		0812 014	1812 014	1412 014	8812 014	6412 014	9812 014	2412 014
			2412 314	4812 014	2412 514	2412 814	5812 014		
9015	I	AH1	0812 015	1812 015	1412 015	8812 015	6412 015	9812 015	2412 015
			2412 315	4812 015	2412 515	2412 815	5812 015		
9016	I	AH1	0812 016	1812 016	1412 016	8812 016	6412 016	9812 016	2412 016
			2412 316	4812 016	2412 516	2412 816	5812 016		
9017	I	AH1	0812 017	1812 017	1412 017	8812 017	6412 017	9812 017	2412 017
			2412 317	4812 017	2412 517	2412 817	5812 017		
9018	I	AH1	0812 018	1812 018	1412 018	8812 018	6412 018	9812 018	2412 018
			2412 318	4812 018	2412 518	2412 818	5812 018		
9019	I	AH1	0812 019	1812 019	1412 019	8812 019	6412 019	9812 019	2412 019
			2412 319	4812 019	2412 519	2412 819	5812 019		
9020	I	AH1	0812 020	1812 020	1412 020	8812 020	6412 020	9812 020	2412 020
			2412 320	4812 020	2412 520	2412 820	5812 020		
9021	I	AH1	0812 021	1812 021	1412 021	8812 021	6412 021	9812 021	2412 021
			2412 321	4812 021	2412 521	2412 821	5812 021		
9022	I	AH1	0812 022	1812 022	1412 022	8812 022	6412 022	9812 022	2412 022
			2412 322	4812 022	2412 522	2412 822	5812 022		
9023	I		0812 023	1812 023	1412 023	8812 023	6412 023	9812 023	2412 023
			2412 323	4812 023	2412 523	2412 823	5812 023		

9024	I	0812 024	1812 024	1412 024	8812 024	6412 024	9812 024	2412 024
		2412 324	4812 024	2412 524	2412 824	5812 024		
9025	I	0812 025	1812 025	1412 025	8812 025	6412 025	9812 025	2412 025
		2412 325	4812 025	2412 525	2412 825	5812 025		
9026	I	0812 026	1812 026	1412 026	8812 026	6412 026	9812 026	2412 026
		2412 326	4812 026	2412 526	2412 826	5812 026		
9027	I	0812 027	1812 027	1412 027	8812 027	6412 027	9812 027	2412 027
		2412 327	4812 027	2412 527	2412 827	5812 027		
9028	I	0812 028	1812 028	1412 028	8812 028	6412 028	9812 028	2412 028
		2412 328	4812 028	2412 528	2412 828	5812 028		
9029	I	0812 029	1812 029	1412 029	8812 029	6412 029	9812 029	2412 029
		2412 329	4812 029	2412 529	2412 829	5812 029		
9030	I	0812 030	1812 030	1412 030	8812 030	6412 030	9812 030	2412 030
		2412 330	4812 030	2412 530	2412 830	5812 030		

Name:

| 9006 | Martin Luther | | 9019 | Freistaat Bayern |

▲ The latest variant of ICE, Class 412, is configured in 12-car formation and features a revised front end design. Set 9001 is seen undergoing trials at the Velim test circuit in the Czech Republic on 1 July 2015, shortly after the unit was built.   **Quintus Vosman**

CLASS 415   ICE-T

These are similar to Class 411 but are only five-car sets and some feature a Swiss pantograph as the units were for working into Switzerland on the Stuttgart–Horb–Singen–Zürich services – a well known route for plenty of curves! Set numbers are carried above the bogies e.g. 1501. In the winter of 2006/07 some intermediate carriages from 411s were swapped with those in 415s; the Swiss trains needed strengthening and as all the Swiss equipment was on the driving trailers this was deemed the easiest solution. These units no longer work from Stuttgart to Zürich as problems with the main ICE3 fleet caused them to be used elsewhere and their intended workings changed to loco-hauled IC trains.

A + BR + B + B + B (DTFO–MRSB–MSO–MSO–DTSO).

Built: 1998–99.
Builders–Mech. Parts: Bombardier/DWA (Ammendorf and Görlitz) (trailers), Siemens (power cars).
Builder–Elec. Parts: Siemens.
Wheel Arrangement: 2-2 + 1A-A1 + 1A-A1 + 1A-A1 + 2-2.
Traction Motors: 6 x 500 kW.
Continuous Rating: 3000 kW.
Length over Couplers: 130 m (driving car 27.45 m, intermediate cars 25.90 m).
Wheel Diameter: 890 mm.
Maximum Speed: 230 km/h.
Tilt: FIAT, hydraulic.

Class 411.5. A (DTFO). With transformer.

Weight: 56 tonnes.   **Accommodation:** 41/–.

Class 415.1. BR (MRSB).

Weight: 53 tonnes.   **Accommodation:** –/22 with children's compartment and bistro with 14 bar seats.

Class 415.7. B (MSO).
Weight: 53 tonnes.   **Accommodation:** –/62 1T with service point.

Class 415.6. B (MSO).
Weight: 52 tonnes.   **Accommodation:** –/62 1W 1TD 1T.

Class 415.5. B (DTSO). With transformer.

Weight: 56 tonnes.   **Accommodation:** –/63.

1501	415 001	415 101	415 701	415 601	415 501	I	FGM	Eisenach
1502	415 002	415 102	415 702	415 602	415 502	I	FGM	Karlsruhe
1503	415 003	415 103	415 703	415 603	415 503	I	FGM	Altenbeken
1504	415 004	415 104	415 704	415 604	415 504	I	FGM	Heidelberg
1505	415 005	415 105	415 705	415 605	415 505	I	FGM	
1506	415 006	415 106	415 706	415 606	415 506	I	FGM	Kassel
1520	415 020	415 180	415 780	415 680	415 520	I	FGM	Gotha
1521	415 021	415 181	415 781	415 681	415 521	I	FGM	Homburg/Saar
1522	415 022	415 182	415 782	415 682	415 522	I	FGM	Torgau
1523	415 023	415 183	415 783	415 683	415 523	I	FGM	Hansestadt Greifswald
1524	415 024	415 184	415 784	415 684	415 524	I	FGM	Hansestadt Rostock

5. ELECTRIC MULTIPLE UNITS

CLASS 420 | 3-CAR UNITS

First introduced for S-Bahn services around München in time for the 1972 Olympics the class later spread to Stuttgart and Frankfurt/M and for a while also in the Rühr. All these areas have received new units in recent years so large numbers of units have now been withdrawn. The most recent units were only built in the 1990s so the class will be around for a while yet, Stuttgart having recently refurbished some of its units. Both Köln and Düsseldorf have received units from Stuttgart allowing services to be increased. In a very surprising move many redundant units have been taken out of store and allocated to München. This city needs more units not only for coping with traffic increases (e.g. S-Bahn extension Dachau–Altomünster) but to replace some of its 423s which will soon be coming up for mid-life refurbishment. Stored 420s at Mukran, Hamm and elsewhere are in fact going first to Nürnberg works for a refresh but also the fitting of PZB/LZB safety system to allow them to work through the core route in the city centre. 421 411[II] was previously 421 401.

B + AB + B (DMSO–MCO–DMSO (non-gangwayed)).

Built: 1969–96.
Builders–Mech. Parts: Linke-Hoffmann-Busch/Messerschmitt-Bölkow-Blohm/Orenstein & Koppel/Uerdingen/Waggon-Union.
Builders–Elec. Parts: AEG/Brown-Boveri/Siemens.
Wheel Arrangement: Bo-Bo + Bo-Bo + Bo-Bo.   **Weight:** 44 + 41 + 44 tonnes.
Traction Motors: 4 x 200 kW.   **Length over Couplers:** 23.30 + 20.80 + 23.30 m.
Accommodation: –/63 + 17/49 + –/65.   **Maximum Speed:** 120 km/h.

420 265	421 265	420 765	FD (Z)	420 449	421 449	420 949	MH6
420 402	421 402	420 902	KD	420 450	421 450	420 950	MH6
420 406	421 406	420 906	EHM (Z)	420 451	421 451	420 951	MH6
420 411	421 411[II]	420 911	EHM (Z)	420 452	421 452	420 952	MH6
420 413	421 413	420 913	KD	420 455	421 455	420 955	KD
420 415	421 415	420 915	KD	420 456	421 456	420 956	MH6
420 417	421 417	420 917	KD	420 457	421 457	420 957	KKN (Z)
420 418	421 418	420 918	KD	420 458	421 458	420 958	KKN
420 419	421 419	420 919	KD	420 459	421 459	420 959	MH6
420 422	421 422	420 922	KD	420 460	421 460	420 960	MH6
420 423	421 423	420 923	KKN	420 461	421 461	420 961	MH6
420 424	421 424	420 924	KD	420 462	421 462	420 962	MH6
420 425	421 425	420 925	MH6	420 463	421 463	420 963	MH6
420 426	421 426	420 926	KKN	420 464	421 464	420 964	KKN
420 427	421 427	420 927	MH6	420 465	421 465	420 965	MH6
420 431	421 431	420 931	MH6	420 466	421 466	420 966	KD
420 432	421 432	420 932	MH6	420 467	421 467	420 967	MH6
420 433	421 433	420 933	KD	420 468	421 468	420 968	MH6
420 434	421 434	420 934	KKN	420 470	421 470	420 970	MH6
420 435	421 435	420 935	KD	420 471	421 471	420 971	MH6
420 436	421 436	420 936	KKN	420 472	421 472	420 972	MH6
420 437	421 437	420 937	MH6	420 474	421 474	420 974	MH6
420 438	421 438	420 938	MH6	420 476	421 476	420 976	MH6
420 439	421 439	420 939	MH6	420 477	421 477	420 977	MH6
420 440	421 440	420 940	KKN	420 478	421 478	420 978	MH6
420 441	421 441	420 941	KKN	420 479	421 479	420 979	KD
420 442	421 442	420 942	KD	420 482	421 482	420 982	KD
420 443	421 443	420 943	KKN	420 483	421 483	420 983	KD
420 444	421 444	420 944	MH6	420 484	421 484	420 984	KKN (Z)
420 445	421 445	420 945	MH6	420 485	421 485	420 985	MH6
420 446	421 446	420 946	MH6	420 486	421 486	420 986	KKN
420 447	421 447	420 947	MH6	420 487	421 487	420 987	KKN
420 448	421 448	420 948	MH6	420 489	421 489	420 989	MH6

CLASS 422   4-SECTION ARTICULATED UNITS

This class can be regarded as a follow-on to Class 423, for which the number series was all but complete. DB Regio Nordrheinwestfalen ordered 78 units in 2005 for services on the Rhein-Ruhr S-Bahn. There was an option for 72 more units but this was not taken up, although 84 units have been built. The original order was shared between Alstom and Bombardier with originally 27 trains being erected at the Bombardier plant in Hennigsdorf and 51 at the Alstom plant in Salzgitter. Electrical equipment came from Bombardier in Mannheim with Bombardier Siegen providing the bogies for the articulation, whilst Alstom provided the end bogies. The Verkehrsverbund Rhein-Ruhr was going to order another 116 sets but changed its mind and decided to wait to see the results from Class 430. However, with some of the S-Bahn lines being offered up for franchising it was later decided to cancel any further orders pending the results of the franchise competition. Like other new EMUs the Class 422 has had its "teething problems". In particular software problems with the on-board computers, especially those concerned with Automatic Train Protection (in this case Ebicab 500 PZB), were brought to light after two instances of signals being passed at danger. The EBA reduced the maximum speed to 100 km/h and insisted on two drivers in the cab! This led to many train services being covered by Class 143 and classic S-Bahn stock. All the problems were sorted by a software update. Another change from Class 423 concerns the unpowered bogie which on the 423s was un-braked. On the 422 it is braked and also has supplementary magnetic brakes. Recently there have been several fires on these units causing yet another problem and no doubt another modification.

AB + B + B + AB (DMCO–TSO–TSO–DMCO).

Built: 2007–10.
Builder–Mech. Parts: Alstom.
Builder–Elec. Parts: Bombardier.
Wheel Arrangement: Bo-Bo-2-Bo-Bo.
Traction Motors: 8 x 293 kW three-phase asynchronous motors per set.
Wheel Diameter: 850 mm.
Width: 3.02 m.   **Weight:** 112 tonnes.
Floor Height: 1025 mm.   **Length over Couplers:** 69.43 m.
Accommodation: 8/40 + –/48 + –/48 + 8/40.   **Maximum Speed:** 140 km/h.
Non-Standard Livery: N   Green and white – new Rhein-Ruhr S-Bahn livery.

422 001	432 001	432 501	422 501	N	EE	
422 002	432 002	432 502	422 502	N	EE	
422 003	432 003	432 503	422 503		EE	
422 004	432 004	432 504	422 504	N	EE	
422 005	432 005	432 505	422 505	N	EE	
422 006	432 006	432 506	422 506	N	EE	
422 007	432 007	432 507	422 507	N	EE	
422 008	432 008	432 508	422 508	N	EE	
422 009	432 009	432 509	422 509	N	EE	Dortmund
422 010	432 010	432 510	422 510	N	EE	
422 011	432 011	432 511	422 511	N	EE	
422 012	432 012	432 512	422 512		EE	
422 013	432 013	432 513	422 513		EE	
422 014	432 014	432 514	422 514		EE	
422 015	432 015	432 515	422 515		EE	
422 016	432 016	432 516	422 516		EE	
422 017	432 017	432 517	422 517		KD	
422 018	432 018	432 518	422 518		KD	
422 019	432 019	432 519	422 519		KD	
422 020	432 020	432 520	422 520		KD	
422 021	432 021	432 521	422 521		KD	
422 022	432 022	432 522	422 522		KD	
422 023	432 023	432 523	422 523		KD	
422 024	432 024	432 524	422 524		KD	
422 025	432 025	432 525	422 525		KD	
422 026	432 026	432 526	422 526		KD	
422 027	432 027	432 527	422 527		KD	
422 028	432 028	432 528	422 528	N	KD	
422 029	432 029	432 529	422 529		KD	
422 030	432 030	432 530	422 530		KD	
422 031	432 031	432 531	422 531		KD	
422 032	432 032	432 532	422 532		KD	

422 033	432 033	432 533	422 533		KD	
422 034	432 034	432 534	422 534		KD	
422 035	432 035	432 535	422 535	N	EE	
422 036	432 036	432 536	422 536		EE	
422 037	432 037	432 537	422 537	N	EE	
422 038	432 038	432 538	422 538		EE	
422 039	432 039	432 539	422 539		EE	
422 040	432 040	432 540	422 540		EE	
422 041	432 041	432 541	422 541		EE	
422 042	432 042	432 542	422 542		EE	
422 043	432 043	432 543	422 543	N	EE	
422 044	432 044	432 544	422 544	N	EE	
422 045	432 045	432 545	422 545	N	KD	
422 046	432 046	432 546	422 546	N	KD	
422 047	432 047	432 547	422 547	N	KD	
422 048	432 048	432 548	422 548		KD	
422 049	432 049	432 549	422 549		KD	
422 050	432 050	432 550	422 550		KD	
422 051	432 051	432 551	422 551		KD	
422 052	432 052	432 552	422 552		KD	
422 053	432 053	432 553	422 553		KD	
422 054	432 054	432 554	422 554		KD	
422 055	432 055	432 555	422 555		KD	
422 056	432 056	432 556	422 556		KD	
422 057	432 057	432 557	422 557		KD	
422 058	432 058	432 558	422 558		KD	
422 059	432 059	432 559	422 559		KD	
422 060	432 060	432 560	422 560		KD	
422 061	432 061	432 561	422 561		KD	
422 062	432 062	432 562	422 562		KD	
422 063	432 063	432 563	422 563		KD	
422 064	432 064	432 564	422 564		KD	
422 065	432 065	432 565	422 565		KD	
422 066	432 066	432 566	422 566		KD	
422 067	432 067	432 567	422 567		KD	
422 068	432 068	432 568	422 568		KD	
422 069	432 069	432 569	422 569		EE	
422 070	432 070	432 570	422 570		EE	
422 071	432 071	432 571	422 571		EE	
422 072	432 072	432 572	422 572		EE	
422 073	432 073	432 573	422 573		EE	
422 074	432 074	432 574	422 574		EE	
422 075	432 075	432 575	422 575		EE	Wuhan China
422 076	432 076	432 576	422 576		EE	
422 077	432 077	432 577	422 577		EE	
422 078	432 078	432 578	422 578		EE	
422 079	432 079	432 579	422 579		EE	Haltern am See
422 080	432 080	432 580	422 580		EE	
422 081	432 081	432 581	422 581		EE	Solingen
422 082	432 082	432 582	422 582		EE	Hilden
422 083	432 083	432 583	422 583		EE	Düsseldorf
422 084	432 084	432 584	422 584		EE	Essen

CLASS 423 4-SECTION ARTICULATED UNITS

Introduced in 1998 this class was the first of a new generation of S-Bahn unit intended to replace Class 420/421 in the München and Stuttgart areas, and provide new services in the Köln and Ruhr areas. Three-phase asynchronous motors are used with water cooled rectifiers. Another break with previous units was the use of articulation to reduce weight and length of the train. There are three sets of doors per carriage which feature an aluminium alloy body, which is wider than the bodies of units of Classes 424, 425 and 426. LCD display units inside and outside are provided for passenger information. The München area units have LZB fitted so that closer intervals can be worked along the core section of the city route from München Hbf to München Ostbahhof. Set 423 025 was withdrawn after accident damage. There have been problems with these units, especially in the autumn leaf period, which has led to additional braking being provided and sanding equipment.

AB + B + B + AB (DMCO–TSO–TSO–DMCO).

Built: 1998–2004.
Builder–Mech. Parts: Alstom LHB.
Builder–Elec. Parts: Adtranz.
Wheel Arrangement: Bo-Bo-2-Bo-Bo.
Traction Motors: 8 x 295 kW three-phase asynchronous motors per set.
Wheel Diameter: 850 mm.
Width: 3.02 m. **Weight:** 105 tonnes.
Floor Height: 995 mm. **Length over Couplers:** 18.24 + 15.46 + 15.46 + 18.24 m.
Accommodation: 8/40 + –/48 + –/48 + 8/40. **Maximum Speed:** 140 km/h.

423 001	433 001	433 501	423 501	TP
423 002	433 002	433 502	423 502	TP
423 003	433 003	433 503	423 503	TP
423 004	433 004	433 504	423 504	TP
423 005	433 005	433 505	423 505	TP
423 006	433 006	433 506	423 506	TP
423 007	433 007	433 507	423 507	TP
423 008	433 008	433 508	423 508	TP
423 009	433 009	433 509	423 509	TP
423 010	433 010	433 510	423 510	TP
423 011	433 011	433 511	423 511	TP
423 012	433 012	433 512	423 512	TP
423 013	433 013	433 513	423 513	TP
423 014	433 014	433 514	423 514	TP
423 015	433 015	433 515	423 515	TP
423 016	433 016	433 516	423 516	TP
423 017	433 017	433 517	423 517	TP
423 018	433 018	433 518	423 518	TP
423 019	433 019	433 519	423 519	TP
423 020	433 020	433 520	423 520	TP
423 021	433 021	433 521	423 521	TP
423 022	433 022	433 522	423 522	TP
423 023	433 023	433 523	423 523	TP
423 024	433 024	433 524	423 524	TP
423 026	433 026	433 526	423 526	TP
423 027	433 027	433 527	423 527	TP
423 028	433 028	433 528	423 528	TP
423 029	433 029	433 529	423 529	TP
423 030	433 030	433 530	423 530	TP
423 031	433 031	433 531	423 531	TP
423 032	433 032	433 532	423 532	TP
423 033	433 033	433 533	423 533	TP
423 034	433 034	433 534	423 534	KKN
423 035	433 035	433 535	423 535	KKN
423 036	433 036	433 536	423 536	KKN
423 037	433 037	433 537	423 537	KKN
423 038	433 038	433 538	423 538	KKN
423 039	433 039	433 539	423 539	KKN
423 040	433 040	433 540	423 540	KKN
423 041	433 041	433 541	423 541	KKN

423 042	433 042	433 542	423 542	KKN
423 043	433 043	433 543	423 543	KKN
423 044	433 044	433 544	423 544	KKN
423 045	433 045	433 545	423 545	KKN
423 046	433 046	433 546	423 546	KKN
423 047	433 047	433 547	423 547	KKN
423 048	433 048	433 548	423 548	KKN
423 049	433 049	433 549	423 549	KKN
423 050	433 050	433 550	423 550	KKN
423 051	433 051	433 551	423 551	KKN
423 052	433 052	433 552	423 552	KKN
423 053	433 053	433 553	423 553	KKN
423 054	433 054	433 554	423 554	KKN
423 055	433 055	433 555	423 555	KKN
423 056	433 056	433 556	423 556	KKN
423 057	433 057	433 557	423 557	KKN
423 058	433 058	433 558	423 558	MH6
423 059	433 059	433 559	423 559	MH6
423 060	433 060	433 560	423 560	MH6
423 061	433 061	433 561	423 561	MH6
423 062	433 062	433 562	423 562	MH6
423 063	433 063	433 563	423 563	MH6
423 064	433 064	433 564	423 564	MH6
423 065	433 065	433 565	423 565	MH6
423 066	433 066	433 566	423 566	MH6
423 067	433 067	433 567	423 567	MH6
423 068	433 068	433 568	423 568	MH6
423 069	433 069	433 569	423 569	MH6
423 070	433 070	433 570	423 570	MH6
423 071	433 071	433 571	423 571	MH6
423 072	433 072	433 572	423 572	MH6
423 073	433 073	433 573	423 573	MH6

▲ A number of former Stuttgart-based Class 420 EMUs are now being used on Köln S-Bahn route S12 services. Shortly after its move north, 420 434 is seen at Horrem on 29 January 2016 with a service to Hennef. **Keith Fender**

423 074	433 074	433 574	423 574		MH6
423 075	433 075	433 575	423 575		MH6
423 076	433 076	433 576	423 576		MH6
423 077	433 077	433 577	423 577		MH6
423 078	433 078	433 578	423 578		MH6
423 079	433 079	433 579	423 579		MH6
423 080	433 080	433 580	423 580		MH6
423 081	433 081	433 581	423 581		MH6
423 082	433 082	433 582	423 582		MH6
423 083	433 083	433 583	423 583		MH6
423 084	433 084	433 584	423 584		MH6
423 085	433 085	433 585	423 585		MH6
423 086	433 086	433 586	423 586		MH6
423 087	433 087	433 587	423 587		MH6
423 088	433 088	433 588	423 588		MH6
423 089	433 089	433 589	423 589		MH6
423 090	433 090	433 590	423 590		MH6
423 091	433 091	433 591	423 591		MH6
423 092	433 092	433 592	423 592		MH6
423 093	433 093	433 593	423 593		MH6
423 094	433 094	433 594	423 594		MH6
423 095	433 095	433 595	423 595		MH6
423 096	433 096	433 596	423 596		MH6
423 097	433 097	433 597	423 597		MH6
423 098	433 098	433 598	423 598		MH6
423 099	433 099	433 599	423 599		MH6
423 100	433 100	433 600	423 600		MH6
423 101	433 101	433 601	423 601		MH6
423 102	433 102	433 602	423 602		MH6
423 103	433 103	433 603	423 603		MH6
423 104	433 104	433 604	423 604		MH6
423 105	433 105	433 605	423 605		MH6
423 106	433 106	433 606	423 606		MH6
423 107	433 107	433 607	423 607		MH6
423 108	433 108	433 608	423 608		MH6
423 109	433 109	433 609	423 609		MH6
423 110	433 110	433 610	423 610		MH6
423 111	433 111	433 611	423 611	**A**	MH6
423 112	433 112	433 612	423 612	**A**	MH6
423 113	433 113	433 613	423 613		MH6
423 114	433 114	433 614	423 614		MH6
423 115	433 115	433 615	423 615		MH6
423 116	433 116	433 616	423 616		MH6
423 117	433 117	433 617	423 617	**A**	MH6
423 118	433 118	433 618	423 618		MH6
423 119	433 119	433 619	423 619		MH6
423 120	433 120	433 620	423 620		MH6
423 121	433 121	433 621	423 621		MH6
423 122	433 122	433 622	423 622		MH6
423 123	433 123	433 623	423 623		MH6
423 124	433 124	433 624	423 624		MH6
423 125	433 125	433 625	423 625		MH6
423 126	433 126	433 626	423 626		MH6
423 127	433 127	433 627	423 627		MH6
423 128	433 128	433 628	423 628		MH6
423 129	433 129	433 629	423 629		MH6
423 130	433 130	433 630	423 630		MH6
423 131	433 131	433 631	423 631		MH6
423 132	433 132	433 632	423 632		MH6
423 133	433 133	433 633	423 633		MH6
423 134	433 134	433 634	423 634		MH6
423 135	433 135	433 635	423 635		MH6
423 136	433 136	433 636	423 636		MH6
423 137	433 137	433 637	423 637		MH6

423 138	433 138	433 638	423 638		MH6
423 139	433 139	433 639	423 639		MH6
423 140	433 140	433 640	423 640		MH6
423 141	433 141	433 641	423 641		MH6
423 142	433 142	433 642	423 642		MH6
423 143	433 143	433 643	423 643		MH6
423 144	433 144	433 644	423 644		MH6
423 145	433 145	433 645	423 645		MH6
423 146	433 146	433 646	423 646		MH6
423 147	433 147	433 647	423 647		MH6
423 148	433 148	433 648	423 648		MH6
423 149	433 149	433 649	423 649		MH6
423 150	433 150	433 650	423 650		MH6
423 151	433 151	433 651	423 651		MH6
423 152	433 152	433 652	423 652		MH6
423 153	433 153	433 653	423 653		MH6
423 154	433 154	433 654	423 654		MH6
423 155	433 155	433 655	423 655		MH6
423 156	433 156	433 656	423 656		MH6
423 157	433 157	433 657	423 657		MH6
423 158	433 158	433 658	423 658		MH6
423 159	433 159	433 659	423 659		MH6
423 160	433 160	433 660	423 660		MH6
423 161	433 161	433 661	423 661		MH6
423 162	433 162	433 662	423 662		MH6
423 163	433 163	433 663	423 663		MH6
423 164	433 164	433 664	423 664		MH6
423 165	433 165	433 665	423 665	A	MH6
423 166	433 166	433 666	423 666		MH6
423 167	433 167	433 667	423 667		MH6
423 168	433 168	433 668	423 668		MH6
423 169	433 169	433 669	423 669		MH6
423 170	433 170	433 670	423 670		MH6
423 171	433 171	433 671	423 671		MH6
423 172	433 172	433 672	423 672		MH6
423 173	433 173	433 673	423 673		MH6
423 174	433 174	433 674	423 674		MH6
423 175	433 175	433 675	423 675		MH6
423 176	433 176	433 676	423 676		MH6
423 177	433 177	433 677	423 677		MH6
423 178	433 178	433 678	423 678		MH6
423 179	433 179	433 679	423 679		MH6
423 180	433 180	433 680	423 680		MH6
423 181	433 181	433 681	423 681		MH6
423 182	433 182	433 682	423 682		MH6
423 183	433 183	433 683	423 683		MH6
423 184	433 184	433 684	423 684		MH6
423 185	433 185	433 685	423 685		MH6
423 186	433 186	433 686	423 686		MH6
423 187	433 187	433 687	423 687		MH6
423 188	433 188	433 688	423 688		MH6
423 189	433 189	433 689	423 689		MH6
423 190	433 190	433 690	423 690		MH6
423 191	433 191	433 691	423 691		MH6
423 192	433 192	433 692	423 692		KKN
423 193	433 193	433 693	423 693		KKN
423 194	433 194	433 694	423 694		KKN
423 195	433 195	433 695	423 695		KKN
423 196	433 196	433 696	423 696		KKN
423 197	433 197	433 697	423 697		KKN
423 198	433 198	433 698	423 698		KKN
423 199	433 199	433 699	423 699		KKN
423 200	433 200	433 700	423 700	A	MH6
423 201	433 201	433 701	423 701		MH6

423 202	433 202	433 702	423 702	**A**	MH6	
423 203	433 203	433 703	423 703	**A**	MH6	
423 204	433 204	433 704	423 704	**A**	MH6	
423 205	433 205	433 705	423 705	**A**	MH6	
423 206	433 206	433 706	423 706		MH6	
423 207	433 207	433 707	423 707	**A**	MH6	
423 208	433 208	433 708	423 708	**A**	MH6	
423 209	433 209	433 709	423 709	**A**	MH6	
423 210	433 210	433 710	423 710	**A**	MH6	
423 211	433 211	433 711	423 711	**A**	MH6	
423 212	433 212	433 712	423 712		MH6	
423 213	433 213	433 713	423 713	**A**	MH6	
423 214	433 214	433 714	423 714	**A**	MH6	
423 215	433 215	433 715	423 715	**A**	MH6	
423 216	433 216	433 716	423 716	**A**	MH6	
423 217	433 217	433 717	423 717	**A**	MH6	
423 218	433 218	433 718	423 718		MH6	
423 219	433 219	433 719	423 719		MH6	
423 220	433 220	433 720	423 720	**A**	MH6	
423 221	433 221	433 721	423 721		MH6	
423 222	433 222	433 722	423 722		MH6	Markt Altomünster
423 223	433 223	433 723	423 723		MH6	
423 224	433 224	433 724	423 724		MH6	
423 225	433 225	433 725	423 725		MH6	
423 226	433 226	433 726	423 726		MH6	
423 227	433 227	433 727	423 727	**A**	MH6	
423 228	433 228	433 728	423 728		MH6	
423 229	433 229	433 729	423 729		MH6	
423 230	433 230	433 730	423 730		MH6	
423 231	433 231	433 731	423 731		MH6	
423 232	433 232	433 732	423 732		MH6	
423 233	433 233	433 733	423 733		MH6	
423 234	433 234	433 734	423 734		MH6	
423 235	433 235	433 735	423 735		MH6	
423 236	433 236	433 736	423 736		MH6	
423 237	433 237	433 737	423 737		MH6	
423 238	433 238	433 738	423 738		MH6	
423 239	433 239	433 739	423 739		MH6	
423 240	433 240	433 740	423 740		MH6	
423 241	433 241	433 741	423 741		MH6	
423 242	433 242	433 742	423 742		MH6	
423 243	433 243	433 743	423 743		MH6	
423 244	433 244	433 744	423 744		MH6	
423 245	433 245	433 745	423 745		KKN	
423 246	433 246	433 746	423 746		KKN	
423 247	433 247	433 747	423 747		KKN	
423 248	433 248	433 748	423 748		KD	
423 249	433 249	433 749	423 749		KD	
423 250	433 250	433 750	423 750		KD	
423 251	433 251	433 751	423 751		KD	
423 252	433 252	433 752	423 752		KD	
423 253	433 253	433 753	423 753		KD	
423 254	433 254	433 754	423 754		KD	
423 255	433 255	433 755	423 755		KD	
423 256	433 256	433 756	423 756		KD	
423 257	433 257	433 757	423 757		KD	
423 258	433 258	433 758	423 758		KD	
423 259	433 259	433 759	423 759		KD	
423 260	433 260	433 760	423 760		KD	
423 261	433 261	433 761	423 761		KD	
423 262	433 262	433 762	423 762		KD	
423 263	433 263	433 763	423 763		KD	
423 264	433 264	433 764	423 764		MH6	
423 265	433 265	433 765	423 765		MH6	

423 266	433 266	433 766	423 766		MH6
423 267	433 267	433 767	423 767		MH6
423 268	433 268	433 768	423 768		MH6
423 269	433 269	433 769	423 769		MH6
423 270	433 270	433 770	423 770		MH6
423 271	433 271	433 771	423 771		MH6
423 272	433 272	433 772	423 772		MH6
423 273	433 273	433 773	423 773		MH6
423 274	433 274	433 774	423 774		MH6
423 275	433 275	433 775	423 775		MH6
423 276	433 276	433 776	423 776		MH6
423 277	433 277	433 777	423 777		MH6
423 278	433 278	433 778	423 778		MH6
423 279	433 279	433 779	423 779		MH6
423 280	433 280	433 780	423 780		MH6
423 281	433 281	433 781	423 781	A	MH6
423 282	433 282	433 782	423 782		MH6
423 283	433 283	433 783	423 783	A	MH6
423 284	433 284	433 784	423 784		MH6
423 285	433 285	433 785	423 785		MH6
423 286	433 286	433 786	423 786		MH6
423 287	433 287	433 787	423 787		MH6
423 288	433 288	433 788	423 788		MH6
423 289	433 289	433 789	423 789		MH6
423 290	433 290	433 790	423 790		KD
423 291	433 291	433 791	423 791		KD
423 292	433 292	433 792	423 792		KD
423 293	433 293	433 793	423 793		KD
423 294	433 294	433 794	423 794		KD
423 295	433 295	433 795	423 795		KD
423 296	433 296	433 796	423 796		KD
423 297	433 297	433 797	423 797		KD
423 298	433 298	433 798	423 798		KD
423 299	433 299	433 799	423 799		KD
423 300	433 300	433 800	423 800		KD
423 301	433 301	433 801	423 801		FF
423 302	433 302	433 802	423 802		FF
423 303	433 303	433 803	423 803		FF
423 304	433 304	433 804	423 804		FF
423 305	433 305	433 805	423 805		FF
423 306	433 306	433 806	423 806		TP
423 307	433 307	433 807	423 807		TP
423 308	433 308	433 808	423 808		TP
423 309	433 309	433 809	423 809		TP
423 310	433 310	433 810	423 810		TP
423 311	433 311	433 811	423 811		TP
423 312	433 312	433 812	423 812		MH6
423 313	433 313	433 813	423 813		MH6
423 314	433 314	433 814	423 814		MH6
423 315	433 315	433 815	423 815		MH6
423 316	433 316	433 816	423 816		MH6
423 317	433 317	433 817	423 817	A	MH6
423 318	433 318	433 818	423 818		MH6
423 319	433 319	433 819	423 819		MH6
423 320	433 320	433 820	423 820		MH6
423 321	433 321	433 821	423 821		MH6
423 322	433 322	433 822	423 822		TP
423 323	433 323	433 823	423 823		TP
423 324	433 324	433 824	423 824		TP
423 325	433 325	433 825	423 825		FF
423 326	433 326	433 826	423 826		FF
423 327	433 327	433 827	423 827		FF
423 328	433 328	433 828	423 828		FF
423 329	433 329	433 829	423 829		FF

423 330	433 330	433 830	423 830	FF
423 331	433 331	433 831	423 831	FF
423 332	433 332	433 832	423 832	FF
423 333	433 333	433 833	423 833	FF
423 334	433 334	433 834	423 834	FF
423 335	433 335	433 835	423 835	TP
423 336	433 336	433 836	423 836	TP
423 337	433 337	433 837	423 837	TP
423 338	433 338	433 838	423 838	TP
423 339	433 339	433 839	423 839	TP
423 340	433 340	433 840	423 840	TP
423 341	433 341	433 841	423 841	TP
423 342	433 342	433 842	423 842	TP
423 343	433 343	433 843	423 843	TP
423 344	433 344	433 844	423 844	TP
423 345	433 345	433 845	423 845	TP
423 346	433 346	433 846	423 846	TP
423 347	433 347	433 847	423 847	MH6
423 348	433 348	433 848	423 848	MH6
423 349	433 349	433 849	423 849	MH6
423 350	433 350	433 850	423 850	MH6
423 351	433 351	433 851	423 851	MH6
423 352	433 352	433 852	423 852	MH6
423 353	433 353	433 853	423 853	MH6
423 354	433 354	433 854	423 854	MH6
423 355	433 355	433 855	423 855	MH6
423 356	433 356	433 856	423 856	MH6
423 357	433 357	433 857	423 857	MH6
423 358	433 358	433 858	423 858	MH6
423 359	433 359	433 859	423 859	MH6
423 360	433 360	433 860	423 860	MH6
423 361	433 361	433 861	423 861	MH6
423 362	433 362	433 862	423 862	MH6
423 363	433 363	433 863	423 863	MH6
423 364	433 364	433 864	423 864	MH6
423 365	433 365	433 865	423 865	MH6
423 366	433 366	433 866	423 866	MH6
423 367	433 367	433 867	423 867	TP
423 368	433 368	433 868	423 868	TP
423 369	433 369	433 869	423 869	TP
423 370	433 370	433 870	423 870	TP
423 371	433 371	433 871	423 871	TP
423 372	433 372	433 872	423 872	FF
423 373	433 373	433 873	423 873	FF
423 374	433 374	433 874	423 874	FF
423 375	433 375	433 875	423 875	FF
423 376	433 376	433 876	423 876	FF
423 377	433 377	433 877	423 877	FF
423 378	433 378	433 878	423 878	FF
423 379	433 379	433 879	423 879	FF
423 380	433 380	433 880	423 880	FF
423 381	433 381	433 881	423 881	FF
423 382	433 382	433 882	423 882	FF
423 383	433 383	433 883	423 883	FF
423 384	433 384	433 884	423 884	FF
423 385	433 385	433 885	423 885	FF
423 386	433 386	433 886	423 886	FF
423 387	433 387	433 887	423 887	FF
423 388	433 388	433 888	423 888	FF
423 389	433 389	433 889	423 889	FF
423 390	433 390	433 890	423 890	FF
423 391	433 391	433 891	423 891	FF
423 392	433 392	433 892	423 892	FF
423 393	433 393	433 893	423 893	FF

423 394	433 394	433 894	423 894	FF	
423 395	433 395	433 895	423 895	FF	
423 396	433 396	433 896	423 896	FF	
423 397	433 397	433 897	423 897	FF	
423 398	433 398	433 898	423 898	FF	
423 399	433 399	433 899	423 899	FF	
423 400	433 400	433 900	423 900	FF	
423 401	433 401	433 901	423 901	FF	
423 402	433 402	433 902	423 902	FF	
423 403	433 403	433 903	423 903	FF	
423 404	433 404	433 904	423 904	FF	
423 405	433 405	433 905	423 905	FF	
423 406	433 406	433 906	423 906	FF	
423 407	433 407	433 907	423 907	FF	
423 408	433 408	433 908	423 908	FF	
423 409	433 409	433 909	423 909	FF	
423 410	433 410	433 910	423 910	FF	
423 411	433 411	433 911	423 911	FF	
423 412	433 412	433 912	423 912	FF	
423 413	433 413	433 913	423 913	FF	
423 414	433 414	433 914	423 914	FF	
423 415	433 415	433 915	423 915	FF	
423 416	433 416	433 916	423 916	FF	
423 417	433 417	433 917	423 917	FF	
423 418	433 418	433 918	423 918	FF	
423 419	433 419	433 919	423 919	FF	
423 420	433 420	433 920	423 920	FF	
423 421	433 421	433 921	423 921	FF	
423 422	433 422	433 922	423 922	FF	
423 423	433 423	433 923	423 923	FF	
423 424	433 424	433 924	423 924	FF	
423 425	433 425	433 925	423 925	FF	
423 426	433 426	433 926	423 926	FF	
423 427	433 427	433 927	423 927	FF	
423 428	433 428	433 928	423 928	FF	
423 429	433 429	433 929	423 929	FF	
423 430	433 430	433 930	423 930	FF	
423 431	433 431	433 931	423 931	FF	
423 432	433 432	433 932	423 932	FF	
423 433	433 433	433 933	423 933	FF	
423 434	433 434	433 934	423 934	FF	
423 435	433 435	433 935	423 935	FF	
423 436	433 436	433 936	423 936	FF	
423 437	433 437	433 937	423 937	FF	
423 438	433 438	433 938	423 938	FF	
423 439	433 439	433 939	423 939	FF	
423 440	433 440	433 940	423 940	FF	
423 441	433 441	433 941	423 941	FF	
423 442	433 442	433 942	423 942	FF	
423 443	433 443	433 943	423 943	FF	
423 444	433 444	433 944	423 944	FF	
423 445	433 445	433 945	423 945	FF	
423 446	433 446	433 946	423 946	FF	
423 447	433 447	433 947	423 947	FF	
423 448	433 448	433 948	423 948	FF	
423 449	433 449	433 949	423 949	FF	
423 450	433 450	433 950	423 950	FF	
423 451	433 451	433 951	423 951	FF	
423 452	433 452	433 952	423 952	FF	
423 453	433 453	433 953	423 953	FF	Heusenstamm
423 454	433 454	433 954	423 954	FF	
423 455	433 455	433 955	423 955	FF	
423 456	433 456	433 956	423 956	FF	
423 457	433 457	433 957	423 957	MH6	

423 458	433 458	433 958	423 958	MH6	
423 459	433 459	433 959	423 959	MH6	
423 460	433 460	433 960	423 960	MH6	Ebersberg
423 461	433 461	433 961	423 961	TP	
423 462	433 462	433 962	423 962	TP	

CLASS 424   4-SECTION ARTICULATED UNITS

These articulated units are a variant of Class 425 (below) for duties around Hannover. They have a lower maximum speed and are fitted with bridge plates which stick out under the doors at stations instead of the folding steps on Class 425.

AB + B + B + AB (DMCO–TSO–TSO–DMCO).

Built: 1998–99.
Builders–Mech. Parts: Bombardier/DWA Ammendorf; Siemens.
Builder–Elec. Parts: Adtranz Hennigsdorf.
Wheel Arrangement: Bo-Bo-2-Bo-Bo.
Traction Motors: 8 x 295 kW three-phase asynchronous motors per set.
Wheel Diameter: 850 mm.   **Weight:** 35 + 21 + 21 + 36 tonnes.
Width: 2.84 m.   **Length over Couplers:** 18.24 + 15.46 + 15.46 + 18.24 m.
Floor Height: 798 mm.   **Maximum Speed:** 140 km/h.
Accommodation: 12/24(14) + –/56 + –/56 + 12/16(16) 1TD.

424 001	434 001	434 501	424 501	HHL	Burgdorf
424 002	434 002	434 502	424 502	HHL	Bad Pyrmont
424 003	434 003	434 503	424 503	HHL	
424 004	434 004	434 504	424 504	HHL	Lehrte
424 005	434 005	434 505	424 505	HHL	Wedemark
424 006	434 006	434 506	424 506	HHL	Neustadt am Rübenberge
424 007	434 007	434 507	424 507	HHL	Bad Nenndorf
424 008	434 008	434 508	424 508	HHL	
424 009	434 009	434 509	424 509	HHL	
424 010	434 010	434 510	424 510	HHL	
424 011	434 011	434 511	424 511	HHL	Stadthagen
424 012	434 012	434 512	424 512	HHL	
424 013	434 013	434 513	424 513	HHL	
424 014	434 014	434 514	424 514	HHL	Springe
424 015	434 015	434 515	424 515	HHL	
424 016	434 016	434 516	424 516	HHL	Wenningsten (Deister)
424 017	434 017	434 517	424 517	HHL	Bad Münder am Deister
424 018	434 018	434 518	424 518	HHL	Stadt Celle
424 019	434 019	434 519	424 519	HHL	Stadt Minden
424 020	434 020	434 520	424 520	HHL	
424 021	434 021	434 521	424 521	HHL	Wunstorf
424 022	434 022	434 522	424 522	HHL	
424 023	434 023	434 523	424 523	HHL	
424 024	434 024	434 524	424 524	HHL	Stadt Seelze
424 025	434 025	434 525	424 525	HHL	Stadt Nienburg
424 026	434 026	434 526	424 526	HHL	
424 027	434 027	434 527	424 527	HHL	Landeshauptstadt Hannover
424 028	434 028	434 528	424 528	HHL	
424 029	434 029	434 529	424 529	HHL	
424 030	434 030	434 530	424 530	HHL	
424 031	434 031	434 531	424 531	HHL	
424 032	434 032	434 532	424 532	HHL	Fürstenbad Pyrmont
424 033	434 033	434 533	424 533	HHL	
424 034	434 034	434 534	424 534	HHL	Rattenfängerstadt Hameln
424 035	434 035	434 535	424 535	HHL	Häste
424 036	434 036	434 536	424 536	HHL	
424 037	434 037	434 537	424 537	HHL	Stadt Langenhagen
424 038	434 038	434 538	424 538	HHL	Stadt Barsinghausen
424 039	434 039	434 539	424 539	HHL	Ronneburg
424 040	434 040	434 540	424 540	HHL	

CLASS 425 4-SECTION ARTICULATED UNITS

These units were a new standard DB local EMU for what can be called "outer suburban" or regional services. They differ from Class 423 in that they are narrower and have only two sets of doors per carriage side. Other features include regenerative braking, Scharfenberg couplers and controlled-emission toilets. Most units are with DB Regio but the units at Ludwigshafen belong to S-Bahn Rhein-Neckar, whilst those at Hannover are with S-Bahn Hannover (both DB subsidiaries).

AB + B + B + AB (DMCO–TSO–TSO–DMCO).

Built: 1999–2004.
Builders–Mech. Parts: Bombardier/DWA Ammendorf, Siemens.
Builder–Elec. Parts: Adtranz Hennigsdorf.
Wheel Arrangement: Bo-Bo-2-Bo-Bo.
Traction Motors: 8 x 293 kW three-phase asynchronous motors per set.
Wheel Diameter: 850 mm.   **Weight:** 35 + 21 + 21 + 36 tonnes.
Width: 2.84 m.   **Length over Couplers:** 18.24 + 15.46 + 15.46 + 18.24 m.
Floor Height: 798 mm.   **Maximum Speed:** 160 km/h.
Accommodation: 12/24(14) + –/56 + –/56 + 12/16(16) 1TD.

Class 425.0.

425 001	435 001	435 501	425 501	LMB	
425 002	435 002	435 502	425 502	LMB	
425 003	435 003	435 503	425 503	LMB	
425 004	435 004	435 504	425 504	LMB	
425 005	435 005	435 505	425 505	LMB	
425 006	435 006	435 506	425 506	LMB	
425 007	435 007	435 507	425 507	LMB	
425 008	435 008	435 508	425 508	LMB	
425 009	435 009	435 509	425 509	LMB	
425 010	435 010	435 510	425 510	LMB	
425 011	435 011	435 511	425 511	LMB	
425 012	435 012	435 512	425 512	LMB	
425 013	435 013	435 513	425 513	HHL	Emmertha
425 014	435 014	435 514	425 514	HHL	
425 015	435 015	435 515	425 515	RL	
425 016	435 016	435 516	425 516	RL	
425 017	435 017	435 517	425 517	RL	
425 018	435 018	435 518	425 518	RL	
425 019	435 019	435 519	425 519	RL	
425 020	435 020	435 520	425 520	RL	
425 021	435 021	435 521	425 521	EE	
425 022	435 022	435 522	425 522	EE	
425 023	435 023	435 523	425 523	FF	
425 024	435 024	435 524	425 524	EE	
425 025	435 025	435 525	425 525	EE	
425 026	435 026	435 526	425 526	RL	
425 027	435 027	435 527	425 527	RL	
425 028	435 028	435 528	425 528	FF	
425 029	435 029	435 529	425 529	RL	
425 030	435 030	435 530	425 530	FF	
425 031	435 031	435 531	425 531	FF	
425 032	435 032	435 532	425 532	FF	
425 033	435 033	435 533	425 533	FF	
425 034	435 034	435 534	425 534	FF	
425 035	435 035	435 535	425 535	FF	
425 036	435 036	435 536	425 536	RL	
425 037	435 037	435 537	425 537	FF	
425 038	435 038	435 538	425 538	RL	
425 039	435 039	435 539	425 539	RL	
425 040	435 040	435 540	425 540	RL	
425 041	435 041	435 541	425 541	RL	
425 042	435 042	435 542	425 542	HHL	
425 043	435 043	435 543	425 543	HHL	

425 044	435 044	435 544	425 544	FF	
425 045	435 045	435 545	425 545	MH6	
425 046	435 046	435 546	425 546	NWH	
425 047	435 047	435 547	425 547	NWH	
425 048	435 048	435 548	425 548	RL	
425 049	435 049	435 549	425 549	RL	
425 050	435 050	435 550	425 550	HHL	Altenbeken
425 051	435 051	435 551	425 551	HHL	
425 052	435 052	435 552	425 552	NWH	
425 053	435 053	435 553	425 553	HHL	
425 054	435 054	435 554	425 554	RL	
425 055	435 055	435 555	425 555	EE	
425 056	435 056	435 556	425 556	EE	
425 057	435 057	435 557	425 557	EE	
425 058	435 058	435 558	425 558	EE	
425 059	435 059	435 559	425 559	EE	
425 060	435 060	435 560	425 560	EE	
425 061	435 061	435 561	425 561	EE	
425 062	435 062	435 562	425 562	EE	
425 063	435 063	435 563	425 563	RL	
425 064	435 064	435 564	425 564	EE	
425 065	435 065	435 565	425 565	EE	
425 066	435 066	435 566	425 566	EE	
425 067	435 067	435 567	425 567	EE	
425 068	435 068	435 568	425 568	RL	
425 069	435 069	435 569	425 569	RL	
425 070	435 070	435 570	425 570	RL	
425 071	435 071	435 571	425 571	EE	
425 072	435 072	435 572	425 572	RL	
425 073	435 073	435 573	425 573	RL	
425 074	435 074	435 574	425 574	RL	
425 075	435 075	435 575	425 575	RL	
425 076	435 076	435 576	425 576	RL	
425 077	435 077	435 577	425 577	RL	
425 078	435 078	435 578	425 578	EE	
425 079	435 079	435 579	425 579	EE	
425 080	435 080	435 580	425 580	EE	
425 081	435 081	435 581	425 581	EE	
425 082	435 082	435 582	425 582	RL	
425 083	435 083	435 583	425 583	RL	
425 084	435 084	435 584	425 584	RL	
425 085	435 085	435 585	425 585	FF	
425 086	435 086	435 586	425 586	RL	
425 087	435 087	435 587	425 587	HHL	
425 088	435 088	435 588	425 588	RL	
425 089	435 089	435 589	425 589	HHL	
425 090	435 090	435 590	425 590	STR	Saarlouis
425 091	435 091	435 591	425 591	KKN	
425 092	435 092	435 592	425 592	KKN	
425 093	435 093	435 593	425 593	KKN	
425 094	435 094	435 594	425 594	KKN	
425 095	435 095	435 595	425 595	KKN	
425 096	435 096	435 596	425 596	KKN	
425 097	435 097	435 597	425 597	KKN	
425 098	435 098	435 598	425 598	KKN	
425 099	435 099	435 599	425 599	KKN	
425 100	435 100	435 600	425 600	KKN	
425 101	435 101	435 601	425 601	KKN	
425 102	435 102	435 602	425 602	KKN	
425 103	435 103	435 603	425 603	KKN	
425 104	435 104	435 604	425 604	KKN	
425 105	435 105	435 605	425 605	RL	
425 106	435 106	435 606	425 606	KKN	
425 107	435 107	435 607	425 607	RL	

425 108	435 108	435 608	425 608	KKN	
425 109	435 109	435 609	425 609	RL	
425 110	435 110	435 610	425 610	RL	
425 111	435 111	435 611	425 611	RL	
425 112	435 112	435 612	425 612	STR	
425 113	435 113	435 613	425 613	RL	
425 114	435 114	435 614	425 614	RL	
425 115	435 115	435 615	425 615	RL	
425 116	435 116	435 616	425 616	KKN	
425 117	435 117	435 617	425 617	RL	
425 118	435 118	435 618	425 618	RL	
425 119	435 119	435 619	425 619	RL	
425 120	435 120	435 620	425 620	RL	
425 121	435 121	435 621	425 621	RL	
425 122	435 122	435 622	425 622	RL	
425 123	435 123	435 623	425 623	RL	
425 124	435 124	435 624	425 624	RL	
425 125	435 125	435 625	425 625	MH6	
425 126	435 126	435 626	425 626	FF	Markt Bruckmühl
425 127	435 127	435 627	425 627	STR	
425 128	435 128	435 628	425 628	STR	
425 129	435 129	435 629	425 629	STR	
425 130	435 130	435 630	425 630	STR	Jägersfreunde
425 131	435 131	435 631	425 631	STR	Metlach
425 132	435 132	435 632	425 632	STR	Homburg
425 133	435 133	435 633	425 633	STR	
425 134	435 134	435 634	425 634	STR	
425 135	435 135	435 635	425 635	STR	
425 136	435 136	435 636	425 636	STR	Ottweiler
425 137	435 137	435 637	425 637	STR	Balterweiler
425 138	435 138	435 638	425 638	STR	Merzig
425 139	435 139	435 639	425 639	STR	Fremersdorf
425 140	435 140	435 640	425 640	STR	Ensdorf
425 141	435 141	435 641	425 641	STR	Bous
425 142	435 142	435 642	425 642	STR	Türkismühle
425 143	435 143	435 643	425 643	STR	
425 144	435 144	435 644	425 644	NWH	
425 145	435 145	435 645	425 645	NWH	
425 146	435 146	435 646	425 646	NWH	
425 147	435 147	435 647	425 647	FF	
425 148	435 148	435 648	425 648	MH6	
425 149	435 149	435 649	425 649	FF	
425 150	435 150	435 650	425 650	HHL	Paderborn
425 151	435 151	435 651	425 651	HHL	
425 152	435 152	435 652	425 652	HHL	Hannover Airport Line
425 153	435 153	435 653	425 653	HHL	
425 154	435 154	435 654	425 654	HHL	
425 155	435 155	435 655	425 655	HHL	Hannover Airport
425 156	435 156	435 656	425 656	RL	

Class 425.2. New units for S-Bahn Rhein–Neckar. These units are similar to Class 425.0, but the maximum speed is 140 km/h.

425 201	435 201	435 701	425 701	RL	Mosbach
425 202	435 202	435 702	425 702	RL	Neustadt an der Weinstrasse
425 203	435 203	435 703	425 703	RL	Wiesloch Walldorf
425 204	435 204	435 704	425 704	RL	Hassloch
425 205	435 205	435 705	425 705	RL	Germersheim
425 206	435 206	435 706	425 706	RL	Mannheim
425 207	435 207	435 707	425 707	RL	Ludwigshafen am Rhein
425 208	435 208	435 708	425 708	RL	Eberbach am Neckar
425 209	435 209	435 709	425 709	RL	Speyer
425 210	435 210	435 710	425 710	RL	Heidelberg
425 211	435 211	435 711	425 711	RL	Bruchsal
425 212	435 212	435 712	425 712	RL	Kaiserslautern

▲ 425 210 and 425 229 are seen at Limburgerhof on 1 April 2013 with a Rhein-Neckar S-Bahn route S1 service from Luwigshafen. The train will split at Kaiserslautern with the front unit going forward to Homburg (Saar) and the rear unit terminating, to later form a return service towards Ludwigshafen. **Quintus Vosman**

▼ Stadler FLIRT 3 units 1428 002 and 1428 014 are forming an RB42 service from Münster to Essen Hbf, seen here near Bösensell on 23 November 2015. **Matthias Müller**

425 213	435 213	435 713	425 713	RL	Sinsheim (Elsenz)
425 214	435 214	435 714	425 714	RL	Seckach
425 215	435 215	435 715	425 715	RL	Osterburken
425 216	435 216	435 716	425 716	RL	Meckesheim
425 217	435 217	435 717	425 717	RL	Schifferstadt
425 218	435 218	435 718	425 718	RL	Homburg (Saar)
425 219	435 219	435 719	425 719	RL	
425 220	435 220	435 720	425 720	RL	
425 221	435 221	435 721	425 721	RL	
425 222	435 222	435 722	425 722	RL	
425 223	435 223	435 723	425 723	RL	
425 224	435 224	435 724	425 724	RL	
425 225	435 225	435 725	425 725	RL	
425 226	435 226	435 726	425 726	RL	
425 227	435 227	435 727	425 727	RL	
425 228	435 228	435 728	425 728	RL	
425 229	435 229	435 729	425 729	RL	
425 230	435 230	435 730	425 730	RL	
425 231	435 231	435 731	425 731	RL	
425 232	435 232	435 732	425 732	RL	
425 233	435 233	435 733	425 733	RL	
425 234	435 234	435 734	425 734	RL	
425 235	435 235	435 735	425 735	RL	
425 236	435 236	435 736	425 736	RL	
425 237	435 237	435 737	425 737	RL	
425 238	435 238	435 738	425 738	RL	
425 239	435 239	435 739	425 739	RL	
425 240	435 240	435 740	425 740	RL	
425 250	435 250	435 750	425 750	RL	
425 251	435 251	435 751	425 751	RL	
425 252	435 252	435 752	425 752	RL	
425 253	435 253	435 753	425 753	RL	
425 254	435 254	435 754	425 754	RL	
425 255	435 255	435 755	425 755	RL	
425 256	435 256	435 756	425 756	RL	
425 257	435 257	435 757	425 757	RL	
425 258	435 258	435 758	425 758	RL	
425 259	435 259	435 759	425 759	RL	
425 260	435 260	435 760	425 760	RL	
425 261	435 261	435 761	425 761	RL	
425 262	435 262	435 762	425 762	RL	
425 263	435 263	435 763	425 763	RL	
425 264	435 264	435 764	425 764	RL	
425 265	435 265	435 765	425 765	RL	
425 266	435 266	435 766	425 766	RL	
425 267	435 267	435 767	425 767	RL	
425 268	435 268	435 768	425 768	RL	
425 269	435 269	435 769	425 769	RL	
425 271	435 271	435 771	425 771	HHL	Laatzen
425 272	435 272	435 772	425 772	HHL	Sehnde
425 273	435 273	435 773	425 773	HHL	
425 274	435 274	435 774	425 774	HHL	
425 275	435 275	435 775	425 775	HHL	Sarstedt
425 276	435 276	435 776	425 776	HHL	Algermissen
425 277	435 277	435 777	425 777	HHL	
425 278	435 278	435 778	425 778	HHL	
425 279	435 279	435 779	425 779	HHL	
425 280	435 280	435 780	425 780	HHL	
425 281	435 281	435 781	425 781	HHL	Hildesheim
425 282	435 282	435 782	425 782	HHL	
425 283	435 283	435 783	425 783	HHL	Lindhorst

Class 425.3. New units for S-Bahn Rhein-Neckar and Rheinland Pfalz–Saarland. These units are similar to Class 425.0, but the maximum speed is 140 km/h.

425 301	435 301	435 801	425 801	RL	
425 302	435 301	435 801	425 802	TP	
425 303	435 301	435 801	425 803	TP	
425 304	435 301	435 801	425 804	TP	
425 305	435 301	435 801	425 805	TP	
425 306	435 301	435 801	425 806	TP	
425 307	435 301	435 801	425 807	RL	Fornsbach
425 308	435 301	435 801	425 808	RL	
425 309	435 301	435 801	425 809	RL	
425 310	435 301	435 801	425 810	RL	
425 311	435 301	435 801	425 811	RL	
425 312	435 301	435 801	425 812	RL	
425 313	435 301	435 801	425 813	TP	
425 314	435 301	435 801	425 814	TP	
425 315	435 301	435 801	425 815	RL	
425 316	435 301	435 801	425 816	RL	
425 317	435 301	435 801	425 817	RL	
425 318	435 301	435 801	425 818	RL	
425 319	435 301	435 801	425 819	RL	
425 320	435 301	435 801	425 820	RL	

CLASS 426   2-SECTION ARTICULATED UNITS

These sets are two-car versions of Class 425 and have similar features.

AB + B (DMCO–DMSO).

Built: 1999–2002.
Builders–Mech. Parts: Bombardier/DWA Ammendorf; Siemens/Duewag.
Builder–Elec. Parts: Adtranz Hennigsdorf.
Wheel Arrangement: Bo-2-Bo.
Traction Motors: 4 x 293 kW three-phase asynchronous motors per set.
Wheel Diameter: 850 mm.
Width: 2.84 m.   **Weight:** 35 + 35 tonnes.
Floor Height: 798 mm.   **Length over Couplers:** 18.245 + 18.245 m.
Accommodation: 12/16(16) 1TD + –/40(14).   **Maximum Speed:** 160 km/h.

426 001	426 501	STR			426 023	426 523	STR	
426 002	426 502	FF			426 024	426 524	EMST	
426 003	426 503	FF			426 025	426 525	EMST	
426 004	426 504	STR	Wahlhausen		426 026	426 526	EMST	
426 005	426 505	STR	Limbach		426 027	426 527	EMST	
426 006	426 506	STR	Oberlinxweiler		426 028	426 528	MH6	Traunstein
426 007	426 507	STR	Kirkel		426 029	426 529	NWH	Reutte
426 008	426 508	STR	Besseringen		426 030	426 530	MH6	Oberammergau
426 009	426 509	TP			426 031	426 531	NWH	Siegsdorf
426 010	426 510	TP			426 032	426 532	NWH	
426 011	426 511	TP			426 033	426 533	MH6	Ruhpolding
426 012	426 512	TP			426 034	426 534	NWH	
426 013	426 513	TP			426 035	426 535	NWH	
426 014	426 514	TP			426 036	426 536	STR	Rohrbach
426 015	426 515	STR			426 037	426 537	STR	Illingen
426 016	426 516	EMST			426 038	426 538	STR	
426 017	426 517	EMST			426 039	426 539	STR	Wemmetsweiler
426 018	426 518	EMST			426 040	426 540	STR	Namborn
426 019	426 519	EMST			426 041	426 541	STR	Rentrisch
426 020	426 520	STR			426 042	426 542	STR	Hofeld
426 021	426 521	STR			426 043	426 543	STR	Niederlinxweiler
426 022	426 522	STR						

CLASS 1428   4-SECTION ARTICULATED UNITS

In 2012 DB Regio NRW ordered 14 FLIRT EMUs from Stadler to be based at Münster as replacements for the 425s working from there on RB42/RE42 services. These are FLIRT 3 sets slightly modified from earlier versions to meet new European TSI and crash standards (EN 15227). These lightweight sets are aluminium and feature all the latest fittings expected these days – air conditioned, two vacuum toilets (one disabled), three multi-purpose areas, information displays, laptop sockets, CCTV etc and automatic couplings.

AB + B +B + B (DMCOL- TSO–TSOL -DMSO).

Built: 2014.
Builders–Mech. Parts: Stadler.
Builder–Elec. Parts:
Wheel Arrangement: Bo-2-2-2-Bo.
Traction Motors: 4 x 500 kW.
Wheel Diameter: 920 mm, (powered), 760 mm (unpowered).
Width: 2.88 m.   **Weight:** 132.9 tonnes.
Floor Height: 780 mm.   **Length over Couplers:** 74.70 m.
Accommodation: 24/201 1T 1TD.   **Maximum Speed:** 160 km/h.

1428 001	1828 001	1828 501	1428 501	EMST
1428 002	1828 002	1828 502	1428 502	EMST
1428 003	1828 003	1828 503	1428 503	EMST
1428 004	1828 004	1828 504	1428 504	EMST
1428 005	1828 005	1828 505	1428 505	EMST
1428 006	1828 006	1828 506	1428 506	EMST
1428 007	1828 007	1828 507	1428 507	EMST
1428 008	1828 008	1828 508	1428 508	EMST
1428 009	1828 009	1828 509	1428 509	EMST
1428 010	1828 010	1828 510	1428 510	EMST
1428 011	1828 011	1828 511	1428 511	EMST
1428 012	1828 012	1828 512	1428 512	EMST
1428 013	1828 013	1828 513	1428 513	EMST
1428 014	1828 014	1828 514	1428 514	EMST

▲ 429 115 and 429 103 leave Kaiserslautern on 2 May 2018, with a Mannheim to Koblenz RE service. These units carry a special Südwest Express livery for duties in Rheinland Pfalz. **Brian Garvin**

CLASS 429.0   5-SECTION ARTICULATED UNITS

These units are the well liked Stadler FLIRT low floor articulated EMUs originally designated Class 427 by DB. The class number was changed by the EBA from 01/01/09 to 429 when European numbering came along, so the DB sets were given running numbers following those sets already with private operators. Like other Stadler products, these EMUs are fine sets but surprisingly only have one set of doors per carriage. Air conditioned, disabled toilet, multi-purpose area (tip up seats and catering machines), in fact everything you would expect to find on a modern unit (including plugs for laptops). All five sets are allocated to Rostock and work Rostock–Stralsund–Sassnitz/Ostseebad Binz.

AB + B + B + B + AB (DMCO–TSO–TSO-TSO–DMCO).

Built: 2007.
Builder–Mech. Parts: Stadler
Builder–Elec. Parts:
Wheel Arrangement: Bo-2-2-2-2-Bo.
Traction Motors: 4 x 500 kW three-phase asynchronous motors per set.
Wheel Diameter: 860 mm (powered), 750 mm (non-powered).
Width: 2.88 m.   **Weight:** 145 tonnes.
Floor Height: 600 mm. (90%), 1120 mm (10%).   **Length over Couplers:**
Accommodation: 15/225 (33).   **Maximum Speed:** 160 km/h.

429 026	829 026	829 326	829 626	429 526	WR	
429 027	829 027	829 327	829 627	429 527	WR	
429 028	829 028	829 328	829 628	429 528	WR	Hansestadt Stralsund
429 029	829 029	829 329	829 629	429 529	WR	
429 030	829 030	829 330	829 630	429 530	WR	

CLASS 429.1   5-SECTION ARTICULATED UNITS

DB Regio ordered 28 five car articulated EMUs from Stadler for services in Rheinland Pfalz. Like other units from this builder aluminium construction provides a lightweight unit which is fitted with air conditioning, vacuum toilets, laptop sockets, CCTV, etc. The design is modified from the earlier version to meet new European TSI and crash standards. Each vehicle has one set of doors per side except the middle vehicle which has none. The sets work Mannheim–Saarbrücken–Trier–Koblenz combining at Trier with a CFL Stadler double-deck set that works Luxembourg–Koblenz Hbf. The sets also work Koblenz–Mainz–Frankfurt/M.

B + B + B + B + AB (DMSO- TSOL-TSO-TSOL-DMCO)

Built: 2013–14.
Builders–Mech. Parts: Stadler.
Builder–Elec. Parts:
Wheel Arrangement: Bo-2-2-2-2-Bo.
Traction Motors: 4 x 500 kW.
Wheel Diameter: 920 mm, (powered), 760 mm (unpowered).
Width: 2.88 m.   **Weight:** circa 156 tonnes.
Floor Height: 780/1200 mm.   **Length over Couplers:** 90.80 m.
Accommodation: 21/249 1T 1TD.   **Maximum Speed:** 160 km/h.
Non-Standard Livery: N A new "Rheinland-Pfalz" livery of white with red logos on the body-side of the driving vehicles and branded SÜWEX = Süd West Express. The cab front is also white.

429 100	829 100	829 400	829 700	429 600	N	STR
429 101	829 101	829 401	829 701	429 601	N	STR
429 102	829 102	829 402	829 702	429 602	N	STR
429 103	829 103	829 403	829 703	429 603	N	STR
429 104	829 104	829 404	829 704	429 604	N	STR
429 105	829 105	829 405	829 705	429 605	N	STR
429 106	829 106	829 406	829 706	429 606	N	STR
429 107	829 107	829 407	829 707	429 607	N	STR
429 108	829 108	829 408	829 708	429 608	N	STR
429 109	829 109	829 409	829 709	429 609	N	STR
429 110	829 110	829 410	829 710	429 610	N	STR
429 111	829 111	829 411	829 711	429 611	N	STR

429 112	829 112	829 412	829 712	429 612	N	STR
429 113	829 113	829 413	829 713	429 613	N	STR
429 114	829 114	829 414	829 714	429 614	N	STR
429 115	829 115	829 415	829 715	429 615	N	STR
429 116	829 116	829 416	829 716	429 616	N	STR
429 117	829 117	829 417	829 717	429 617	N	STR
429 118	829 118	829 418	829 718	429 618	N	STR
429 119	829 119	829 419	829 719	429 619	N	STR
429 120	829 120	829 420	829 720	429 620	N	STR
429 121	829 121	829 421	829 721	429 621	N	STR
429 122	829 122	829 422	829 722	429 622	N	STR
429 123	829 123	829 423	829 723	429 623	N	STR
429 124	829 124	829 424	829 724	429 624	N	STR
429 125	829 125	829 425	829 725	429 625	N	STR
429 126	829 126	829 426	829 726	429 626	N	STR
429 127	829 127	829 427	829 727	429 627	N	STR

CLASS 430 4-SECTION ARTICULATED UNITS

Class 430 is yet another S-Bahn unit, this time for the Stuttgart and Frankfurt/M systems. 83 sets were ordered to replace the remaining Class 420s on the Stuttgart system. 29 sets were built by Alstom in Salzgitter and 54 by Bombardier in Aachen. Later the Stuttgart area order was increased by another 10 sets. Frankfurt/M decided to have 91 sets.

AB + B + B + AB (DMCO–TSO–TSO–DMCO).

Built: 2011–17.
Builder–Mech. Parts: Alstom.
Builder–Elec. Parts: Bombardier.
Wheel Arrangement: Bo-Bo-2-Bo-Bo.
Traction Motors: 8 x 295 kW three-phase asynchronous motors per set.
Wheel Diameter:
Width: 3.03 m.
Floor Height: 1025 mm.
Accommodation: 8/40 + –/48 + –/48 + 8/40.

Weight: 119 tonnes.
Length over Couplers: 15.14 + 14.894 + 14.894 + 15.14 m.
Maximum Speed: 140 km/h.

430 001	431 001	431 501	430 501	TP
430 002	431 002	431 502	430 502	TP
430 003	431 003	431 503	430 503	TP
430 004	431 004	431 504	430 504	TP
430 005	431 005	431 505	430 505	TP
430 006	431 006	431 506	430 506	TP
430 007	431 007	431 507	430 507	TP
430 008	431 008	431 508	430 508	TP
430 009	431 009	431 509	430 509	TP
430 010	431 010	431 510	430 510	TP
430 011	431 011	431 511	430 511	TP
430 012	431 012	431 512	430 512	TP
430 013	431 013	431 513	430 513	TP
430 014	431 014	431 514	430 514	TP
430 015	431 015	431 515	430 515	TP
430 016	431 016	431 516	430 516	TP
430 017	431 017	431 517	430 517	TP
430 018	431 018	431 518	430 518	TP
430 019	431 019	431 519	430 519	TP
430 020	431 020	431 520	430 520	TP
430 021	431 021	431 521	430 521	TP
430 022	431 022	431 522	430 522	TP
430 023	431 023	431 523	430 523	TP
430 024	431 024	431 524	430 524	TP
430 025	431 025	431 525	430 525	TP
430 026	431 026	431 526	430 526	TP
430 027	431 027	431 527	430 527	TP
430 028	431 028	431 528	430 528	TP

430 029	431 029	431 529	430 529	TP
430 030	431 030	431 530	430 530	TP
430 031	431 031	431 531	430 531	TP
430 032	431 032	431 532	430 532	TP
430 033	431 033	431 533	430 533	TP
430 034	431 034	431 534	430 534	TP
430 035	431 035	431 535	430 535	TP
430 036	431 036	431 536	430 536	TP
430 037	431 037	431 537	430 537	TP
430 038	431 038	431 538	430 538	TP
430 039	431 039	431 539	430 539	TP
430 040	431 040	431 540	430 540	TP
430 041	431 041	431 541	430 541	TP
430 042	431 042	431 542	430 542	TP
430 043	431 043	431 543	430 543	TP
430 044	431 044	431 544	430 544	TP
430 045	431 045	431 545	430 545	TP
430 046	431 046	431 546	430 546	TP
430 047	431 047	431 547	430 547	TP
430 048	431 048	431 548	430 548	TP
430 049	431 049	431 549	430 549	TP
430 050	431 050	431 550	430 550	TP
430 051	431 051	431 551	430 551	TP
430 052	431 052	431 552	430 552	TP
430 053	431 053	431 553	430 553	TP
430 054	431 054	431 554	430 554	TP
430 055	431 055	431 555	430 555	TP
430 056	431 056	431 556	430 556	TP
430 057	431 057	431 557	430 557	TP
430 058	431 058	431 558	430 558	TP
430 059	431 059	431 559	430 559	TP
430 060	431 060	431 560	430 560	TP
430 061	431 061	431 561	430 561	TP

▲ S-Bahn unit 430 036 is seen on display at the Innotrans exhibition in Berlin on 29 September 2012. **Quintus Vosman**

430 062	431 062	431 562	430 562		TP
430 063	431 063	431 563	430 563		TP
430 064	431 064	431 564	430 564		TP
430 065	431 065	431 565	430 565		TP
430 066	431 066	431 566	430 566		TP
430 067	431 067	431 567	430 567		TP
430 068	431 068	431 568	430 568		TP
430 069	431 069	431 569	430 569		TP
430 070	431 070	431 570	430 570		TP
430 071	431 071	431 571	430 571		TP
430 072	431 072	431 572	430 572		TP
430 073	431 073	431 573	430 573		TP
430 074	431 074	431 574	430 574		TP
430 075	431 075	431 575	430 575		TP
430 076	431 076	431 576	430 576		TP
430 077	431 077	431 577	430 577		TP
430 078	431 078	431 578	430 578		TP
430 079	431 079	431 579	430 579		TP
430 080	431 080	431 580	430 580		TP
430 081	431 081	431 581	430 581		TP
430 082	431 082	431 582	430 582		TP
430 083	431 083	431 583	430 583		TP
430 084	431 084	431 584	430 584		TP
430 085	431 085	431 585	430 585		TP
430 086	431 086	431 586	430 586		TP
430 087	431 087	431 587	430 587		TP
430 088	431 088	431 588	430 588		TP
430 089	431 089	431 589	430 589		TP
430 090	431 090	431 590	430 590		TP
430 091	431 091	431 591	430 591		TP
430 092	431 092	431 592	430 592		TP
430 093	431 093	431 593	430 593		TP
430 094	431 094	431 594	430 594		TP
430 095	431 095	431 595	430 595		TP
430 096	431 096	431 596	430 596		TP
430 097	431 097	431 597	430 597		TP
430 100	431 100	431 600	430 600	A	FF
430 101	431 101	431 601	430 601		FF
430 102	431 102	431 602	430 602		FF
430 103	431 103	431 603	430 603		FF
430 104	431 104	431 604	430 604		FF
430 105	431 105	431 605	430 605		FF
430 106	431 106	431 606	430 606		FF
430 107	431 107	431 607	430 607		FF
430 108	431 108	431 608	430 608		FF
430 109	431 109	431 609	430 609		FF
430 110	431 110	431 610	430 610		FF
430 111	431 111	431 611	430 611		FF
430 112	431 112	431 612	430 612		FF
430 113	431 113	431 613	430 613		FF
430 114	431 114	431 614	430 614		FF
430 115	431 115	431 615	430 615		FF
430 116	431 116	431 616	430 616		FF
430 117	431 117	431 617	430 617		FF
430 118	431 118	431 618	430 618		FF
430 119	431 119	431 619	430 619		FF
430 120	431 120	431 620	430 620		FF
430 121	431 121	431 621	430 621		FF
430 122	431 122	431 622	430 622		FF
430 123	431 123	431 623	430 623		FF
430 124	431 124	431 624	430 624		FF
430 125	431 125	431 625	430 625		FF
430 126	431 126	431 626	430 626		FF

430 127	431 127	431 627	430 627	FF
430 128	431 128	431 628	430 628	FF
430 129	431 129	431 629	430 629	FF
430 130	431 130	431 630	430 630	FF
430 131	431 131	431 631	430 631	FF
430 132	431 132	431 632	430 632	FF
430 133	431 133	431 633	430 633	FF
430 134	431 134	431 634	430 634	FF
430 135	431 135	431 635	430 635	FF
430 136	431 136	431 636	430 636	FF
430 137	431 137	431 637	430 637	FF
430 138	431 138	431 638	430 638	FF
430 139	431 139	431 639	430 639	FF
430 140	431 140	431 640	430 640	FF
430 141	431 141	431 641	430 641	FF
430 142	431 142	431 642	430 642	FF
430 143	431 143	431 643	430 643	FF
430 144	431 144	431 644	430 644	FF
430 145	431 145	431 645	430 645	FF
430 146	431 146	431 646	430 646	FF
430 147	431 147	431 647	430 647	FF
430 148	431 148	431 648	430 648	FF
430 149	431 149	431 649	430 649	FF
430 150	431 150	431 650	430 650	FF
430 151	431 151	431 651	430 651	FF
430 152	431 152	431 652	430 652	FF
430 153	431 153	431 653	430 653	FF
430 154	431 154	431 654	430 654	FF
430 155	431 155	431 655	430 655	FF
430 156	431 156	431 656	430 656	FF
430 157	431 157	431 657	430 657	FF
430 158	431 158	431 658	430 658	FF
430 159	431 159	431 659	430 659	FF
430 160	431 160	431 660	430 660	FF
430 161	431 161	431 661	430 661	FF
430 162	431 162	431 662	430 662	FF
430 163	431 163	431 663	430 663	FF
430 164	431 164	431 664	430 664	FF
430 165	431 165	431 665	430 665	FF
430 166	431 166	431 666	430 666	FF
430 167	431 167	431 667	430 667	FF
430 168	431 168	431 668	430 668	FF
430 169	431 169	431 669	430 669	FF
430 170	431 170	431 670	430 670	FF
430 171	431 171	431 671	430 671	FF
430 172	431 172	431 672	430 672	FF
430 173	431 173	431 673	430 673	FF
430 174	431 174	431 674	430 674	FF
430 175	431 175	431 675	430 675	FF
430 176	431 176	431 676	430 676	FF
430 177	431 177	431 677	430 677	FF
430 178	431 178	431 678	430 678	FF
430 179	431 179	431 679	430 679	FF
430 180	431 180	431 680	430 680	FF
430 181	431 181	431 681	430 681	FF
430 182	431 182	431 682	430 682	FF
430 183	431 183	431 683	430 683	FF
430 184	431 184	431 684	430 684	FF
430 185	431 185	431 685	430 685	FF
430 186	431 186	431 686	430 686	FF
430 187	431 187	431 687	430 687	FF
430 188	431 188	431 688	430 688	FF
430 189	431 189	431 689	430 689	FF
430 190	431 190	431 690	430 690	FF

CLASS 440   3-, 4- & 5-SECTION ARTICULATED UNITS

Class 440 is known as the Alstom Coradia Continental incorporating ideas learnt from the Class 618 LIREX experimental DMU. Just like Bombardier, Alstom offered this product in 2-, 3-, 4- and 5-car versions. A big change is that to accomplish the low floor, a lot of electrical equipment is on the roof! In 2006 DB Regio ordered 26 3-car, 48 4-car and 6 5-car sets for various services around Augsburg, München, Nürnberg and Würzburg. The 440 has also been ordered by private operators Agilis and Nord West Bahn, details of which appear in German Railways Part 2. The driving cars have differing lengths, sets being "short" or "long". All DB sets so far are "short". Teething problems ensued with air-conditioning, toilets and couplings. The EBA had its own concerns which also helped to delay entry into service of the units. The problems overcome, the Augsburg area units entered service in December 2009 one year late. Further units have been ordered for the Nürnberg S-Bahn and the RE8 service Mönchengladbach – Köln – Koblenz both orders meaning the replacement of 143s at Nürnberg and Trier.

CLASS 440.0   4-SECTION ARTICULATED UNITS

For its *E-Netz Augsburg*, DB Regio ordered 37 4-section 440s so that services from München via Augsburg to Treutchlingen and Ulm could be improved. Using EMUs the *"Fugger Express"* as the new service is called allowed trains from München to split at Augsburg for the above destinations. 440 002 experienced a fire with some roof equipment whilst standing in Augsburg on 23/06/2009 but was back in service by the end of that year. Later DB Regio ordered five more sets for the Würzburg area and six sets for München–Passau.

AB + B + B + AB (DMCO–TSO–TSO–DMCO).

Built: 2008–10.
Builder–Mech. Parts: Alstom
Builder–Elec. Parts:
Wheel Arrangement: Bo-Bo-2-Bo-Bo.
Traction Motors: 8 x 360 kW three phase asynchronous motors per set.
Wheel Diameter: 850 mm.
Width: 2.92 m.   **Weight:** 140 tonnes.
Floor Height: 600 mm (entrance), 730 mm (saloons).   **Length over Couplers:** 70.90 m.
Accommodation: 8/40 + –/48 + –/48 + 8/40.   **Maximum Speed:** 160 km/h.

440 001	441 001	441 501	440 501	MH6	
440 002	441 002	441 502	440 502	MH6	
440 003	441 003	441 503	440 503	MH6	
440 004	441 004	441 504	440 504	MH6	
440 005	441 005	441 505	440 505	MH6	
440 006	441 006	441 506	440 506	MH6	
440 007	441 007	441 507	440 507	MH6	
440 008	441 008	441 508	440 508	MH6	
440 009	441 009	441 509	440 509	MH6	
440 010	441 010	441 510	440 510	MH6	
440 011	441 011	441 511	440 511	MH6	
440 012	441 012	441 512	440 512	MH6	
440 013	441 013	441 513	440 513	MH6	Stadt Nördlingen
440 014	441 014	441 514	440 514	MH6	
440 015	441 015	441 515	440 515	MH6	
440 016	441 016	441 516	440 516	MH6	
440 017	441 017	441 517	440 517	MH6	
440 018	441 018	441 518	440 518	MH6	
440 019	441 019	441 519	440 519	MH6	
440 020	441 020	441 520	440 520	MH6	
440 021	441 021	441 521	440 521	MH6	
440 022	441 022	441 522	440 522	MH6	
440 023	441 023	441 523	440 523	MH6	
440 024	441 024	441 524	440 524	MH6	
440 025	441 025	441 525	440 525	MH6	
440 026	441 026	441 526	440 526	MH6	
440 027	441 027	441 527	440 527	MH6	
440 028	441 028	441 528	440 528	MH6	
440 029	441 029	441 529	440 529	MH6	
440 030	441 030	441 530	440 530	MH6	

440 031	441 031	441 531	440 531	MH6	
440 032	441 032	441 532	440 532	MH6	
440 033	441 033	441 533	440 533	MH6	
440 034	441 034	441 534	440 534	MH6	
440 035	441 035	441 535	440 535	MH6	
440 036	441 036	441 536	440 536	MH6	
440 037	441 037	441 537	440 537	MH6	
440 038	441 038	441 538	440 538	NWH	
440 039	441 039	441 539	440 539	NWH	
440 040	441 040	441 540	440 540	NWH	
440 041	441 041	441 541	440 541	NWH	
440 042	441 042	441 542	440 542	NWH	
440 043	441 043	441 543	440 543	MH6	
440 044	441 044	441 544	440 544	MH6	Plattling Niebelungenstadt
440 045	441 045	441 545	440 545	MH6	
440 046	441 046	441 546	440 546	MH6	
440 047	441 047	441 547	440 547	MH6	
440 048	441 048	441 548	440 548	MH6	Wallersdorf

▲ 3-section Class 440.3 unit 440 324 "Gunzenhausen" forms service RB 58023 from Jossa to Schweinfurt. It is seen passing Himmelstadt on 21 May 2016. **Matthias Müller**

CLASS 440.2   5-SECTION ARTICULATED UNITS

These five section sets were ordered by DB Regio for the *Donau–Isar Express* service *(DIEX)* which is the name given to the RE service from München to Passau. A mixture of 4- and 5- section units was ordered.

AB + B + B + B + AB (DMCO–TSO–TSO–TSO–DMCO).

Built: 2009–10.
Builder–Mech. Parts: Alstom.
Builder–Elec. Parts:
Wheel Arrangement: Bo-Bo-2-2-Bo-Bo.
Traction Motors: 8 x 360 kW three-phase asynchronous motors per set.
Wheel Diameter: 850 mm.
Width: 2.92 m.   **Weight:**
Floor Height: 600 mm (entrance), 730 mm (saloons).   **Length over Couplers:** 87.90 m.
Accommodation: 24/266 per set.   **Maximum Speed:** 160 km/h.

440 201	441 201	841 201	441 701	440 701	MH6	
440 202	441 202	841 202	441 702	440 702	MH6	Moosburg a.d. Isar
440 203	441 203	841 203	441 703	440 703	MH6	Passau
440 204	441 204	841 204	441 704	440 704	MH6	Landshut
440 205	441 205	841 205	441 705	440 705	MH6	Landau a.d. Isar
440 206	441 206	841 206	441 706	440 706	NWH	

CLASS 440.3   3-SECTION ARTICULATED UNITS

The third type of Coradia Continental ordered by DB Regio is a three-section train for services based on Würzburg. Routes covered include Nürnberg–Würzburg, Nürnberg–Aisch and from Würzburg to Kitzingen, Bamberg and Treutchlingen. These units are short sets.

AB + B + AB (DMCO–TSO–DMCO).

Built: 2008–10, 2012–14.
Builder–Mech. Parts: Alstom.
Builder–Elec. Parts:
Wheel Arrangement: Bo-2-Bo-Bo.
Traction Motors: 6 x 360 kW three-phase asynchronous motors per set.
Wheel Diameter: 850 mm.
Width: 2.92 m.   **Weight:** 112 tonnes.
Floor Height: 600 mm (entrance), 730 mm (saloons).   **Length over Couplers:** 54.50 m.
Accommodation: **Maximum Speed:** 160 km/h.

440 301	441 801	440 801	NWH	440 314	441 814	440 814	NWH
440 302	441 802	440 802	NWH	440 315	441 815	440 815	NWH
440 303	441 803	440 803	NWH	440 316	441 816	440 816	NWH
440 304	441 804	440 804	NWH	440 317	441 817	440 817	NWH
440 305	441 805	440 805	NWH	440 318	441 818	440 818	NWH
440 306	441 806	440 806	NWH	440 319	441 819	440 819	NWH
440 307	441 807	440 807	NWH	440 320	441 820	440 820	NWH
440 308	441 808	440 808	NWH	440 321	441 821	440 821	NWH
440 309	441 809	440 809	NWH	440 322	441 822	440 822	NWH
440 310	441 810	440 810	NWH	440 323	441 823	440 823	NWH
440 311	441 811	440 811	NWH	440 324	441 824	440 824	NWH
440 312	441 812	440 812	NWH	440 325	441 825	440 825	NWH
440 313	441 813	440 813	NWH	440 326	441 826	440 826	NWH

Names:

440 324	Gunzenhausen		440 325	Neustadt an der Aisch

CLASS 1440.3   3-SECTION ARTICULATED UNITS

DB Regio Nordrheinwestfalen ordered 28 3-car EMUs from Alstom to operate on S5 and S8 services As the design has been updated to meet the new European TSI and crash standards these units have been given the 1440 classification.

Built: 2014–15.
Builder–Mech. Parts: Alstom.
Builder–Elec. Parts:
Wheel Arrangement: Bo-2-Bo-Bo.
Traction Motors: 6 x 315 kW.
Wheel Diameter: 850mm
Width: 2.92 m.
Floor Height:
Accommodation: –/170.

Weight: 116 tonnes.
Length over Couplers: 56.90 m.
Maximum Speed: 160 km/h.

1440 300	1441 300	1440 800	KD		1440 314	1441 314	1440 814	KD
1440 301	1441 301	1440 801	KD		1440 315	1441 315	1440 815	KD
1440 302	1441 302	1440 802	KD		1440 316	1441 316	1440 816	KD
1440 303	1441 303	1440 803	KD		1440 317	1441 317	1440 817	KD
1440 304	1441 304	1440 804	KD		1440 318	1441 318	1440 818	KD
1440 305	1441 305	1440 805	KD		1440 319	1441 319	1440 819	KD
1440 306	1441 306	1440 806	KD		1440 320	1441 320	1440 820	KD
1440 307	1441 307	1440 807	KD		1440 321	1441 321	1440 821	KD
1440 308	1441 308	1440 808	KD		1440 322	1441 322	1440 822	KD
1440 309	1441 309	1440 809	KD		1440 323	1441 323	1440 823	KD
1440 310	1441 310	1440 810	KD		1440 324	1441 324	1440 824	KD
1440 311	1441 311	1440 811	KD		1440 325	1441 325	1440 825	KD
1440 312	1441 312	1440 812	KD		1440 326	1441 326	1440 826	KD
1440 313	1441 313	1440 813	KD		1440 327	1441 327	1440 827	KD

▲ 1442 204 features the Leipzig-Halle area S-Bahn livery. Here it is seen at Zwickau with an S5X working for Halle/Leipzig Flughafen on 25 February 2017.   **Brian Garvin**

FURTHER ALSTOM ORDERS FOR CLASS 440s

On 27/10/2016 Alstom announced an order from DB Regio for Coradia Continental EMUs for Breisgau S-Bahn services. The order is for 11 3-section units with 164 seats and 13 4-section units with 249 seats that are expected to enter service in December 2019 on the following routes: Freiburg–Endingen/Breisach; Freiburg –Titisee–Seebrugg; Freiburg–Titisee–Donaueschingen. These units are to be in the Baden-Württemberg white and yellow livery.

On 31/03/2017 Alstom announced an order from DB Regio for 53 Coradia Continental EMUs for entry into service in 2019/20. 27 sets will be 4-section units with 230 seats (second class) with a power rating of 2900 kW for the Nürnberg S-Bahn. These are expected to be 1440.2 sets and will be used on S3, S4, and S5 routes. The other 26 units are 10 3-Section units and 16 5-section units for Nordrhein-Westfalen and Rheinland Pfalz areas. The units are expected to have 155 and 266 second class seats and be rated at 2400 kW and 2900 kW respectively; they will be used on RE8 services Mönchengladbach–Köln–Koblenz.

CLASS 442   2-, 3-, 4- & 5-SECTION ARTICULATED UNITS

This class is the Talent 2 – Bombardier's EMU train offered in various versions. It is an updated version of the Talent EMUs delivered to Austria but has been bedevilled with problems. Whilst the first units were being built regulations were changed which the EBA insisted had to apply to these units. A dispute situation arose but construction never stopped. DB Regio had entered a framework contract for up to 321 EMUs ordering the first sets in 2007 followed by more and more with the total being 295 by the end of 2011. The first 4-car unit appeared at Innotrans in Berlin in 2008 but by late 2011 no units had entered traffic (over 100 built!). There are reports that Bombardier itself had to dismantle (scrap?) some sets as construction defects were found. In March 2011 the EBA authorised the sets for Nürnberg to enter traffic but not in multiple and not to exceed 140 km/h. DB Regio refused to accept these conditions. In July 2011 the EBA agreed for the Nürnberg sets to run in multiple but still restricted to 140 km/h. DB Regio would not accept the units as they had ordered sets for 160 km/h! Meanwhile there had been other problems as these units also had the Ebicab 500 safety system as on the Ruhr 430s where problems had been encountered, so all the 442s had to have software updates. During autumn 2011 the EBA authorised the 4-car sets for Nürnberg and Trier to run without restriction but there was no clearance for the other versions. The following years saw the various problems overcome and further orders placed for other areas. In 2018 the next version, Talent 3, was expected to appear.

CLASS 442.0   2-SECTION ARTICULATED UNITS

DB Regio, having won some franchise contracts, ordered new 2-car EMUs from Bombardier for use around Trier, Cottbus and München. Because of the problems outlined above entry into service was delayed.

AB + B (DMCO–DMSO).

Built: 2008–09.
Builder–Mech. Parts: Bombardier.
Builder–Elec. Parts: Bombardier.
Wheel Arrangement: Bo-2-Bo.
Traction Motors: 4 x 505 kW three-phase asynchronous motors per set.
Wheel Diameter: 850 mm.
Width: 2.926 m.   **Weight:**
Floor Height: 800 mm (entrance), 695/1250 (saloons).   **Length over Couplers:** 20.05 + 20.05 m.
Accommodation: 8/46 –/45 (10).   **Maximum Speed:** 160 km/h.

442 001	442 501	STR	442 007	442 507	BCS
442 002	442 502	STR	442 008	442 508	BCS
442 003	442 503	STR	442 009	442 509	MH2
442 004	442 504	STR	442 010	442 510	MH2
442 005	442 505	STR	442 011	442 511	MH2
442 006	442 506	BCS			

Names:

442 001	Oberbillig	442 004	Klotten
442 002	Ediger-Eller	442 005	Lehman
442 003	Nittel		

CLASS 442.1 3-SECTION ARTICULATED UNITS

As part of the framework contract with Bombardier, DB Regio ordered several batches of 3-car sets as follows: Rhein-Sieg Express (3); Saxonia Dresden–Leipzig (4); E-Netz Franken (5); Mittelhessen Express (6); Berlin/Brandenburg (26); Elbe-Elster Netz (8) and S-Bahn Leipzig/Halle (36). As mentioned above, acceptance problems have delayed entrance into service. For these units the design has already been updated as they have the latest form of anti-climb buffers, whereas the 442.2 has not.

AB + B + B (DMCO–TSO–DMSO).

Built: 2009–13.
Builder–Mech. Parts: Bombardier.
Builder–Elec. Parts: Bombardier.
Wheel Arrangement: Bo-2-2-Bo.
Traction Motors: 4 x 505 kW three-phase asynchronous motors per set.
Wheel Diameter: 850 mm.
Width: 2.926 m.
Floor Height: 800 mm (entrance), 695/1250 (saloons).
Accommodation: 8/160 (10).
Weight:
Length over Couplers: 56.20 m.
Maximum Speed: 160 km/h.

442 101	843 101	442 601	LH2	442 127	843 127	442 627	BCS
442 102	843 102	442 602	LH2	442 128	843 128	442 628	BCS
442 103	843 103	442 603	LH2	442 129	843 129	442 629	BLO
442 104	843 104	442 604	NN1	442 130	843 130	442 630	BLO
442 105	843 105	442 605	NN1	442 131	843 131	442 631	BLO
442 106	843 106	442 606	NN1	442 132	843 132	442 632	BLO
442 107	843 107	442 607	NN1	442 133	843 133	442 633	BLO
442 108	843 108	442 608	NN1	442 134	843 134	442 634	BLO
442 109	843 109	442 609	FGM	442 135	843 135	442 635	BLO
442 110	843 110	442 610	FGM	442 136	843 136	442 636	BLO
442 111	843 111	442 611	FGM	442 137	843 137	442 637	BLO
442 112	843 112	442 612	FGM	442 138	843 138	442 638	BLO
442 113	843 113	442 613	FGM	442 139	843 139	442 639	BLO
442 114	843 114	442 614	FGM	442 140	843 140	442 640	BLO
442 115	843 115	442 615	DA	442 141	843 141	442 641	BLO
442 116	843 116	442 616	DA	442 142	843 142	442 642	BCS
442 117	843 117	442 617	DA	442 143	843 143	442 643	BCS
442 118	843 118	442 618	DA	442 144	843 144	442 644	BCS
442 119	843 119	442 619	BLO	442 145	843 145	442 645	BCS
442 120	843 120	442 620	BLO	442 146	843 146	442 646	BCS
442 121	843 121	442 621	BLO	442 147	843 147	442 647	BCS
442 122	843 122	442 622	BLO	442 148	843 148	442 648	BCS
442 123	843 123	442 623	BLO	442 149	843 149	442 649	BCS
442 124	843 124	442 624	BLO	442 150	843 150	442 650	BCS
442 125	843 125	442 625	BLO	442 151	843 151	442 651	BCS
442 126	843 126	442 626	BLO	442 152	843 152	442 652	BCS

Names:

442 105	Stockheim		442 131	Oranienburg
442 107	Markt Küps		442 145	Schwarzer Elster
442 108	Förtschendorf		442 146	Elbe
442 119	Potsdam Park Sanssouc			

CLASS 1442.1   3-SECTION ARTICULATED UNITS

These Talent 2 EMUs were ordered for S-Bahn Mitteldeutschland covering the areas around Leipzig and Halle, getting to quite a few places further away such as Oschatz, Hoyerswerda, Zwickau, Eilenburg on S-Bahn routes S1 – S9, plus RE13/14 and RB 42, 51, 75, 80, and 81.

Non-Standard Livery: N Silver.

1442 100	1843 100	1442 600	N	LH2		1442 128	1843 128	1442 628	N	LH2
1442 101	1843 101	1442 601	N	LH2		1442 129	1843 129	1442 629	N	LH2
1442 102	1843 102	1442 602	N	LH2		1442 130	1843 130	1442 630	N	LH2
1442 103	1843 103	1442 603	N	LH2		1442 131	1843 131	1442 631	N	LH2
1442 104	1843 104	1442 604	N	LH2		1442 132	1843 132	1442 632	N	LH2
1442 105	1843 105	1442 605	N	LH2		1442 133	1843 133	1442 633	N	LH2
1442 106	1843 106	1442 606	N	LH2		1442 134	1843 134	1442 634	N	LH2
1442 107	1843 107	1442 607	N	LH2		1442 135	1843 135	1442 635	N	LH2
1442 108	1843 108	1442 608	N	LH2						
1442 109	1843 109	1442 609	N	LH2		1442 160	1843 160	1442 660	N	LH2
1442 110	1843 110	1442 610	N	LH2		1442 161	1843 161	1442 661	N	LH2
1442 111	1843 111	1442 611	N	LH2		1442 162	1843 162	1442 662	N	LH2
1442 112	1843 112	1442 612	N	LH2		1442 163	1843 163	1442 663	N	LH2
1442 113	1843 113	1442 613	N	LH2		1442 164	1843 164	1442 664	N	LH2
1442 114	1843 114	1442 614	N	LH2		1442 165	1843 165	1442 665	N	LH2
1442 115	1843 115	1442 615	N	LH2		1442 166	1843 166	1442 666	N	LH2
1442 116	1843 116	1442 616	N	LH2		1442 167	1843 167	1442 667	N	LH2
1442 117	1843 117	1442 617	N	LH2		1442 168	1843 168	1442 668	N	LH2
1442 118	1843 118	1442 618	N	LH2		1442 169	1843 169	1442 669	N	LH2
1442 119	1843 119	1442 619	N	LH2		1442 170	1843 170	1442 670	N	LH2
1442 120	1843 120	1442 620	N	LH2		1442 171	1843 171	1442 671	N	LH2
1442 121	1843 121	1442 621	N	LH2		1442 172	1843 172	1442 672	N	LH2
1442 122	1843 122	1442 622	N	LH2		1442 173	1843 173	1442 673	N	LH2
1442 123	1843 123	1442 623	N	LH2		1442 174	1843 174	1442 674	N	LH2
1442 124	1843 124	1442 624	N	LH2		1442 175	1843 175	1442 675	N	LH2
1442 125	1843 125	1442 625	N	LH2		1442 176	1843 176	1442 676	N	LH2
1442 126	1843 126	1442 626	N	LH2		1442 177	1843 177	1442 677	N	LH2
1442 127	1843 127	1442 627	N	LH2		1442 178	1843 178	1442 678	N	LH2

CLASS 442.2   4-SECTION ARTICULATED UNITS

The first Talent 2 to appear was a 4-car set for the Nürnberg S-Bahn, 442 212 being exhibited at Innotrans in Berlin in 2008.

AB + B + B + B (DMCO–TSO–TSO–DMSO).

Built: 2008–15.
Builder–Mech. Parts: Bombardier.
Builder–Elec. Parts: Bombardier.
Wheel Arrangement: Bo-2-Bo-2-Bo.
Traction Motors: 6 x 505 kW three-phase asynchronous motors per set.
Wheel Diameter: 850 mm.   **Weight:**
Width: 2.926 m.   **Length over Couplers:** 20.05 + 16.10 + 16.10 + 20.05 m.
Floor Height: 800 mm (entrance), 695/1250 (saloons).
Accommodation: 8/241.   **Maximum Speed:** 160 km/h.
Non-Standard Livery: N Silver and dark grey, green doors.

442 200	443 200	443 700	442 700	STR	Hatzenport
442 202	443 202	443 702	442 702	STR	Moselkern
442 203	443 203	443 703	442 703	STR	Pommern
442 204	443 204	443 704	442 704	STR	Müden
442 205	443 205	443 705	442 705	STR	Ürzig
442 206	443 206	443 706	442 706	STR	Neef
442 207	443 207	443 707	442 707	STR	Kobern-Gondorf
442 208	443 208	443 708	442 708	STR	Winningen

442 209	443 209	443 709	442 709	BCS	
442 210	443 210	443 710	442 710	BCS	
442 211	443 211	443 711	442 711	BCS	
442 217	443 217	443 717	442 717	NN1	Hartmannshof
442 218	443 218	443 718	442 718	NN1	Röthenbach a.d. Pegnitz
442 219	443 219	443 719	442 719	NN1	Neumarkt i. d. Oberpflalz
442 220	443 220	443 720	442 720	NN1	Ansbach
442 221	443 221	443 721	442 721	NN1	Sachsen bei Ansbach
442 222	443 222	443 722	442 722	NN1	Stadt Baiersdorf
442 223	443 223	443 723	442 723	NN1	Petersaurach
442 224	443 224	443 724	442 724	NN1	Lauf a.d. Pegnitz
442 225	443 225	443 725	442 725	NN1	Münsterstadt Heilsbronn
442 226	443 226	443 726	442 726	NN1	Erlangen
442 227	443 227	443 727	442 727	NN1	Markt Feucht
442 228	443 228	443 728	442 728	NN1	
442 229	443 229	443 729	442 729	NN1	
442 230	443 230	443 730	442 730	NN1	
442 231	443 231	443 731	442 731	NN1	
442 232	443 232	443 732	442 732	NN1	
442 233	443 233	443 733	442 733	NN1	
442 234	443 234	443 734	442 734	NN1	
442 235	443 235	443 735	442 735	NN1	
442 236	443 236	443 736	442 736	NN1	
442 237	443 237	443 737	442 737	NN1	
442 238	443 238	443 738	442 738	NN1	
442 239	443 239	443 739	442 739	NN1	
442 240	443 240	443 740	442 740	NN1	
442 241	443 241	443 741	442 741	NN1	
442 242	443 242	443 742	442 742	NN1	
442 243	443 243	443 743	442 743	NN1	
442 244	443 244	443 744	442 744	NN1	
442 245	443 245	443 745	442 745	NN1	
442 246	443 246	443 746	442 746	NN1	
442 247	443 247	443 747	442 747	NN1	
442 248	443 248	443 748	442 748	NN1	
442 249	443 249	443 749	442 749	NN1	
442 250	443 250	443 750	442 750	NN1	
442 251	443 251	443 751	442 751	NN1	
442 252	443 252	443 752	442 752	NN1	
442 253	443 253	443 753	442 753	NN1	
442 254	443 254	443 754	442 754	KA	
442 255	443 255	443 755	442 755	KA	
442 256	443 256	443 756	442 756	KA	
442 257	443 257	443 757	442 757	KA	
442 258	443 258	443 758	442 758	KA	
442 259	443 259	443 759	442 759	KA	
442 260	443 260	443 760	442 760	KA	
442 261	443 261	443 761	442 761	KA	
442 262	443 262	443 762	442 762	FGM	
442 263	443 263	443 763	442 763	FGM	
442 264	443 264	443 764	442 764	NN1	
442 265	443 265	443 765	442 765	NN1	
442 266	443 266	443 766	442 766	NN1	
442 267	443 267	443 767	442 767	NN1	
442 268	443 268	443 768	442 768	NN1	
442 269	443 269	443 769	442 769	NN1	Ludwigsstadt
442 270	443 270	443 770	442 770	NN1	Grub am Forst
442 271	443 271	443 771	442 771	NN1	
442 272	443 272	443 772	442 772	NN1	
442 273	443 273	443 773	442 773	NN1	
442 274	443 274	443 774	442 774	NN1	
442 275	443 275	443 775	442 775	NN1	Pressig-Rothenkirchen
442 276	443 276	443 776	442 776	NN1	Marktzeuln
442 277	443 277	443 777	442 777	NN1	

442 278	443 278	443 778	442 778		FGM
442 279	443 279	443 779	442 779		FGM
442 280	443 280	443 780	442 780		FGM
442 281	443 281	443 781	442 781		FGM
442 282	443 282	443 782	442 782		FGM
442 283	443 283	443 783	442 783		FGM
442 284	443 284	443 784	442 784		FGM
442 285	443 285	443 785	442 785		FGM
442 286	443 286	443 786	442 786		FGM
442 287	443 287	443 787	442 787		FGM
442 288	443 288	443 788	442 788		FGM
442 289	443 289	443 789	442 789		FGM
442 290	443 290	443 790	442 790		FGM
442 291	443 291	443 791	442 791		FGM
442 292	443 292	443 792	442 792		FGM
442 293	443 293	443 793	442 793		FGM
1442 200	1443 200	1443 200	1442 700	N	LH2
1442 201	1443 201	1443 201	1442 701	N	LH2
1442 202	1443 202	1443 202	1442 702	N	LH2
1442 203	1443 203	1443 203	1442 703	N	LH2
1442 204	1443 204	1443 204	1442 704	N	LH2
1442 205	1443 205	1443 205	1442 705	N	LH2
1442 206	1443 206	1443 206	1442 706	N	LH2
1442 207	1443 207	1443 207	1442 707	N	LH2
1442 208	1443 208	1443 208	1442 708	N	LH2
1442 209	1443 209	1443 209	1442 709	N	LH2
1442 210	1443 210	1443 210	1442 710	N	LH2

▲ 445 030 arrives at Hamburg Hbf on 8 May 2018. The unit belongs to Schleswig Holstein Land but is operated by DB. Note the leading power car is all First Class upstairs whilst the opposite end is composite. **Brian Garvin**

1442 211	1443 211	1443 211	1442 711	N	LH2	
1442 212	1443 212	1443 212	1442 712	N	LH2	
1442 213	1443 213	1443 213	1442 713	N	LH2	
1442 214	1443 214	1443 214	1442 714	N	LH2	
2442 200	2443 200	2443 700	2442 700		MH2	
2442 201	2443 201	2443 701	2442 701		MH2	
2442 202	2443 202	2443 702	2442 702		MH2	
2442 203	2443 203	2443 703	2442 703		MH2	
2442 204	2443 204	2443 704	2442 704		MH2	
2442 205	2443 205	2443 705	2442 705		MH2	
2442 206	2443 206	2443 706	2442 706		MH2	
2442 207	2443 207	2443 707	2442 707		MH2	
2442 208	2443 208	2443 708	2442 708		MH2	
2442 209	2443 209	2443 709	2442 709		MH2	
2442 210	2443 210	2443 710	2442 710		MH2	
2442 211	2443 211	2443 711	2442 711		MH2	
2442 212	2443 212	2443 712	2442 712		MH2	
2442 213	2443 213	2443 713	2442 713		MH2	
2442 214	2443 214	2443 714	2442 714		MH2	
2442 215	2443 215	2443 715	2442 715		MH2	
2442 216	2443 216	2443 716	2442 716		MH2	
2442 217	2443 217	2443 717	2442 717		MH2	
2442 218	2443 218	2443 718	2442 718		MH2	
2442 219	2443 219	2443 719	2442 719		MH2	
2442 220	2443 220	2443 720	2442 720		MH2	
2442 221	2443 221	2443 721	2442 721		MH2	
2442 222	2443 222	2443 722	2442 722		MH2	
2442 223	2443 223	2443 723	2442 723		MH2	
2442 224	2443 224	2443 724	2442 724		MH2	
2442 225	2443 225	2443 725	2442 725		MH2	
2442 226	2443 226	2443 726	2442 726		MH2	
2442 227	2443 227	2443 727	2442 727		MH2	
2442 228	2443 228	2443 728	2442 728		MH2	
2442 229	2443 229	2443 729	2442 729		MH2	
2442 230	2443 230	2443 730	2442 730		MH2	
2442 231	2443 231	2443 731	2442 731		MH2	
2442 232	2443 232	2443 732	2442 732		MH2	
2442 233	2443 233	2443 733	2442 733		MH2	
3442 200	3443 200	3443 700	3442 700	N	TS	Crailsheim
3442 201	3443 201	3443 701	3442 701	N	TS	
3442 202	3443 202	3443 702	3442 702	N	TS	
3442 203	3443 203	3443 703	3442 703	N	TS	
3442 204	3443 204	3443 704	3442 704	N	TS	
3442 205	3443 205	3443 705	3442 705	N	TS	
3442 206	3443 206	3443 706	3442 706	N	TS	
3442 207	3443 207	3443 707	3442 707	N	TS	
3442 208	3443 208	3443 708	3442 708	N	TS	
3442 209	3443 209	3443 709	3442 709	N	TS	
3442 210	3443 210	3443 710	3442 710	N	TS	
3442 211	3443 211	3443 711	3442 711	N	TS	
3442 212	3443 212	3443 712	3442 712	N	TS	
3442 213	3443 213	3443 713	3442 713	N	TS	Horb am Neckar
3442 214	3443 214	3443 714	3442 714	N	TS	
3442 215	3443 215	3443 715	3442 715	N	TS	Freudenstadt

CLASS 442.3   5-SECTION ARTICULATED UNITS

59 sets were ordered for the following areas: Rhein-Sieg Express (2); Saxonia Dresden–Leipzig (4); E-Netz Franken (8); Berlin area (22) and Rostock area (23).

AB + B + B +B + B (DMCO + TSO + MSO + TSO + DMSO).

Built: 2009–12.
Builder–Mech. Parts: Bombardier.
Builder–Elec. Parts: Bombardier.
Wheel Arrangement: Bo-2-Bo-2-2-Bo.
Traction Motors: 6 x 505 kW three-phase asynchronous motors per set.
Wheel Diameter: 850 mm.   **Weight:** 163.8 tonnes.
Width: 2.926 m.   **Length over Couplers:** 20.05 + 16.10 + 16.10 +16.10 + 20.05 m.
Floor Height: 800 mm (entrance), 695/1250 (saloons).
Accommodation: **Maximum Speed:** 160 km/h.

442 301	843 301	443 301	443 801	442 801	KA	
442 302	843 302	443 302	443 802	442 802	KA	
442 303	843 303	443 303	443 803	442 803	NN1	Bad Staffelstein
442 304	843 304	443 304	443 804	442 804	NN1	
442 305	843 305	443 305	443 805	442 805	NN1	
442 306	843 306	443 306	443 806	442 806	NN1	
442 307	843 307	443 307	443 807	442 807	NN1	Markt Ebensfeld
442 308	843 308	443 308	443 808	442 808	NN1	Ebersdorf b.Coburg
442 309	843 309	443 309	443 809	442 809	NN1	
442 310	843 310	443 310	443 810	442 810	NN1	
442 311	843 311	443 311	443 811	442 811	DA	
442 312	843 312	443 312	443 812	442 812	DA	
442 313	843 313	443 313	443 813	442 813	DA	
442 314	843 314	443 314	443 814	442 814	DA	
442 315	843 315	443 315	443 815	442 815	BLO	
442 316	843 316	443 316	443 816	442 816	BLO	
442 317	843 317	443 317	443 817	442 817	BLO	
442 318	843 318	443 318	443 818	442 818	BLO	
442 319	843 319	443 319	443 819	442 819	BLO	
442 320	843 320	443 320	443 820	442 820	BLO	
442 321	843 321	443 321	443 821	442 821	BLO	
442 322	843 322	443 322	443 822	442 822	BLO	
442 323	843 323	443 323	443 823	442 823	BLO	
442 324	843 324	443 324	443 824	442 824	BLO	
442 325	843 325	443 325	443 825	442 825	BLO	
442 326	843 326	443 326	443 826	442 826	BLO	
442 327	843 327	443 327	443 827	442 827	BLO	
442 328	843 328	443 328	443 828	442 828	BLO	Wildau
442 329	843 329	443 329	443 829	442 829	BLO	
442 330	843 330	443 330	443 830	442 830	BLO	Dessau-Roßlau
442 331	843 331	443 331	443 831	442 831	BLO	
442 332	843 332	443 332	443 832	442 832	BLO	
442 333	843 333	443 333	443 833	442 833	BLO	
442 334	843 334	443 334	443 834	442 834	BLO	
442 335	843 335	443 335	443 835	442 835	BLO	
442 336	843 336	443 336	443 836	442 836	BLO	
442 337	843 337	443 337	443 837	442 837	WR	
442 338	843 338	443 338	443 838	442 838	WR	
442 339	843 339	443 339	443 839	442 839	WR	
442 340	843 340	443 340	443 840	442 840	WR	
442 341	843 341	443 341	443 841	442 841	WR	
442 342	843 342	443 342	443 842	442 842	WR	
442 343	843 343	443 343	443 843	442 843	WR	
442 344	843 344	443 344	443 844	442 844	WR	
442 345	843 345	443 345	443 845	442 845	WR	
442 346	843 346	443 346	443 846	442 846	WR	
442 347	843 347	443 347	443 847	442 847	WR	
442 348	843 348	443 348	443 848	442 848	WR	

442 349	843 349	443 349	443 849	442 849		WR
442 350	843 350	443 350	443 850	442 850		WR
442 351	843 351	443 351	443 851	442 851		WR
442 352	843 352	443 352	443 852	442 852		WR
442 353	843 353	443 353	443 853	442 853		WR
442 354	843 354	443 354	443 854	442 854	A	WR
442 355	843 355	443 355	443 855	442 855		WR
442 356	843 356	443 356	443 856	442 856		WR
442 357	843 357	443 357	443 857	442 857		WR
442 358	843 358	443 358	443 858	442 858		WR
442 359	843 359	443 359	443 859	442 859		WR

CLASS 1442.3   5-SECTION ARTICULATED UNITS

These 5-section units work with Class 1442.1 on Mittel Deutschland S-Bahn services around Halle and Leipzig.

Non-Standard Livery: N Silver.

1442 301	1843 301	1443 301	1443 801	1442 801	N	LH2
1442 302	1843 302	1443 302	1443 802	1442 802	N	LH2
1442 303	1843 303	1443 303	1443 803	1442 803	N	LH2
1442 304	1843 304	1443 304	1443 804	1442 804	N	LH2
1442 305	1843 305	1443 305	1443 805	1442 805	N	LH2
1442 306	1843 306	1443 306	1443 806	1442 806	N	LH2
1442 307	1843 307	1443 307	1443 807	1442 807	N	LH2
1442 308	1843 308	1443 308	1443 808	1442 808	N	LH2
1442 309	1843 309	1443 309	1443 809	1442 809	N	LH2
1442 310	1843 310	1443 310	1443 810	1442 810	N	LH2

CLASS 0445/0446   BOMBARDIER TWINDEXX VARIO 160DE   4-CAR UNITS

Bombardier calls these units TWINDEXX VARIO 160DE. Twindexx is explained as **Twinde**ck Fahrzeuge mit e**X**tremer fle**X**ibilität – double-deck vehicles with extreme flexibility. In Germany, double-deck carriages have quite a long history with loco-hauled vehicles being produced in the former DDR for many years and indeed exported to other Eastern Bloc countries. Some push-pull trains had been produced but it was under the Bombardier regime in the 1990s that a three-car double-deck EMU was produced (also Class 445) but there were no takers at that time and the unit was later scrapped. As ever with railways, wheels eventually turn full circle and now the double-deck EMU is back in favour.

There is, however, a big difference. The EVN starts with 91 denoting an electric locomotive, despite the vehicle being a double-deck power car; the Germans call them powered driving trailers! The main reasoning behind the classification seems to be the intermediate vehicles are ordinary carriages that can work with a locomotive or with these new units. It may be a computer logic problem in as much as ordinary carriages must work with a locomotive! The concept allows for additional intermediate trailers to be added as necessary e.g. in tourist areas in summer; so not necessarily in fixed formations.

There are three possible train formations:
1) formed with a 445 power car and a driving trailer at the other end;
2) formed with a 445 at each end;
3) a locomotive can replace a power car or indeed a driving trailer.

In October 2012 an order was placed by DB Regio for five sets to work from Rostock to Berlin etc on RE3 and RE5 routes. The trains were due to enter service in the summer of 2014 but there have been lots of problems with the power cars and getting them authorised for service. The permission only came through in late summer 2017 with the trains entering service with the winter 2017 timetable.

Although a standard vehicle, actual accommodation inside can be varied according to the customer's wishes. The units for Schleswig Holstein, also ordered in 2012, have more first class accommodation, reflecting commuter traffic into Hamburg. So for this area the top deck of one power car is all first class (445 027–42), whilst the power car at the other end (445 011–26) is half first and half second on the top deck. The intention in this area is for two sets to work together from Hamburg to Neumünster and split there for Flensburg and Kiel.

Those based at Würzburg for the "Main-Spessart Express" service have larger multi-purpose areas so that up to 50 bicycles can be accommodated. The München area is different again as it is expected that the trains will operate as 15 six-car and 3 four-car sets in the "Ringzug West" area (München–Treuchtlingen and München–Augsburg).

At a late stage it was found the Frankfurt/M units were to be Class 446 as the trains will serve stations with different platform heights. It is expected there will be 7 three-car and 17 four-car sets.

NB. All train sets will have a multi-purpose area and a disabled WC which when not in a power car will be found in one of the trailer vehicles. As all the trailer vehicles are ordinary carriages, details of these are not included in this book.

Built: 2015–18.
Builder–Mech. Parts: Bombardier.
Builder–Elec. Parts: Bombardier.
Continuous Rating:
Wheel Arrangement: Bo-Bo.
Traction Motors: 4 x 575 kW. **Weight:** 66 tonnes.
Maximum Tractive Effort: 200 kN. **Length Over Couplers:** 25.975 m.
Wheel Diameter: 920 mm. **Door Step Height:** 600 (445); 730 (446) mm.
Accommodation: See below for variations. **Maximum Speed:** 160 km/h.
Non-Standard Livery: N Dark blue and light green for Schleswig Holstein.

Note: Bodies are from Görlitz, bogies are from Siegen, traction motors are from Västerås (all are Bombardier factories).

Accommodation Notes:

Rostock: –/68 (23) 1T; space for 12 bicycles.

Kiel: Two variants: 445 011–026 are 21/22 (17) 1TD. There is a multi-purpose area with space for two wheelchairs; 445 027–042 are 14/43 (24); multipurpose area has space for 12 bicycles. No WC.

Frankfurt/M/Würzburg/München: –/68 (23) 1T; space for 16 bicycles.

Class 0445

445 001	WR	445 027	N AK	445 053	NWH	445 078	MH2
445 002	WR	445 028	N AK	445 054	MH2	445 079	MH2
445 003	WR	445 029	N AK	445 055	NWH	445 080	MH2
445 004	WR	445 030	N AK	445 056	NWH	445 081	MH2
445 005	WR	445 031	N AK	445 057	NWH	445 082	MH2
445 006	WR	445 032	N AK	445 058	NWH	445 083	MH2
445 007	WR	445 033	N AK	445 059	NWH	445 084	MH2
445 008	WR	445 034	N AK	445 060	NWH	445 085	MH2
445 009	WR	445 035	N AK	445 061	MH2	445 086	MH2
445 010	WR	445 036	N AK	445 062	NWH	445 087	MH2
445 011	N AK	445 037	N AK	445 063	NWH	445 088	MH2
445 012	N AK	445 038	N AK	445 064	MH2	445 089	MH2
445 013	N AK	445 039	N AK	445 065	NWH	445 090	MH2
445 014	N AK	445 040	N AK	445 066	MH2	445 091	MH2
445 015	N AK	445 041	N AK	445 067	MH2	445 092	MH2
445 016	N AK	445 042	N AK	445 068	MH2	445 093	MH2
445 017	N AK	445 043	NWH	445 069	MH2	445 094	MH2
445 018	N AK	445 044	NWH	445 070	MH2	445 095	MH2
445 019	N AK	445 045	NWH	445 071	MH2	445 096	MH2
445 020	N AK	445 046	NWH	445 072	MH2	445 097	MH2
445 021	N AK	445 047	NWH	445 073	MH2	445 098	MH2
445 022	N AK	445 048	NWH	445 074	MH2	445 099	MH2
445 023	N AK	445 049	NWH	445 075	MH2	445 100	MH2
445 024	N AK	445 050	NWH	445 076	MH2	445 101	MH2
445 025	N AK	445 051	NWH	445 077	MH2	445 102	MH2
445 026	N AK	445 052	NWH				

Class 0446

446 001	FGM	446 009		446 017	FGM	446 025	FGM
446 002	FGM	446 010	FGM	446 018	FGM	446 026	FGM
446 003	FGM	446 011	FGM	446 019	FGM	446 027	FGM
446 004	FGM	446 012	FGM	446 020	FGM	446 028	FGM
446 005	FGM	446 013	FGM	446 021	FGM	446 029	FGM
446 006	FGM	446 014	FGM	446 022	FGM	446 030	FGM
446 007	FGM	446 015	FGM	446 023	FGM	446 031	FGM
446 008	FGM	446 016	FGM	446 024	FGM	446 032	FGM

446 033	FGM	446 037		446 041		446 045	FGM
446 034	FGM	446 038	FGM	446 042		446 046	FGM
446 035	FGM	446 039	FGM	446 043	FGM	446 047	FGM
446 036	FGM	446 040	FGM	446 044	FGM	446 048	FGM

CLASS 450

DB owns some trams! DB financed some of the vehicles for the Karlsruhe S-Bahn service which are worked by the Albtalbahn. The vehicles are numbered in the Albtalbahn series but carry in addition the DB logo and DB numbers. Further details are in German Railways Part 2.

450 001	RK	450 003	RK	450 004	RK	450 005	RK

CLASS 462   SIEMENS DESIRO HC   4-CAR UNITS

Siemens has delivered to various companies its Desiro ML (Main Line) EMU and has now gone one step further with the Desiro HC – High Capacity. The high capacity is gained by making the intermediate cars double-deck, whilst the outer cars are single-deck! DB Regio has ordered 15 4-car units for RE trains Karlsruhe–Basel. Three units can work in multiple; the double-deck vehicles each have a standard toilet; one universal access toilet is located in one of the driving cars, both of which have a multi purpose area, LED lighting throughout, air conditioning, CCTV and two double doors each side of each vehicle. Each power car has a pantograph and also has electrical equipment on the roof. Note that these units are not articulated. Numbering details not yet available.

Built: 2018–
Builder–Mech. Parts: Siemens Krefeld (outer cars), Wien (intermediate cars).
Builder–Elec. Parts: Siemens.
Wheel Arrangement: Bo-Bo + 2-2 + 2-2 + Bo-Bo.
Traction Motors: 8 x 500 kW.   **Weight:** 200 tonnes.
Wheel Diameter: **Length over Couplers:** 105.252 m (outer cars 26.226 m, intermediate cars 25.20 m).
Width: 2.82 m.   **Maximum Speed:** 160 km/h.
Floor Height: 800 mm (end car entrance), 730 mm (intermediate car entrance).
Accommodation: 36/374 2T 1TD 18 bicycles.

▲ It is nearly rush hour at Hamburg Hbf on 6 May 2018. In the foreground a Class 472 arrives on an S21 working to Aumühle, whilst alongside and in the background Class 474 units are busy on other routes.   **Brian Garvin**

CLASS 463   SIEMENS MIREO   3-SECTION ARTICULATED UNITS

This class is the latest offering from Siemens to replace the Desiro Main Line EMUs and features articulation and aluminium construction. There are quite a few innovations, such as inside frames for the bogies and a shorter wheelbase for the articulated bogies which will also feature hollow axles. All this is to reduce weight. The use of lightweight materials and various other innovations including the traction control system allows Siemens to quote a reduction in energy consumption of up to 25%. Units can be formed of up to seven vehicles. DB Regio has ordered 24 3-section units for the Süd Baden area to be used on RB services from Offenburg to Basel. Another order from DB Regio is for 57 3-section units for S-Bahn services in the Mannheim and Heidelberg areas. With this design Siemens has put all electrical equipment either under the floor or on the roof, so making all the floor space available to operators. Full details of set numbering are still awaited

Built: 2018–
Builder–Mech. Parts: Siemens.
Builder–Elec. Parts: Siemens.
Wheel Arrangement:
Traction Motors:
Wheel Diameter:
Width: **Weight:**
Floor Height: 760 mm (entrance).   **Maximum Speed:** 160 km/h.
Accommodation: 220 seats.   **Length over Couplers:** 26.00 + 19.00 + 26.00 m.

Süd Baden units

463 001	463 007	463 013	463 019
463 002	463 008	463 014	463 020
463 003	463 009	463 015	463 021
463 004	463 010	463 016	463 022
463 005	463 011	463 017	463 023
463 006	463 012	463 018	463 024

S-Bahn Rhein – Neckar units. To be used on S5 Mannheim–Eppingen/Bad Rappenau, S6 Wiesbaden–Mainz–Worms–Mannheim–Bensheim, S8 Mannheim–Karlsruhe and S9 Mannheim–Gross Rohrheim/Mannheim–Waldhof routes.

463 025	463 040	463 054	463 068
463 026	463 041	463 055	463 069
463 027	463 042	463 056	463 070
463 028	463 043	463 057	463 071
463 029	463 044	463 058	463 072
463 030	463 045	463 059	463 073
463 031	463 046	463 060	463 074
463 032	463 047	463 061	463 075
463 033	463 048	463 062	463 076
463 034	463 049	463 063	463 077
463 035	463 050	463 064	463 078
463 036	463 051	463 065	463 079
463 037	463 052	463 066	463 080
463 038	463 053	463 067	463 081
463 039			

CLASS 472   HAMBURG S-BAHN 3-CAR UNITS

This class is now getting old; its replacements have been ordered (Class 490 q.v.).

B + A + B (DMSO–MFO–DMSO (non-gangwayed)).

Built: 1974–84.
Builders–Mech. Parts: Linke-Hofmann-Busch/Messerschmitt-Bölkow-Blohm.
Builder–Elec. Parts: Brown-Boveri.
System: 1200 V DC bottom contact third rail.
Wheel Arrangement: Bo-Bo + Bo-Bo + Bo-Bo.   **Weight:** 40 + 34 + 40 tonnes.
Traction Motors: 4 x 125 kW per power car.   **Length over Couplers:** 65.82 m.
Accommodation: –/65 + 66/– + –/65.   **Maximum Speed:** 100 km/h.

w   Windows in ends of all vehicles.

472 001	473 001	472 501		AOP
472 002	473 002	472 502		AOP
472 003	473 003	472 503		AOP
472 004	473 004	472 504		AOP
472 005	473 005	472 505		AOP
472 009	473 009	472 009		AOP
472 012	473 012	472 512		AOP
472 013	473 013	472 513		AOP
472 014	473 014	472 514		AOP
472 015	473 015	472 515		AOP
472 016	473 016	472 516		AOP
472 017	473 017	472 517		AOP
472 018	473 018	472 518		AOP
472 019	473 019	472 519		AOP
472 020	473 020	472 520		AOP
472 023	473 023	472 523		AOP
472 024	473 024	472 524		AOP
472 025	473 025	472 525		AOP
472 026	473 026	472 526		AOP
472 027	473 027	472 527		AOP
472 028	473 028	472 528		AOP (Z)
472 029	473 029	472 529		AOP
472 030	473 030	472 530		AOP (Z)
472 031	473 031	472 531		AOP
472 032	473 032	472 532	w	AOP
472 033	473 033	472 533	w	AOP
472 034	473 034	472 534	w	AOP
472 035	473 035	472 535	w	AOP (Z)
472 036	473 036	472 536	w	AOP
472 037	473 037	472 537	w	AOP
472 038	473 038	472 538	w	AOP
472 039	473 039	472 539	w	AOP
472 040	473 040	472 540	w	AOP
472 041	473 041	472 541	w	AOP
472 042	473 042	472 542	w	AOP
472 043	473 043	472 543	w	AOP
472 044	473 044	472 544	w	AOP
472 045	473 045	472 545	w	AOP
472 046	473 046	472 546	w	AOP
472 047	473 047	472 547	w	AOP
472 048	473 048	472 548	w	AOP
472 049	473 049	472 549	w	AOP
472 050	473 050	472 550	w	AOP
472 053	473 053	472 553	w	AOP
472 054	473 054	472 554	w	AOP
472 055	473 055	472 555	w	AOP
472 056	473 056	472 556	w	AOP
472 057	473 057	472 557	w	AOP
472 058	473 058	472 558	w	AOP
472 059	473 059	472 559	w	AOP
472 060	473 060	472 560	w	AOP
472 061	473 061	472 561	w	AOP
472 062	473 062	472 562	w	AOP

▲ A surprise in the main line section of Hamburg Harburg station on 13 August 2015, was to find 474 131 and 474 136 on test under the AC wiring. The destination indicator shows "Leerfahrt" – empty run. **Brian Garvin**

CLASS 474   HAMBURG S-BAHN 3-CAR UNITS

These units allowed Classes 470 (1959–70) and 471 (1939–1958) to be withdrawn. Like other modern units three-phase asynchronous motors are provided as are water cooled GTO thyristors and Scharfenberg couplers. Some units have been rebuilt as dual-voltage for the S-Bahn service to Stade where the line was already electrified at 15 kV AC. To get a head start, nine additional units were built as dual voltage and their entry into service allowed older units to go into works for conversion. 474 104–112 are the new sets whilst 474 113–145 are converted from 474 059–091. Technically speaking all the dual-voltage sets should have been given a new class number! Currently units are being refreshed at Neumünster works during which work carriages are being fitted with gangways. This programme is likely to last until 2021.

Built: 1996–2001, 2006.
Builder–Mech. Parts: LHB later Alstom/LHB.
Builder–Elec. Parts: ABB Henschel (Later Adtranz, Kassel).
Systems: 1200 V DC bottom contact third rail and 15 kV AC 16.7 Hz (d).
Wheel Arrangement: Bo-Bo + 2-2 + Bo-Bo.   **Weight:** 102 tonnes.
Traction Motors: 4 x 115 kW.   **Length over Couplers:** 22.895 + 19.77 + 22.895 m.
Accommodation: –/71 + –/66 + –/71.   **Maximum Speed:** 100 km/h.

d   Dual voltage

474 001	874 001	474 501	AOP		474 045	874 045	474 545		AOP
474 002	874 002	474 502	AOP		474 046	874 046	474 546		AOP
474 003	874 003	474 503	AOP		474 047	874 047	474 547		AOP
474 004	874 004	474 504	AOP		474 048	874 048	474 548		AOP
474 005	874 005	474 505	AOP		474 049	874 049	474 549		AOP
474 006	874 006	474 506	AOP		474 050	874 050	474 550		AOP
474 007	874 007	474 507	AOP		474 051	874 051	474 551		AOP
474 008	874 008	474 508	AOP		474 052	874 052	474 552		AOP
474 009	874 009	474 509	AOP		474 053	874 053	474 553		AOP
474 010	874 010	474 510	AOP		474 054	874 054	474 554		AOP
474 011	874 011	474 511	AOP		474 055	874 055	474 555		AOP
474 012	874 012	474 512	AOP		474 056	874 056	474 556		AOP
474 013	874 013	474 513	AOP		474 057	874 057	474 557		AOP
474 014	874 014	474 514	AOP		474 058	874 058	474 558		AOP
474 015	874 015	474 515	AOP		474 092	874 092	474 592		AOP
474 016	874 016	474 516	AOP		474 093	874 093	474 593		AOP
474 017	874 017	474 517	AOP		474 094	874 094	474 594		AOP
474 018	874 018	474 518	AOP		474 095	874 095	474 595		AOP
474 019	874 019	474 519	AOP		474 096	874 096	474 596		AOP
474 020	874 020	474 520	AOP		474 097	874 097	474 597		AOP
474 021	874 021	474 521	AOP		474 098	874 098	474 598		AOP
474 022	874 022	474 522	AOP		474 099	874 099	474 599		AOP
474 023	874 023	474 523	AOP		474 100	874 100	474 600		AOP
474 024	874 024	474 524	AOP		474 101	874 101	474 601		AOP
474 025	874 025	474 525	AOP		474 102	874 102	474 602		AOP
474 026	874 026	474 526	AOP		474 103	874 103	474 603		AOP
474 027	874 027	474 527	AOP		474 104	874 104	474 604	d	AOP
474 028	874 028	474 528	AOP		474 105	874 105	474 605	d	AOP
474 029	874 029	474 529	AOP		474 106	874 106	474 606	d	AOP
474 030	874 030	474 530	AOP		474 107	874 107	474 607	d	AOP
474 031	874 031	474 531	AOP		474 108	874 108	474 608	d	AOP
474 032	874 032	474 532	AOP		474 109	874 109	474 609	d	AOP
474 033	874 033	474 533	AOP		474 110	874 110	474 610	d	AOP
474 034	874 034	474 534	AOP		474 111	874 111	474 611	d	AOP
474 035	874 035	474 535	AOP		474 112	874 112	474 612	d	AOP
474 036	874 036	474 536	AOP		474 113	874 113	474 613	d	AOP
474 037	874 037	474 537	AOP		474 114	874 114	474 614	d	AOP
474 038	874 038	474 538	AOP		474 115	874 115	474 615	d	AOP
474 039	874 039	474 539	AOP		474 116	874 116	474 616	d	AOP
474 040	874 040	474 540	AOP		474 117	874 117	474 617	d	AOP
474 041	874 041	474 541	AOP		474 118	874 118	474 618	d	AOP
474 042	874 042	474 542	AOP		474 119	874 119	474 619	d	AOP
474 043	874 043	474 543	AOP		474 120	874 120	474 620	d	AOP
474 044	874 044	474 544	AOP		474 121	874 121	474 621	d	AOP

474 122	874 122	474 622	d	AOP	474 134	874 134	474 634	d	AOP
474 123	874 123	474 623	d	AOP	474 135	874 135	474 635	d	AOP
474 124	874 124	474 624	d	AOP	474 136	874 136	474 636	d	AOP
474 125	874 125	474 625	d	AOP	474 137	874 137	474 637	d	AOP
474 126	874 126	474 626	d	AOP	474 138	874 138	474 638	d	AOP
474 127	874 127	474 627	d	AOP	474 139	874 139	474 639	d	AOP
474 128	874 128	474 628	d	AOP	474 140	874 140	474 640	d	AOP
474 129	874 129	474 629	d	AOP	474 141	874 141	474 641	d	AOP
474 130	874 130	474 630	d	AOP	474 142	874 142	474 642	d	AOP
474 131	874 131	474 631	d	AOP	474 143	874 143	474 643	d	AOP
474 132	874 132	474 632	d	AOP	474 144	874 144	474 644	d	AOP
474 133	874 133	474 633	d	AOP	474 145	874 145	474 645	d	AOP

CLASS 479.2 — SINGLE CAR

These units operate on an isolated line which runs from Lichtenhain to Cursdorf in Thüringen, which is part of the Oberweissbacher Bergbahn, an odd funicular which runs in open country from Obstfelderschmiede to Lichtenhain. Opened in 1923, the line received modernised vehicles in the 1980s. The Berlin S-Bahn workshops did the rebuilding and used a lot of S-Bahn equipment. A visit to this line and its funicular connection to the rest of the DB network is a must!

Built: 1981.
Builder: RAW Schöneweide.
System: 600 V DC overhead.
Wheel Arrangement: A-A.
Traction Motors: 2 x 60 kW.
Accommodation: –/24.
Former DR Class: 279.2.

Weight: 14.4 tonnes.
Length over Couplers: 11.50 m.
Maximum Speed: 50 km/h.

Originally Class ET 188.

479 201	UE		479 203	UE		479 205	UE

▲ Berlin S-Bahn unit 480 021 leads an S42 Ringbahn service away from Berlin Messe Nord/ICC on 23 September 2016. **Quintus Vosman**

BERLIN S-BAHN

The Berlin S-Bahn is a third-rail 800 V DC system and was operated by the DR. The part of the S-Bahn which operated solely in the former West Berlin was transferred to the former West Berlin Transport Authority (the BVG) in 1984, but the whole operation is now a subsidiary of DB. The BVG received the very oldest units to operate its part of the system, and in 1987 took delivery of some new units of Class 480. The DR also ordered new units, now known as Class 485, but these were of much more spartan design. Upon unification, plans that had gathered dust on shelves for years were brought out and the task started of restoring the S-Bahn to its former glory. Routes that had been cut or abandoned were restored to use. Many S-Bahn units dated from the 1940s and were over 50 years old, so new S-Bahn units were needed; Class 481/2 sets were decided upon as the new standard. However, 2018 will see the appearance of the first of a new generation of S-Bahn trains to be built by Siemens and Stadler which will become series 483, 484 (q.v.).

Berliners refer to 8-car trains as *Vollzüge* (full trains), and thus a four-car train is known as a *Halbzüg* (half-train) and a two-car unit as a *Viertelzüg* (quarter-train). Since most units consist of a driving motor and a non-driving trailer, the smallest train which can be operated is a four-car. However, the inner units of a six or eight-car train can face either direction. Units consisting of two power cars (Class 480) and driving motor/ driving trailer can, of course, operate as a 2-car train.

In the early part of the 21st century the Berlin S-Bahn was in a mess. When privatisation was the way forward several depots and workshops were closed as an efficiency measure, but train availability dropped and some serious maintenance problems ensued. Train services had to be reorganised and many trains ran with short formations. The end result was that privatisation plans were dropped and some depots and workshops reopened; train working only got back to normal levels after many withdrawn sets were reinstated and overhauled at Dessau and/or Wittenberge workshops, as Schöneweide works could not cope. Depots reopened were Friedrichsfelde and Oranienburg

Since 2014 several Class 481 sets have been named after the localities they serve.

Livery: Red and ochre.

CLASS 480   BERLIN S-BAHN   2-CAR UNITS

Units to BVG design. 480 001–004 were prototypes and have been withdrawn. 480 053 and 480 573 were scrapped after accidents. Set 480 025 was burnt out in 2000 and 480 554 was scrapped after hitting a tree in 2002. 480 554[II] has been renumbered from 480 553 and 480 573[II] has been renumbered from 480 525; 480 556[II] is ex 480 570.

B + B (DMSO–DMSO) Non-gangwayed.

Built: 1986–94.
Builders–Mech. Parts: Waggon-Union, ABB Henschel, AEG Hennigsdorf.
Builders–Elec. Parts: AEG, Siemens.   **Weight:** 30 + 30 tonnes.
Wheel Arrangement: Bo-Bo + Bo-Bo.   **Length over Couplers:** 18.40 + 18.40 m.
Traction Motors: 4 x 90 kW three-phase asynchronous motors per power car.
Accommodation: –/44 + – /44.   **Maximum Speed:** 100 km/h.

480 005	480 505	BGA	480 028	480 528	BGA
480 006	480 506	BGA	480 029	480 529	BGA
480 007	480 507	BGA	480 030	480 530	BGA
480 008	480 508	BGA	480 032	480 532	BGA
480 009	480 509	BGA	480 033	480 533	BGA
480 011	480 511	BGA	480 034	480 534	BGA
480 013	480 513	BGA	480 035	480 535	BGA
480 014	480 514	BGA	480 036	480 536	BGA
480 015	480 515	BGA	480 037	480 537	BGA
480 016	480 516	BGA	480 038	480 538	BGA
480 017	480 517	BGA	480 040	480 540	BGA
480 018	480 518	BGA	480 041	480 541	BGA
480 019	480 519	BGA	480 042	480 542	BGA
480 021	480 521	BGA	480 044	480 544	BGA
480 022	480 522	BGA	480 045	480 545	BGA
480 023	480 523	BGA	480 046	480 546	BGA
480 026	480 526	BGA	480 047	480 547	BGA
480 027	480 527	BGA	480 048	480 548	BGA

480 049	480 549	BGA		480 068	480 568	BGA
480 051	480 551	BGA		480 069	480 569	BGA
480 052	480 552	BGA		480 071	480 571	BGA
480 054	480 554[II]	BGA		480 072	480 572	BGA
480 055	480 555	BGA		480 073	480 573[II]	BGA
480 056	480 556[II]	BGA		480 074	480 574	BGA
480 057	480 557	BGA		480 075	480 575	BGA
480 058	480 558	BGA		480 076	480 576	BGA
480 059	480 559	BGA		480 077	480 577	BGA
480 060	480 560	BGA		480 078	480 578	BGA
480 061	480 561	BGA		480 079	480 579	BGA
480 062	480 562	BGA		480 080	480 580	BGA
480 063	480 563	BGA		480 081	480 581	BGA
480 064	480 564	BGA		480 082	480 582	BGA
480 065	480 565	BGA		480 083	480 583	BGA
480 066	480 566	BGA		480 084	480 584	BGA
480 067	480 567	BGA		480 085	480 585	BGA

CLASS 481   BERLIN S-BAHN   2-CAR UNITS

Following the unification of Germany the S-Bahn network of Berlin was brought back under unified control and many sections that had lain dormant for many years were reactivated. Large numbers of new S-Bahn units were required, consequently some 500 units of Class 481 were ordered. They have now replaced all pre-war units.

B + AB (DMSO–MCO) Non-gangwayed.

Built: 1995–2004.
Builders: Adtranz Hennigsdorf, Bombardier/DWA Ammendorf.
Wheel Arrangement: Bo-2 + Bo-Bo   **Weight:** 31 + 28 tonnes.
Traction Motors: One 200 kW and two 200 kW.   **Length over Couplers:** 18.40 m + 18.40 m.
Accommodation: –/30 (14) + 12/38.   **Maximum Speed:** 100 km/h.

481 001	482 001	BWS	Bernau		481 031	482 031	BFF
481 002	482 002	BWS			481 032	482 032	BWS
481 003	482 003	BWS			481 033	482 033	BFF
481 004	482 004	BWS			481 034	482 034	BOR
481 005	482 005	BWS			481 035	482 035	BWS
481 006	482 006	BOR			481 036	482 036	BWS
481 007	482 007	BWS			481 037	482 037	BFF
481 008	482 008	BWS			481 038	482 038	BOR
481 009	482 009	BGA			481 039	482 039	BOR
481 010	482 010	BOR			481 040	482 040	BWS
481 011	482 011	BWS			481 041	482 041	BFF
481 012	482 012	BFF			481 042	482 042	BFF
481 013	482 013	BFF			481 043	482 043	BFF
481 014	482 014	BWS			481 044	482 044	BWS
481 015	482 015	BFF			481 045	482 045	BWS
481 016	482 016	BFF			481 046	482 046	BWS
481 017	482 017	BFF			481 047	482 047	BFF
481 018	482 018	BFF			481 048	482 048	BOR
481 019	482 019	BOR			481 049	482 049	BOR
481 020	482 020	BOR			481 050	482 050	BWS
481 021	482 021	BWS			481 051	482 051	BWS
481 022	482 022	BOR			481 052	482 052	BWS
481 023	482 023	BGA			481 053	482 053	BFF
481 024	482 024	BFF			481 054	482 054	BFF
481 025	482 025	BFF			481 055	482 055	BFF
481 026	482 026	BFF			481 056	482 056	BFF
481 027	482 027	BWS			481 057	482 057	BFF
481 028	482 028	BWS			481 058	482 058	BFF
481 029	482 029	BFF			481 059	482 059	BFF
481 030	482 030	BOR			481 060	482 060	BFF

481 061	482 061	BFF		481 125	482 125	BWS	
481 062	482 062	BFF		481 126	482 126	BWS	
481 063	482 063	BWS		481 127	482 127	BWS	
481 064	482 064	BFF		481 128	482 128	BWS	
481 065	482 065	BOR		481 129	482 129	BWS	
481 066	482 066	BFF		481 130	482 130	BFF	
481 067	482 067	BFF		481 131	482 131	BFF	
481 068	482 068	BWS		481 132	482 132	BWS	
481 069	482 069	BOR		481 133	482 133	BFF	
481 070	482 070	BFF		481 134	482 134	BWS	
481 071	482 071	BWS		481 135	482 135	BOR	
481 072	482 072	BWS	Teltow	481 136	482 136	BFF	
481 073	482 073	BWS		481 137	482 137	BFF	
481 074	482 074	BWS		481 138	482 138	BOR	
481 075	482 075	BWS		481 139	482 139	BWS	
481 076	482 076	BOR		481 140	482 140	BFF	
481 077	482 077	BFF		481 141	482 141	BFF	
481 078	482 078	BWS		481 142	482 142	BWS	
481 079	482 079	BWS		481 143	482 143	BWS	
481 080	482 080	BFF		481 144	482 144	BWS	
481 081	482 081	BFF		481 145	482 145	BWS	
481 082	482 082	BWS		481 146	482 146	BWS	
481 083	482 083	BFF		481 147	482 147	BFF	
481 084	482 084	BFF		481 148	482 148	BWS	
481 085	482 085	BWS		481 149	482 149	BWS	
481 086	482 086	BOR		481 150	482 150	BOR	
481 087	482 087	BWS		481 151	482 151	BWS	
481 088	482 088	BOR		481 152	482 152	BOR	
481 089	482 089	BFF		481 153	482 153	BWS	
481 090	482 090	BFF	Erkner	481 154	482 154	BWS	
481 091	482 091	BWS		481 155	482 155	BWS	
481 092	482 092	BGA		481 156	482 156	BOR	
481 093	482 093	BFF		481 157	482 157	BWS	
481 094	482 094	BFF		481 158	482 158	BWS	
481 095	482 095	BWS		481 159	482 159	BWS	
481 096	482 096	BFF		481 160	482 160	BWS	
481 097	482 097	BWS		481 161	482 161	BOR	
481 098	482 098	BFF		481 162	482 162	BOR	
481 099	482 099	BWS		481 163	482 163	BOR	
481 100	482 100	BGA		481 164	482 164	BOR	
481 101	482 101	BWS		481 165	482 165	BWS	
481 102	482 102	BFF		481 166	482 166	BOR	
481 103	482 103	BOR		481 167	482 167	BOR	
481 104	482 104	BFF		481 168	482 168	BFF	
481 105	482 105	BFF		481 169	482 169	BFF	
481 106	482 106	BWS		481 170	482 170	BOR	
481 107	482 107	BFF		481 171	482 171	BOR	
481 108	482 108	BWS		481 172	482 172	BWS	
481 109	482 109	BWS		481 173	482 173	BFF	
481 110	482 110	BOR		481 174	482 174	BWS	
481 111	482 111	BFF		481 175	482 175	BOR	
481 112	482 112	BWS		481 176	482 176	BOR	
481 113	482 113	BFF		481 177	482 177	BWS	
481 114	482 114	BFF		481 178	482 178	BWS	
481 115	482 115	BOR		481 179	482 179	BWS	Blankenfelde-Mahlow
481 116	482 116	BWS					
481 117	482 117	BOR		481 180	482 180	BFF	
481 118	482 118	BOR		481 181	482 181	BWS	
481 119	482 119	BFF		481 182	482 182	BOR	
481 120	482 120	BOR		481 183	482 183	BOR	
481 121	482 121	BFF		481 184	482 184	BOR	
481 122	482 122	BWS		481 185	482 185	BFF	
481 123	482 123	BOR		481 186	482 186	BFF	Strausberg
481 124	482 124	BWS		481 187	482 187	BFF	

481 188	482 188	BFF		481 215	482 215	BWS	
481 189	482 189	BWS		481 216	482 216	BOR	
481 190	482 190	BFF	Spandau	481 217	482 217	BFF	
481 191	482 191	BWS		481 218	482 218	BGA	
481 192	482 192	BWS		481 219	482 219	BFF	
481 193	482 193	BWS	Potsdam	481 220	482 220	BFF	Mitte
481 194	482 194	BWS		481 221	482 221	BFF	
481 195	482 195	BWS		481 222	482 222	BFF	
481 196	482 196	BOR		481 223	482 223	BFF	
481 197	482 197	BWS		481 224	482 224	BWS	
481 198	482 198	BWS		481 225	482 225	BFF	
481 199	482 199	BFF		481 226	482 226	BFF	
481 200	482 200	BFF		481 227	482 227	BWS	
481 201	482 201	BFF		481 228	482 228	BFF	
481 202	482 202	BOR		481 229	482 229	BFF	
481 203	482 203	BOR		481 230	482 230	BGA	
481 204	482 204	BWS		481 231	482 231	BGA	
481 205	482 205	BFF		481 232	482 232	BGA	
481 206	482 206	BFF		481 233	482 233	BGA	
481 207	482 207	BFF		481 234	482 234	BFF	
481 208	482 208	BWS		481 235	482 235	BGA	
481 209	482 209	BFF		481 236	482 236	BGA	
481 210	482 210	BWS		481 237	482 237	BGA	
481 211	482 211	BWS	Hohen Neuendorf	481 238	482 238	BGA	
481 212	482 212	BWS		481 239	482 239	BGA	
481 213	482 213	BFF		481 240	482 240	BGA	
481 214	482 214	BFF		481 241	482 241	BGA	

▲ Nearly 500 examples of Class 481 are in use on the Berlin S-Bahn. 481 053 departs from Berlin Alexanderplatz on 21 June 2015.
Antony Guppy

481 242	482 242	BWS	
481 243	482 243	BWS	
481 244	482 244	BGA	
481 245	482 245	BFF	
481 246	482 246	BGA	
481 247	482 247	BGA	
481 248	482 248	BGA	
481 249	482 249	BGA	
481 250	482 250	BWS	
481 251	482 251	BGA	
481 252	482 252	BGA	
481 253	482 253	BGA	
481 254	482 254	BGA	
481 255	482 255	BWS	
481 256	482 256	BWS	
481 257	482 257	BWS	
481 258	482 258	BGA	
481 259	482 259	BWS	
481 260	482 260	BGA	
481 261	482 261	BGA	
481 262	482 262	BGA	
481 263	482 263	BGA	
481 264	482 264	BGA	
481 265	482 265	BGA	
481 266	482 266	BGA	
481 267	482 267	BWS	
481 268	482 268	BFF	
481 269	482 269	BWS	
481 270	482 270	BGA	
481 271	482 271	BGA	
481 272	482 272	BGA	
481 273	482 273	BGA	
481 274	482 274	BGA	
481 275	482 275	BGA	
481 276	482 276	BGA	
481 277	482 277	BWS	
481 278	482 278	BFF	
481 279	482 279	BGA	
481 280	482 280	BWS	
481 281	482 281	BGA	
481 282	482 282	BWS	
481 283	482 283	BGA	
481 284	482 284	BWS	
481 285	482 285	BGA	
481 286	482 286	BFF	
481 287	482 287	BGA	
481 288	482 288	BFF	
481 289	482 289	BWS	
481 290	482 290	BFF	
481 291	482 291	BFF	
481 292	482 292	BFF	
481 293	482 293	BWS	
481 294	482 294	BGA	
481 295	482 295	BGA	
481 296	482 296	BWS	
481 297	482 297	BWS	
481 298	482 298	BWS	
481 299	482 299	BOR	
481 300	482 300	BFF	
481 301	482 301	BWS	
481 302	482 302	BWS	
481 303	482 303	BWS	
481 304	482 304	BWS	
481 305	482 305	BFF	
481 306	482 306	BFF	
481 307	482 307	BWS	
481 308	482 308	BOR	
481 309	482 309	BFF	
481 310	482 310	BFF	
481 311	482 311	BWS	
481 312	482 312	BWS	Oranienburg
481 313	482 313	BWS	
481 314	482 314	BWS	
481 315	482 315	BWS	
481 316	482 316	BWS	
481 317	482 317	BWS	
481 318	482 318	BFF	
481 319	482 319	BFF	
481 320	482 320	BFF	
481 321	482 321	BFF	
481 322	482 322	BWS	
481 323	482 323	BWS	
481 324	482 324	BWS	
481 325	482 325	BWS	
481 326	482 326	BOR	
481 327	482 327	BFF	
481 328	482 328	BWS	
481 329	482 329	BWS	
481 330	482 330	BFF	
481 331	482 331	BWS	
481 332	482 332	BGA	
481 333	482 333	BFF	
481 334	482 334	BFF	
481 335	482 335	BFF	
481 336	482 336	BFF	
481 337	482 337	BWS	
481 338	482 338	BOR	
481 339	482 339	BWS	
481 340	482 340	BWS	
481 341	482 341	BWS	
481 342	482 342	BFF	
481 343	482 343	BFF	
481 344	482 344	BFF	
481 345	482 345	BFF	
481 346	482 346	BWS	
481 347	482 347	BWS	
481 348	482 348	BWS	
481 349	482 349	BWS	
481 350	482 350	BOR	
481 351	482 351	BWS	
481 352	482 352	BOR	
481 353	482 353	BFF	
481 354	482 354	BFF	
481 355	482 355	BWS	
481 356	482 356	BFF	
481 357	482 357	BWS	
481 358	482 358	BOR	
481 359	482 359	BWS	
481 360	482 360	BWS	
481 361	482 361	BWS	
481 362	482 362	BWS	
481 363	482 363	BWS	
481 364	482 364	BWS	
481 365	482 365	BWS	
481 366	482 366	BWS	
481 367	482 367	BWS	
481 368	482 368	BOR	
481 369	482 369	BOR	

481 370	482 370	BWS		481 432	482 432	BOR	Velten
481 371	482 371	BWS		481 433	482 433	BFF	
481 372	482 372	BOR		481 434	482 434	BOR	
481 373	482 373	BWS		481 435	482 435	BFF	
481 374	482 374	BFF		481 436	482 436	BOR	
481 375	482 375	BGA		481 437	482 437	BWS	
481 376	482 376	BWS		481 438	482 438	BFF	
481 377	482 377	BWS		481 439	482 439	BWS	
481 378	482 378	BFF		481 440	482 440	BFF	
481 379	482 379	BOR		481 441	482 441	BOR	
481 380	482 380	BFF		481 442	482 442	BGA	
481 381	482 381	BWS		481 443	482 443	BOR	
481 382	482 382	BWS		481 444	482 444	BOR	
481 383	482 383	BFF		481 445	482 445	BOR	
481 384	482 384	BOR	Charlottenburg-Wilmersdorf	481 446	482 446	BFF	
481 385	482 385	BFF		481 447	482 447	BFF	
481 386	482 386	BWS		481 448	482 448	BOR	
481 387	482 387	BWS		481 449	482 449	BOR	
481 388	482 388	BFF		481 450	482 450	BFF	
481 389	482 389	BWS		481 451	482 451	BFF	
481 390	482 390	BWS		481 452	482 452	BOR	
481 391	482 391	BFF		481 453	482 453	BWS	
481 392	482 392	BFF		481 454	482 454	BFF	
481 393	482 393	BOR		481 455	482 455	BWS	
481 394	482 394	BWS		481 456	482 456	BWS	
481 395	482 395	BGA		481 457	482 457	BOR	
481 396	482 396	BOR		481 458	482 458	BFF	
481 397	482 397	BWS	Steglitz-Zehlendorf	481 459	482 459	BFF	
481 398	482 398	BFF		481 460	482 460	BWS	
481 399	482 399	BWS		481 461	482 461	BFF	
481 400	482 400	BFF		481 462	482 462	BOR	
481 401	482 401	BFF		481 463	482 463	BWS	
481 402	482 402	BFF		481 464	482 464	BOR	
481 403	482 403	BFF		481 465	482 465	BGA	
481 404	482 404	BGA		481 466	482 466	BFF	
481 405	482 405	BOR		481 467	482 467	BFF	
481 406	482 406	BFF		481 468	482 468	BFF	
481 407	482 407	BFF		481 469	482 469	BWS	
481 408	482 408	BOR		481 470	482 470	BFF	
481 409	482 409	BFF		481 471	482 471	BFF	
481 410	482 410	BOR		481 472	482 472	BWS	
481 411	482 411	BFF		481 473	482 473	BWS	Hennigsdorf
481 412	482 412	BGA		481 474	482 474	BFF	
481 413	482 413	BOR		481 475	482 475	BFF	
481 414	482 414	BFF		481 476	482 476	BOR	
481 415	482 415	BFF		481 477	482 477	BOR	
481 416	482 416	BFF		481 478	482 478	BFF	
481 417	482 417	BFF		481 479	482 479	BOR	
481 418	482 418	BFF		481 480	482 480	BFF	
481 419	482 419	BFF		481 481	482 481	BFF	
481 420	482 420	BFF		481 482	482 482	BFF	
481 421	482 421	BFF		481 483	482 483	BFF	
481 422	482 422	BWS	Reinickendorf	481 484	482 484	BFF	
481 423	482 423	BWS		481 485	482 485	BFF	
481 424	482 424	BWS		481 486	482 486	BFF	
481 425	482 425	BOR		481 487	482 487	BWS	
481 426	482 426	BFF		481 488	482 488	BFF	
481 427	482 427	BFF		481 489	482 489	BFF	
481 428	482 428	BFF		481 490	482 490	BFF	
481 429	482 429	BFF		481 491	482 491	BWS	
481 430	482 430	BOR		481 492	482 492	BFF	
481 431	482 431	BOR		481 493	482 493	BWS	
				481 494	482 494	BFF	

CLASS 481.5   BERLIN S-BAHN   4-CAR UNITS

An innovation in 2003 was the delivery of three complete *Halbzüge*. These differ from previous practice in being gangwayed within the set. Details are as given for other Class 481 vehicles.

481 501	482 501	482 601	481 601	BOR	Berlin
481 502	482 502	482 602	481 602	BOR	Brandenburg
481 503	482 503	482 603	481 603	BOR	

CLASS 483   BERLIN S-BAHN   2-CAR UNITS

These new units will allow withdrawals of Classes 480 and 485 to start again. A consortium made up of Siemens AG and Stadler Pankow GmbH won the tender for the construction of the new units. 21 new 2-car sets will be provided with construction of the first vehicles starting in late 2017, with a view to service entry in late 2020. These sets continue the Berlin tradition of a *Viertelzug* which can operate back to back as a 4-car train or by the addition of another unit a 6-car train can be formed. Each carriage has three sets of doors, whilst the area behind the driving cabs will have tip up seats to allow bicycles and prams to be conveyed. Bodies are made at the Stadler works in Hungary, with the fitting out and completion taking place in Berlin. First use is expected to be on Ringbahn S41 and S42, S46, S47 and S48 routes. In a departure from previous practise there is only one number allocated for the complete set with suffix letters denoting the different carriage in this case 483 001 A and 483 001 B. It is considered an EVN is not needed as the trains do not normally leave the Berlin S-Bahn network.

B + B (DMSO–DMSO). Gangwayed within set.

Built: 2018 onwards.
Builder–Mech. Parts: Stadler Pankow.
Builder–Elec. Parts: Siemens.
Continuous Rating: 840 kW.
Wheel Arrangement: 1A-Bo + Bo-A1.
Traction Motors: 6 x 140 = 840 kW.
Maximum Tractive Effort: 104 kN.
Wheel Diameter: 820 mm.
Accommodation: –/60 (20).

Weight:
Length over Couplers: 36.80 m (per set).
Door Step Height: 1000 mm.
Maximum Speed: 100 km/h.

483 001	483 008	483 015
483 002	483 009	483 016
483 003	483 010	483 017
483 004	483 011	483 018
483 005	483 012	483 019
483 006	483 013	483 020
483 007	483 014	483 021

CLASS 484   BERLIN S-BAHN   4-CAR UNITS

As well as winning the order for new 2-car units, Siemens AG and Stadler Pankow GmbH also won the order for 85 4-car EMUs. These are similar to Class 483 but the elimination of two driving cabs allows an extra 24 seats to be provided. First use is expected to be on Ringbahn S41 and S42, S46, S47 and S48 routes. As with Class 483, a single number is allocated to each set with suffixes A, B, C & D used to denote the individual carriages

B + B + B + B (DMSO–MSO–MSO–DMSO). Gangwayed within set.

Built: 2018 onwards.
Builder–Mech. Parts: Stadler Pankow.
Builder–Elec. Parts: Siemens.
Wheel Arrangement: 1A-Bo + Bo-A1 + 1A-Bo + Bo-A1.
Continuous Rating:
Traction Motors: 12 x 140 kW.
Maximum Tractive Effort: 208 kN.
Wheel Diameter: 820 mm.
Accommodation: –/31 (10) + –/44 (10) + –/44 (10) + –/31 (10).

Weight:
Length over Couplers: 73.60 m (per set).
Door Step Height: 1000 mm.
Maximum Speed: 100 km/h.

484 001	484 030	484 058
484 002	484 031	484 059
484 003	484 032	484 060
484 004	484 033	484 061
484 005	484 034	484 062
484 006	484 035	484 063
484 007	484 036	484 064
484 008	484 037	484 065
484 009	484 038	484 066
484 010	484 039	484 067
484 011	484 040	484 068
484 012	484 041	484 069
484 013	484 042	484 070
484 014	484 043	484 071
484 015	484 044	484 072
484 016	484 045	484 073
484 017	484 046	484 074
484 018	484 047	484 075
484 019	484 048	484 076
484 020	484 049	484 077
484 021	484 050	484 078
484 022	484 051	484 079
484 023	484 052	484 080
484 024	484 053	484 081
484 025	484 054	484 082
484 026	484 055	484 083
484 027	484 056	484 084
484 028	484 057	484 085
484 029		

▲ The latest addition to the Berlin S-Bahn is Class 484. In a departure from previous practice all cars have been given the same unit number, with the addition of A, B, C and D to distinguish the four cars making up a unit. Brand new **484 002** is seen on display at the Innotrans exhibition in Berlin on 17 September 2018. **Keith Fender**

CLASS 485   BERLIN S-BAHN   2-CAR UNITS

Units built to DR design. Many sets were withdrawn and scrapped after Class 481 was introduced, but the problems of recent years have seen some sets taken back from scrap yards or storage lines and reinstated after a thorough overhaul.

B + B (DMSO–TSO) Non-gangwayed.

Built: 1987–92.
Builder: LEW.
Wheel Arrangement: Bo-Bo + 2-2.
Traction Motors: 4 x 150 kW.
Accommodation: –/44 + –/56.
Former DR Class: 285.

Weight: 34 + 26 tonnes.
Length over Couplers: 18.00 + 18.00 m.
Maximum Speed: 90 km/h.

485 014	885 014	BGA		485 092	885 092	BGA
485 015	885 015	BGA		485 093	885 093	BGA
485 016	885 016	BGA		485 094	885 094	BGA
485 019	885 019	BGA		485 095	885 095	BGA
485 022	885 022	BGA		485 096	885 096	BGA
485 026	885 026	BGA		485 097	885 097	BGA
485 027	885 027	BGA		485 099	885 099	BGA (Z)
485 028	885 028	BGA		485 102	885 102	BGA
485 029	885 029	BGA		485 104	885 104	BGA
485 030	885 030	BGA		485 108	885 108	BGA
485 031	885 031	BGA		485 109	885 109	BGA
485 033	885 033	BGA		485 110	885 110	BGA
485 034	885 034	BGA		485 111	885 111	BGA
485 038	885 038	BGA		485 112	885 112	BGA
485 040	885 040	BGA		485 114	885 114	BGA
485 041	885 041	BGA		485 115	885 115	BGA
485 042	885 042	BGA		485 117	885 117	BGA
485 043	885 043	BGA		485 118	885 118	BGA
485 044	885 044	BGA		485 119	885 119	BGA
485 048	885 048	BGA		485 120	885 120	BGA
485 050	885 050	BGA		485 121	885 121	BGA
485 054	885 054	BGA (Z)		485 122	885 122	BGA
485 055	885 055	BGA		485 123	885 123	BGA
485 059	885 059	BGA		485 126	885 126	BGA
485 061	885 061	BGA		485 127	885 127	BGA
485 062	885 062	BGA		485 128	885 128	BGA
485 066	885 066	BGA		485 129	885 129	BGA
485 068	885 068	BGA		485 137	885 137	BGA
485 069	885 069	BGA		485 138	885 138	BGA (Z)
485 070	885 070	BGA		485 140	885 140	BGA (Z)
485 072	885 072	BGA		485 141	885 141	BGA
485 074	885 074	BGA		485 142	885 142	BGA
485 076	885 076	BGA		485 143	885 143	BGA (Z)
485 078	885 078	BGA		485 147	885 147	BGA
485 079	885 079	BGA		485 149	885 149	BGA
485 080	885 080	BGA		485 152	885 152	BGA
485 082	885 082	BGA		485 156	885 156	BGA
485 083	885 083	BGA		485 158	885 158	BGA
485 085	885 085	BGA		485 160	885 160	BGA
485 088	885 088	BGA		485 161	885 161	BGA
485 089	885 089	BGA		485 162	885 162	BGA
485 090	885 090	BGA		485 164	885 164	BGA
485 091	885 091	BGA		485 168	885 168	BGA

CLASS 490   HAMBURG S-BAHN 3-CAR UNITS

Some of the Hamburg S-Bahn sets are older than those in Berlin so it is no surprise that the city wishes to update its fleet. Bombardier won the contract and is to provide two types of unit to replace the existing Class 472 sets. Sets 490 001–041 will be single-voltage sets whilst 490 101–130 will be dual-voltage. Each carriage will have three sets of doors and for the first time in Hamburg there will be air conditioning. There are multi-purpose areas in each driving vehicle to accommodate wheelchairs, prams and bikes. The sets are gangwayed within the set. CCTV is provided as well as screens showing travel information. Some prototypes have been built for service testing, to be followed by the production run. All are painted in standard DB red but interestingly the front end has a silver surround to the cab window which also covers the dummy buffers, giving the appearance head on of a letter "H" for Hamburg! Class 472 is expected to disappear when the production units settle in.

B + B + B (DMBSO–PMSO–DMBSO)

Built: 2016 onwards.
Builder: Bombardier, Hennigsdorf.
System: 1200 V DC bottom contact third rail and 15 kV AC 16.7 Hz.
Wheel Arrangement: 2-Bo + Bo-Bo + Bo-2.
Traction Motors: 8 x 200 kW.
Maximum Tractive Effort: 104 kN.
Wheel Diameter:
Accommodation: –/172 (50/72/50) plus 18 tip up. Standing room for 279.
Weight: 127.7 tonnes (490.0); 132.7 tonnes (490.1).
Length over Couplers: 66.00 m (per set) (DMSO 21.59 m, PMSO 20.75 m).
Door Step Height: 990 mm.
Maximum Speed: 100 km/h (490.0); 140 km/h (490.1).

DC Units

490 001	1490 001	490 501		490 022	1490 022	490 522
490 002	1490 002	490 502		490 023	1490 023	490 523
490 003	1490 003	490 503		490 024	1490 024	490 524
490 004	1490 004	490 504		490 025	1490 025	490 525
490 005	1490 005	490 505		490 026	1490 026	490 526
490 006	1490 006	490 506	AOP	490 027	1490 027	490 527
490 007	1490 007	490 507	AOP	490 028	1490 028	490 528
490 008	1490 008	490 508	AOP	490 029	1490 029	490 529
490 009	1490 009	490 509	AOP	490 030	1490 030	490 530
490 010	1490 010	490 510		490 031	1490 031	490 531
490 011	1490 011	490 511		490 032	1490 032	490 532
490 012	1490 012	490 512		490 033	1490 033	490 533
490 013	1490 013	490 513		490 034	1490 034	490 534
490 014	1490 014	490 514		490 035	1490 035	490 535
490 015	1490 015	490 515		490 036	1490 036	490 536
490 016	1490 016	490 516		490 037	1490 037	490 537
490 017	1490 017	490 517		490 038	1490 038	490 538
490 018	1490 018	490 518		490 039	1490 039	490 539
490 019	1490 019	490 519		490 040	1490 040	490 540
490 020	1490 020	490 520		490 041	1490 041	490 541
490 021	1490 021	490 521				

Dual-voltage units

490 100	1490 100	490 630		490 112	1490 112	490 642
490 101	1490 101	490 631		490 113	1490 113	490 643
490 102	1490 102	490 632		490 114	1490 114	490 644
490 103	1490 103	490 633		490 115	1490 115	490 645
490 104	1490 104	490 634		490 116	1490 116	490 646
490 105	1490 105	490 635		490 117	1490 117	490 647
490 106	1490 106	490 636		490 118	1490 118	490 648
490 107	1490 107	490 637		490 119	1490 119	490 649
490 108	1490 108	490 638		490 120	1490 120	490 650
490 109	1490 109	490 639		490 121	1490 121	490 651
490 110	1490 110	490 640		490 122	1490 122	490 652
490 111	1490 111	490 641		490 123	1490 123	490 653

490 124	1490 124	490 654
490 125	1490 125	490 655
490 126	1490 126	490 656
490 127	1490 127	490 657

490 128	1490 128	490 658
490 129	1490 129	490 659
490 130	1490 130	490 660

BERLIN S-BAHN DEPARTMENTAL UNITS

The Berlin S-Bahn has several departmental units which are grouped into the 478 series whether they are EMUs or locomotives.

SHUNTING LOCOMOTIVE   Bo

This electric locomotive is used for shunting at the main Berlin S-Bahn workshops at Berlin-Schöneweide and has never been numbered in the main stock list.

Built: 1932.   **Maximum Tractive Effort:** 44 kN.
Builder: AEG.   **Weight:** 29.1 tonnes.
Power: 220 kW.   **Maximum Speed:** 50 km/h.

E176 11

BREAKDOWN TRAIN VEHICLES

Converted in 1994. One vehicle is the breakdown vehicle containing jacks, packing etc whilst the other vehicle is the staff messroom etc.

478 521	(475 137)	478 523	(478 021)	BWS
478 522	(475 148)	478 524	(478 022)	BFF (Z)

▲ A brand new 3-car dual-voltage unit for the Hamburg S-Bahn, 490 101 stands outside the Bombardier factory at Hennigsdorf on 20 September 2018. **Keith Fender**

6. DIESEL MULTIPLE UNITS

CLASS 605   ICE-TD   4-CAR UNITS

This DMU is a diesel version of an ICE3 unit intended to bring ICE comfort and standards to non-electrified lines. It was intended to be used on services between Nürnberg and Dresden and also München and Lindau/Zürich but in traffic they were deemed unsuitable. The tilt system is an electro-mechanical version by Siemens. At one point all the units were in store but problems with the electric ICE fleet saw some 605s standing in for them. Then the Danes came to the rescue! Danish railways had ordered a new batch of IC DMUs from Italy but deliveries have been seriously delayed. DSB hired in some DB 605s to cover for their existing IC DMUs on services from København to Hamburg. This use ceased in 2017 and now all the units are out of service and stored awaiting a buyer or another emergency. During spring 2018 two sets were moved from storage at Mukran to the privatised works at Halle-Ammendorf where they are expected to be converted into automatic operation for trials in the Annaberg-Buchholz area.

B + B + B + A (DMSO–MSO–MSORMB–DMFO).

Built: 1998–99.
Builders: Siemens-Duewag, SGP.
Wheel Arrangement: 2-Bo + Bo-2 + 2-Bo + Bo-2.
Engine: Four Cummins QSK 19R750 engines of 560 kW at 1800 rpm.
Transmission: Electric. 4 x 425 kW three-phase asynchronous traction motors.
Wheel Diameter: 860 mm.
Accommodation: –/63 + –/51 with children's compartment 1W 1T 1TD + –/40 with bistro & conductor's office 1T 1 staff T + 41/–.
Weight: 54 + 54 + 55 + 56 tonnes.
Length over Couplers: 27.45 + 25.90 + 25.90 + 27.45 m.
Maximum Speed: 200 km/h.

DK   Fitted with Danish safety equipment.

605 001		605 201	605 501		LHAD (Z)
605 002	605 102	605 202	605 502		WM (Z)
605 003	605 103	605 203	605 503	DK	WM (Z)
605 004	605 104	605 204	605 504	DK	WM (Z)
605 005	605 105	605 205	605 505	DK	WM (Z)
605 006	605 106	605 206	605 506	DK	WM (Z)
605 007	605 107	605 207	605 507	DK	WM (Z)
605 008	605 108	605 208	605 508		WM (Z)
605 010	605 110	605 210	605 510	DK	WM (Z)
605 011	605 111	605 211	605 511	DK	WM (Z)
605 012	605 112	605 212	605 512		WM (Z)
605 014	605 114	605 214	605 514	DK	WM (Z)
605 015	605 115	605 215	605 515		WM (Z)
605 016	605 116	605 216	605 516	DK	WM (Z)
605 017	605 117	605 217	605 517	DK	LHAD (Z)
605 018	605 118	605 218	605 518	DK	KKROX (Z)
605 019	605 119	605 219	605 519	DK	LHAD (Z)

CLASS 610   2-CAR UNITS

These tilting units were inspired by the Italian "Pendolino" trains. DB wanted some new DMUs for its route from Nürnberg to Hof and Bayreuth where there are many curves. The units operated quite successfully since introduction but in 2000 the bogies started to show signs of strain. The units were all withdrawn from service; a solution was found and the sets were back at work by late 2001. The whole class has now been taken out of service and stored. Their former duties are now worked by class 612s or have been taken over by private operators.

BD + AB (DMBSO–DMCO).

Built: 1991–92 for DB.
Builders: Duewag (610.0), MAN (610.5).
Wheel Arrangement: 2-A1 + 1A-A1.   **Weight:** 47.45 + 47.90 tonnes.
Engine: 1 MTU 12V183TD12 of 485 kW.   **Length over Buffers:** 25.40 + 25.40 m.
Transmission: Electric. Three-phase asynchronous motors.
Accommodation: –/68 (4) + 16/46 (2).   **Maximum Speed:** 160 km/h.

610 001	610 501	EHM (Z)	
610 002	610 502	EHM (Z)	PEGNITZ
610 003	610 503	EHM (Z)	
610 004	610 504	EHM (Z)	STADT HOF
610 005	610 505	EHM (Z)	HERZOG STADT SULZBACH-ROSENBERG
610 006	610 506	EHM (Z)	MARKT-NEUHAUS A.D. PEGNITZ
610 007	610 507	EHM (Z)	MARKTREDWITZ
610 008	610 508	EHM (Z)	LANDKREIS CHAM
610 009	610 509	EHM (Z)	
610 010	610 510	EHM (Z)	STADT HERSBRUCK
610 013	610 513	EHM (Z)	
610 014	610 514	EHM (Z)	STADT AMBERG
610 015	610 515	EHM (Z)	
610 016	610 516	EHM (Z)	
610 017	610 517	EHM (Z)	STADT SCHWANDORF
610 018	610 518	EHM (Z)	STADT WEIDEN
610 019	610 519	EHM (Z)	
610 020	610 520	EHM (Z)	

CLASS 611   2-CAR UNITS

These tilting DMUs can be considered a German version of the Italian-inspired, but German built, Class 610s. However, the tilting system used on the 611s is based on the military system used in Leopard tanks! Five years after delivery the trains were still giving problems often associated with the tilt which means slower running speeds have to apply and consequently trains are late. Rhineland-Pfalz refused to pay subsidies to DB Regio and had all the units allocated to Kaiserslautern transferred away, being replaced by Class 612 units. The Germans, instead of calling the units Pendolinos often refer to them as "Pannelinos" (Panne = a breakdown!). They are currently in use on the following routes: Basel–Lindau, Ulm–Aulendorf–Tübingen–Stuttgart and Ulm–Friedrichshafen but are still giving problems and are being replaced by 612s. All are likely to be withdrawn soon rather than having a mid-life refurbishment.

B + AB (DMSO–DMCO).

Built: 1996–97.
Builders: AEG/Adtranz, Hennigsdorf.
Wheel Arrangement: 2-B + B-2.   **Weight:** 116 tonnes.
Engine: Two 12 cylinder MTU 183TD13 engines of 540 kW.
Transmission: Hydraulic – Voith.   **Length over Couplers:** 25.87 + 25.87 m.
Accommodation: –/77 + 24/37 1T.   **Maximum Speed:** 160 km/h.

611 001	611 501	WM (Z)		611 006	611 506	WM (Z)
611 002	611 502	WM (Z)		611 007	611 507	WM (Z)
611 003	611 503	WM (Z)		611 008	611 508	WM (Z)
611 004	611 504	WM (Z)		611 009	611 509	WM (Z)
611 005	611 505	WM (Z)		611 010	611 510	TU

611 011	611 511	WM (Z)	611 031	611 531	TU (Z)
611 012	611 512	WM (Z)	611 032	611 532	WM (Z)
611 013	611 513	WM (Z)	611 033	611 533	WM (Z)
611 014	611 514	WM (Z)	611 034	611 534	TU
611 015	611 515	WM (Z)	611 035	611 535	WM (Z)
611 016	611 516	WM (Z)	611 036	611 536	TU (Z)
611 017	611 517	WM (Z)	611 037	611 537	WM (Z)
611 018	611 518	WM (Z)	611 038	611 538	WM (Z)
611 019	611 519	WM (Z)	611 039	611 539	WM (Z)
611 020	611 520	TU (Z)	611 040	611 540	WM (Z)
611 021	611 521	TU	611 041	611 541	WM (Z)
611 022	611 522	WM (Z)	611 042	611 542	WM (Z)
611 023	611 523	TU (Z)	611 043	611 543	WM (Z)
611 024	611 524	WM (Z)	611 044	611 544	WM (Z)
611 025	611 525	WM (Z)	611 045	611 545	TU
611 026	611 526	WM (Z)	611 046	611 546	TU
611 027	611 527	WM (Z)	611 047	611 547	WM (Z)
611 028	611 528	WM (Z)	611 048	611 548	WM (Z)
611 029	611 529	WM (Z)	611 049	611 549	WM (Z)
611 030	611 530	WM (Z)	611 050	611 550	WM (Z)

▲ 611 043 stands at Ulm Hbf on 12 February 2018 having arrived with a service from Sigmaringen. Operation of Ulm to Neustadt (Schwarzwald) via Sigmaringen services was due to switch to Class 612 in early 2018, although a shortage of available Class 612 units delayed this by a few weeks.
Keith Fender

CLASS 612   REGIO SWINGER   2-CAR UNITS

This class was designed as a follow-on order to the 611s and again tilt is featured. An extra set was provided as a mobile laboratory with car 612 902 fitted with a pantograph and camera. When there were problems with Class 605s on the Nürnberg–Hof route they were replaced by 612s which were painted in IC livery and renumbered by adding 300 to the number. These are back in Regio use now and back in red. However the numbers never reverted back to the original ones. Over the years there have been various problems with the tilt, with the apparatus being isolated and then reinstated many times. Currently it is understood that the apparatus is back in use. Ulm units have had a major refresh and have been turned out in the new Baden-Württemberg livery. Seating has been altered with accommodation now reported as 8/138 in a two-car set with the second class vehicle now incorporating a multi-purpose area with space for bicycles. Other new features are a wheelchair lift, wifi and CCTV.

Set 612 016 was involved in a fire and withdrawn, with 612 516 becoming 612 508[II]. Set 612 063 was withdrawn following a crash at a level crossing.

AB + B (DMCO–DMSO).

Built: 1998–2003.
Builder: Adtranz Hennigsdorf.
Wheel Arrangement: 2-B + B-2.
Engine: One 12 cylinder Cummins QSK 19 of 559 kW. **Weight:** 119 tonnes.
Transmission: Hydraulic.   **Length over Couplers:** 30.875 + 30.875 m.
Accommodation: 24/37 (10) + –/71 (4) 1TD.   **Maximum Speed:** 160 km/h.
Non-Standard Livery: N New Baden-Württemberg livery of white, black and yellow.

612 001	612 501		MKP	612 041			FK
612 002	612 502		MKP	612 042	612 542		FK
612 003	612 503		MKP	612 043	612 543		FK
612 004	612 504		MKP	612 044	612 544		FK
612 005	612 505	N	TU	612 045	612 545		FK
612 006	612 506	N	TU	612 046	612 546		FK
612 007	612 507		MKP	612 047	612 547		FK
612 008	612 508[II]	N	TU	612 048	612 548		FK
612 009	612 509		TU	612 049	612 549		FK
612 010	612 510		FK	612 050	612 550		FK
612 011	612 511		MKP	612 051	612 551	N	TU
612 012	612 512		MKP	612 052	612 552		WM (Z)
612 013	612 513		MKP	612 053	612 553	N	TU
612 014	612 514		TU	612 054	612 554	N	TU
612 015	612 515	N	TU	612 055	612 555		NHO
612 017	612 517		MKP	612 056	612 556		NHO
612 018	612 518		TU	612 057	612 557		MKP
612 019	612 519		TU	612 058	612 558		MKP
612 020	612 520		TU	612 059	612 559		MKP
612 021	612 521		TU	612 061	612 561		NHO
612 022	612 522		UE	612 062	612 562		NHO
612 023	612 523		UE	612 064	612 564		NHO
612 024	612 524		UE	612 065	612 565		NHO
612 025	612 525		UE	612 066	612 566		NHO
612 026	612 526		UE	612 067	612 567		NHO
612 027	612 527		UE	612 069	612 569		TU
612 028	612 528		UE	612 071	612 571		TU
612 029	612 529		UE	612 072	612 572		TU
612 030	612 530		UE	612 073	612 573		MKP
612 031	612 531		UE	612 074	612 574		MKP
612 032	612 532		UE	612 075	612 575		MKP
612 033	612 533		UE	612 076	612 576		MKP
612 034	612 534		UE	612 077	612 577		MKP
612 035	612 535		UE	612 078	612 578		FK (Z)
612 036	612 536		UE	612 079	612 579		MKP
612 037	612 537		TU	612 080	612 580		MKP
612 038	612 538		FK	612 081	612 581		MKP
612 039	612 539		FK	612 082	612 582		LHAD (Z)
612 040	612 540		FK	612 083	612 583		MKP

612 084	612 584		MKP	612 114	612 614		NHO
612 085	612 585		MKP	612 115	612 615		NHO
612 086	612 586		MKP	612 116	612 616		UE
612 087	612 587		MKP	612 117	612 617		UE
612 088	612 588		MKP	612 118	612 618		MKP
612 089	612 589		MKP	612 119	612 619		MKP
612 090	612 590		MKP	612 120	612 620		MKP
612 091	612 591		MKP	612 121	612 621		MKP
612 092	612 592		NHO	612 122	612 622		TU
612 093	612 593		NHO	612 123	612 623		MKP
612 094	612 594		NHO	612 124	612 624		MKP
612 095	612 595		NHO	612 125	612 625		TU
612 096	612 596		NHO	612 126	612 626		UE
612 097	612 597		NHO	612 127	612 627		TU
612 098	612 598		NHO	612 128	612 628		TU
612 099	612 599		UE	612 129	612 629	N	TU
612 100	612 600		UE	612 130	612 630		UE
612 101	612 601		UE	612 131	612 631		TU
612 102	612 602		UE	612 132	612 632		NHO
612 103	612 603	N	TU	612 133	612 633		TU
612 104	612 604	N	TU	612 134	612 634		UE
612 105	612 605	N	TU	612 135	612 635		UE
612 106	612 606		TU	612 136	612 636		TU
612 107	612 607		TU	612 137	612 637		TU
612 108	612 608	N	TU	612 138	612 638		MKP
612 109	612 609	N	TU	612 139	612 639		TU
612 110	612 610	N	TU	612 140	612 640		NHO
612 111	612 611		TU	612 141	612 641		NHO
612 112	612 612	N	TU	612 142	612 642		TU
612 113	612 613		TU	612 143	612 643		MKP

▲ 612 054 in the new Baden-Württemberg livery is bringing up the rear of a Regional Express service leaving Stuttgart Hbf on 8 December 2017. **Keith Fender**

612 144	612 644	UE (Z)		612 169	612 669	NHO
612 145	612 645	UE		612 170	612 670	NHO
612 146	612 646	UE		612 471	612 971	NHO
612 147	612 647	UE		612 472	612 972	NHO
612 148	612 648	UE		612 173	612 673	UE
612 149	612 649	MKP		612 174	612 674	UE
612 150	612 650	MKP		612 175	612 675	UE
612 151	612 651	MKP		612 176	612 676	UE
612 152	612 652	MKP		612 477	612 977	NHO
612 153	612 653	MKP		612 178	612 678	UE
612 154	612 654	MKP		612 479	612 979	NHO
612 155	612 655	NHO		612 480	612 980	NHO
612 156	612 656	NHO		612 481	612 981	NHO
612 157	612 657	NHO		612 482	612 982	NHO
612 158	612 658	NHO		612 183	612 683	UE
612 159	612 659	MKP		612 184	612 684	UE
612 160	612 660	NHO		612 485	612 985	NHO
612 161	612 661	MKP		612 486	612 986	NHO
612 162	612 662	MKP		612 487	612 987	NHO
612 463	612 963	NHO		612 488	612 988	NHO
612 464	612 964	NHO		612 489	612 989	NHO
612 165	612 665	NHO		612 490	612 990	NHO
612 166	612 666	NHO		612 491	612 991	NHO
612 167	612 667	NHO		612 492	612 992	NHO
612 168	612 668	NHO		612 901	612 902	STMI

Names:

612 055	Bergunstadt	612 090	LINDAU
612 058	STADT HOF	612 096	MARKT NEUHAUS A.D. PEGNITZ
612 062	Stadt Schweinfurt	612 098	Landkreis Bamberg
612 074	IMMENSTADT im ALLGÄU	612 115	LANDKREIS KRONACH
612 075	Oberstdorf	612 156	Landkreis Amberg-Sulzbach
612 078	Markt Oberstaufen	612 157	LANDKREIS HOF
612 081	Buchloe	612 158	STADT HOF
612 084	Heimenkirch	612 170	LANDKREIS HOF
612 089	Sonthofen		

CLASS 614 — 3-CAR UNITS

All these units are now out of service with most remaining sets being in store at Hamm awaiting a purchaser. Some sets have been sold to eastern European countries with a view to being used by intending private operators. Sales have been few over the last five years and the scrap yards must be the eventual destination.

ABD + B + ABD (DMBCso–TSO–DMBCso).

Built: 1971–76 for DB.
Builders: Orenstein & Koppel/Uerdingen.
Wheel Arrangement: B–2 + 2–2 + 2–B.   **Weight:** 45.5 + 32 + 45.5 tonnes.
Engine: One MAN (Cummins QSK18*) of 335 kW (450 hp).
Transmission: Hydraulic.   **Length over Buffers:** 26.65 + 26.16 + 26.65 m.
Accommodation: 12/58 1T + –/88 2T + 12/58 1T.   **Maximum Speed:** 140 km/h.

	914 007		EHM (Z)		614 057		614 058	EHM (Z)
614 027	914 014	614 028	EHM (Z)		614 059		*	EHM (Z)
	914 020		EHM (Z)			914 040		EHM (Z)
614 053		*	EHM (Z)		614 083	914 035	614 084	BGD (Z)

CLASS 620   LINT 81H   3-CAR UNITS

These new units from Alstom are part of the Coradia family of DMUs but differ from previous versions as no articulation is involved so the sets are longer. In fact these would appear to be the first Alstom three car units. 38 sets were ordered for the Köln area. Surprisingly these three-car sets have four engines! The extra engine, unlike the principal engines, is for traction only not providing any power to auxiliaries and is capable of being switched off whilst in transit to save fuel. The MTU engines meet EU Stage IIIB emissions. The units additionally are fitted with selective catalytic reduction equipment that cleans exhaust gases. Soon after entering service it was realised that there was unacceptable overcrowding on some services, so it was decided to make some 622s into three-car sets by building some additional intermediate vehicles. The first publicity for the 620/621 sets called them VAREO units – Voreifel Ahrtal Rhein Eifel Oberbergisches Land und Oberes Volmetal.

ABD + B + AB (DMBCso–MSO–DMBCso).

Built: 2012–13.
Builder: Alstom Salzgitter.
Wheel Arrangement: B-2 + B-2 + B-B.   **Weight:** 45.5 + 32 + 45.5 tonnes.
Engine: MTU 6H 1800 R85L of 390kW (620.0 1 engine, 621 1 engine, 620.5 2 engines).
Transmission: Hydraulic, Voith T 320 rz.   **Length over Couplers:** 26.65 + 26.16 + 26.65 m.
Accommodation: 12/58 1T + –/88 2T + 12/58 1T.   **Maximum Speed:** 140 km/h.

620 001	621 001	620 501	KK2	620 025	621 025	620 525	KK2
620 002	621 002	620 502	KK2	620 026	621 026	620 526	KK2
620 003	621 003	620 503	KK2	620 027	621 027	620 527	KK2
620 004	621 004	620 504	KK2	620 028	621 028	620 528	KK2
620 005	621 005	620 505	KK2	620 029	621 029	620 529	KK2
620 006	621 006	620 506	KK2	620 030	621 030	620 530	KK2
620 007	621 007	620 507	KK2	620 031	621 031	620 531	KK2
620 008	621 008	620 508	KK2	620 032	621 032	620 532	KK2
620 009	621 009	620 509	KK2	620 033	621 033	620 533	KK2
620 010	621 010	620 510	KK2	620 034	621 034	620 534	KK2
620 011	621 011	620 511	KK2	620 035	621 035	620 535	KK2
620 012	621 012	620 512	KK2	620 036	621 036	620 536	KK2
620 013	621 013	620 513	KK2	620 037	621 037	620 537	KK2
620 014	621 014	620 514	KK2	620 038	621 038	620 538	KK2
620 015	621 015	620 515	KK2	620 041	621 041	620 541	KK2
620 016	621 016	620 516	KK2	620 042	621 042	620 542	KK2
620 017	621 017	620 517	KK2	620 043	621 043	620 543	KK2
620 018	621 018	620 518	KK2	620 044	621 044	620 544	KK2
620 019	621 019	620 519	KK2	620 045	621 045	620 545	KK2
620 020	621 020	620 520	KK2	620 046	621 046	620 546	KK2
620 021	621 021	620 521	KK2	620 047	621 047	620 547	KK2
620 022	621 022	620 522	KK2	620 048	621 048	620 548	KK2
620 023	621 023	620 523	KK2	620 049	621 049	620 549	KK2
620 024	621 024	620 524	KK2				

CLASS 622   LINT 54H   2-CAR UNITS

This is another new version of the Alstom Coradia family but does not feature articulation so a two-car set is longer. 18 sets were ordered for the Köln area and 24 for the Dieselnetz Südwest. The units have 3 engines, one of which may be shut down in transit to save fuel. The MTU engines meet EU Stage IIIB emissions. The units additionally are fitted with selective catalytic reduction equipment that cleans exhaust gases. As mentioned under Class 620 sets 622 010–018 had new intermediate cars added and became 620 041–49 etc. DB Regio has won the contract for Dieselnetz Ulm. 12 Lint 54s have been ordered for delivery by December 2020.

B + AB (DMSO–DMCO).

Built: 2012–13.
Builder: Alstom Salzgitter.
Wheel Arrangement: B-2 + B-B.   **Weight:**
Engine: MTU 6H 1800 R85L of 390kW (622.0 1 engine, 622.5 2 engines).
Transmission: Hydraulic, Voith T 320 rz.   **Length over Couplers:** 22.70 + 22.70 m.
Accommodation: –/64 (8) 1T + 8/48 (13).   **Maximum Speed:** 140 km/h.
Non-Standard Livery N: New "Rheinland Pfalz" livery of white giving way to red patterns and a red front end.

▲ Alstom-built 620 026 is seen forming an RB service from Köln Hbf. to Gerolstein, passing Wisskirchen, a liitle village near Euskirchen on 3 October 2015. **Matthias Müller**

▼ 622 023 is seen stabled at Kaiserslautern depot on 2 May 2018. **Brian Garvin**

622 001	622 501		KK2		622 029	622 529	N	SKL
622 002	622 502		KK2		622 030	622 530	N	SKL
622 003	622 503		KK2		622 031	622 531	N	SKL
622 004	622 504		KK2		622 032	622 532	N	SKL
622 005	622 505		KK2		622 033	622 533	N	SKL
622 006	622 506		KK2		622 034	622 534	N	SKL
622 007	622 507		KK2		622 035	622 535	N	SKL
622 008	622 508		KK2		622 036	622 536	N	SKL
622 009	622 509		KK2		622 037	622 537	N	SKL
622 021	622 521	N	SKL		622 038	622 538	N	SKL
622 022	622 522	N	SKL		622 039	622 539	N	SKL
622 023	622 523	N	SKL		622 040	622 540	N	SKL
622 024	622 524	N	SKL		622 041	622 541	N	SKL
622 025	622 525	N	SKL		622 042	622 542	N	SKL
622 026	622 526	N	SKL		622 043	622 543	N	SKL
622 027	622 527	N	SKL		622 044	622 544	N	SKL
622 028	622 528	N	SKL					

CLASS 623   LINT 42H   2-SECTION ARTICULATED UNITS

For this class the Lint 41 unit had a stronger and lengthened front end and became class 623 rather than Class 1648. The batch in northern Germany, allocated at first to Rostock, is understood to be actually based in the former private depot in Neubrandenburg. Some of the units are fitted out for working into Poland on services to Szczecin. The Kaiserslautern units work on lines in the area but also cover the branch from Weinheim (Bergstrasse) to Furth (Odenwald). Note that these units are articulated and only have two engines as opposed to three on class 622. DB Regio has won the contract for Dieselnetz Ulm. Eight Lint 42s have been ordered for delivery by December 2020.

B + AB (DMSO–DMCO).

Built: 2015.
Builder: Alstom Salzgitter.
Wheel Arrangement: B-2-B.
Engine: MTU 6H 1800 R83L of 315kW.   **Weight:** 68 tonnes.
Transmission: Mechanical.   **Length over Couplers:** 42.17 m (set).
Accommodation: –/64 (8) 1T + 8/48 (13).   **Maximum Speed:** 140 km/h.
Non-Standard Livery N: New "Rheinland Pfalz" livery of white giving way to red patterns and a red front end.

623 001	623 501	N	SKL		623 017	623 517	WN
623 002	623 502	N	SKL		623 018	623 518	WN
623 003	623 503	N	SKL		623 019	623 519	WN
623 004	623 504	N	SKL		623 020	623 520	WN
623 005	623 505	N	SKL		623 021	623 521	WN
623 006	623 506	N	SKL		623 022	623 522	WN
623 007	623 507	N	SKL		623 023	623 523	WN
623 008	623 508	N	SKL		623 024	623 524	WN
623 009	623 509	N	SKL		623 025	623 525	WN
623 010	623 510	N	SKL		623 026	623 526	WN
623 011	623 511	N	SKL		623 027	623 527	WN
623 012	623 512	N	SKL		623 028	623 528	WN
623 013	623 513	N	SKL		623 029	623 529	WN
623 014	623 514	N	SKL		623 030	623 530	WN
623 015	623 515		WN		623 031	623 531	WN
623 016	623 516		WN				

Names:

623 026   Seebad Ueckermünde | 623 031   Szczecin

CLASS 628.2   2-CAR UNITS

The production series of lightweight DMUs for branch line use based on the 628.0 and 628.1 prototypes. Most units are fitted out for driver only operation whereby the driver can issue tickets as passengers join, but with the installation of ticket machines at stations this is rarely the case these days. Some power cars have been rebuilt as Class 629 and paired with another 628 power car. The displaced trailers are spare or scrapped. The early units are now being replaced by more modern units from Alstom resulting in most of the early 628.2 being withdrawn and stored at Hamm or Karsdorf awaiting sale or scrapping.

B + AB (DMSO–DTCO).

Built: 1987 onwards for DB.
Builders: Duewag, Uerdingen, LHB Salzgitter, MBB Donauwörth, AEG Hennigsdorf.
Wheel Arrangement: 2–B + 2–2.   **Weight:** 40 + 28 tonnes.
Engine: 12 cylinder Daimler Benz OM 444A of 410 kW.
Transmission: Hydraulic, Voith T 320 rz.   **Length over Couplers:** 22.70 + 22.70 m.
Accommodation: –/64 (8) 1T + 10/48 (13).   **Maximum Speed:** 120 km/h.

628 202	928 202	UKF (Z)		628 260	928 260	UKF (Z)
628 203	928 203	UKF (Z)			928 261	RL (Z)
628 204	928 204	UKF (Z)		628 262	928 262	UKF (Z)
628 205	928 205	UKF (Z)		628 264	928 264	UKF (Z)
628 206	928 206	UKF (Z)		628 265	928 265	FSK (Z)
628 207	928 207	RL		628 266	928 266	UKF (Z)
628 208	928 208	UKF (Z)		628 267	928 267	FSK
628 209	928 209	UKF (Z)		628 268	928 268	UKF (Z)
628 210	928 210	UKF (Z)		628 269	928 269	FL (Z)
628 211	928 211	UKF (Z)		628 270	928 270	FSK (Z)
628 213	928 213	UKF (Z)		628 271	928 271	RL (Z)
628 214	928 214	RL		628 272	928 272	UKF (Z)
628 215	928 215	EHM (Z)		628 273	928 273	UKF (Z)
628 216	928 216	UKF (Z)		628 274	928 274	UKF (Z)
628 217	928 217	UKF (Z)		628 278	928 278	TU
628 218	928 218	UKF (Z)		628 280	928 280	RL (Z)
628 220	928 220	UKF (Z)		628 281	928 281	UKF (Z)
628 222	928 349	UKF (Z)		628 282	928 282	UKF (Z)
628 223	928 223	FK (Z)			928 284	UKF (Z)
628 224	928 224	FSK		628 287	928 287	UKF (Z)
628 225	928 225	FK		628 288	928 288	RL (Z)
628 226	928 226	FK (Z)		628 289	928 289	FSK (Z)
628 227	928 227	FK		628 290	928 290	UKF (Z)
628 228	928 228	FK		628 291	928 291	UKF (Z)
628 229	928 229	FSK		628 292	928 292	UKF (Z)
628 230	928 230	UKF (Z)		628 293	928 293	UKF (Z)
628 231	928 231	FSK		628 294	928 294	UKF (Z)
628 232	928 232	FSK		628 295	928 295	RL (Z)
628 234	928 234	FSK		628 296	928 296	UKF (Z)
628 235	928 235	FK (Z)		628 297	928 297	UKF (Z)
628 236	928 236	TU		628 298	928 298	FSK
628 237	928 237	UKF (Z)		628 299	928 299	UKF (Z)
628 238	928 238	UKF (Z)		628 300	928 300	UKF (Z)
628 240	928 240	UKF (Z)		628 301		UKF (Z)
628 243	928 243	UKF (Z)		628 303		UKF (Z)
628 245	928 245	UKF (Z)		628 305		UKF (Z)
628 247	928 247	UKF (Z)		628 308	928 308	UKF (Z)
628 248	928 248	UKF (Z)		628 309	928 309	UKF (Z)
628 249	928 249	UKF (Z)		628 310		UKF (Z)
628 250	928 250	FK		628 311	928 311	FL
628 251	928 251	FSK		628 312	928 312	UKF (Z)
628 252	928 252	FK		628 313		TU
	928 253	UKF (Z)		628 314	928 314	FSK
628 254	928 254	UKF (Z)		628 316	928 316	UKF (Z)
628 255	928 255	FK		628 317	928 317	UKF (Z)
628 256	928 256	UKF (Z)		628 318	928 318	TU
	928 259	RL (Z)		628 320	928 320	UKF (Z)

628 321	928 321	UKF (Z)		628 335		UKF (Z)
628 322	928 322	UKF (Z)		628 336	928 336	UKF (Z)
628 323		UKF (Z)		628 337	928 337	TU (Z)
	928 323	RL (Z)			928 338	UKF (Z)
	928 324	RL (Z)		628 339	928 339	UKF (Z)
628 325	928 325	FSK		628 340		UKF (Z)
628 326	928 326	UKF (Z)		628 342	928 342	UKF (Z)
628 327	928 327	FSK		628 345	928 345	UKF (Z)
628 328	928 328	UKF (Z)		628 346	928 346	UKF (Z)
628 329	928 329	FL (Z)		628 347		TU
628 330	928 330	UKF (Z)			928 347	UKF (Z)
628 331	928 331	UKF (Z)		628 348	928 348	TU
628 332	928 332	FSK			928 349	RL
	928 333	UKF (Z)		628 350	928 350	UKF (Z)
628 334	928 334	UKF (Z)				

Names:

628 206	Niedersachsen	628 255	Stadt Bad Laasphe
628 223	Gemeinde Burgwald	628 328	Landkreis Limburg-Weilburg
628 228	Region Siegen-Wittgenstein	628 345	Landkreis Altenkirchen
628 250	Region Burgwald-Ederbergland		

▲ 628 507 is used on Sylt Shuttle plus services from Westerland (Sylt) to Bredstedt, as can be seen from the markings applied to the unit's bodyside. It is seen on just such a working leaving Westerland on 26 September 2016. **Matthias Müller**

CLASS 628.4   2-CAR UNITS

The Class 628/4 features a more powerful engine, wider middle-entry doors and a different, more comfortable seat design. Sets 405–408 were not taken into DB stock being diverted to the EVB (Eisenbahnen und Verkehrsbetriebe Elbe-Weser GmbH). An interesting development in recent years has been the transfer of some units to Fernverkehr which uses them attached to car shuttles between Westerland and Niebüll, which on arrival at Niebüll shunt off into the station with some continuing south as ordinary passenger trains. Note that these are Fernverkehr services and local tickets may not be valid. Many units are now stored by DB as a result of losing services to private operators.

B + AB (DMSO–DTCO).

Built: 1993–95.
Builders: Duewag, Uerdingen, LHB Salzgitter, MBB Donauwörth, AEG Hennigsdorf.
Wheel Arrangement: B–2 + 2–2.
Engine: 12 cyl MTU of 485 kW.   **Weight:** 40 + 29 tonnes.
Transmission: Hydraulic, Voith T 320 rz.   **Length over Couplers:** 23.20 + 23.20 m.
Accommodation: –/62 (8) 1T + 12/48 (14).   **Maximum Speed:** 120 km/h.
Non-Standard Livery N: White and red.

628 401	928 401		UKF (Z)	628 450	928 450		UKF (Z)
628 402	928 402		FK (Z)	628 451	928 451		RL (Z)
628 403	928 403		UKF (Z)	628 452	928 452		RL
628 404	928 404		UKF (Z)	628 453	928 453		RL
628 409	928 409		UKF (Z)	628 454	928 454		SKL (Z)
628 410	928 410		UKF (Z)	628 455	928 455		RL
628 411	928 411		UKF (Z)	628 457	928 457		EHM (Z)
628 412	928 412		UKF (Z)	628 458	928 458		EHM (Z)
628 413	928 413		UKF (Z)	628 459	928 459		UKF (Z)
628 414	928 414		UKF (Z)	628 460	928 460		EHM (Z)
628 415	928 415		UKF (Z)	628 461	928 461		EHM (Z)
628 416	928 416		UKF (Z)	628 462	928 462		EHM (Z)
628 417	928 417		S KL (Z)	628 464	928 464		UKF (Z)
628 418	928 418		UKF (Z)	628 465	928 465		SKL
628 419	928 419		FK (Z)	628 466	928 466		SKL
628 420	928 420		UKF (Z)	628 467	928 467		SKL
628 421	928 421		UKF (Z)	628 468	928 468		UKF (Z)
628 422	928 422		MMF	628 469	928 469		UKF (Z)
628 423	928 423		MMF	628 470	928 470		SKL
628 424	928 424	A	MMF	628 471	928 471		SKL
628 425	928 425		MMF	628 472	928 472		SKL
628 426	928 426		MMF	628 473	928 473		SKL
628 427	928 427		UKF (Z)	628 474	928 474		SKL
628 428	928 428		UKF (Z)	628 475	928 475		SKL
628 429	928 429		FK (Z)	628 476	928 476		RL
628 430	928 430		UKF (Z)	628 477	928 477		SKL
628 431	928 431		FSK	628 478	928 478		UKF (Z)
628 432	928 432		MMF	628 479	928 479		SKL
628 433	928 433		MMF	628 480	928 480		SKL
628 434	928 434		EDO	628 483	928 483		FSK
628 435	928 435		BLO	628 484	928 484		UKF (Z)
628 436	928 436		FSK	628 485	928 485		UKF (Z)
628 437	928 437		UKF (Z)	628 486	928 486		FSK
628 438	928 438		TU	628 487	928 487		SKL
628 439	928 439		UKF (Z)	628 488	928 488		SKL (Z)
628 440	928 440		UKF (Z)	628 489	928 489		UKF (Z)
628 441	928 441		RL	628 490	928 490		FSK
628 442	928 442		EHM (Z)	628 491	928 491		FSK (Z)
628 443	928 443		UKF (Z)	628 492	928 492		RL (Z)
628 444	928 444		RL (Z)	628 494	928 494		RL (Z)
628 445	928 445		RL	628 495	928 495	N	AN
628 446	928 446		UKF (Z)	628 496	928 496		FSK
628 447	928 447		RL	628 497	928 497		UKF (Z)
628 448	928 448		UKF (Z)	628 498	928 498		UKF (Z)
628 449	928 449		UKF (Z)	628 499	928 499		EHM (Z)

628	928	N		628	928	
628 500	928 500		UKF (Z)	628 573	928 573	MMF (Z)
628 501	928 501	N	AN	628 574	928 574	MMF
628 502	928 502	N	AN	628 575	928 575	MMF
628 503	928 503	N	AN (Z)	628 576	928 576	MMF
628 504	928 504		UKF (Z)	628 577	928 577	MMF
628 507	928 507	N	AN	628 578	928 578	MMF
628 508	928 508		UKF (Z)	628 579	928 579	UKF (Z)
628 509	928 509	N	AN	628 580	928 580	MMF
628 510	928 510		UKF (Z)	628 581	928 581	MMF
628 511	928 511		EDO (Z)	628 582	928 582	RL (Z)
628 512	928 512	N	AN	628 583	928 583	UKF (Z)
628 514	928 514		UKF (Z)	628 584	928 584	MMF
628 515	928 515		UKF (Z)	628 585	928 585	MMF
628 516	928 516		UKF (Z)	628 586	928 586	BLO
628 517	928 517		EDO (Z)	628 587	928 587	UKF (Z)
628 518	928 518		EDO	628 588	928 588	UKF (Z)
628 519	928 519		FSK	628 589	928 589	MMF
628 521	928 521	N	AN	628 591	928 591	MMF
628 522	(628 696)		SKL	628 592	928 592	RL (Z)
628 523	928 523		TU	628 593	928 593	MMF
628 526	928 526		FSK (Z)	628 594	928 594	FSK
628 527	928 527		EDO (Z)	628 595	928 595	UKF (Z)
628 528	928 528		UKF (Z)	628 596	928 596	MMF
628 529	928 529		UKF (Z)	628 597	928 597	DC
628 530	928 530		UKF (Z)	628 598	928 598	RL (Z)
628 531	928 531		UKF (Z)	628 599	928 599	UKF (Z)
628 532	928 532	N	AN	628 600	928 600	HBS
628 533	928 533		FSK	628 601	928 601	RL (Z)
628 534	928 534		UKF (Z)	628 602	928 602	RL (Z)
628 535	928 535	N	AN	628 603	928 603	RL (Z)
628 536	928 536		EDO (Z)	628 604	928 604	RL (Z)
628 537	928 537		UKF (Z)	628 605	928 605	RL (Z)
628 538	928 538		UKF (Z)	628 606	928 606	UKF (Z)
628 539	928 539		UKF (Z)	628 607	928 607	FL (Z)
628 540	928 540	N	AN	628 608	928 608	HBS (Z)
628 541	928 541		UKF (Z)	628 609	928 609	UKF (Z)
628 542	928 542		TU	628 610	928 610	UKF (Z)
628 543	928 543		MMF	628 611	928 611	RL
628 544	928 544		MMF	628 612	928 612	MMF
628 546	928 546		UKF (Z)	628 613	928 613	UKF (Z)
628 547	928 547		UKF (Z)	628 614	928 614	RL (Z)
628 548	928 548		TU	628 615	928 615	RL (Z)
628 549	928 549		TU	628 616	928 616	RL (Z)
628 550	928 550		UKF (Z)	628 617	928 617	EHM (Z)
628 551	928 551		FSK	628 618	928 618	MMF
628 552	928 552		UKF (Z)	628 620	928 620	UKF (Z)
628 553	928 553		FSK	628 622	928 622	FK (Z)
628 554	928 554		UKF (Z)	628 623	928 623	FSK
628 555	928 555		UKF (Z)	628 624	928 624	EHM (Z)
628 556	928 556		BLO	628 625	928 625	HBS
628 558	928 558		MMF	628 626	928 626	SKL
628 559	928 559		MMF	628 627	928 627	MMF
628 560	928 560		MMF (Z)	628 628	928 628	MMF
628 561	928 561		UKF (Z)	628 629	928 629	MMF
628 562	928 562		UKF (Z)	628 630	928 630	MMF
628 563	928 563		AK	628 632	928 632	UKF (Z)
628 564	928 564		MMF	628 633	928 633	BLO
628 565	928 565		MMF	628 634	928 634	RL (Z)
628 566	928 566		MMF	628 636	928 636	RL
628 567	928 567		MMF	628 637	928 637	UKF (Z)
628 568	928 568		MMF	628 638	928 638	UKF (Z)
628 570	928 570		MMF	628 639	928 639	MMF
628 571	928 571		MMF	628 640	928 640	HBS
628 572	928 572		MMF	628 641	928 641	UKF (Z)

628 643	928 643	HBS (Z)		628 675	928 675	UKF (Z)
628 644	928 644	FSK		628 676	928 676	UKF (Z)
628 645	928 645	FSK		628 678	928 678	MMF
628 646	928 646	MMF		628 681	928 681	UKF (Z)
628 647	928 647	UKF (Z)		628 682	928 682	UKF (Z)
628 648	928 648	UKF (Z)		628 683	928 683	UKF (Z)
628 649	928 649	MMF		628 684	928 684	EHM (Z)
628 650	928 650	WR		628 685	928 685	FSK
628 653	928 653	MMF		628 686	928 686	FSK
628 655	928 655	RL		628 687	928 687	EHM (Z)
628 656	928 656	BLO		628 688	928 688	FSK
628 657	928 657	BLO		628 689	928 689	UKF (Z)
628 660	928 660	EDO (Z)		628 691	928 691	UKF (Z)
628 661	928 661	UKF (Z)		628 693	928 693	RL
628 662	928 662	UKF (Z)		628 694	928 694	UKF (Z)
628 663	928 663	UKF (Z)		628 695	928 695	UKF (Z)
628 664	928 664	UKF (Z)		628 696	628 253	TU
628 665	928 665	UKF (Z)		628 697	928 697	UKF (Z)
628 666	928 666	UKF (Z)		628 698	928 698	EDO
628 667	928 667	UKF (Z)		628 699	928 699	UKF (Z)
628 668	928 668	FSK		628 700	928 700	UKF (Z)
628 669	928 669	EHM (Z)		628 701	928 701	TU
628 670	928 670	UKF (Z)		628 702	928 702	MMF
628 671	928 671	EHM (Z)		628 703	928 703	TU
628 672	928 672	EHM (Z)		628 704	928 704	EHM (Z)
628 673	928 673	FSK		628 705	928 705	UKF (Z)
628 674	928 674	EHM (Z)				

Names:

628 423	Stadt Bogen		628 576	Garching a.d. Alz
628 432	STADT RIED IM INNKREIS		628 577	LANDKREIS STRAUBING BOGEN
628 501	Hörnum		628 578	GEMEINDE ZUBEN
628 502	Keitum		628 591	Pfarrkirchen
628 509	Westerland(Sylt)		628 593	WALD KRAIBURG
628 512	Kampen		628 612	STADT TRAUNREUT
628 521	Archsum		628 626	Waging am See
628 535	Wenningstedt-Braderup		628 627	MARKT TÜSSLING
628 540	Rantum		628 628	STADT MÜHLDORF AM INN
628 560	LANDKREIS ALTÖTTLING		628 629	Julbach
628 572	STADT WALDKRAIBURG		628 630	Stadt Traunstein

CLASS 628.9/629   2-CAR UNITS

When first introduced these units were two Class 628.4 back to back. They replaced the last of the original order for 628.4 as it was found a power car + trailer were under-powered when working on the Mainz–Alzey line. Thus the order was changed for extra power cars. Later, as 628.2 units became spare, pairs of these power cars were put together with the trailers being made spare or scrapped. Some sets have been created for use in other areas.

B + AB (DMSO–DMCO).

Built: 1995 (1999*).
Builders: Duewag, Uerdingen, LHB Salzgitter, MBB Donauwörth, AEG Hennigsdorf.
Wheel Arrangement: B–2 + 2–B.
Engine: 12 cylinder MTU of 485 kW.   **Weight:** 40 + 40 tonnes.
Transmission: Hydraulic, Voith T 320 rz.   **Length over Couplers:** 23.20 + 23.20 m.
Accommodation: –/64 1T (8) + 10/48 (13).   **Maximum Speed:** 120 km/h.

628 906 ex 628 522, 629 006 ex 928 607.

Class 628.9

628 901	629 001	TU		628 904	629 004		TU
628 902	629 002	TU		628 905	629 005		TU
628 903	629 003	TU (Z)		628 906	629 006	*	TU

Class 629

629 288	(628 259)	RL	629 313	(628 276)	STR
629 301	(628 257)	UKF (Z)	629 335	(628 345)	TU
629 303	(628 233)	UKF (Z)	629 340	(628 341)	UKF (Z)
629 305	(628 263)	UKF (Z)	629 347	(628 333)	TU

CLASS 632　　　PESA LINK II　　　2-SECTION ARTICULATED UNITS

The Polish firm of PESA received an order from Regentalbahn AG for 12 2-car DMUs for its Oberpfalzbahn network. The prototype was shown at Innotrans 2012. The trains started to arrive in 2014, but the units had not been cleared for operation by the EBA. This process was so drawn out that the order was eventually cancelled and replaced by Alstom units. In the meantime DB had contracted to acquire many units ranging from single cars to three-car sets, ordering 20 sets for the Sauerland services from Dortmund in 2013 for delivery in 2016. But the authority to run in Germany for the DB units was still outstanding. It eventually came in 2018. Other units on order by DB are two for the DB Dreiech services.

Built: 2015–
Builder: PESA.
Wheel Arrangement: B-2-B.
Engine: Two MTU 6H 1800 R85L of 390 kW.
Transmission: Hydrodynamic.
Maximum Tractive Effort:
Wheel Diameter:
Accommodation: 8/102 1TD 2W, 12 bicycles.

Weight: 86.5 tonnes.
Length Over Couplers: 43.73 m.
Door Step Height: 600 mm.
Maximum Speed: 140 km/h

632 101	632 601		632 111	632 611	EDO
632 102	632 602	EDO	632 112	632 612	EDO
632 103	632 603	EDO	632 113	632 613	EDO
632 104	632 604	EDO	632 114	632 614	
632 105	632 605	EDO	632 115	632 615	
632 106	632 606	EDO	632 116	632 616	
632 107	632 607	EDO	632 117	632 617	
632 108	632 608	EDO	632 118	632 618	
632 109	632 609	EDO	632 119	632 619	
632 110	632 610	EDO	632 120	632 620	

▲ After several years of teething troubles, PESA-built Class 632 finally received clearance for operation by the EBA and began to enter service in July 2018. 632 107 leaves Ludenscheid Brügge with an RB52 service from Ludenscheid to Dortmund on 13 September 2018. **Keith Fender**

CLASS 633 PESA LINK III 3-SECTION ARTICULATED UNITS

As mentioned above, DB ordered 16 3-section units for the Sauerland services in 2013. Now that the 2-section units have arrived, perhaps the 633s will soon follow – but have they been authorized to run in Germany? Two other orders are known, being seven sets for the DB Dreiech services and 26 for the Diesel Netz Allgau although the latter were ordered for delivery in 2020.

Built: 2015–
Builder: PESA.
Wheel Arrangement: B-2-2-B.
Engine: Two (?) of 625 kW.
Transmission: Hydrodynamic.
Maximum Tractive Effort:
Wheel Diameter:
Accommodation: 12/148 1TD 2W, 36 bicycles.

Weight: 120.4 tonnes.
Length Over Couplers: 60.77 m.
Door Step Height: 600 mm.
Maximum Speed: 140 km/h.

633 001	933 001	633 501	633 009	933 009	633 509
633 002	933 002	633 502	633 010	933 010	633 510
633 003	933 003	633 503	633 011	933 011	633 511
633 004	933 004	633 504	633 012	933 012	633 512
633 005	933 005	633 505	633 013	933 013	633 513
633 006	933 006	633 506	633 014	933 014	633 514
633 007	933 007	633 507	633 015	933 015	633 515
633 008	933 008	633 508	633 016	933 016	633 516

CLASS 640 LINT 27 SINGLE CAR

30 of these single car LINT 27 were ordered on 21/06/96 (LINT = *Leichter Innovativer Nahverkehrs Triebwagen*; 27 = length in metres and now given the brand name Coradia). They were ordered along with many others to re-equip local services and give a good start to the 21st Century, not to mention the State giving the soon-to-be privatised railways lots of modern stock to be inherited by private buyers! They have welded stainless steel bodies, low floors, magnetic brakes, Scharfenberg couplers, and vacuum-toilets. Two sets of access doors. The cabs also have modern safety fittings etc including Sifa STG 545, Indusi I60R, Zugbahnfunk ZFM 90. Originally all were based at Dortmund but now Limburg and Braunschweig have allocations. Most at the latter place are already stored.

AB (DMCO).

Built: 2000–01.
Builders: Alstom/LHB.
Wheel Arrangement: B-2.
Engine: Two six-cylinder MTU 6R 183 TD 13H of 315 kW at 1900 rpm.
Transmission: Hydrodynamic, Voith T211rzze.
Wheel Diameter: 770 mm.
Accommodation: 8/52 (13).

Weight: 40.5 tonnes.
Floor Height: 580 mm.
Length over Couplers: 27.21 m.
Maximum Speed: 120 km/h.

640 001	EDO	640 011	EDO	640 021	EDO
640 002	EDO	640 012	UE	640 022	HBS
640 003	EDO	640 013	FL	640 023	HBS
640 004	EDO	640 014	EDO	640 024	HBS
640 005	WM (Z)	640 015	FL	640 025	EDO
640 006	FL	640 016	EDO	640 026	HBS
640 007	WM (Z)	640 017	FL	640 027	HBS
640 008	EDO	640 018	EDO	640 028	EDO
640 009	EDO	640 019	FL	640 029	EDO
640 010	FL	640 020	HBS	640 030	HBS

CLASS 641 SINGLE CAR

40 of these units were ordered on 21/06/96 with the Limburg area expected to get the first units. In fact it got none and instead the units took over stopping services from Basel to Waldshut and similar work in Thüringen. The units are in fact basically the same as the SNCF TER sets of Class X 73500. Features include magnetic brakes, Scharfenberg couplers, and a welded aluminium body bolted to steel frames. Cabs are glass reinforced plastic. Magnetic brakes. 641 024/30 have been withdrawn following accident damage. The Germans called these units "Whales"

AB (DMCO).

Built: 2000–02.
Builders: Alstom/LHB, De Dietrich.
Wheel Arrangement: 1A-A1.
Engine: Two MAN D2866 LH21 of 257 kW.   **Weight:** 47 tonnes.
Transmission: Hydrodynamic.   **Length over Couplers:** 28.90 m.
Wheel Diameter: 840 mm.   **Floor Height:**
Accommodation: 8/55 (17).   **Maximum Speed:** 140 km/h.
Non-Standard Livery: N Silver.

641 001	LL1		641 020	UE	
641 002	RHL	Bad Säckingen	641 021	UE	
641 003	LL1		641 022	UE	
641 004	RHL	Laufenburg	641 023	UE	
641 005	WM		641 025	NHO	
641 006	RHL	Schwörstadt	641 026	NHO	Markt Stammbach
641 007	WM		641 027	LL1	
641 008	RHL		641 028	NHO	Kulmbach
641 009	RHL	Albbruck	641 029	RHL	
641 010	RHL	Klettgau	641 031	NHO	Neuenmarkt-Wirsberg
641 011	RHL	Haltingen	641 032	UE	
641 012	UE	Lauchringen	641 034	**N**	LL1
641 013	RHL	Basel	641 035	LL1	
641 014	RHL	Wehr	641 036	UE	
641 015	RHL	Murg	641 037	NHO	
641 016	RHL	Grenzach-Wyhlen	641 038	NHO	Trebgast
641 017	RHL	Dogern	641 039	NHO	
641 018	RHL		641 040	NHO	
641 019	UE				

CLASS 642 2-SECTION ARTICULATED UNITS

150 of these articulated two-car units were ordered on 21/06/96 and were known at that time as the Duewag RVT2.2, but after the Siemens takeover of Duewag the marketing name of "*Desiro*" was applied. Welded aluminium features for the body whilst the cabs are glass-reinforced plastic. There is rubber primary and air secondary suspension; Scharfenberg couplers. SIBAS microprocessor control system allows four sets to work in multiple. The arrival of these units saw off many locos of Classes 202, 211, 212, 215 and 219. At Innotrans 2012, DB presented set 642 129 as a hybrid unit – an electro-diesel. This unit now has two MTU hybrid power packs of 315 kW from MTU 6H1800R75 engines. There is an alternator and an electric motor which is connected to the hydrodynamic gearbox. Additionally there is a lithium phosphate battery charged from the diesel engines but also by kinetic energy from braking. The unit is being tested in various areas with a view to converting more units if the scheme is judged successful. Nothing more has been heard of this project and the unit is now stored at Chemnitz.

B + AB (DMSO–DMCO).

Built: 1999–2003.
Builder: Siemens-Duewag.
Wheel Arrangement: B-2-B.
Engine: Two MTU engines of 275 kW.   **Weight:** 64 + 86 tonnes.
Transmission: Hydrodynamic.   **Length over Couplers:** 20.35 + 20.35 m.
Wheel Diameter: 770 mm.   **Floor height:**
Accommodation: –/45 (13) + 12/53.   **Maximum Speed:** 120 km/h.

*   Fitted with PKP safety systems for working between Dresden and Wrocław.

642 001	642 501		SKL	642 066	642 566		FGM
642 002	642 502		FGM	642 067	642 567		FGM
642 003	642 503		FGM	642 068	642 568		FGM
642 004	642 504		FGM	642 069	642 569		FGM
642 005	642 505		MKP	642 070	642 570		FGM
642 006	642 506		FSK	642 071	642 571		FGM
642 007	642 507		SKL	642 072	642 572		UE
642 008	642 508		MKP	642 073	642 573		SKL
642 009	642 509		UE	642 074	642 574		NN1
642 010	642 510		MKP	642 075	642 575		NN1
642 011	642 511		MKP	642 076	642 576		NN1
642 012	642 512		FGM	642 077	642 577		MKP
642 013	642 513		FGM	642 078	642 578		WR
642 014	642 514		NN1	642 079	642 579		WR
642 015	642 515		FGM	642 080	642 580		NN1
642 017	642 517		FGM	642 081	642 581		NN1
642 018	642 518		UE	642 082	642 582		MKP
642 019	642 519		SKL	642 083	642 583		MKP
642 020	642 520		UE	642 084	642 584		MKP
642 021	642 521		FGM	642 085	642 585		MKP
642 022	642 522		UE	642 086	642 586		MKP
642 023	642 523		UE	642 087	642 587		MKP
642 024	642 524		SKL	642 088	642 588		MKP
642 025	642 525		UE	642 089	642 589		MKP
642 026	642 526		FGM	642 090	642 590		MKP
642 027	642 527		FGM	642 091	642 591		MKP
642 028	642 528		DCX	642 092	642 592		RL
642 029	642 529		SKL	642 093	642 593		MKP
642 030	642 530		UE	642 094	642 594		MKP
642 031	642 531		UE	642 095	642 595		SKL
642 032	642 532		DA	642 096	642 596		NN1
642 033	642 533	*	DA	642 097	642 597		MKP
642 034	642 534	*	DA	642 098	642 598		MKP
642 035	642 535		DA	642 099	642 599		MKP
642 036	642 536		SKL	642 100	642 600		MKP
642 037	642 537	A	DA	642 101	642 601		MKP
642 038	642 538		DA	642 102	642 602		SKL
642 039	642 539	*	DA	642 103	642 603		SKL
642 040	642 540		DA	642 104	642 604		SKL
642 041	642 541		DA	642 105	642 605		SKL
642 042	642 542		FK	642 106	642 606		SKL
642 043	642 543	*	DA	642 107	642 607		SKL
642 044	642 544		FK	642 108	642 608		SKL
642 045	642 545		FK	642 109	642 609		SKL
642 046	642 546		FK	642 110	642 610		SKL
642 047	642 547		FK	642 111	642 611		SKL
642 048	642 548		WR	642 112	642 612		SKL
642 049	642 549		WR	642 113	642 613		NN1
642 050	642 550		WR	642 114	642 614		NN1
642 051	642 551		WR	642 115	642 615		NN1
642 052	642 552		WR	642 116	642 616		NN1
642 053	642 553		WR	642 117	642 617		NN1
642 054	642 554		WR	642 118	642 618		NN1
642 055	642 555		DCX	642 119	642 619		NN1
642 056	642 556		DCX	642 120	642 620		MKP
642 057	642 557		DCX (Z)	642 121	642 621		MKP
642 058	642 558		DCX	642 122	642 622		MKP
642 059	642 559		DCX	642 123	642 623		MKP
642 060	642 560		FK	642 124	642 624		FSK
642 061	642 561		FSK	642 125	642 625	A	FSK
642 062	642 562		FK	642 126	642 626		FSK
642 063	642 563		FGM	642 127	642 627		FSK
642 064	642 564		FGM	642 128	642 628		FSK
642 065	642 565		MKP	642 129	642 629		DCX (Z)

642 130	642 630	DA		642 165	642 665	LMB
642 131	642 631	FGM		642 166	642 666	LMB
642 132	642 632	MKP		642 167	642 667	FSK
642 133	642 633	FGM		642 168	642 668	LMB
642 134	642 634	FGM		642 169	642 669	LMB (Z)
642 135	642 635	FK		642 170	642 670	LMB
642 136	642 636	NN1		642 171	642 671	LMB
642 137	642 637	FK		642 172	642 672	DCX (Z)
642 138	642 638	FGM		642 173	642 673	LMB
642 139	642 639	FGM		642 174	642 674	LMB
642 140	642 640	NN1		642 175	642 675	RL
642 141	642 641	NN1		642 176	642 676	LMB
642 142	642 642	RL		642 177	642 677	SKL
642 143	642 643	FK		642 178	642 678	MKP
642 144	642 644	FK		642 179	642 679	FK
642 145	642 645	FGM		642 180	642 680	SKL
642 146	642 646	FGM		642 181	642 681	SKL
642 147	642 647	FGM		642 182	642 682	FK
642 148	642 648	FK		642 183	642 683	WR
642 149	642 649	FK		642 184	642 684	WR
642 156	642 656	MKP		642 185	642 685	WR
642 157	642 657	FK		642 186	642 686	LMB
642 158	642 658	MKP		642 187	642 687	LMB
642 159	642 659	MKP		642 188	642 688	LMB
642 160	642 660	RL		642 189	642 689	LMB
642 161	642 661	DA		642 190	642 690	LMB
642 162	642 662	LMB		642 191	642 691	LMB
642 163	642 663	LMB		642 192	642 692	LMB
642 164	642 664	FSK		642 193	642 693	LMB

▲ 642 225 "Schloss Hundisburg" waits to leave Braunschweig Hbf with the 10.24 to Stendal on 13 August 2015. **Brian Garvin**

642 194	642 694	FSK		642 216	642 716	MKP
642 195	642 695	LMB		642 217	642 717	MKP
642 196	642 696	DC		642 218	642 718	MKP
642 197	642 697	FK		642 219	642 719	LMB
642 198	642 698	FSK		642 220	642 720	LMB
642 199	642 699	LMB		642 221	642 721	LMB
642 200	642 700	FK		642 222	642 722	LMB
642 201	642 701	DC		642 223	642 723	LMB
642 202	642 702	FSK		642 224	642 724	LMB
642 203	642 703	LMB		642 225	642 725	LMB
642 204	642 704	FK		642 227	642 727	LMB
642 205	642 705	FSK		642 228	642 728	DC
642 206	642 706	FSK		642 229	642 729	LMB
642 207	642 707	FSK		642 230	642 730	LMB
642 208	642 708	MKP		642 231	642 731	DC
642 209	642 709	MKP		642 232	642 732	DC
642 210	642 710	MKP		642 233	642 733	LMB
642 211	642 711	MKP		642 234	642 734	DC
642 212	642 712	MKP		642 235	642 735	DC
642 213	642 713	MKP		642 236	642 736	DC
642 214	642 714	MKP		642 237	642 737	DC
642 215	642 715	MKP		642 238	642 738	DC

Names:

642 029	Hinterweidenthal
642 036	Albersweiler
642 055	Stadt Augustusburg
642 056	Gemeinde Pockau
642 057	Stadt Wilkau-Haßlau
642 058	Berg und Adam Ries Stadt Annaberg-Buchholz
642 059	Schwarzenberg – Perle des Erzgebirge
642 082	Wittelsbacher Land
642 085	Landsberg am Lech
642 088	Bobingen
642 089	Bad Wörishofen im Allgau
642 095	Kandel
642 102	Steinalben
642 103	Bierbach
642 104	Dellfeld
642 105	Hassel
642 106	Rieschweiler – Mühlbach
642 107	Zweibrücken
642 108	Winnweiler
642 109	Langenlonsheim
642 110	Hochspeyer
642 111	Stadt Gräfenberg
642 112	Münchweiler/Alsenz
642 114	Neustadt (Aisch)
642 115	Stadt Amorbach
642 116	Markt Heroldsberg
642 117	Bad Kissingen
642 118	Stadt Roth
642 124	Liebliches Taubertal
642 127	Bad Mergentheim
642 142	Rinnthal
642 160	Hauenstein (Pfalz)
642 162	Hansestadt Gardelegen
642 164	Strasse der Romantik
642 171	Schloss Bernburg (Eulenspiegel-Express)
642 172	Anhaltisches Theater Dessau
642 173	Bioshärenreservat Karstlandschaft Südharz
642 175	Wilgartswiesen
642 180	Landau (Pfalz)
642 188	Joseph von Fraunhofer
642 190	Biosphärenreservat Mittelelbe
642 192	Gartenräume Sachsen Anhalt
642 196	Olbernhau Spielzugland im Erzgebirge
642 197	Thermalbad Wiesenbad
642 198	Zoo Magdeburg
642 199	Kaiser und Hansestadt Tangermünde
642 200	Bergstadt Langenfeld
642 201	Gemeinde Burghardtsdorf
642 202	Johann Sebastian Bach
642 203	Solepark Schönebeck/Bad Salzelmen
642 205	Stadt Miltenberg
642 206	Aschaffenburg
642 207	Amorbach
642 214	Stadt Krumbach
642 219	Sachsen Anhalt
642 220	Hansestadt Stendal
642 225	Schloss Hundisburg
642 228	Stadt Zwönitz/Erzgebirge
642 229	Naturpark Drömling
642 230	Katharina die Grosse
642 231	Kreisstadt Aue
642 232	Johanngeorgenstadt
642 233	Local Heros
642 234	Bergstadt Zschopau
642 237	Thalheim/Erzgebirge
642 238	Stadt Zwickau

CLASS 643.0   TALENT   3-SECTION ARTICULATED UNITS

Knowing that orders for new local trains were in the pipeline, Talbot got a head start by producing a prototype set which it called the TALENT (= **T**albots **Le**ichtbau **N**iederflur **T**riebwagen). The unit was sent on promotional tours and Talbot was subsequently rewarded with many orders for the units. DB Regio ordered 75 diesel mechanical and 45 diesel-electric units on 21/06/96. Steel bodies have aluminium roofs and glass-reinforced cabs. There is only one set of doors per vehicle.

B + B + AB (DMSO–TSO–DMCO).

Built: 1999–2001.
Builder: Bombardier Talbot.
Wheel Arrangement: B-2-2-B.
Engine: Two 6 cylinder MAN D2866 LH21 of 257 kW each.
Transmission: Hydrodynamic, Voith T311r.
Wheel Diameter:
Accommodation: –/24 1TD + –/40 (8) + 16/32.

Weight: 89.3 tonnes.

Length over Couplers: 48.86 m.
Floor Height: 590 mm.
Maximum Speed: 120 km/h.

643 001	943 001	643 501	SKL		643 039	943 039	643 539	FL
643 002	943 002	643 502	RK		643 040	943 040	643 540	EMST
643 003	943 003	643 503	RK		643 041	943 041	643 541	FL
643 004	943 004	643 504	RK		643 042	943 042	643 542	EMST
643 005	943 005	643 505	SKL		643 043	943 043	643 543	FL
643 006	943 006	643 506	SKL		643 044	943 044	643 544	EMST
643 007	943 007	643 507	RK		643 045	943 045	643 545	EMST
643 008	943 008	643 508	SKL		643 046	943 046	643 546	FL
643 009	943 009	643 509	RK		643 047	943 047	643 547	FL
643 010	943 010	643 510	SKL		643 048	943 048	643 548	EMST
643 011	943 011	643 511	RK		643 049	943 049	643 549	EMST
643 012	943 012	643 512	RK		643 050	943 050	643 550	FL
643 013	943 013	643 513	RK		643 051	943 051	643 551	EMST
643 014	943 014	643 514	RK		643 052	943 052	643 552	EMST
643 015	943 015	643 515	SKL		643 053	943 053	643 553	EMST (Z)
643 016	943 016	643 516	SKL		643 054	943 054	643 554	EMST
643 017	943 017	643 517	RK		643 055	943 055	643 555	EMST
643 018	943 018	643 518	RK		643 056	943 056	643 556	EMST
643 019	943 019	643 519	SKL		643 057	943 057	643 557	EMST
643 020	943 020	643 520	SKL		643 058	943 058	643 558	EMST
643 021	943 021	643 521	SKL		643 059	943 059	643 559	EMST
643 022	943 022	643 522	SKL		643 060	943 060	643 560	EMST
643 023	943 023	643 523	SKL		643 061	943 061	643 561	EMST
643 024	943 024	643 524	SKL		643 062	943 062	643 562	EMST
643 025	943 025	643 525	SKL		643 063	943 063	643 563	EMST
643 026	943 026	643 526	SKL		643 064	943 064	643 564	EMST
643 027	943 027	643 527	SKL		643 065	943 065	643 565	EMST
643 028	943 028	643 528	SKL		643 066	943 066	643 566	EMST
643 029	943 029	643 529	SKL		643 067	943 067	643 567	EMST
643 030	943 030	643 530	SKL		643 068	943 068	643 568	EMST
643 031	943 031	643 531	SKL		643 069	943 069	643 569	EMST
643 032	943 032	643 532	SKL		643 070	943 070	643 570	EMST
643 033	943 033	643 533	FL		643 071	943 071	643 571	EMST
643 034	943 034	643 534	EMST		643 072	943 072	643 572	EMST
643 035	943 035	643 535	EMST		643 073	943 073	643 573	EMST
643 036	943 036	643 536	EMST		643 074	943 074	643 574	EMST
643 037	943 037	643 537	FL		643 075	943 075	643 575	EMST
643 038	943 038	643 538	EMST					

Names:

643 001	Hochstätten/Pfalz		643 008	Schopp
643 002	Birkweiler		643 009	Steinfeld
643 003	Knöringen		643 010	Pirmasens
643 004	Kapsweyer		643 011	Steinweiler
643 005	Alsenz		643 012	Winden (Pfalz)
643 006	Horst Eckel		643 013	Schweighofen
643 007	Schaidt		643 014	Kirrweiler (Pfalz)

643 015	Ottmar Walter	643 025	Niedermohr
643 016	Fritz Walter	643 026	Landstuhl
643 017	Siebeldingen	643 027	Hirschhorn
643 018	Barbelroth	643 028	Katzweiler
643 019	Wolfstein	643 029	Kreimbach-Kaulbach
643 020	Kusel	643 031	Otterbach
643 021	Rammelsbach	643 032	Lauterecken
643 022	Theisbergstegen	643 064	GEMEENTE ENSCHEDE
643 023	Matzenbach	643 065	STADT GRONAU
643 024	Glan-Münchweiler		

CLASS 643.2   TALENT   2-SECTION ARTICULATED UNITS

This batch of units operates the EUROBAHN service around Aachen. Several freight-only lines have been reactivated for passenger use and in fact an Aachen S-Bahn system has been created which includes the service to Heerlen in the Netherlands. The units are fitted with cab systems including I160R, PZB90, ZBF and GSM-R. Four units can operate in multiple. Eventually these units will be replaced by EMUs as electrification schemes come on line.

B + AB (DMSO–DMCO).

Built: 2002–03.
Builder: Bombardier Talbot.
Wheel Arrangement: B-2-B.   **Weight:** 57 tonnes.
Engine: Two 6-cylinder MAN D2866 LH21 of 315 kW each.
Transmission: Hydrodynamic, Voith T311r.   **Length over Couplers:** 13.465 + 13.465 m.
Wheel Diameter: **Floor Height:** 800 mm.
Accommodation: –/32 (15) + 22/24.   **Maximum Speed:** 120 km/h.

643 201	643 701	KA		643 213	643 713	KA
643 202	643 702	KA		643 214	643 714	KA
643 203	643 703	KA		643 215	643 715	KA
643 204	643 704	KA		643 216	643 716	KA
643 205	643 705	KA		643 217	643 717	KA
643 206	643 706	KA		643 218	643 718	KA
643 207	643 707	KA		643 219	643 719	KA
643 208	643 708	KA		643 220	643 720	KA
643 209	643 709	KA		643 221	643 721	KA
643 210	643 710	KA		643 222	643 722	KA
643 211	643 711	KA		643 223	643 723	KA
643 212	643 712	KA		643 226	643 726	KA

CLASS 644   TALENT   3-SECTION ARTICULATED UNITS

An initial order for 45 sets was placed on 21/06/96 by DB Regio and was later increased to 63. These 3-car articulated Talbot Talents were the first of the new generation DMUs to appear and the design has been taken up by several other railway companies in Germany as well as in other countries. The units have Scharfenberg couplers, dynamic brakes (mounted on roof), welded bodies and GRP cabs. Vacuum toilets are fitted suitable for wheelchair access. The 644 is longer than the 643 and has more doors. Much larger set so thus a bigger engine. Not only that, they are used amongst the Köln area S-Bahn services so a strong acceleration was needed so allow them to stay up there with the electric trains.

AB + B + B (DMCO–TSO–DMSO).

Built: 1998–2000.
Builder: Bombardier Talbot.
Wheel Arrangement: Bo-2-2-Bo.
Engine: Two 12 cylinder MTU 12V183TD13 of 505 kW at 1800 rpm.
Transmission: Electric, Elin Asynchronous 300 kW traction motors.
Wheel Diameter: 760/630 mm.   **Floor Height:** 800 mm.
Accommodation: 16/32 + –/48 + –/24 (16) 1W 1TD.   **Length over Couplers:** 18.705 + 14.75 + 18.705 m.
Weight: 33 + 19 + 33 tonnes.   **Maximum Speed:** 140 km/h.

▲ The Bombardier Talbot 'Talent' was one of the first new generation DMUs when it appeared in the late 1990s. Class 644 is the larger version and features a more powerful engine than its Class 643 counterparts. 644 003 is seen at Köln Hbf on 4 May 2018. **Keith Fender**

▼ Stadler Class 646.2 No. 646 210 forms an RB service from Brilon to Korbach on 12 September 2015, seen on the approach to Korbach. Note the power pack section in the centre of this articulated unit. **Matthias Müller**

644 001	944 001	644 501	KK2
644 002	944 002	644 502	EDO
644 003	944 003	644 503	KK2
644 004	944 004	644 504	EDO
644 005	944 005	644 505	TU
644 006	944 006	644 506	TU
644 007	944 007	644 507	KK2
644 008	944 008	644 508	EDO
644 009	944 009	644 509	TU
644 010	944 010	644 510	KK2
644 011	944 011	644 511	EDO
644 012	944 012	644 512	TU
644 013	944 013	644 513	TU
644 014	944 014	644 514	EDO
644 016	944 016	644 516	KK2
644 017	944 017	644 517	EDO
644 018	944 018	644 518	EDO
644 019	944 019	644 519	KK2
644 021	944 021	644 521	EDO
644 022	944 022	644 522	TU
644 023	944 023	644 523	RHL
644 024	944 024	644 524	RHL
644 025	944 025	644 525	RHL
644 027	944 027	644 527	KK2
644 028	944 028	644 528	KK2
644 029	944 029	644 529	EDO
644 030	944 030	644 530	EDO
644 031	944 031	644 531	KK2
644 032	944 032	644 532	KK2
644 033	944 033[II]	644 533	TU
644 034	944 034	644 534	EDO
644 035	944 035	644 535	RHL
644 036	944 036	644 536	RHL
644 037	944 037	644 537	TU
644 038	944 038	644 538	EDO
644 039	944 039	644 539	RHL
644 040	944 040	644 540	RHL
644 041	944 041	644 541	TU
644 042	944 042	644 542	TU
644 043	944 043	644 543	TU
644 044	944 044	644 544	KK2
644 045	944 045	644 545	EMST (Z)
644 046	944 046	644 546	TU
644 047	944 047	644 547	EDO
644 048	944 048	644 548	TU
644 049	944 049	644 549	RHL
644 050	944 050	644 550	TU
644 051	944 051	644 551	EMST
644 052	944 052	644 552	TU
644 053	944 053	644 553	EDO
644 054	944 054	644 554	RHL
644 055	944 055	644 555	KK2
644 056	944 056	644 556	EMST
644 057	944 057	644 557	TU
644 058	944 058	644 558	RHL
644 059	944 059	644 559	KK2
644 060	944 060	644 560	RHL
644 061	944 061	644 561	TU
644 062	944 062	644 562	TU
644 063	944 063	644 563	TU
644 064	944 064	644 564	EDO

Names:

644 024	Landkreis Waldshut		644 058	Landkreis Lörrach
644 047	EIFEL			

CLASS 646.0　　　GTW2/6　　　3-SECTION ARTICULATED UNITS

This design of articulation stems from the Swiss firm of Stadler. A centre "power pack" is flanked by two passenger coaches. The Swiss classification GTW 2/6 seems to have stuck with the design which has found favour with many railway companies not only in Switzerland! (GTW = *Gelenktriebwagen* = articulated railcar). DB Regio ordered 44 sets (Classes 646.0 and 646.1). Class 646.0 is used on local services in Berlin and Brandenburg. However, there have been problems with the sets in recent years consequently most sets are now stored out of use awaiting a decision on their future.

AB + B (DTCO–M–DTSO).

Built: 1999–2002.
Builders: Stadler, Adtranz, Bombardier/DWA.
Wheel Arrangement: 2-Bo-2.
Engine: 12 cylinder MTU 12V183 TDE2 of 550 kW at 2100 rpm.
Transmission: Electric, two three-phase asynchronous traction motors type Adtranz 6R1A 4548.
Wheel Diameter: DT 680 mm, M 860 mm. **Floor Height:** 760 mm.
Accommodation: 15/39 (5) + 0 + –/39 (10) 1T. **Length over Couplers:** 17.065 + 4.50 + 17.065 m.
Weight: 55.6 tonnes. **Maximum Speed:** 120 km/h.

* Fitted with PKP safety systems for working into Poland.

946 001	646 001	946 501		BLO (Z)	946 009	646 009	946 509	*	WNR (Z)
946 002	646 002	946 502	*	WNR	946 010	646 010	946 510		FK (Z)
946 003	646 003	946 503	*	WNR	946 011	646 011	946 511	*	WNR
946 004	646 004	946 504		WM (Z)	946 012	646 012	946 512	*	WNR
946 005	646 005	946 505	*	WNR	946 013	646 013	946 513		WNR
946 007	646 007	946 507		WM (Z)	946 014	646 014	946 514		WNR
946 008	646 008	946 508		WNR	946 015	646 015	946 515		WM (Z)

946 016	646 016	946 516		WNR	946 024	646 024	946 524		WM (Z)
946 017	646 017	946 517	*	LDLX (Z)	946 025	646 025	946 525		WM (Z)
946 018	646 018	946 518		WM (Z)	946 026	646 026	946 526		BCS (Z)
946 019	646 019	946 519		WM (Z)	946 027[II]	646 027	946 527		WM (Z)
946 020	646 020	946 520		WM (Z)	946 028	646 028	946 528	*	LDLX (Z)
946 021	646 021	946 521		WNR	946 029	646 029	946 529	*	WNR
946 022	646 022	946 522		WNR	946 030	646 030	946 530	*	LDLX (Z)
946 023	646 023	946 523		WM (Z)					

Name:

646 028   Frankfurt (Oder) - Poznan

CLASS 646.1   GTW2/6   3-SECTION ARTICULATED UNITS

This class is similar to Class 646.0 but was specifically ordered for services on the Island of Usedom which have since been set up as a DB Regio subsidiary Usedomer Bäder Bahn. There are subtle differences such as lower floor height, heavier weight, no first class and high density seating (3+2) to cope with holiday crowds. They work all services on the island and the connection to the mainland at Zussow. The units are not in the standard livery, instead they are in a blue and white livery with the blue being formed into "waves" to denote the seaside area the line serves. Services have been extended to Stralsund and even to Barth for which eight additional units were obtained. Recently DB has taken the UBB services back in house.

Details as Class 646/0 except:

B + B (DTSO–M–DTSO).

Accommodation: –/65 + 0 + –/46 (10) 1T.   **Weight:** 56.1 tonnes.
Floor Height: 585 mm.
Non-Standard Livery N: White and blue.

946 101	646 101	946 601	N	WHF	946 112	646 112	946 612	N	WHF
946 102	646 102	946 602	N	WHF	946 113	646 113	946 613	N	WHF
946 103	646 103	946 603	N	WHF	946 114	646 114	946 614	N	WHF
946 104	646 104	946 604	N	WHF	946 121	646 121	946 621	N	WHF
946 105	646 105	946 605	N	WHF	946 122	646 122	946 622	N	WHF
946 106	646 106	946 606	N	WHF	946 123	646 123	946 623	N	WHF
946 107	646 107	946 607	N	WHF	946 124	646 124	946 624	N	WHF
946 108	646 108	946 608	N	WHF	946 125	646 125	946 625	N	WHF
946 109	646 109	946 609	N	WHF	946 126	646 126	946 626	N	WHF
946 110	646 110	946 610	N	WHF	946 127	646 127	946 627	N	WHF
946 111	646 111	946 611	N	WHF					

CLASS 646.2   GTW2/6   3-SECTION ARTICULATED UNITS

In 2003 deliveries began of a further batch of units for local services in Hessen around Darmstadt and for the Kurhessenbahn from Kassel. Units are understood to receive maintenance at the Cantus depot in Kassel pending a new depot being built at Korbach.

946 201	646 201	946 701	FGM	946 208	646 208	946 708	FK
946 202	646 202	946 702	FGM	946 209	646 209	946 709	FK
946 203	646 203	946 703	FGM	946 210	646 210	946 710	FK
946 204	646 204	946 704	FGM	946 211	646 211	946 711	FK
946 205	646 205	946 705	FK	946 212	646 212	946 712	FK
946 206	646 206	946 706	FK	946 213	646 213	946 713	FK
946 207	646 207	946 707	FK				

Name:

646 211   Frankenberg (Eder)

CLASS 648   LINT 41   2-SECTION ARTICULATED UNITS

This railcar set is related to Class 640 (LINT 27). The LINT 41 is the same unit but extended to 41 m in length with two body sections instead of one. These units are similar to some delivered in 2000 to the private operator Nordostbahn that are working services in Schleswig Holstein. DB ordered some similar units to work alongside the private operator so that there is at least a common standard. The sets are known as "Coradia" by Alstom.

AB + B (DMCO–DMSO).

Built: 2000–01.
Builders: Alstom/LHB.
Wheel Arrangement: B-2-B.
Engine: One 6 cylinder MTU 6R 183TD 13H engine giving 315 kW at 1900 rpm.
Transmission: Hydrodynamic.
Wheel Diameter: 770 mm.
Accommodation: 16/46 (5) + –/52 1TD.

Weight: 63.5 tonnes.

Length over Couplers: 20.905 + 20.905 m.
Floor Height: 780 mm.
Maximum Speed: 120 km/h.

Class 648.0

648 001	648 501	EDO		648 004	648 504	EDO
648 002	648 502	EDO		648 005	648 505	EDO
648 003	648 503	EDO		648 006	648 506	EDO

Class 648.1. In February 2003 DB ordered 21 units for Sauerland services such as Dortmund–Iserlohn, Dortmund–Lüdenscheid, Dortmund–Winterberg and Unna–Menden–Fröndenberg–Neuenrade. These units have a floor height of 780 mm.

648 101	648 601	EDO		648 112	648 612	WNR
648 102	648 602	EDO		648 113	648 613	WNR
648 103	648 603	EHM (Z)		648 114	648 614	WNR
648 104	648 604	EDO		648 115	648 615	WNR
648 105	648 605	EDO		648 116	648 616	WNR
648 106	648 606	EDO		648 117	648 617	WNR
648 107	648 607	EDO		648 118	648 618	WNR
648 108	648 608	WNR		648 119	648 619	WNR
648 109	648 609	WNR		648 120	648 620	WNR
648 110	648 610	WNR		648 121	648 621	WNR
648 111	648 611	WNR				

Name:

648 114 Fontanestadt Neuruppin

Class 648.2. At the same time as the 648.1 order, DB ordered seven Class 648.2. These units have a floor height of 598 mm and were intended for Siegen–Bad Berleburg/Dillenburg/Au and Finnentrop–Olpe services. Later DB announced another order; this time for 27 units for the Harz–Weser services. These units work over the following lines Bad Harzburg–Goslar–Kreiensen; Braunschweig–Salzgitter Ringelheim–Kreiensen; Göttingen–Northeim–Nordhausen; Braunschweig–Seesen–Herzberg; Kreiensen–Holzminden; Ottbergen–Northeim/Göttingen.

648 201	648 701	FL		648 261	648 761	HBS
648 202	648 702	FL		648 262	648 762	HBS
648 203	648 703	FL		648 263	648 763	HBS
648 204	648 704	FL		648 264	648 764	HBS
648 205	648 705	FL		648 265	648 765	HBS
648 206	648 706	FL		648 266	648 766	HBS
648 207	648 707	FL		648 267	648 767	HBS
648 251	648 751	HBS		648 268	648 768	HBS
648 252	648 752	HBS		648 269	648 769	HBS
648 253	648 753	HBS		648 270	648 770	HBS
648 254	648 754	HBS		648 271	648 771	HBS
648 255	648 755	HBS		648 272	648 772	HBS
648 256	648 756	HBS		648 273	648 773	HBS
648 257	648 757	HBS		648 274	648 774	HBS
648 258	648 758	HBS		648 275	648 775	HBS
648 259	648 759	HBS		648 276	648 776	HBS
648 260	648 760	HBS		648 277	648 777	HBS

Names:

648 251	Stadt Bad Harzburg	648 258	Walkenried
648 252	Stadt Holzminden	648 259	Stadt Goslar
648 253	Herzberg am Harz	648 260	Seesen
648 254	Stadt Nordheim	648 261	Stadt Ellrich
648 255	Stadt Osterode am Harz	648 262	Katlenburg-Lindau
648 256	Stadt Einbeck	648 264	Eulenspiegelstadt Schöppenstedt
648 257	Kreiensen	648 274	Wulften am Harz

Classes 648.3 & 648.4. DB Regio, in continuing to improve local services, ordered 30 sets for the Nürnberg area followed by further orders for Schleswig Holstein Ost based in Kiel.

648 301	648 801	NN1		648 338	648 838	AK
648 302	648 802	NN1		648 339	648 839	AK
648 303	648 803	NN1		648 340	648 840	AK
648 304	648 804	NN1		648 341	648 841	AK
648 305	648 805	NN1		648 342	648 842	AK
648 306	648 806	NN1		648 343	648 843	AK
648 307	648 807	NN1		648 344	648 844	AK
648 308	648 808	NN1		648 345	648 845	AK
648 309	648 809	NN1		648 346	648 846	AK
648 310	648 810	NN1		648 347	648 847	AK
648 311	648 811	NN1		648 348	648 848	AK
648 312	648 812	NN1		648 349	648 849	AK
648 313	648 813	NN1		648 350	648 850	AK
648 314	648 814	NN1		648 351	648 851	AK
648 315	648 815	NN1		648 352	648 852	AK
648 316	648 816	NN1		648 353	648 853	AK
648 317	648 817	NN1		648 354	648 854	AK
648 318	648 818	NN1		648 355	648 855	AK
648 319	648 819	NN1		648 450	648 950	AK
648 320	648 820	NN1		648 451	648 951	AK
648 321	648 821	NN1		648 452	648 952	AK
648 322	648 822	NN1		648 453	648 953	AK
648 323	648 823	NN1		648 454	648 954	AK
648 324	648 824	NN1		648 455	648 955	AK
648 325	648 825	NN1		648 456	648 956	AK
648 326	648 826	NN1		648 457	648 957	AK
648 327	648 827	NN1		648 458	648 958	AK
648 331	648 831	AK		648 459	648 959	AK
648 332	648 832	AK		648 460	648 960	AK
648 333	648 833	AK		648 461	648 961	AK
648 334	648 834	AK		648 462	648 962	AK
648 335	648 835	AK		648 463	648 963	AK
648 336	648 836	AK		648 464	648 964	AK
648 337	648 837	AK		648 465	648 965	AK (Z)

Names:

648 301	Stadt Lauf	648 335	Büchen
648 302	Gräfenberg	648 336	Echem
648 303	Schnaittachtal	648 337	Großenbrode
648 304	Cadolzburg	648 338	Lauenburg (Elbe)
648 305	Nürnberg	648 339	Lensahn
648 306	Markt Erlbach	648 340	Lüneburg
648 307	Burgbernheim	648 341	Mölln
648 308	Bad Windsheim	648 342	Müssen
648 309	Rupprechtstegen	648 343	Neustadt (Holst.)
648 310	Landkreis Fürth	648 344	Oldenburg (Holst.)
648 311	Stadt Zirndorf	648 345	Plön
648 312	Siegelsdorf	648 346	Preetz
648 331	Ascheberg	648 347	Ratekau
648 332	Aumühle	648 348	Ratzenburg
648 333	Schwentiental	648 349	Schwarzenbek
648 334	Bad Malente-Gremsmühlen	648 355	Fehmarn

CLASS 650   REGIO SHUTTLE   SINGLE CAR

The German private railways were ahead of the field in ordering new equipment and this Adtranz product having caught on well with the private lines, DB Regio just had to have some. The design is a mix of bus, lorry and rail technologies. Waggon Union in Berlin thought out the design as a follow on to their successful NE81 design for the private lines. Waggon Union became part of Adtranz who continued the production with Stadler taking over the plant later. This single car DMU features a welded all-steel frame but the roof, body, and cabs are glued glass fibre reinforced plastic. Bus engines and transmission are provided. MICAS computer controls allow up to five units to run in multiple. The units are air conditioned and have two sets of doorways.

B (DMSO).

Built: 1999–2002.
Builder: Adtranz Berlin Pankow (former Waggon Union) later becoming Stadler.
Wheel Arrangement: B-B.
Engine: Two 6 cylinder MAN D2866 LH21 of 257 kW.   **Weight:** 40 tonnes.
Transmission: Hydrodynamic, Voith - DIWA.   **Length over Buffers:** 25.50 m.
Wheel Diameter: 770 mm.   **Floor Height:**
Accommodation: –/75 (3) 1T.   **Maximum Speed:** 120 km/h.

Class 650/0. Units ordered by DB Zug-Bus, Regionalverkehr Alb-Bodensee.

650 001	TT	650 010	TT	650 019	TT
650 002	TT	650 011	TT	650 020	TU
650 003	TT	650 012	TT	650 021	TT
650 004	TT	650 013	TT	650 022	TT
650 005	TT	650 014	TT	650 023	TT
650 006	TT	650 015	TT	650 024	TT
650 007	TT	650 016	TT	650 025	TT
650 008	TT	650 017	TU	650 026	TT
650 009	TT	650 018	TT	650 027	TT

Class 650/1. Units ordered by Baden-Württemberg. In the Tübingen area sets can be seen working alongside similar ones belonging to the HzL – Hohenzollerische Landesbahn.

650 100	TU	650 108	TU	650 116	TU
650 101	TU	650 109	TU	650 117	TU
650 102	TU	650 110	TU	650 118	TU
650 103	TU	650 111	TU	650 119	TU
650 104	TU	650 112	TU	650 120	TU
650 105	TU	650 113	TU	650 121	TU
650 106	TU	650 114	TU	650 122	TU
650 107	TU	650 115	TU		

Class 650/2. Units with no toilets but instead having a space for bicycles.

650 201	TU	650 202	TU	650 203	TU

Name:

650 203   Seehänsele

Class 650/3. More units for Baden Württemberg and Bayern. These units were of an updated design using LED headlights, fire alarm systems for engines, disabled toilet, armrests, lift for wheelchair and an information display with speech. Two units can work in multiple but this version is understood not to work in multiple with earlier versions.

650 301	TT	650 311	TT	650 320	TU
650 302	TT	650 312	TU	650 321	TU
650 303	TT	650 313	TU	650 322	TU
650 304	TT	650 314	TU	650 323	TU
650 305	TT	650 315	TU	650 324	TU
650 306	TT	650 316	TU	650 325	TU
650 307	TT	650 317	TU	650 326	TU
650 308	TT	650 318	TU	650 327	TU
650 309	TT	650 319	TU	650 997	MMF
650 310	TT				

Names:

650 301	Landkreis Calw	650 305	Stadt Horb
650 302	Stadt Wildberg	650 306	Stadt Nagold
650 303	Stadt Calw	650 307	Bad Teinach-Zavelstein
650 304	Bad Liebenzell	650 308	Stadt Pforzheim

CLASS 672 SINGLE CAR

These units were built for the Burgenlandbahn, which at one time was semi-private, being owned by Karsdorfer Eisenbahn and DB. When the Karsdorfer Eisenbahn went bankrupt all the units passed to DB. Class originally VT3.01–20.

Built: 1998–99.
Builder: DWA Bautzen.
Wheel Arrangement: 1-A.
Engine: 265 kW.
Transmission: Hydraulic.
Wheel Diameter:
Accommodation: –/64 1T.
Non-Standard Livery: N Silver and yellow.

Weight: 40 tonnes.
Length over Couplings: 16.54 m.
Maximum Speed: 120 km/h.

672 901	N	LBW	672 906	N	LBW	672 913	N	LBW
672 902	N	LBW	672 908	N	LBW	672 914	N	LBW
672 903	N	LBW	672 909	N	LBW	672 915	N	LBW
672 904	N	LBW	672 910	N	LBW	672 916	N	LBW
672 905	N	LBW	672 911	N	LBW	672 918	N	LBW

▲ This RB 23 service from Mayen to Limburg/Lahn conveniently affords the opportunity to compare Alstom's single-car LINT 27 (Class 640) and articulated LINT 41 (Class 646) units. 27 and 41 refer to the overall length of the unit. 648 204 and 640 010 are seen arriving at Koblenz-Lützel on 17 March 2016. **Matthias Müller**

Names:

672 901	Querfurt Thaldorfer Pfingstbursche	672 910	Stadt Weissenfels
672 902	Rotkäppchen-Sekt	672 911	Stadt Rossleben
672 903	Stadt Nebra	672 913	Der Querfurter
672 904	Happy Corax	672 914	Mitteldeutscher Verkehrsverbund
672 905	Stadt Naumburg (Saale)	672 915	Mücheln im Geisetal
672 906	Auf den Spuren Otto's des Grossen	672 916	Bergenlandkreis gut in Fahrt
672 908	Kohlebau Deuben	672 918	Finnebahn
672 909	Weissenfelser Schusterjunge		

CLASS 772 SINGLE CAR

These units, amazingly, are still in DB stock. They are based in Erfurt and used on tourist services by subsidiary company Oberweissbacher Berg– und Schwarztalbahn.

Built: 1965–69 for DR.
Former DR Class: 172.
Builder: VEB Waggonbau Görlitz.
Engine: MAN 2866UH of 132 kW (175 hp).
Transmission: Mechanical.

Weight: 19.3 tonnes.
Length over Couplers: 13.55 m.
Maximum Speed: 90 km/h.

772 140	UE		772 141	UE

CLASS 798 SINGLE CAR

This unit is still in DB stock having been reinstated on 01/12/2005 for use on tourist services. Some trailer cars have also been saved to work with the power car.

Built: 19xx for DB.
Builder: Uerdingen.
Engine: 2 x 112 kW.
Transmission: Mechanical.

Weight: 27 tonnes.
Length over Buffers: 13.95 m.
Maximum Speed: 90 km/h.

Class 798. B (DMSO). –/56 1T.

798 652	TU

Class 996.0. B (TSO). –/63 1T. 10.7 tonnes.

996 257	TU

Class 998.8 BD (DTBSO). –/40 1T. 16.7 tonnes.

998 896	TU

180

7. SELF-PROPELLED DEPARTMENTAL VEHICLES

Numbers may be painted on vehicles in this section but small white data panels are increasingly being used and are unreadable unless one is close to the vehicle! The introduction of European Vehicle Numbers has meant completely different numbers being applied in some cases; full details are not known. However, in most cases the old numbers are still shown on the vehicles.

DB is in the process of re-equipping the infrastructure departments with lots of new vehicles expected especially from Plasser & Theurer. The emphasis now is on multi-purpose vehicles under the acronym MISS – Multifunctionale Instandhaltungsfahrzeuge für die Streckeninfrastruktur.

CLASS 701 — A-A

Class 701.0 is the standard type of overhead line maintenance vehicle used by the old DB based on the Class 798 railbus.

The units are allocated to various depots for maintenance purposes but their operating base can be elsewhere at overhead line depots etc. In 1998/99 units marked * were converted to Diagnosetriebwagen (DVT). On these units the overhead work platform has been removed and a second pantograph mounted. These modified units have video and laser fittings for measuring the performance of the pantograph/catenary interface.

Most other units have now been withdrawn but many still exist as maintenance contractors quickly bought them up; some have been sold to other countries. For its part DB has more modern vehicles now or uses road/rail vehicles.

Built: 1955–74.
Builder: WMD, Rathgeber, Uerdingen, MBB.
Engine: Two 6 cylinder Bussing U10 of 110 kW at 1800 rpm. Water cooled.
Transmission: Mechanical.
Accommodation: Two cabs, workshop area, overhead platform, pantograph.
Wheel Diameter: 900 mm.
Weight: 29 tonnes.
Length over Couplers: 13.95 m.
Floor Height:
Maximum Speed: 90 km/h.

| 701 017 | Y | * | HM | 99 80 9236 002 | 701 165 | Y | * | STMI | 99 80 9261 001 |
| 701 079 | Y | | HBH (Z) | | 701 167 | Y | * | STMI | |

CLASS 702 — DIAGNOSE VT — 1A-B

This bogie-vehicle has replaced the old Class 702 units. It is what we in the UK would call a measurement vehicle. Fitted with two pantographs for measuring the contact wire status, there are lots of modern cameras on board to record the state of the infrastructure. Another German name for the unit is *Fahrwegmessung* – track testing

Built: 2014.
Builder: Plasser & Theurer.
Engine: 2 Deutz TCD16.0 V8 giving 480 kW at 1900 rpm.
Transmission: Voith T212 hydrodynamic.
Accommodation: .
Wheel Diameter: 900 mm.
Weight: 78 tonnes.
EVN: 99 80 9163 001.
Length over Couplers: 23.00 m.
Maximum Speed: 140 km/h.

| 702 201 | Y | HMI |

CLASS 703.1   IFO   A-A

IFO = Instandhaltungsfahrzeuge Oberleitungsanlagen = maintenance units for overhead equipment. These OHLE units are based on the GAF 200 engineer's trolley/draisine. The vehicles have one complete frame upon which is mounted a cab with crew room, behind which is a hydraulic lifting platform. The main engine is for traction; there is an auxiliary engine to power the lifting platform. (This is a MAN four cylinder D 8024 LFL 06 of 89 kW).

Built: 2000–01.
Builder: Gleisbaumechanik Brandenburg.
Engine: MAN 6-cylinder D.2876 LOH 01 of 338 kW.
Transmission: Hydraulic. Voith T211 rc3.   **Weight:** 40 tonnes.
Wheel Diameter: 840 mm.   **Length over Couplers:** 14.95 m.
Accommodation: 8 persons.   **Maximum Speed:** 100 km/h.
EVN: 99 80 xxxx xxx.

703 101	Y	KKO	703 105	Y	FH (Z)	703 108	Y	FGM
703 102	Y	BSE	703 106	Y	BGD	703 109	Y	FFU
703 103	Y	FK	703 107	Y	TC	703 110	Y	HO
703 104	Y	FD						

CLASS 705   TIF   B-2

TIF = Tunnelinstandhaltungsfahrzeuge-tunnel maintenance unit. This unit was ordered to cope with all the extra tunnels DB acquired when the NBS lines were built. The unit is based on the Austrian X 552 departmental unit also built by Plasser. At No. 1 end there is a small hydraulic platform to carry two persons whilst No. 2 end has a much larger hydraulic crane arm. Steps are provided to give access to the roof which is also used as a work or inspection area.

Built: 1992.
Builder: Deutsche Plasser 2454/1992.   **Weight:** 52 tonnes.
Engine: One 12 cylinder KHD BF12L513C engine of 367 kW at 2300 rpm for principal traction and one 4 cylinder KHD BF4L1011T of 44 kW at 2500 rpm for the auxiliaries.
Transmission: Hydrodynamic, mechanical.   **Length over Couplers:** 15.92 m.
Accommodation: 2 cabs, mess room with kitchen and washroom, 2 beds, office.
Wheel Diameter: 840 mm.   **Maximum Speed:** 120 km/h (140 km/h hauled).
EVN: 99 80 xxxx xxx.

705 001   Y   Duisburg

CLASS 705.1   TIF   B-2

This is another version for tunnel maintenance with a large cab and workroom at one end and three cranes with a cabin at the other end. Whilst classified as a TIF it is also known as a MISS - Multifunktionales Instandhaltungfahrzeuge (Multi-purpose maintenance vehicle).

Built: 2016.
Builder: Plasser & Theurer.
Engine:
Transmission: **Weight:** 78 tonnes.
Accommodation: 10 staff.   **Length over Couplers:** 23.00 m.
Wheel Diameter: 920 mm.   **Maximum Speed:** 140 km/h.
EVN: 99 80 9146 001 onwards.

705 101   Y   Duisburg | 705 102   Y   BGD

CLASS 705.2   MZF   Bo-Bo

These new vehicles are Mehrzweckfahrzeuge – multi-purpose vehicles and were built for the new high speed line from Erfurt to Nürnberg. As the name suggests they can be used for various purposes. There is a large cab at one end and a smaller one at the opposite end. A working platform for attending to the catenary is provided as well as a crane and a multi-purpose workshop. Other adaptions are possible according to the seasons e.g. snow plough, undergrowth mulcher etc. As the units work on the new high speed line they are fitted with ETCS Level 2. Actual allocations are not clear except it is known the units are stationed at Erfurt, Halle and Nürnberg.

Built: 2016.
Builder: Plasser & Theurer.
Wheel Arrangement:
Engine: 2 x 480 kW.   **Weight:** 80 tonnes.
Transmission: Electric.   **Length over Couplers:** 23.00 m.
Wheel Diameter: **Maximum Speed:** 140 km/h.
EVN: 99 80 9120 xxx.

705 201   Y | 705 202   Y | 705 203   Y

CLASS 707   MTW 100   B

This class is used by DB Bahnbau and should not be confused with a previous Class 707 which was in stock 2000–12. These MTW100 vehicles were built some years ago but were never given a departmental class number as they were regarded as Nebenfahrzeuge. Although built from 2004 onwards the class number first came to light in 2016 but only the first two vehicles have been reported with new numbers. MTW stands for Motor Turm Wagen (Motor Tower Wagons); many similar vehicles exist in Austria. There is only one cab which has a pantograph on top for measuring and testing the overhead catenary contact wire. There is a platform for use when working on the catenary. The mess room/workshop accommodates seven staff. A tail load of up to 80 tonnes can be hauled. 707s can work in multiple with each other.

Built: 2004–06.
Builder: Plasser & Theurer.
Engine: KHD.   **Length over Buffers:**
Transmission: Hydraulic.   **Maximum Speed:** 100 km/h.

▲ Although classified as a tunnel maintenance unit, Class 705.1 is really a multi-purpose maintenance vehicle, as can be appreciated from the multitude of equipment on board. 705 102 is seen on display at the Innotrans exhibition in Berlin on 19 September 2016.   **Keith Fender**

No.	Depot	Plasser Works Number	Original Number	Later Internal Number
707 001	WNT	865/2004	97 99 06 501 17-1	97 99 06 001 17-2
707 002	BCS	877/2004	97 99 06 502 17-9	
		878/2004	97 99 06 503 17-7	
		881/2004	97 99 06 504 17-5	
		883/2004	97 99 06 505 17-2	
		887/2004	97 99 06 506 17-0	
		931/2006	97 99 06 507 17-8	

CLASS 708.3 OBERLEITUNGSREVISIONTRIEBWAGEN (ORT) 1A-2

The oil crisis of the 1980s gave a spurt to DR electrification; consequently there was a need for a new batch of ORTs. Apart from the expected workshop area, a mess room and toilet are also provided. Some units have recently been withdrawn; some have been taken over by private maintenance contractors.

Built: 1987–91 for DR.
Builder: VEB Waggonbau Görlitz. **Weight:** 58 tonnes.
Engine: Rosslau 6VD18/15 AL–2 of 330 kW (* MAN D2876 LUE 604 of 371 kW).
Transmission: Hydraulic. **Length over Buffers:** 22.40 m.
Accommodation: 2 cabs, mess room, workshop and toilet.
Former DR Class: 188.3. **Maximum Speed:** 100 km/h.
EVN: 99 80 xxxx xxx.

708 303	Y		MH4	708 324	0	*	WR	708 331	0		KD
708 306	Y	*	HB	708 325	0	*	EDO	708 332	0		MRO
708 311	Y		LL	708 326	Y		BSE	708 333	Y		AK
708 319	Y	*	RF	708 327	0	*	EHM	708 334	Y	*	AH1
708 320	0	*	DZW	708 329	0		TU	708 336	Y		LLW
708 323	Y		HB	708 330	0	*	AHH	708 337	Y		EHM

CLASS 709 MOTORTURMWAGEN B-B

This class is similar to ÖBB X 552 and in fact was ordered by the DR in 1992. There is a normal cab at one end but at the other end the cab is set back to give space for the work platform. Two hydraulic arms are provided with the larger one supporting the working platform. The smaller arm can support a small platform or be fitted with a crane. A video camera is provided for recording the state of the OHLE.

Built: 1993.
Builder: Plasser.
Engine: One 12 cylinder KHD BF L513C of 367 kW for principal traction and one 4 cylinder KHD BF4L1011T for auxiliaries. **Weight:** 59 tonnes.
Transmission: Hydrodynamic, mechanical. **Length over Couplers:** 15.84 m.
Accommodation: 2 cabs, workshop, office, pantograph, mess room for eight staff.
Wheel Diameter: 840 mm. **Maximum Speed:** 120 km/h (140 km/h hauled).
EVN: 99 80 xxxx xxx.

709 002	Y	LL1	709 003	Y	BSE (Z)

CLASSES 711.0 & 711.1 HIOB B-2

HIOB = Hubarbeitsbuhnen Instandhaltungsfahrzeug Oberleitungsanlagen.

These Windhoff-built units have a pantograph, hydraulic platform and an observation post at roof level. Video recording gear is also provided. Some units have been withdrawn.

Built: 1995–96.
Builder: Windhoff. **Weight:** 66 tonnes.
Engine: One 6 cylinder MAN D 2876 of 338 kW at 1800 rpm for principal traction and one 4 cylinder MAN D 0824 of 118 kW at 2400 rpm for auxiliaries. **Length over Couplers:** 17.24 m.
Transmission: Hydrodynamic, mechanical. **Maximum Speed:** 120 km/h.
Accommodation: 2 cabs, office, mess room, workshop.
Wheel Diameter: 840 mm.
EVN: 99 80 xxxx xxx.

Class 711.0.

711 004	Y	BGD (Z)		711 008	Y	BGD (Z)

Class 711.1.

711 101[II]	Y	NWH		711 112	Y	RF
711 102	Y	LMR		711 113	Y	HG
711 103	Y	AH1		711 114	Y	MA
711 104	Y	EHM		711 115	Y	DF
711 105	Y	NRH		711 116	Y	WP
711 106	Y	RK		711 117	Y	KD
711 107	Y	KK		711 118	Y	EWAN
711 108	Y	WW		711 119	Y	MH2
711 109	Y	HS		711 121	Y	Zuffenhausen
711 110	Y	BCS		711 122	Y	BRG
711 111	Y	HB				

CLASS 711.2   IFO   B-B

Built: 2009–11.
Builder: Robel, type 57.44.
Engine. Two Deutz TCD 2015V08 of 480 kW.   **Weight:** 76 tonnes.
Transmission: Hydraulic.   **Length over Couplers:** 17.24 m.
Accommodation: 2 cabs, office, personnel room for 5, workshop, pantograph, work platform.
Wheel Diameter: 840 mm.   **Maximum Speed:** 140 km/h.
EVN: 99 80 9136 001–008, xxxx xxx.

711 201	Y	KK2		711 205	Y	KKO		711 210	Y	LH1
711 202	Y	DZW		711 206	Y	FMB		711 211	Y	LL
711 203	Y	FF		711 207	Y	HO		711 212	Y	NN2
711 204	Y	FK		711 208	Y	EOB		711 213	Y	UE

▲ Overhead line maintenance vehicle 711 101 is seen heading south through the Main valley near Harrbach on 17 May 2017.   **Matthias Müller**

CLASS 714   RETTUNGSDIENSTFAHRZEUG (RTZ)   B-B

These are Class 212 locomotives converted for use with the RTZ trains. Originally numbered as Class 214 and retaining the original Class 212 running number they have subsequently been renumbered into the departmental series and given completely new numbers. For working with the RTZ trains the locomotives have been given many extra fittings such as two halogen headlights, heat-sensitive cameras fitted at the front as well as video cameras. Yellow flashing lights denote that the train may be approaching remotely controlled from within the train.

The RTZ trains were built for use in emergencies on the NBS lines that have many tunnels and often pass through remote areas. RTZ trains comprise several vehicles usually formed as follows:

1. **Locomotive.**
2. **Transportwagen:** Special containers on a flat wagon. The containers are fitted with a driving position from which the driver can remotely control the locomotive and use TV monitors that are linked to cameras on the front of the locomotives. 60–80 people can be accommodated including 24 on beds and 24 on seats. Loudspeakers provided on the outside.
3. **Gerätewagen:** This is a rebuilt former postal coach for fire brigade use, pumps hoses, etc.
4. **Löschmittelwagen:** This wagon contains 20,000 litres of water.
5. **Sanitätswagen:** This is a hospital coach with an operating theatre.
6. **Transportwagen:** Similar to (2) above.
7. **Locomotive.**

Going into a tunnel where a train has crashed people can be rescued and walk through the train into the rear transport wagon. People can be given instructions and advice over the loudspeakers fixed to the exterior of the vehicles. Having walked through the train to the rear transport wagon the train can be divided and the rear half go out of the tunnel to a point where people can be detrained into waiting ambulances etc. There is an automatic coupling between the two halves of the train.

Note: The formations above are of the original trains; the new trains built by Tatrawagen and Drager have a similar formation.

All Class 714s are based at the DB Netz depot at Fulda but the locos are normally permanently coupled to their trains ready to go at a moment's notice. The emergency trains are normally stationed at Stuttgart (Kornwestheim), Mannheim, Würzburg, Fulda, Kassel and Hildesheim. Taking Kassel as an example the NBS north to Göttingen has 20 km of tunnels (in 50 km) and to the south the NBS to Fulda has 47 km of tunnels in 70 km. Thus if there is an incident on the NBS line it is highly likely that a tunnel would be involved. The EBA has considered Class 714 locomotives to be still Class 212 locomotives and consequently the EVN gives the old 212 number!

In late 2012 it was learnt that some new rescue trains are to be ordered to replace the existing trains. The new trains are likely to be formed of multi-purpose vehicles. With the building of the Erfurt–Nürnberg NBS more trains were needed. Consequently several 212s were rebuilt at Bremen works with new cabs provided by Gmeinder to create a float, after which the older 714s came in for rebuilding. The process continues.

It is unclear whether the new trains have new wagons or simply new containers put onto the old wagons. The formation is the same on one train reported numbered as follows:

Transportwagen 1	99 80 9370 104		Sanitatswagen	99 80 9370 152
Gerätewagen	99 80 9370 018		Transportwagen 2	99 80 9370 157
Löschmittelwagen	99 80 9370 002			

Built: 1963–65, rebuilt 1989–97 and again 2015 –.
Builder: MaK, Deutz, Henschel.
Engine: MTU 12V652TZ.
Power: 990 kW.
Maximum Tractive Effort: 183 kN.
Wheel Diameter: 950 mm.
EVN: 99 80 9170 001 onwards for the 2015 rebuilds.

Weight: 63 tonnes.
Length over Buffers: 12.30 m.
Maximum Speed: 100 km/h.

1989 Version

714 001	(212 033)	FFU		714 008	(212 251)	FFU
714 002	(212 046)	FFU		714 009	(212 257)	FFU
714 003	(212 235)	FFU		714 010	(212 260)	FFU
714 005	(212 244)	FFU		714 012	(212 277)	FFU
714 006	(212 245)	FFU		714 014	(212 269)	FFU
714 007	(212 246)	FFU		714 015	(212 160)	FFU

186

2015 Version

714 101	(212 076)	FFU		714 105	(212 270)	FFU
714 102	(212 343)	FFU		714 106	(714 013)	FFU
714 103	(212 158)	FFU		714 107	(714 011)	FFU
714 104	(714 004)	FFU				

CLASS 716 SCHNEESCHLEUDER B-B

Class 716 is the designation given to two rotary snowploughs specially built for service on the new NBS lines especially Hannover–Würzburg, but they can also see general use. There are three engines; one for traction and the other two for powering the two rotary ploughs. The machine carries its own turntable and can thus turn for ploughing in the reverse direction.

Built: 1994.
Builder: Beilhack/DB Meiningen.
Engine: Three 12 cylinder Daimler Benz OM 4441a of 605 kW at 600 rpm.
Transmission: Hydraulic, Voith T 311. **Weight:** 80 tonnes.
Maximum Tractive Effort: **Length over Buffers:** 16.50 m.
Wheel Diameter: 850 mm. **Maximum Speed:** 120 km/h.
EVN: 99 80 xxxx xxx.

716 001	Y	MP		716 002	Y	FFU

CLASS 719.0/720.0 ULTRASONIC TEST TRAIN 1 3-CAR

This three car set is an ultrasonic test train which is in effect a modified Class 614 DMU. The two power cars contain offices, mess rooms, kitchen and overnight accommodation. The trailer car is the actual test car and has two extra sets of wheels in the centre to support the testing equipment; these can all be raised and locked out of use when the train is in transit and not testing. The train is cleared for use in Austria and Switzerland.

Built: 1974.
Builder: MAN, MBB.
Wheel Arrangement: B-2 + 2-2 + 2-B. **Weight:** 48.5 tonnes (719); 51.3 tonnes (720).
Engine: MAN 12 cylinder D 3560 HM 12 of 360 kW. **Length over Buffers:** 26.65 m + 26.16 m + 26.65 m.
Transmission: Hydraulic. **Maximum Speed:** 140 km/h.
EVN: 99 80 9429 001, 99 80 9529 001, 99 80 9429 002.

719 001	720 001	719 002	Y	HM

CLASS 719.2 LIMEZ III 2-CAR

This two car DMU is formed of the power cars 614 045/046 suitably modified and is a replacement for the former LIMEZ II train of Class 712/713. LIMEZ = *Lichtraumprofil Messtriebwagen*, a profile measuring train. One end of the train still looks like a 614 front end but the other end has all sorts of measuring equipment attached. Recently the unit has been renumbered being previously 719 045/046. The train is permitted to work in Austria and Switzerland.

EVN: 99 80 9160 001 + 002

Technical details as for Class 614.

719 201	719 202	Y	HM

CLASS 719.3/720.3   FAHRWEGMESSZUG   2-CAR

This set is another measurement train, full details of which are awaited. It could well be for measuring the contact between pantograph and catenary as a pantograph is fitted to 719 301 as well as spot lights; this vehicle is also the power car. However, 720 301 is a driving trailer fitted with an ultrasonic measuring unit between the bogies, this assembly also having its own axles thus allowing the track to be monitored simultaneously with the catenary.

Built: 2015.
Builder: Plasser.
Wheel Arrangement:
Engine: **Weight:** 80 tonnes (719); 67 tonnes (720).
Transmission: **Length over Buffers:** 23.00 m.
Wheel Diameter: **Maximum Speed:** 140 km/h.

| 719 301 | HM | 9980 9160 004 | 720 301 | HM | 9980 9360 006 |
| 719 302 | HM | 9980 9160 005 | 720 302 | HM | 9980 9360 008 |

CLASS 720.1   ULTRASONIC TEST TRAIN 1   3-CAR

This is a purpose built ultrasonic test train. Built in 1995, exhibited at the Hannover Fair in 1996. Cab fittings include Sifa, Indusi I60R, ZBF, ZFG90.

Built: 1995.
Builder: Plasser, Linz, Austria.
Wheel Arrangement: B-2 + 2-2 + 2-B.
Engine: One 12 cylinder MTU 12V183TD13 of 540 kW.   **Weight:** 62.6 tonnes (719), 67.5 tonnes (720).
Transmission: Hydraulic.   **Length over couplings:** 23.70 m.
Accommodation: Mess room, working area, WC, washroom.
Wheel Diameter: 920 mm.   **Maximum Speed:** 160 km/h.
EVN: 99 80 9360 005

| 720 101 | Y | HM | 721 101 | Y | HM |

CLASS 725.0   TRACK RECORDING TRAIN   2-CAR

These track recording trains have two vehicles. The 725 is the power car and was converted from older units but the 726 vehicles were built new based on a Class 701 unit. The 725 car has a dormitory. The sets are normally used to test on secondary routes or even private lines where DB has running rights.

Built: 1959–61 (725); 1974 (726).
Builder: MAN, Uerdingen, WMD (725); MBB (726).
Engine: Two 6 cylinder Bussing U10 of 110 kW.   **Weight:** 23 tonnes (725); 18 tonnes (726).
Transmission: Mechanical.   **Length over Couplers:** 13.95 m. (725); 13.40 m. (726).
Wheel Diameter: 900 mm (725); 800 mm (726).   **Maximum Speed:** 90km/h (80 km/h if testing).
EVN: 99 80 xxxx xxx.

| 725 002 | 726 002 | Y | FH | 725 004 | 726 004 | Y | KK |

CLASS 725.1   TRACK RECORDING TRAIN   2-CAR

A relatively new "Gleismesszug" which has allowed some older vehicles to be withdrawn. Cabs at each end, there is a workshop and mess room for 10 staff.

Built: 2014.
Builder: Plasser.
Wheel Arrangement: Bo-Bo + 2-2.   **Weight:** 79.75 tonnes (725); 57.50 tonnes (726).
Engine: Two Deutz TCD16.0/V8/1700/IIIB of 480 kW.   **Length over Buffers:** 23.00 m.
Transmission: Voith Hydrodynamic Turbo T212BRE+HA/MISS.
Wheel Diameter: 920 mm.   **Maximum Speed:** 140 km/h.
EVN: 9980 9160 003 (725); 9980 9560 001 (726).

| 725 101 | Y | HM | 726 101 | Y | HM |

CLASS 730   BREAKDOWN CRANES

730 001   LL | 730 002   EWAN

Name:

730 002   Goliath

CLASS 732   BREAKDOWN CRANES

DB has been re-equipping the departmental fleet and now has some Kirow Multitasker 1200 cranes

Built: 2014–16.
Builder: Kirow, Leipzig.
Wheel Arrangement: 1AA1-A1A1.
Engine: **Weight:** 110 tonnes.
Transmission: **Length over Buffers:** 15.00 m.
Wheel Diameter: **Maximum Speed:** 100 km/h (Hauled), 19 km/h under own power.
EVN: 99 80 9471 001–003.

732 001   FFU | 732 002   LL | 732 003   EWAN

▲ DB Netz is modernising its emergency trains for high-speed lines. 714 103 stands at Fulda with such a train on 2 March 2017.   **Brian Garvin**

CLASS 740   SIGNALDIENST   A-A

These units were converted from Class 798 railbuses when it was realised that more test units would be required in the light of the expanding high speed network. The units cover the testing of NBS signalling and radio. Some have been withdrawn.

Built: 1955–60, Rebuilt 1990–92.
Builder: MAN, Uerdingen, WMD.   **Weight:** 22.40 tonnes.
Engine: Two 6 cylinder Bussing U10 engines of 110 kW.
Transmission: Mechanical.   **Length over Buffers:** 3.95 m.
Wheel Diameter: 900 mm.   **Maximum Speed:** 90 km/h.
EVN: 99 80 xxxx xxx.

740 004   (798 735)   Y   FFU

CLASS 740.101   LEIT & SICHERUNGSTECHNIK FAHRZEUG - LST

Built: 2016–17.
Builder: Plasser.
Wheel Arrangement:
Engine: **Weight:** 74–76 tonnes.
Transmission: **Length over Buffers:** 23.00 m.
Wheel Diameter: **Maximum Speed:** 140 km/h.
EVN: 99 80 9120 002–004.

740 101   FFU | 740 102   FFU | 740 103   FFU

CLASS 746   GLEISARBEITFAHRZEUG – GAF   1A-Bo

DB Netze is gradually re-equipping its on-track plant vehicles. This new GAF vehicle – Gleisarbeitsfahrzeug – is a modern platelayers trolley with all the latest equipment. It has a bit of a strange look as at one end there is a large cab and personnel room which includes a WC whilst at the other end there is a crane. The space in between is a clear area which can be used for loading rails or equipment with space under the vehicle for other equipment. The vehicle can be used for track inspection and maintenance with attachments available for snow clearance, vegetation control, etc.

28 vehicles are understood to be on order with 6 to be delivered in 2018, 13 in 2019 and 9 in 2020.

Built: 2018–.
Builder: Plasser.
Engine: 480 kW.   **Weight:** 65 tonnes.
Transmission: Hydraulic.   **Length over Buffers:** 23.00 m.
Wheel Diameter: 920 mm.   **Maximum Speed:** 100 km/h.
EVN: 99 80 9110 001–.

746 001 Oberhausen	746 011	746 020
746 002	746 012	746 021
746 003	746 013	746 022
746 004	746 014	746 023
746 005	746 015	746 024
746 006	746 016	746 025
746 007	746 017	746 026
746 008	746 018	746 027
746 009	746 019	746 028
746 010		

CLASS 747   GLEISARBEITFAHRZEUG - GAF   1A-B

This is another new GAF unit. It appears to be a general purpose unit, there being two cabs and mess room etc for up to 11 staff. There is a workshop and a lifting work platform. There can be various attachments such as snow ploughs and brushes etc.

Built: 2017.
Builder: Plasser.
Engine: **Weight:** 78 tonnes.
Transmission: **Length over Buffers:** 23.00 m.
Wheel Diameter: 920 mm.   **Maximum Speed:** 140 km/h.
EVN: 99 80 9120 008–010.

747 001	Murnau			
747 101	Leipzig	747 102	Uelzen	

8. INTERNAL USER LOCOMOTIVES

AKKUMULATOR SCHLEPP FAHRZEUGE (ASF)   Bo

ASFs are small battery shunters that the DR used at all its depots and workshops for shunting locomotives into place inside the depot/workshop and thus not fill these places with fumes. With the closure of many former DR depots spare ASFs have moved west where they have been welcomed. Additionally some former industrial ASFs have also been acquired. Regretfully many have lost their workplates and so the identities of the new additions to the list are unclear. Some depots have numbered their locomotives in to their own series adding yet another complication. (WL = Werklok; 17767 = LEW works number). Some of these diminutive shunters still move around with No. 15 having appeared at NN2 when last known to be at the closed depot in Vacha. It is possible that others are still locked away in closed depots

Note: Although referred to as a locomotive, the Germans refer to these and departmental locomotives as a "Gerate" - basically a tool or piece of equipment. Thus, they are not counted as capital stock and presumably not considered for an EVN.

Built: 1966–89.
Builder: LEW.   **Weight:** 12 tonnes.
Power Rating: 17kW.   **Maximum Speed:** 6 km/h.

No.	Location	No.	Location	No.	Location
3	BWS	35	LH2	68	DF?
5	LH1	36	LMR	69	RF
7	FK	37	HS	70	NN2
9	DF ?	38	FB	73	UE
12	BCSX	39	AK	74	TU
13	BCSX	40	BSE	75	WNTX
14	LH2	42	BCS	77	LMR
15	NN2	43	UE	80	LS?
16	BSE	44	US	81	HBS
17	NN1	47	HB1	82	TS
19	DF ?	48	(LF)?	83	TK
20	FL	49	LE	84	LH2
21	HBS	50	LH2	85	LH1
25	BSN	52	WR	86	BSE
26	BHF	55	WNT?	87	BFG
27	DG	56	WRS	88	DZW?
28	WNTX	58	LH2	89	DF?
29	BCSX	61	EHG	90	WA?
31	HBS	62	AK	92	NN2
33	UN	64	BRG	96	AH1
34	UE	66	BRG	97	LS

99	LMR	121	TS	143	UE
100	MH1	123	UN?	145	NN1
102	BFG	124	WM?	148	AK
103	WR	125	LS?	149	BCS
104	BSE	126	WRS	150	WRS WL3
105	WNR	127	WM?	151	UG?
106	WR	128	WA?	152	HB1
107	WR	130	DF?	153	BSE
108	US?	131	BLO	155	AH1
109	HO	132	LE	156	US?
110	US?	133	UE	157	WHF
111	DZW?	134	BLO	158	LL2
112	BSN	135	BRG	159	LL1
114	LL2	136	BSE	161	LDX
116	RHL	137	BFG	162	LL2
117	NN1	138	BSN	163	LMR
118	LH1	140	NN2	164	FK
119	LS?	141	DZW?	165	MH1
120	BSE	142	AH1	166	LH2

Duplicates

1	WRS	5	WM?	1001	FF1
001	NN2	6	WRS	1002	FF1
1	AM	7	WRS	1003	FF1
01	HS	9	WRS	1004	LL2
01	M. NORD	20	DA	1005	LE
02	HS	20	FLX	1006	BF
2	WRS	192	FLX	404 001	MH1
03	HS	200	UE	14868	TK
04	HS	222	UG?	17767	TK
4	WRS	303	AM	17230	KD
5	WRS	333	US?	383 001	KK2

9. PRESERVED LOCOMOTIVES AND RAILCARS

DB Museum seems to be out on a limb. Having been under Fernverkehr for a while and until recently using its locomotives and stock for excursion and relief trains this has now ceased. Amazingly the Class 103 electric locomotive it was using has been taken back into active stock! The main museum remains in Nürnberg with the nearby shed at Lichtenfels being used to store locomotives. It was thought that once the new Regio depot opened in Nürnberg the museum would take over the old depot but this has not happened. DB Museum has in the meantime taken over the old wagon shop at Koblenz Lützel as an annexe but this building is too small and many locomotives are stored in the open. It appears DB does not wish to bite the bullet and get something properly organised for its vast collection. Just as in Britain some locomotives are loaned to museum groups to be looked after particularly at Halle and Leipzig. More recently the museums at Bahnpark Augsburg and Horb have received stock on loan. The situation needs careful attention as some interesting relics could fall by the wayside.

The current status of motive power is indicated at follows:

M	Museum, on display (not active)
MA	Museum, active
MR	Museum, under repair
MS	Museum, stored
P	Plinthed
S	Stored

9.1. STEAM LOCOMOTIVES

Old No.	Computer No.	Co.	Wheel	Type	Built	Status	Location
01 005	-	DR	4-6-2	2C1h2	1925	M	VMD, Stassfurt.
01 008	001 008	DB	4-6-2	2C1h2	1925	M	Stiftung Eisenbahnmuseum. Bochum Dahlhausen.
01 066	01 2066	DR	4-6-2	2C1h2	1928	MA	BEM. Nördlingen.
01 111	001 111	DB	4-6-2	2C1h2	1934	M	DDM. Neuenmarkt Wirsberg.
01 118	01 2118	DR	4-6-2	2C1h2	1934	MA	HE. Frankfurt/Main.
01 137	01 2137	DR	4-6-2	2C1h2	1935	M	DBM. Dresden Altstadt.
01 150	001 150	DB	4-6-2	2C1h2	1935	MA	DBM. Hanau.
01 164	001 164	DB	4-6-2	2C1h2	1935	MS	Lichtenfels.
01 173	001 173	DB	4-6-2	2C1h2	1936	M	DTM. Berlin.
01 180	001 180	DB	4-6-2	2C1h2	1936	MA	BEM Nördlingen.
01 202	001 202	DB	4-6-2	2C1h2	1936	MA	Lyss, Switzerland.
01 204	01 2204	DR	4-6-2	2C1h2	1936	M	Hermeskeil.
01 220	001 220	DB	4-6-2	2C1h2	1937	P	Treuchtlingen.
01 509	01 0509	DR	4-6-2	2C1h2	1963	MA	UEF. Heilbronn.
01 514	01 1514	DR	4-6-2	2C1h2	1964	M	TM. Speyer.
01 519	01 1519	DR	4-6-2	2C1h2	1964	MA	EFZ. Rottweil.
01 531	01 1531	DR	4-6-2	2C1h2	1964	M	DBM. Arnstadt.
01 533	01 1533	DR	4-6-2	2C1h2	1964	MA	ÖGEG. Ampflwang, (A)
01 1056	011 056	DB	4-6-2	2C1h3	1940	M	DME. Darmstadt Kranichstein.
01 1061	012 061	DB	4-6-2	2C1h3	1940	M	DDM. Neuenmarkt Wirsberg.
01 1063	012 063	DB	4-6-2	2C1h3	1940	P	Braunschweig Hbf.
01 1066	012 066	DB	4-6-2	2C1h3	1940	MA	UEF. Heilbronn.
01 1075	012 075	DB	4-6-2	2C1h3	1940	MA	SSN. Rotterdam Noord, (NL)
01 1081	012 081	DB	4-6-2	2C1h3	1940	M	SEH Heilbronn.
01 1082	012 082	DB	4-6-2	2C1h3	1940	M	DTM. Berlin.
01 1100	012 100	DB	4-6-2	2C1h3	1940	MR	DBM. Koblenz Lützel.
01 1102	012 102	DB	4-6-2	2C1h3	1940	MR	UEF/SEH Heilbronn.
01 1104	012 104	DB	4-6-2	2C1h3	1940	MR	DBK Crailsheim.
03 001	03 2001	DR	4-6-2	2C1h2	1930	M	DBM. Dresden Altstadt.
03 002	03 2002	DR	4-6-2	2C1h2	1930	M	TM. Prora.
03 098	03 2098	DR	4-6-2	2C1h2	1933	M	TM. Speyer.
03 131	003 131	DB	4-6-2	2C1h2	1933	M	DDM. Neuenmarkt Wirsberg.
03 155	03 2155	DR	4-6-2	2C1h2	1934	MA	WFL, Nossen.

03 188	003 188	DB	4-6-2	2C1h2	1935	P	DBM. Kirchheim (Teck).
03 204	03 2204	DR	4-6-2	2C1h2	1936	MR	LDC. Cottbus.
03 295	03 2295	DR	4-6-2	2C1h2	1937	M	BEM. Bahnpark Augsburg.
03 1010	03 1010	DR	4-6-2	2C1h3	1940	MA	DBM. Halle P.
03 1090	03 0090	DR	4-6-2	2C1h3	1940	M	DBM. Schwerin.
05 001	-	DB	4-6-4	2C2h3	1935	M	DBM. Nürnberg.
10 001	010 001	DB	4-6-2	2C1h3	1957	M	DDM. Neuenmarkt Wirsberg.
15 001	-3201	DRG	4-4-4	2B2h4v	1906	M	DBM. Nürnberg.
17 008	-	DRG	4-6-0	2Ch4	1911	M	DTM. Berlin.
17 1055	-	DR	4-6-0	2Ch4v	1913	M	VMD. Dresden Altstadt.
18 201	02 0201	DR	4-6-2	2C1h3	1961	MA	Dampf Plus, Lutherstadt Wittenberg.
18 314	02 0314	DR	4-6-2	2C1h4v	1919	M	TM. Sinsheim.
18 316	018 316	DB	4-6-2	2C1h4v	1919	M	Technosum, Mannheim.
18 323	018 323	DB	4-6-2	2C1h4v	1920	P	DBM. Offenburg.
18 451	-	DB	4-6-2	2C1h4v	1912	M	Deutsches Museum, München.
18 478	-	DB	4-6-2	2C1h4v	1918	MA	BEM. Nördlingen.
18 505	018 505	DB	4-6-2	2C1h4v	1924	M	DGEG Neustadt (Weinstrasse).
18 508	-	DB	4-6-2	2C1h4v	1924	M	Locorama, Romanshorn, (CH)
18 528	-	DB	4-6-2	2C1h4v	1928	M	Siemens, München Allach.
18 612	-	DB	4-6-2	2C1h4v	1926	M	DDM. Neuenmarkt Wirsberg.
19 017	-	DR	2-8-2	1D1h4v	1922	M	VMD. Dresden Altstadt.
22 029	39 1029	DR	2-8-2	1D1h3	1959	MS	BEM. Nördlingen.
22 047	39 1047	DR	2-8-2	1D1h3	1960	M	Falkenberg/Elster.
22 064	39 1064	DR	2-8-2	1D1h3	1960	MS	BEM Nördlingen.
22 066	39 1066	DR	2-8-2	1D1h3	1960	M	Hermeskeil.
22 073	39 1073	DR	2-8-2	1D1h3	1961	M	Falkenberg/Elster.
23 019	023 019	DB	2-6-2	1C1h2	1952	M	DDM. Neuenmarkt Wirsberg.
23 023	023 023	DB	2-6-2	1C1h2	1952	MA	SSN. Rotterdam Noord, (NL)
23 029	023 029	DB	2-6-2	1C1h2	1954	P	Aalen.
23 042	023 042	DB	2-6-2	1C1h2	1954	MA	DME. Darmstadt Kranichstein.
23 058	023 058	DB	2-6-2	1C1h2	1955	MR	Eurovapor, SEH Heilbronn.
23 071	023 071	DB	2-6-2	1C1h2	1956	MA	VSM. Beekbergen, (NL)
23 076	023 076	DB	2-6-2	1C1h2	1956	MA	VSM. Beekbergen, (NL)
23 105	023 105	DB	2-6-2	1C1h2	1959	MS	DBM. SEH, Heilbronn.
23 1019	35 1019	DR	2-6-2	1C1h2	1958	MA	LDC. Cottbus.
23 1021	35 1021	DR	2-6-2	1C1h2	1958	M	TM. Prora.
23 1074	35 1074	DR	2-6-2	1C1h2	1959	MS	Eisenbahnwelt, Gera.
23 1097	35 1097	DR	2-6-2	1C1h2	1959	MA	IG. Glauchau.
23 1113	35 1113	DR	2-6-2	1C1h2	1959	MS	DBM. Nossen.
24 004	37-1004	DR	2-6-0	1Ch2	1928	M	VMD. Dresden Altstadt.
24 009	37 1009	DR	2-6-0	1Ch2	1928	MS	Gelsenkirchen Bismarck.
24 083	(Oi2-22)	PKP	2-6-0	1Ch2	1938	MA	DBG, Loburg.
38 205	38 5205	DR	4-6-0	2Ch2	1910	M	DBM, SEM Chemnitz Hilbersdorf.
38 1182	38 1182	DR	4-6-0	2Ch2	1910	M	DBM. Arnstadt.
38 1444	-	DB	4-6-0	2Ch2	1913	M	LHB. Salzgitter.
38 1772	038 772	DB	4-6-0	2Ch2	1915	M	Hanau.
38 2267	38 2267	DR	4-6-0	2Ch2	1918	MA	Stiftung Eisenbahnmuseum Bochum Dahlhausen.
38 2383	038 382	DB	4-6-0	2Ch2	1918	M	DDM. Neuenmarkt Wirsberg.
38 2425	(Ok1-296)	PKP	4-6-0	2Ch2	1919	M	DTM. Berlin.
38 2460	(230 094)	CFR	4-6-0	2Ch2	1919	MA	Bahnpark, Augsburg. Restored as Posen 2455.
38 2884	038 884	DB	4-6-0	2Ch2	1921	M	DBM. Nürnberg.
38 3180	(230 105)	CFR	4-6-0	2Ch2	1921	MA	BEM Nördlingen.
38 3199	(230 106)	CFR	4-6-0	2Ch2	1921	MA	SEH Heilbronn.
38 3650	038 650	DB	4-6-0	2Ch2	1922	P	Böblingen.
38 3711	038 711	DB	4-6-0	2Ch2	1922	P	Berebostel.
38 3999	(230 111)	CFR	4-6-0	2Ch2	1923	MA	DME Darmstadt.
39 184	-	DB	2-8-2	1D1h3	1924	M	LHB. Salzgitter.
39 230	-	DB	2-8-2	1D1h3	1925	M	DBM. Neuenmarkt Wirsberg
41 018	042 018	DB	2-8-2	1D1h2	1938	MA	IG 41 018. Bahnpark Augsburg.
41 024	042 024	DB	2-8-2	1D1h2	1938	M	DME. Darmstadt Kranichstein.
41 025	41 1025	DR	2-8-2	1D1h2	1938	M	Hermeskeil.

41 052	042 052	DB	2-8-2	1D1h2	1938	MR	Osnabrück.
41 073	042 073	DB	2-8-2	1D1h2	1939	MR	Club 41 073, SEH Heilbronn.
41 096	042 096	DB	2-8-2	1D1h2	1938	MA	IG 41 096. Salzgitter.
41 105	042 105	DB	2-8-2	1D1h2	1938	MR	SSN. Rotterdam Noord, (NL)
41 113	042 113	DB	2-8-2	1D1h2	1938	M	TM. Sinsheim.
41 122	41 1122	DR	2-8-2	1D1h2	1938	MS	Meiningen Works.
41 125	41 1125	DR	2-8-2	1D1h2	1938	MS	Falkenberg/Elster.
41 137	41 1137	DR	2-8-2	1D1h2	1938	M	Hermeskeil.
41 144	41 1144	DR	2-8-2	1D1h2	1938	MA	IG Werrabahn, Eisenach.
41 150	41 1150	DR	2-8-2	1D1h2	1938	MA	BEM. Nördlingen.
41 185	41 1185	DR	2-8-2	1D1h2	1938	M	DBM Halle P.
41 186	042 186	DB	2-8-2	1D1h2	1938	M	Dieringhausen.
41 225	41 1225	DR	2-8-2	1D1h2	1938	M	SEM. Chemnitz Hilbersdorf.
41 226	042 226	DB	2-8-2	1D1h2	1938	M	Tuttlingen.
41 231	41 1231	DR	2-8-2	1D1h2	1939	M	Stassfurt.
41 241	042 241	DB	2-8-2	1D1h2	1939	M	DBM Oberhausen Osterfeld Süd.
41 271	042 271	DB	2-8-2	1D1h2	1939	S	EF Rendsburg. Neumünster.
41 289	41 1289	DR	2-8-2	1D1h2	1939	M	Falkenberg/Elster.
41 303	41 1303	DR	2-8-2	1D1h2	1939	S	Lubbenau.
41 360	042 360	DB	2-8-2	1D1h2	1939	MA	DBM Oberhausen Osterfeld Süd.
41 364	042 364	DB	2-8-2	1D1h2	1941	M	Bahnpark, Augsburg.
42 1504	(Ty43-127)	PKP	2-10-0	1Eh2	1944	M	TM. Speyer.
42 2754	(16.15)	BDZ	2-10-0	1Eh2	1949	M	Hermeskeil.
42 2768	(16.18)	BDZ	2-10-0	1Eh2	1949	M	BEM Nördlingen.
43 001	-	DR	2-10-0	1Eh2	1926	M	VMD. Chemnitz Hilbersdorf.
44 100	043 100	DB	2-10-0	1Eh3	1937	M	TM. Sinsheim.
44 105	44 2105	DR	2-10-0	1Eh3	1938	M	Falkenberg/Elster.
44 140	44 2140	DR	2-10-0	1Eh3	1938	M	Falkenberg/Elster.
44 154	44 2154	DR	2-10-0	1Eh3	1938	M	Falkenberg/Elster.
44 167	44 2167	DR	2-10-0	1Eh3	1939	M	Hermeskeil.
44 177	44 2177	DR	2-10-0	1Eh3	1939	M	Hermeskeil.
44 196	44 2196	DR	2-10-0	1Eh3	1939	M	Hermeskeil.
44 225	44 2225	DR	2-10-0	1Eh3	1939	M	IG. Glauchau.
44 264	44 2264	DR	2-10-0	1Eh3	1939	M	Hermeskeil.
44 276	044 276	DB	2-10-0	1Eh3	1940	M	DDM. Neuenmarkt Wirsberg.
44 351	44 0351	DR	2-10-0	1Eh3	1941	S	VSE. Wülknitz.
44 381	043 381	DB	2-10-0	1Eh3	1941	M	BEM. Nördlingen.
44 389	044 389	DB	2-10-0	1Eh3	1941	P	Altenbeken.
44 394	44 2394	DR	2-10-0	1Eh3	1941	M	Falkenberg/Elster.
44 397	44 2397	DR	2-10-0	1Eh3	1941	M	TM. Prora.
44 404	044 404	DB	2-10-0	1Eh3	1941	M	DME. Darmstadt Kranichstein.
44 434	044 434	DB	2-10-0	1Eh3	1941	M	Hermeskeil.
44 481	044 481	DB	2-10-0	1Eh3	1941	M	Technikmuseum, Kassel.
44 500	44 2500	DR	2-10-0	1Eh3	1941	M	Hermeskeil.
44 508	044 508	DB	2-10-0	1Eh3	1941	MS	Westerburg.
44 546	44 2546	DR	2-10-0	1Eh3	1941	M	BEM. Nördlingen.
44 594	044 594	DB	2-10-0	1Eh3	1941	M	Wittenberge.
44 606	043 606	DB	2-10-0	1Eh3	1941	M	Bahnpark, Augsburg.
44 635	44 2635	DR	2-10-0	1Eh3	1941	M	Hermeskeil.
44 661	44 2661	DR	2-10-0	1Eh3	1941	MA	ÖGEG. Ampflwang (A)
44 663	44 2663	DR	2-10-0	1Eh3	1941	M	Stassfurt.
44 687	44 2687	DR	2-10-0	1Eh3	1941	M	Altenbeken.
44 903	043 903	DB	2-10-0	1Eh3	1943	P	Emden Hbf.
44 1040	44 1040	DR	2-10-0	1Eh3	1942	M	Hermeskeil.
44 1056	44 1056	DR	2-10-0	1Eh3	1942	M	Hermeskeil.
44 1085	043 085	DB	2-10-0	1Eh3	1942	M	VSM Beekbergen, (NL)
44 1093	44 1093	DR	2-10-0	1Eh3	1942	M	DBM Arnstadt.
44 1106	44 1106	DR	2-10-0	1Eh3	1942	M	Hermeskeil.
44 1121	043 121	DB	2-10-0	1Eh3	1942	M	Tuttlingen.
44 1182	44 1182	DR	2-10-0	1Eh3	1942	MA	Stassfurt.
44 1203	043 196	DB	2-10-0	1Eh3	1942	P	Salzbergen Bhf.
44 1251	44 1251	DR	2-10-0	1Eh3	1942	M	Hermeskeil.
44 1315	043 315	DB	2-10-0	1Eh3	1943	P	Märklin, Göppingen
44 1338	44 1338	DR	2-10-0	1Eh3	1943	M	SEM Chemnitz Hilbersdorf.

44 1377	044 377	DB	2-10-0	1Eh3	1943	M	Stiftung Eisenbahnmuseum Bochum Dahlhausen.
44 1378	44 1378	DR	2-10-0	1Eh3	1943	MR	Crailsheim.
44 1412	44 1412	DR	2-10-0	1Eh3	1943	M	Hermeskeil.
44 1424	044 424	DB	2-10-0	1Eh3	1943	MS	Altenbeken.
44 1486	44 1486	DR	2-10-0	1Eh3	1943	MA	Stassfurt.
44 1489	44 1489	DR	2-10-0	1Eh3	1943	M	Glauchau
44 1537	44 1537	DR	2-10-0	1Eh3	1943	M	Hermeskeil.
44 1558	044 556	DB	2-10-0	1Eh3	1943	M	Gelsenkirchen Bismarck
44 1593	44 1593	DR	2-10-0	1Eh3	1943	MA	VSM. Beekbergen, (NL)
44 1595	44 1595	DR	2-10-0	1Eh3	1943	S	ÖGEG. Ampflwang. (A)
44 1614	44 1614	DR	2-10-0	1Eh3	1943	S	ÖGEG. Ampflwang. (A)
44 1616	44 1616	DR	2-10-0	1Eh3	1943	S	SEH Heilbronn.
44 1681	043 681	DB	2-10-0	1Eh3	1942	MS	Altenbeken.
45 010	045 010	DB	2-10-2	1E1h3	1941	S	DBM. NN2
50 001	050 001	DB	2-10-0	1Eh2	1939	M	DTM. Berlin.
50 413	050 413	DB	2-10-0	1Eh2	1940	M	TM. Sinsheim.
50 607	050 607	DB	2-10-0	1Eh2	1940	M	Hermeskeil.
50 622	050 622	DB	2-10-0	1Eh2	1940	MS	DBM. NN2
50 682	050 682	DB	2-10-0	1Eh2	1940	P	Grafenwöhr.
50 685	50.685	GKB	2-10-0	1Eh2	1940	M	TM. Speyer.
50 778	050 778	DB	2-10-0	1Eh2	1941	M	BEM. Nördlingen.
50 794	050 794	DB	2-10-0	1Eh2	1941	P	Tolk, Kreis Schleswig.
50 849	50 1849	DR	2-10-0	1Eh2	1941	MA	DBM Glauchau.
50 904	050 904	DB	2-10-0	1Eh2	1940	MS	DDM. Neuenmarkt Wirsberg.
50 955	50 1955	DR	2-10-0	1Eh2	1941	S	BEM. Nördlingen.
50 975	050 975	DB	2-10-0	1Eh2	1941	M	DDM. Neuenmarkt Wirsberg.
50 1002	50 1002	DR	2-10-0	1Eh2	1941	MS	ÖGEG. Ampflwang. (A)
50 1255	051 255	DB	2-10-0	1Eh2	1941	MR	SSN. Rotterdam Noord, (NL)
50 1446	051 446	DB	2-10-0	1Eh2	1941	M	Hermeskeil.
50 1650	051 650	DB	2-10-0	1Eh2	1942	MS	Moers, Rheinkamp.
50 1724	051 724	DB	2-10-0	1Eh2	1941	MS	Altenbeken.
50 1832	051 832	DB	2-10-0	1Eh2	1941	M	Hermeskeil.
50 2146	50 2146	DR	2-10-0	1Eh2	1943	P	Weiden.
50 2404	052 404	DB	2-10-0	1Eh2	1942	MS	Gelsenkirchen Bismarck.
50 2429	052 429	DB	2-10-0	1Eh2	1942	MS	Oberhausen.
50 2613	052 613	DB	2-10-0	1Eh2	1942	P	Seifertshofen.
50 2652	50 2652	DR	2-10-0	1Eh2	1943	P	Kaiserslautern.
50 2740	50 2740	DR	2-10-0	1Eh2	1942	MR	UEF Menzingen.
50 2838	052 838	DB	2-10-0	1Eh2	1943	M	Tuttlingen.
50 2908	052 908	DB	2-10-0	1Eh2	1942	P	Lauda (Bhf).
50 2988	052 988	DB	2-10-0	1Eh2	1942	MA	Dampfbahn Schwarzwald Baar
50 3014	50 3014	DR	2-10-0	1Eh2	1942	M	Hermeskeil.
50 3031	053 031	DB	2-10-0	1Eh2	1942	MR	SEH. Heilbronn.
50 3075	053 075	DB	2-10-0	1Eh2	1943	M	Stiftung Eisenbahnmuseum Bochum Dahlhausen.
50 3502	50 0072	DR	2-10-0	1Eh2	1957	MA	BEM. Nördlingen.
50 3506	50 3506	DR	2-10-0	1Eh2	1957	MS	ÖGEG. Ampflwang. (A)
50 3517	50 3517	DR	2-10-0	1Eh2	1958	M	Falkenberg/Elster,
50 3518	50 3518	DR	2-10-0	1Eh2	1958	M	Falkenberg/Elster,
50 3519	50 3519	DR	2-10-0	1Eh2	1958	MS	ÖGEG. Ampflwang. (A)
50 3520	50 3520	DR	2-10-0	1Eh2	1958	M	VSM. Beekbergen, (NL)
50 3521	50 3521	DR	2-10-0	1Eh2	1958	P	Meyenberg.
50 3522	50 3522	DR	2-10-0	1Eh2	1958	MS	Röbel.
50 3523	50 3523	DR	2-10-0	1Eh2	1958	M	Selb.
50 3527	50 3527	DR	2-10-0	1Eh2	1958	M	Pasewalk.
50 3539	50 3539	DR	2-10-0	1Eh2	1958	MA	SEH. Heilbronn.
50 3540	50 3540	DR	2-10-0	1Eh2	1958	M	Tuttlingen.
50 3545	50 3545	DR	2-10-0	1Eh2	1958	MA	Crailsheim.
50 3552	50 3552	DR	2-10-0	1Eh2	1958	MA	Hanau.
50 3553	50 3553	DR	2-10-0	1Eh2	1958	M	Hermeskeil.
50 3554	50 3554	DR	2-10-0	1Eh2	1959	MS	Tuttlingen.
50 3555	50 3555	DR	2-10-0	1Eh2	1959	M	Hermeskeil.
50 3556	50 3556	DR	2-10-0	1Eh2	1958	M	Stassfurt.

50 3557	50 3557	DR	2-10-0	1Eh2	1959	M	Falkenberg/Elster.
50 3559	50 3559	DR	2-10-0	1Eh2	1959	P	Liblar/Erfstadt.
50 3562	50 3562	DR	2-10-0	1Eh2	1959	P	Kirchweyhe.
50 3564	50 3564	DR	2-10-0	1Eh2	1959	MA	VSM. Beekbergen, (NL)
							(Restored as 50 307).
50 3568	50 3568	DR	2-10-0	1Eh2	1959	M	Falkenberg/Elster.
50 3570	50 3570	DR	2-10-0	1Eh2	1959	M	Wittenberge.
50 3576	50 3576	DR	2-10-0	1Eh2	1959	MA	NTB. Wiesbaden.
50 3580	50 3580	DR	2-10-0	1Eh2	1960	P	Triberg Bhf (Restored as 50 245).
50 3600	50 3600	DR	2-10-0	1Eh2	1960	MA	BEM. Nördlingen.
50 3603	50 3603	DR	2-10-0	1Eh2	1960	M	Tuttlingen.
50 3604	50 3604	DR	2-10-0	1Eh2	1960	M	Tuttlingen.
50 3606	50 3606	DR	2-10-0	1Eh2	1960	MA	Stassfurt.
50 3610	50 3610	DR	2-10 0	1Eh2	1960	MA	Nossen.
50 3616	50 3616	DR	2-10-0	1Eh2	1960	MA	VSE. Schwarzenberg.
50 3618	50 3618	DR	2-10-0	1Eh2	1960	MS	VSM Apeldoorn (NL)
50 3624	50 3624	DR	2-10-0	1Eh2	1960	M	Wittenberge.
50 3626	50 3626	DR	2-10-0	1Eh2	1960	M	Weimar.
50 3628	50 3628	DR	2-10-0	1Eh2	1960	M	SEM Chemnitz Hilbersdorf.
50 3631	50 3631	DR	2-10-0	1Eh2	1960	M	Falkenberg/Elster.
50 3635	50 3635	DR	2-10-0	1Eh2	1960	M	Falkenberg/Elster.
50 3636	50 3636	DR	2-10-0	1Eh2	1960	MA	GES. Kornwestheim.
50 3638	50 3638	DR	2-10-0	1Eh2	1960	MS	Röbel.
50 3642	50 3642	DR	2-10-0	1Eh2	1960	M	Falkenberg/Elster.
50 3645	50 3645	DR	2-10-0	1Eh2	1961	MS	STAR, Stadskanaal, (NL)
50 3648	50 3648	DR	2-10-0	1Eh2	1961	MA	SEM Chemnitz Hilbersdorf.
50 3649	50 3649	DR	2-10-0	1Eh2	1961	M	Hermeskeil.
50 3652	50 3652	DR	2-10-0	1Eh2	1961	M	Falkenberg/Elster.
50 3654	50 3654	DR	2-10-0	1Eh2	1961	MA	VSM. Beekbergen, (NL)
50 3655	50 3655	DR	2-10-0	1Eh2	1961	MA	ET. Lengerich.
50 3657	50 3657	DR	2-10-0	1Eh2	1961	M	Tuttlingen.

▲ 01 1066, carrying its computer number 012 066, storms into Landshut station with an IGE special from Augsburg Hbf to Nürnberg Hbf on 9 August 2015. **Brian Garvin**

50 3658	50 3659	DR	2-10-0	1Eh2	1961	P	Biblis-Wattenheim Golfpark.
50 3661	50 3661	DR	2-10-0	1Eh2	1961	MS	CFT Pontarlier – Vallorbe, (F).
50 3662	50 3662	DR	2-10-0	1Eh2	1961	M	Hermeskeil.
50 3666	50 3666	DR	2-10-0	1Eh2	1961	MA	VSM Apeldoorn, (NL).
50 3670	50 3670	DR	2-10-0	1Eh2	1961	MS	Fischamend, (A)
50 3673	50 3673	DR	2-10-0	1Eh2	1961	MA	Luino, (I).
50 3680	50 3680	DR	2-10-0	1Eh2	1961	P	Linde bei Lindlar.
50 3681	50 3681	DR	2-10-0	1Eh2	1961	MA	VSM. Beekbergen, (NL).
50 3682	50 3682	DR	2-10-0	1Eh2	1961	M	Wittenberge.
50 3684	50 3684	DR	2-10-0	1Eh2	1961	P	Rosengarten (or Buchholz?).
50 3685	50 3685	DR	2-10-0	1Eh2	1961	M	Wittenberge.
50 3688	50 3688	DR	2-10-0	1Eh2	1961	M	DBM. Arnstadt.
50 3689	50 3689	DR	2-10-0	1Eh2	1961	M	ÖGEG Ampflwang, (A).
50 3690	50 3690	DR	2-10-0	1Eh2	1961	MR	Nossen.
50 3691	50 3691	DR	2-10-0	1Eh2	1961	M	Falkenberg/Elster.
50 3693	50 3693	DR	2-10-0	1Eh2	1961	M	Falkenberg/Elster.
50 3694	50 3694	DR	2-10-0	1Eh2	1961	M	Schwerin.
50 3695	50 3695	DR	2-10-0	1Eh2	1961	MA	Stassfurt.
50 3696	50 3696	DR	2-10-0	1Eh2	1961	MA	CFV3V. Mariembourg,(B).
50 3700	50 3700	DR	2-10-0	1Eh2	1961	M	Stassfurt.
50 3703	50 3703	DR	2-10-0	1Eh2	1961	M	Prora.
50 3705	50 3705	DR	2-10-0	1Eh2	1962	M	Treysa.
50 3707	50 3707	DR	2-10-0	1Eh2	1962	P	Berlin Naturpark Süd.
50 3708	50 3708	DR	2-10-0	1Eh2	1962	MA	Blankenburg.
50 4073	50 4073	DR	2-10-0	1Eh2	1959	MR	BEM. Nördlingen.
52 360	52 1360	DR	2-10-0	1Eh2	1942	MA	Vienenburg.
52 662	52 1662	DR	2-10-0	1Eh2	1944	M	Hermeskeil.
52 1423	52 1423	DR	2-10-0	1Eh2	1943	M	Hermeskeil.
52 2093	52 2093	DR	2-10-0	1Eh2	1943	M	Hermeskeil.
52 2195	52 2195	DR	2-10-0	1Eh2	1943	M	BEM. Nördlingen.
52 2751	52 2751	DR	2-10-0	1Eh2	1943	M	Marl.
52 3109	-152.3109	GKB	2-10-0	1Eh2	1943	M	TM. Sinsheim.
52 3548	52 3548	DR	2-10-0	1Eh2	1943	M	BEM. Nördlingen.
52 3915	(TE-3915)	SZD	2-10-0	1Eh2	1944	M	Speyer (ex TE-3915).
52 4544	(Ty2-4544)	PMP	2-10-0	1Eh2	1943	MR	Naumburg.
52 4867	-152.4867	GKB	2-10-0	1Eh2	1943	MA	HEF.Frankfurt/M.
52 4900	52 9900	DR	2-10-0	1Eh2	1943	M	Halle P.
52 4924	52 4924	DR	2-10-0	1Eh2	1943	M	SEM Chemnitz Hilbersdorf.
52 4966	52 4966	DR	2-10-0	1Eh2	1943	M	DTM. Berlin.
52 5448	52 5448	DR	2-10-0	1Eh2	1943	MS	Leipzig Hbf.
52 5679	52 5679	DR	2-10-0	1Eh2	1943	P	Falkenberg/Elster.
52 5804	-52.5804	ÖBB	2-10-0	1Eh2	1943	M	DDM. Neuenmarkt Wirsberg.
52 5933	(TE-5933)	SZD	2-10-0	1Eh2	1943	MA	STAR, Stadskanaal, (NL)
52 6666	52 6666	DR	2-10-0	1Eh2	1943	MS	DBM Berlin Schöneweide.
52 6721	52 6721	DR	2-10-0	1Eh2	1943	M	Hermeskeil.
52 7409	-52.7409	ÖBB	2-10-0	1Eh2	1943	MA	Würzburg.
52 7596	-52.7596	ÖBB	2-10-0	1Eh2	1944	MA	EFZ. Rottweil.
52 8001	52 8001	DR	2-10-0	1Eh2	1960	M	Eisenbahnwelt, Gera.
52 8003	52 8003	DR	2-10-0	1Eh2	1960	MS	ÖGEG Ampflwang, (A).
52 8006	52 8006	DR	2-10-0	1Eh2	1960	M	Hermeskeil.
52 8008	52 8008	DR	2-10-0	1Eh2	1960	M	Falkenberg/Elster.
52 8009	52 8009	DR	2-10-0	1Eh2	1961	M	Falkenberg/Elster.
52 8010	52 8010	DR	2-10-0	1Eh2	1961	MR	VSM. Beekbergen, (NL).
52 8012	52 8012	DR	2-10-0	1Eh2	1961	P	Zollhaus Blumberg.
52 8013	52 8013	DR	2-10-0	1Eh2	1961	M	Falkenberg/Elster.
52 8015	52 8015	DR	2-10-0	1Eh2	1961	P	Lehrte.
52 8017	52 8017	DR	2-10-0	1Eh2	1961	P	Kirchmoser.
52 8019	52 8019	DR	2-10-0	1Eh2	1961	M	Tuttlingen.
52 8020	52 8020	DR	2-10-0	1Eh2	1961	M	Tuttlingen.
52 8021	52 8021	DR	2-10-0	1Eh2	1961	M	Falkenberg/Elster.
52 8023	52 8023	DR	2-10-0	1Eh2	1961	M	Falkenberg/Elster.
52 8028	52 8028	DR	2-10-0	1Eh2	1961	MS	Belzig.
52 8029	52 8029	DR	2-10-0	1Eh2	1961	MS	Klostermansfeld
52 8030	52 8030	DR	2-10-0	1Eh2	1961	MS	Falkenberg/Elster.

52 8034	52 8034	DR	2-10-0	1Eh2	1961	P	Simbach (Inn).
52 8035	52 8035	DR	2-10-0	1Eh2	1961	M	Falkenberg/Elster.
52 8036	52 8036	DR	2-10-0	1Eh2	1961	M	Falkenberg/Elster.
52 8037	52 8037	DR	2-10-0	1Eh2	1961	M	Falkenberg/Elster.
52 8038	52 8038	DR	2-10-0	1Eh2	1961	MA	DEW Rinteln.
52 8039	52 8039	DR	2-10-0	1Eh2	1962	MS	AKO, Scharzerden.
52 8041	52 8041	DR	2-10-0	1Eh2	1962	MS	Lutherstadt Wittenberg.
52 8042	52 8042	DR	2-10-0	1Eh2	1962	M	Falkenberg/Elster.
52 8043	52 8043	DR	2-10-0	1Eh2	1962	M	Tuttlingen.
52 8044	52 8044	DR	2-10-0	1Eh2	1962	M	Falkenberg/Elster.
52 8047	52 8047	DR	2-10-0	1Eh2	1962	MS	Nossen.
52 8051	52 8051	DR	2-10-0	1Eh2	1962	M	Tuttlingen.
52 8053	52 8053	DR	2-10-0	1Eh2	1962	MA	VSM. Beekbergen, (NL).
52 8055	52 8055	DR	2-10-0	1Eh2	1962	MA	DLM. Schaffhausen, (CH)
52 8056	52 8056	DR	2-10-0	1Eh2	1962	P	Bautzen.
52 8057	52 8057	DR	2-10-0	1Eh2	1962	M	Tuttlingen.
52 8058	52 8058	DR	2-10-0	1Eh2	1962	M	Falkenberg/Elster.
52 8060	52 8060	DR	2-10-0	1Eh2	1962	MS	STAR, Stadskanaal, (NL).
52 8062	52 8062	DR	2-10-0	1Eh2	1962	P	Treuenbritzen.
52 8064	52 8064	DR	2-10-0	1Eh2	1962	MR	Krefeld.
52 8068	52 8068	DR	2-10-0	1Eh2	1962	M	SEM. Chemnitz Hilbersdorf.
52 8070	52 8070	DR	2-10-0	1Eh2	1962	P	Peitz.
52 8072	52 8072	DR	2-10-0	1Eh2	1963	M	Falkenberg/Elster.
52 8075	52 8075	DR	2-10-0	1Eh2	1963	MA	IG Werrabahn. Eisenach.
52 8077	52 8077	DR	2-10-0	1Eh2	1963	MS	DBK. Crailsheim.
52 8079	52 8079	DR	2-10-0	1Eh2	1963	MA	Dampf Plus, Glauchau.
52 8080	52 8080	DR	2-10-0	1Eh2	1963	MA	Löbau.
52 8082	52 8082	DR	2-10-0	1Eh2	1963	MR	STAR, Stadskanaal, (NL)
52 8083	52 8083	DR	2-10-0	1Eh2	1963	MS	Falkenberg/Elster.
52 8085	52 8085	DR	2-10-0	1Eh2	1963	M	Falkenberg/Elster.
52 8086	52 8086	DR	2-10-0	1Eh2	1963	M	Dalhausen (Wupper).
52 8087	52 8087	DR	2-10-0	1Eh2	1963	MS	Gladenbach
52 8089	52 8089	DR	2-10-0	1Eh2	1963	M	Falkenberg/Elster.
52 8090	52 8090	DR	2-10-0	1Eh2	1963	M	Hermeskeil.
52 8091	52 8091	DR	2-10-0	1Eh2	1963	M	VSM Beekbergen, (NL)
52 8092	52 8092	DR	2-10-0	1Eh2	1963	M	Falkenberg/Elster.
52 8095	52 8095	DR	2-10-0	1Eh2	1963	MA	VEB, Gerolstein, (Restored as 52 6106).
52 8096	52 8096	DR	2-10-0	1Eh2	1963	M	ÖGEG. Ampflwang, (A)
52 8098	52 8098	DR	2-10-0	1Eh2	1963	M	Leipzig Plagwitz.
52 8100	52 8100	DR	2-10-0	1Eh2	1963	M	Falkenberg/Elster.
52 8102	52 8102	DR	2-10-0	1Eh2	1964	M	Falkenberg/Elster.
52 8104	52 8104	DR	2-10-0	1Eh2	1964	M	Falkenberg/Elster.
52 8106	52 8106	DR	2-10-0	1Eh2	1964	MR	Treysa.
52 8109	52 8109	DR	2-10-0	1Eh2	1964	M	Weimar.
52 8111	52 8111	DR	2-10-0	1Eh2	1964	M	Tuttlingen.
52 8113	52 8113	DR	2-10-0	1Eh2	1964	M	Hermeskeil.
52 8115	52 8115	DR	2-10-0	1Eh2	1964	M	Knappenrode.
52 8116	52 8116	DR	2-10-0	1Eh2	1964	P	Bielefeld-Brake
52 8117	52 8117	DR	2-10-0	1Eh2	1964	M	Falkenberg/Elster.
52 8118	52 8118	DR	2-10-0	1Eh2	1964	MS	Brandenburg Hafen
52 8120	52 8120	DR	2-10-0	1Eh2	1964	M	Hermeskeil.
52 8122	52 8122	DR	2-10-0	1Eh2	1964	M	Falkenberg/Elster.
52 8123	52 8123	DR	2-10-0	1Eh2	1965	M	Hermeskeil.
52 8124	52 8124	DR	2-10-0	1Eh2	1965	M	ÖGEG Ampflwang, (A)
52 8125	52 8125	DR	2-10-0	1Eh2	1965	M	Tuttlingen.
52 8126	52 8126	DR	2-10-0	1Eh2	1965	M	Falkenberg/Elster.
52 8130	52 8130	DR	2-10-0	1Eh2	1965	M	Tuttlingen.
52 8131	52 8131	DR	2-10-0	1Eh2	1965	MR	Nossen.
52 8132	52 8132	DR	2-10-0	1Eh2	1965	M	Falkenberg/Elster.
52 8133	52 8133	DR	2-10-0	1Eh2	1965	M	Falkenberg/Elster.
52 8134	52 8134	DR	2-10-0	1Eh2	1965	MA	ÖGEG Ampflwang, (A)
52 8135	52 8135	DR	2-10-0	1Eh2	1965	P	Wildau.
52 8137	52 8137	DR	2-10-0	1Eh2	1965	M	Stassfurt.

52 8138	52 8138	DR	2-10-0	1Eh2	1965	M	Tuttlingen.
52 8139	52 8139	DR	2-10-0	1Eh2	1965	MA	VSM Beekbergen, (NL)
52 8141	52 8141	DR	2-10-0	1Eh2	1965	MS	Löbau.
52 8147	52 8147	DR	2-10-0	1Eh2	1965	MR	Schwarzerden.
52 8148	52 8148	DR	2-10-0	1Eh2	1965	MR	Walheim
52 8149	52 8149	DR	2-10-0	1Eh2	1965	M	SEM Chemnitz Hilbersdorf.
52 8150	52 8150	DR	2-10-0	1Eh2	1965	MS	VSM Beekbergen, (NL)
52 8152	52 8152	DR	2-10-0	1Eh2	1965	MS	Brandenburg Hafen
52 8154	52 8154	DR	2-10-0	1Eh2	1965	MA	Leipzig-Plagwitz.
52 8156	52 8156	DR	2-10-0	1Eh2	1966	MS	Belzig.
52 8157	52 8157	DR	2-10-0	1Eh2	1966	S	Falkenberg/Elster.
52 8160	52 8160	DR	2-10-0	1Eh2	1966	MA	VSM Beekbergen, (NL)
52 8161	52 8161	DR	2-10-0	1Eh2	1966	M	Stassfurt.
52 8163	52 8163	DR	2-10-0	1Eh2	1966	MS	Pontarlier, France.
52 8168	52 8168	DR	2-10-0	1Eh2	1966	M	BEM. Nördlingen.
52 8169	52 8169	DR	2-10-0	1Eh2	1966	M	Tuttlingen.
52 8170	52 8170	DR	2-10-0	1Eh2	1966	M	Falkenberg/Elster.
52 8173	52 8173	DR	2-10-0	1Eh2	1966	MS	Berlin Schöneweide.
52 8174	52 8174	DR	2-10-0	1Eh2	1966	M	Flakenberg/Elster.
52 8175	52 8175	DR	2-10-0	1Eh2	1966	M	Falkenberg/Elster.
52 8176	52 8176	DR	2-10-0	1Eh2	1966	M	Tuttlingen.
52 8177	52 8177	DR	2-10-0	1Eh2	1966	MA	Berlin Schöneweide.
52 8183	52 8183	DR	2-10-0	1Eh2	1967	M	VSE Schwarzenberg.
52 8184	52 8184	DR	2-10-0	1Eh2	1967	MA	Stassfurt.
52 8186	52 8186	DR	2-10-0	1Eh2	1967	M	ÖGEG Ampflwang, (A)
52 8187	52 8187	DR	2-10-0	1Eh2	1967	M	Falkenberg/Elster.
52 8189	52 8189	DR	2-10-0	1Eh2	1967	M	Stassfurt.
52 8190	52 8190	DR	2-10-0	1Eh2	1967	M	Prora.
52 8191	52 8191	DR	2-10-0	1Eh2	1967	M	Tuttlingen.
52 8194	52 8194	DR	2-10-0	1Eh2	1967	M	Falkenberg/Elster.
52 8195	52 8195	DR	2-10-0	1Eh2	1967	MA	FME. Nürnberg.
52 8196	52 8196	DR	2-10-0	1Eh2	1967	M	ÖGEG Ampflwang, (A)
52 8197	52 8197	DR	2-10-0	1Eh2	1967	M	Hermeskeil.
52 8198	52 8198	DR	2-10-0	1Eh2	1967	M	Tuttlingen.
52 8199	52 8199	DR	2-10-0	1Eh2	1967	M	Oelsnitz.
52 8200	52 8200	DR	2-10-0	1Eh2	1967	MA	CFV3V. Mariembourg, (B).
							(Restored as 52 467).
53 7002	-	DRG	0-6-0	Cn2	1884	M	DBM. Nürnberg.
55 669	-	DR	0-8-0	Dn2	1905	M	VMD. Dresden Altstadt.
55 3345	055 345	DB	0-10-0	DH2	1915	M	DGEG. Bochum Dahlhausen.
55 3528	055 528	DB	0-10-0	DH2	1915	M	TM. Speyer.
56 3007	-	DB	0-10-0	1DH2	1928	M	DME. Darmstadt Kranichstein.
57 1841	50.259	CFR	0-10-0	Eh2	1919	MR	Dieringhausen
57 3088	057 088	DB	0-10-0	Eh2	1922	M	DBM Siegen.
57 3297		DR	0-10-0	Eh2	1923	M	VMD. Dresden Altstadt.
"57 3525"	50.277	CFR	0-10-0	Eh2	1926	M	BEM Nördlingen.
"57 3597"	50.397	CFR	0-10-0	Eh2	1930	M	SEH. Heilbronn.
58 261	58 1261	DR	2-10-0	1Eh3	1921	M	VMD. Chemnitz Hilbersdorf.
58 311	58 1111	DR	2-10-0	1Eh3	1921	MR	UEF. Menzingen.
58 1616	58 1616	DR	2-10-0	1Eh3	1920	M	Hermeskeil.
58 3047	58 3047	DR	2-10-0	1Eh3	1963	MS	DBM Glauchau.
58 3049	52 3049	DR	2-10-0	1Eh3	1963	MR	VSE Schwarzenberg.
62 015	62 1015	DR	4-6-4T	2C2h2t	1928	M	DBM Dresden Altstadt.
64 006	064 006	DB	2-6-2T	1C1h2t	1926	M	DGEG. Neustadt/Weinstr.
64 007	64 1007	DR	2-6-2T	1C1h2t	1928	M	DBM Schwerin.
64 019	064 019	DB	2-6-2T	1C1h2t	1927	M	Selb.
64 094	064 094	DB	2-6-2T	1C1h2t	1928	MS	GES. Kornwestheim.
64 250	064 250	DB	2-6-2T	1C1h2t	1932	MA	CFV3V. Mariembourg, (B)
64 289	064 289	DB	2-6-2T	1C1h2t	1933	M	EFZ. Rottweil.
64 295	064 295	DB	2-6-2T	1C1h2t	1933	M	DDM. Neuenmarkt Wirsberg.
64 305	064 305	DB	2-6-2T	1C1h2t	1934	MR	NVR Peterborough, UK.
64 317	64 1317	DR	2-6-2T	1C1h2t	1934	P	Frankfurt/Oder Hbf.
64 344	064 344	DB	2-6-2T	1C1h2t	1934	M	DBM. Passau.
64 355	064 355	DB	2-6-2T	1C1h2t	1934	P	Hillstedt.

64 393	064 393	DB	2-6-2T	1C1h2t	1935	P	Konz.
64 415	064 415	DB	2-6-2T	1C1h2t	1935	MA	VSM Beekbergen, (NL).
64 419	064 419	DB	2-6-2T	1C1h2t	1935	MA	DBK. Crailsheim.
64 446	064 446	DB	2-6-2T	1C1h2t	1938	M	DBM. Bahnpark, Augsburg.
64 491	064 491	DB	2-6-2T	1C1h2t	1940	MA	DFS Ebermannstadt.
64 518	064 518	DB	2-6-2T	1C1h2t	1940	MA	Eurovapor, Huttwil, (CH).
64 520	064 520	DB	2-6-2T	1C1h2t	1940	MR	BEM Nördlingen.
65 018	065 018	DB	2-8-4T	1D2h2t	1955	MA	SSN. Rotterdam Noord, (NL)
65 1008	65 1008	DR	2-8-4T	1D2h2t	1955	M	Pasewalk.
65 1049	65 1049	DR	2-8-4T	1D2h2t	1956	MA	DBM Arnstadt.
65 1057	65 1057	DR	2-8-4T	1D2h2t	1956	M	Basdorf.
66 002	066 002	DB	2-6-4T	1C2h2t	1955	M	Stiftung Eisenbahnmuseum Bochum Dahlhausen.
70 083	-	DB	2-4-0T	1Bn2t	1913	MA	BLV, Tegernsee.
74 231	-	DR	2-6-0T	1Ch2t	1908	MA	MEM, Minden.
74 1192	-	DR	2-6-0T	1Ch2t	1915	M	Stiftung Eisenbahnmuseum Bochum Dahlhausen.
74 1230	74 1230	DR	2-6-0T	1Ch2t	1916	MS	DBM Berlin Schöneweide.
75 501	-	DR	2-6-2T	1C1h2t	1916	M	DDM. Neuenmarkt Wirsberg
75 515	-	DR	2-6-2T	1C1h2t	1911	M	VMD. SEM. Chemnitz Hilbersdorf.
75 634	-	DB	2-6-2T	1C1h2t	1929	M	VVM. Aumühle.
75 1118	-	DR	2-6-2T	1C1h2t	1921	MA	UEF. Gerstetten.
78 009		DR	4-6-4T	2C2h2t	1912	M	VMD. Dresden Altstadt.
78 192	078 192	DB	4-6-4T	2C2h2t	1920	M	Tuttlingen.
78 246	078 246	DB	4-6-4T	2C2h2t	1922	MR	DDM/EFZ. Rottweil.
78 468	078 468	DB	4-6-4T	2C2h2t	1923	MA	Lengerich.
78 510	078 510	DB	4-6-4T	2C2h2t	1924	M	DBM. Nürnberg.
80 009	-	DR	0-6-0T	Ch2t	1928	P	Berlin Bohnsdorf.
80 013	-	DB	0-6-0T	Ch2t	1928	M	DDM. Neuenmarkt Wirsberg.
80 014	-	DB	0-6-0T	Ch2t	1928	M	SEH. Heilbronn.
80 023	-	DR	0-6-0T	Ch2t	1928	M	VMD. Chemnitz Hilbersdorf.
80 030	-	DR	0-6-0T	Ch2t	1929	M	Stiftung Eisenbahnmuseum Bochum Dahlhausen.
80 036	-	DB	0-6-0T	Ch2t	1929	M	VSM. Beekbergen, (NL).
80 039	-	DB	0-6-0T	Ch2t	1929	MA	Hamm.
81 004	-	DB	0-8-0T	DH2t	1928	MS	Naumburg.
82 008	082-008	DB	0-10-0T	Eh2t	1950	M	DBM. Koblenz
85 007		DB	2-10-2T	1E1h3t	1932	P	DBM. Freiburg/Brsg.
86 001	86 1001	DR	2-8-2T	1D1h2t	1928	M	DBM, SEM Chemnitz Hilbersdorf.
86 049	86 1049	DR	2-8-2T	1D1h2t	1932	M	VSE Schwarzenberg.
86 056	86 1056	DR	2-8-2T	1D1h2t	1932	M	ÖGEG Ampflwang, (A).
86 283	086 283	DB	2-8-2T	1D1h2t	1937	M	DDM. Neuenmarkt Wirsberg.
86 333	86 1333	DR	2-8-2T	1D1h2t	1939	MA	PRESS, Glauchau
86 346	086 346	DB	2-8-2T	1D1h2t	1939	MS	UEF. Menzingen.
86 348	086 348	DB	2-8-2T	1D1h2t	1939	MS	Kornwestheim.
86 457	086 457	DB	2-8-2T	1D1h2t	1942	M	DBM Heilbronn.
86 501	86 1501	DR	2-8-2T	1D1h2t	1942	MA	ÖGEG Ampflwang, (A)
86 607	86 1607	DR	2-8-2T	1D1h2t	1942	M	Adorf.
86 744	86 1744	DR	2-8-2T	1D1h2t	1942	MR	MEM. Prussisch Oldendorf.
88 7306		DB	0-4-0T	Bn2t	1892	M	DGEG. Neustadt/Weinstr
88 "7405"		DB	0-4-0T	Bn2t	1899	M	DTM, Berlin.
89 008		DR	0-6-0T	Ch2t	1938	M	VMD. Schwerin.
89 312		DB	0-6-0T	Cn2t	1896	M	Technoseum. Mannheim.
89 339		DB	0-6-0T	Cn2t	1901	M	DME. Darmstadt Kranichstein.
89 357		DB	0-6-0T	Cn2t	1903	P	Kornwestheim.
89 363		DB	0-6-0T	Cn2t	1905	MA	GES, Neuffen.
89 407		DB	0-6-0T	Cn2t	1912	M	SEH. Heilbronn.
89 801		DB	0-6-0T	Cn2t	1921	M	DBM. Koblenz Lützel.
89 837	789.837	ÖBB	0-6-0T	Cn2t	1921	M	BEM Nördlingen.
89 1004	89 1004	DR	0-6-0T	Ch2t	1906	M	DBM Halle P.
89 6009	89 6009	DR	0-6-0T	Ch2t	1902	MA	DBM Dresden Altstadt.
89 6024		DR	0-6-0T	Ch2t	1914	MA	DDM. Neuenmarkt Wirsberg.
89 6237		DR	0-6-0T	Ch2t	1924	MA	MEM. Prussisch Oldendorf.
"89 6311"	-	DR	0-6-0T	Ch2t	1936	M	DBM Arnstadt.

89 7005			0-6-0T	Ch2t	1882	M	Hochdahl.
89 7077		DB	0-6-0T	Ch2t	1899	MS	Lübeck (Private).
89 7159			0-6-0T	Ch2t	1910	MA	DGEG. Neustadt/Weinstr.
89 7220			0-6-0T	Ch2t	1896	M	MBS. Haaksbergen, (NL).
89 7296		DB	0-6-0T	Ch2t	1899	M	Gramzow.
89 7462		DB	0-6-0T	Ch2t	1904	M	DBM. Koblenz.
89 7513		DB	0-6-0T	Ch2t	1911	M	Loburg.
89 7531		DB	0-6-0T	Ch2t	1898	M	SEH. Heilbronn.
89 7538		DB	0-6-0T	Ch2t	1914	MS	Moers-Rheinkamp
90 009			0-6-2T	C1n2t	1893	M	Stiftung Eisenbahnmuseum Bochum Dahlhausen.
90 042			0-6-2T	C1n2t	1895	M	SHE, Heilbronn.
91 134		DR	2-6-0T	1Cn2t	1898	M	DBM. Schwerin.
91 319			2-6-0T	1Cn2t	1902	P	Münster-Gremmendorf (Westf.)
91 896II		DR	2-6-0T	1Cn2t	1912	M	SEM, Chemnitz Hilbersdorf.
91 936	(TKi3-112)	PKP	2-6-0T	1Cn2t	1903	M	DTM. Berlin.
(T9.3)	Sbr 7318	(CFR)	2-6-0T	1Cn2t		MR	Moers-Rheinkamp
91 6580	-	DR	2-6-0T	1Ch2t	1939	M	DBM Arnstadt.
92 011	-	DRG	0-8-0T	DH2t	1917	P	Rust/Lahr.
92 442	-	DRG	0-8-0T	DH2t	1928	MR	GES, Kornwestheim.
92 503	-	DR	0-8-0T	DH2t	1910	M	VMD. Dresden Altstadt.
92 638	-	DR	0-8-0T	DH2t	1912	M	MEM. Minden.
92 739	-	DB	0-8-0T	DH2t	1914	M	DBM/DGEG. Neustadt/Weinstr.
93 230	-	DR	2-8-2T	1D1h2t	1917	M	VMD. Dieringhausen.
93 526	093 526	DB	2-8-2T	1D1h2t	1918	M	DDM. Neuenmarkt Wirsberg.
94 002	-	DRG	0-10-0T	Eh2t	1907	M	DGEG. Neustadt/Weinstr.
94 249	-	DR	0-10-0T	Eh2t	1908	M	Heiligenstadt Ost.
94 1184	094 184	DB	0-10-0T	Eh2t	1921	MR	Crailsheim.
94 1292	94 1292	DR	0-10-0T	Eh2t	1922	MA	DBM. Ilmenau.
94 1538	094 538	DB	0-10-0T	Eh2t	1922	MR	Ilmenau.
94 1640	094 640	DB	0-10-0T	Eh2t	1923	P	Gennep, (NL).
94 1692	094 692	DB	0-10-0T	Eh2t	1924	M	DBM. Ilmenau.
94 1697	094 697	DB	0-10-0T	Eh2t	1924	M	BEM Nördlingen.
94 1730	094 730	DB	0-10-0T	Eh2t	1924	M	DDM. Neuenmarkt Wirsberg.
94 2105	-	DR	0-10-0T	Eh2t	1923	M	VMD. Schwarzenberg.
95 009	95 0009	DR	2-10-2T	1E1h2t	1922	M	Glauchau
95 016	95 1016	DR	2-10-2T	1E1h2t	1922	M	Neuenmarkt Wirsberg.
95 020	95 0020	DR	2-10-2T	1E1h2t	1923	M	TM. Speyer (As "95 007").
95 027	95 1027	DR	2-10-2T	1E1h2t	1923	MA	DBM Blankenberg.
95 028	95 0028	DR	2-10-2T	1E1h2t	1923	M	Stiftung Eisenbahnmuseum Bochum Dahlhausen.
95 6676	95 6676	DR	2-10-2T	1E1h2t	1919	MS	Rubeland.
97 501	-	DB	0-10-0RT	Ezzh2t	1923	MA	ZHL, Reutlingen.
97 502	-	DB	0-10-0RT	Ezzh2t	1923	M	Stiftung Eisenbahnmuseum Bochum Dahlhausen.
97 504	-	DB	0-10-0RT	Ezzh2t	1925	M	DTM. Berlin
98 001	-	DR	0-4-4-0T	BBn4vt	1910	M	VMD. Industrie Museum, Chemnitz.
98 307	-	DB	0-4-0T	Bh2t	1909	M	DBM. Neuenmarkt Wirsberg
98 507	-	DB	0-6-2T	C1h2t	1903	P	DBM. Ingolstadt, Bhf.
98 727	-	DRG	0-4-4-0T	BBn4vt	1903	M	DME. Darmstadt Kranichstein.
98 812	098 812	DB	0-8-0T	DH2t	1914	MA	UEF. Gerstetten.
98 886	098 886	DB	0-8-0T	DH2t	1924	MA	Fladungen.
98 7056	-	DR	0-4-0T	Bn2t	1886	M	VMD. Dresden Altstadt.
98 7508	-	DRG	0-4-0T	Bn2t	1883	M	DGEG. Neustadt/Weinstr.
98 7658	-	DRG	0-6-0T	Cn2t	1892	M	Bayerische Eisenstein.
99 162	-	DR	0-4-4-0T	BBn4vt	1902	M	Oberhainsdorf.
99 193	-	DB	0-10-0T	Eh2t	1927	MA	Blonay Chamby, (CH).
99 211	-	DB	0-6-0T	Ch2t	1929	P	Wangerooge.
99 253	-	DB	0-6-2T	C1n2t	1908	P	Regensburg.
99 516	99 1516	DR	0-4-4-0T	BBn4vt	1892	MA	Schöneheide Mitte.
99 534	99 1534	DR	0-4-4-0T	BBn4vt	1898	P	Geyer.
99 535	99 1535	DR	0-4-4-0T	BBn4vt	1898	M	VMD. Dresden.
99 539	99 1539	DR	0-4-4-0T	BBn4vt	1899	MS	Radeburg.
99 542	99 1542	DR	0-4-4-0T	BBn4vt	1899	MA	Jöhstadt.

99 555	99 1555	DR	0-4-4-0T	BBn4vt	1908	MS	Bertsdorf.
99 562	99 1562	DR	0-4-4-0T	BBn4vt	1909	M	DDM. Neuenmarkt Wirsberg.
99 564	99 1564	DR	0-4-4-0T	BBn4vt	1909	MR	Radebeul Ost.
99 566	99 1566	DR	0-4-4-0T	BBn4vt	1909	M	SEM. Chemnitz Hilbersdorf.
99 568	99 1568	DR	0-4-4-0T	BBn4vt	1910	MA	Jöhstadt.
99 579	99 1579	DR	0-4-4-0T	BBn4vt	1912	P	Oberrittersgrün.
99 582	99 1582	DR	0-4-4-0T	BBn4vt	1912	MA	Schöneheide Mitte.
99 585	99 1585	DR	0-4-4-0T	BBn4vt	1913	MS	Schöneheide Mitte.
99 586	99 1586	DR	0-4-4-0T	BBn4vt	1913	MA	Radebeul Ost.
99 590	99 1590	DR	0-4-4-0T	BBn4vt	1913	MA	Jöhstadt.
99 594	99 1594	DR	0-4-4-0T	BBn4vt	1913	MS	Putbus.
99 604	99 1604	DR	0-4-4-0T	BBn4vt	1914	MA	VSSB, Radebeul.
99 606	99 1606	DR	0-4-4-0T	BBn4vt	1916	MR	VSSB Carlsfeld.
99 633	-	DB	0-4-4-0T	BBn4vt	1899	MA	Ochsenhausen.
99 637	-	DB	0-4-4-0T	BBn4vt	1904	P	Bad Buchau.
99 651	-	DB	0-10-0T	Eh2t	1919	MR	Ochsenhausen.
99 713	99 1713	DR	0-10-0T	Eh2t	1927	MA	Radebeul.
99 715	99 1715	DR	0-10-0T	Eh2t	1927	MR	Jöhstadt.
99 716	-	DB	0-10-0T	Eh2t	1927	MA	Ochsenhausen.
99 750	99 1750	DR	2-10-2T	1E1h2t	1929	P	Trixipark, Gross Schönau.
99 759	99 1759	DR	2-10-2T	1E1h2t	1933	M	Oberrittersgrün.
99 788	99 1788	DR	2-10-2T	1E1h2t	1955	MA	Ochsenhausen.
99 790	99 1790	DR	2-10-2T	1E1h3	1957	P	Freital Hainsberg.
99 3301	99 3301	DR	0-6-0T	Cn2t	1895	MA	Cottbus Park.
99 3310	99 3310	DR	0-8-0T	Dn2t	1917	MA	Ohs Bruk Jvg. (S).
99 3311	99 3311	DR	0-8-0T	Dn2t	1917	MR	Schinznach, (CH).
99 3312	99 3312	DR	0-8-0T	Dn2t	1912	MA	Weisswasser.
99 3313	99 3313	DR	0-8-0T	Dn2t	1914	MA	DRM. Frankfurt/M.
99 3314	99 3314	DR	0-8-0T	Dn2t	1917	M	MPSF. Schwichtenberg.
99 3315	99 3315	DR	0-8-0T	Dn2t	1917	MA	DKM. Muhlenstroth.
99 3316	99 3316	DR	0-8-0T	Dn2t	1919	M	TM. Speyer.
99 3317	99 3317	DR	0-8-0T	Dn2t	1918	MS	Weisswasser.
99 3318	99 3318	DR	0-8-0T	Dn2t	1918	MR	DKM. Muhlenstroth.
99 3351	99 3351	DR	0-6-2T	C1n2t	1906	MR	DRM. Frankfurt/M.
99 3352	99 3352	DR	0-6-2TT	C1n2t	1907	P	Friedland.
99 3353	99 3353	DR	0-6-2T	C1n2t	1908	MA	Brecon, (UK).
99 3361	99 3361	DR	0-8-0	Dn2t	1938	MA	Hesston, Indiana, (USA).
99 3461	99 3461	DR	0-8-0	Dn2t	1934	MA	Froissy, France.
99 3462	99 3462	DR	0-8-0	Dn2t	1934	MA	DKM. Muhlenstroth.
99 4301		DR	0-6-0T	Cn2t	1920	P	Gommern.
99 4503		DR	0-6-0T	Cn2t	1920	P	Gramzow.
99 4511		DR	0-6-2T	C1n2t	1899	MA	Jöhstadt.
99 4532	99 4532	DR	0-8-0T	Dn2t	1924	M	Bertsdorf.
99 4631	99 4631	DR	0-8-0T	Dh2t	1913	MS	Kanzach.
99 4644	99 4644	DR	0-8-0T	Dh2t	1923	MR	Lindenberg.
99 4652		DR	0-6-0TT	Cn2t	1941	MS	Putbus.
99 4701		DR	0-6-0T	Cn2t	1914	P	Wollstein.
99 5001		DR	0-6-0T	Bn2t	1922	MS	Portes la Valence, (F).
99 5605	99 5605	DR	0-4-0T	Bn2t	1925	MA	DEV. Bruchhausen Vilsen.
99 5606	99 5606	DR	0-4-0T	Bn2t	1894	MR	Wim Pater. (NL).
99 5611		DR	0-6-0T	Cn2t	1925	MS	Tence, (F).
99 5633		DR	2-6-0T	1Cn2t	1917	MA	DEV. Bruchhausen Vilsen.
99 5703		DR	0-6-0T	Cn2t	1897	M	Lubbenau.
99 7201		DB	0-6-0T	Cn2t	1904	MR	Tambach-Dietharz.
99 7202		DB	0-6-0T	Cn2t	1904	P	Mudau.
99 7203		DB	0-6-0T	Cn2t	1904	MA	UEF. Amstetten.
99 7204		DB	0-6-0T	Cn2t	1904	M	MME. Hersheid-Hünigshause.

9.2. ELECTRIC LOCOMOTIVES

Old No.	Computer No.	Co.	Wheel	Built	Status	Location
E03 001	103 001	DB	Co-Co	1965	MA	DBM. Koblenz Lützel.
E03 002	103 002	DB	Co-Co	1965	P	Herrnried.
E03 004	103 004	DB	Co-Co	1966	MS	DBM. Lichtenfels.
	103 101	DB	Co-Co	1971	M	DME. Darmstadt.
	103 113	DB	Co-Co	1971	MA	DBM. Koblenz Lützel.
	103 132	DB	Co-Co	1971	MS	LDX (Spares for 103 235/245).
	103 136	DB	Co-Co	1971	M	BEM Nördlingen.
	103 167	DB	Co-Co	1971	M	Lokwelt Freilassing, Freilassing.
	103 184	DB	Co-Co	1972	MS	FF1.
	103 197	DB	Co-Co	1972	MS	Paderborn
	103 220	DB	Co-Co	1973	M	DBM. Koblenz Lützel.
	103 224	DB	Co-Co	1973	M	DBM. Glauchau
	103 226	DB	Co-Co	1973	MS	Wildenrath.
	103 233	DB	Co-Co	1973	MS	DBM. Koblenz Lützel.
	103 235	DB	Co-Co	1973	M	DBM. Koblenz Lützel.
E04 01	204 001	DR	1Co1	1932	M	Leipzig Hbf.
E04 07	204 007	DR	1Co1	1933	M	Stassfurt.
E04 11	204 011	DR	1Co1	1934	M	Weimar.
E04 20	104 020	DB	1Co1	1934	P	DB HQ Frankfurt/Main.
E10 002	110 002	DB	Bo-Bo	1952	M	DBM. Nürnberg
E10 005	110 005	DB	Bo-Bo	1952	M	DBM Koblenz Lützel.
E10 121	110 121	DB	Bo-Bo	1957	M	DB Regio. Köln Bbf.
E10 152	110 152	DB	Bo-Bo	1956	MS	DBM Koblenz Lützel.
E10 210	110 210	DB	Bo-Bo	1957	M	DBM Koblenz Lützel.
E10 223	110 223	DB	Bo-Bo	1961	M	DBM Lichtenfels.
E10 228	110 228	DB	Bo-Bo	1961	MA	DBM Stuttgart (TS).
E10 281	110 281	DB	Bo-Bo	1963	M	Eisenbahn Erlebniswelt, Horb.
E10 292	110 292	DB	Bo-Bo	1964	M	DBM Koblenz Lützel.
E10 300	110 300	DB	Bo-Bo	1963	MS	Baureihe E10 e.V. Koblenz Lützel.
E10 348	110 348	DB	Bo-Bo	1964	MA	DBM Koblenz Lützel.
E10 468	110 468	DB	Bo-Bo	1966	MS	BSW Freizeit Gruppe, Rottweil.
E10 488	110 488	DB	Bo-Bo	1968	MS	BSW Freizeit Gruppe, Rottweil.
E10 1239	110 239	DB	Bo-Bo	1961	MA	Lokomotive 103 e.V. Wegberg Wildenrath.
E10 1311	113 311	DB	Bo-Bo	1963	MS	DBM. NN2.
E11 001	211 001	DR	Bo-Bo	1961	MS	Halle P.
E11 049	109 049	DR	Bo-Bo	1970	M	Weimar.
	111 001	DB	Bo-Bo	1975	M	DBM. Koblenz Lützel.
	111 003	DB	Bo-Bo	1975	MR	Euskirchen.
E16 03	116 003	DB	1Do1	1926	M	DBM. Koblenz Lützel.
E16 07	116 007	DB	1Do1	1926	M	Lokwelt Freilassing.
E16 08	116 008	DB	1Do1	1926	M	DME, Darmstadt Kranichstein.
E16 09	116 009	DB	1Do1	1926	M	Bahnpark Augsburg.
E17 103	117 103	DB	1Do1	1929	MS	Lichtenfels.
E17 113	117 113	DB	1Do1	1928	M	DGEG. Neustadt (Weinstr).
E18 03	118 003	DB	1Do1	1935	MS	DBM. Koblenz Lützel.
E18 08	118 008	DB	1Do1	1936	M	Bahnpark Augsburg.
E18 19	218 019	DB	1Do1	1936	MS	Glauchau.
E18 24	118 024	DR	1Do1	1936	M	Weimar.
E18 31	218 031	DR	1Do1	1937	M	Halle P.
E18 047	118 047	DB	1Do1	1939	MA	DBM, Halle P.
E19 01	119 001	DB	1Do1	1938	M	DTM. Berlin.
E19 12	119 012	DB	1Do1	1939	MS	DBM. NN2
-	120 003	DB	Bo-Bo	1979	M	Bahnpark Augsburg.
	120 004	DB	Bo-Bo	1979	M	DBM. Koblenz Lützel.
-	120 005	DB	Bo-Bo	1979	M	TEV, Weimar.
-	128 001		Bo-Bo	1994	M	Bombardier, TEV Weimar
E32 27	132 027	DB	1C1	1925	M	Stiftung Eisenbahnmuseum Bochum Dahlhausen.
	140 128	DB	Bo-Bo	1959	M	DBM. Koblenz Lützel.

▲ E10 1239, owned by Lokomotiv 103 eV, heads the historic TEE stock from Freundeskreis Eisenbahn Köln on a dining special from Köln to Mainz on 8 November 2015, seen here near Hammerstein.
Matthias Müller

▼ 140 423 and 212 372 top and tail an excursion from Koblenz Hbf to the DB Museum at Koblenz-Lützel on 18 June 2017. Both locomotives are based at the museum site. They are seen passing the signal box at Koblenz-Lützel yard.
Matthias Müller

	140 423	DB	Bo-Bo	1963	M	DBM. Koblenz Lützel.
	140 844	DB	Bo-Bo	1972	M	DBM. DDM Neuenmarkt Wirsberg
E41 001	141 001	DB	Bo-Bo	1956	M	DBM. Koblenz Lützel.
E41 006	141 006	DB	Bo-Bo	1956	M	Dieringhausen.
E41 011	141 011	DB	Bo-Bo	1956	MR	Private. NN1.
E41 055	141 055	DB	Bo-Bo	1958	MS	Koblenz Lützel.
E41 068	141 068	DB	Bo-Bo	1958	MS	Private. FF1.
	141 083	DB	Bo-Bo	1958	M	DBM, Nördlingen
E41 228	141 228	DB	Bo-Bo	1962	M	DBM/DME. Darmstadt.
E41 248	141 248	DB	Bo-Bo	1963	M	DBM/ Siegen.
E41 366	141 366	DB	Bo-Bo	1965	M	DBM, Wegberg Wildenrath
E41 401	141 401	DB	Bo-Bo	1965	M	Technikmuseum, Kassel
E42 001	142 001	DR	Bo-Bo	1963	MA	Glauchau.
E42 002	142 002	DR	Bo-Bo	1963	M	SEM. Chemnitz Hilbersdorf.
E42 151	142 151	DR	Bo-Bo	1968	MA	Weimar.
E42 255	142 255	DR	Bo-Bo	1976	M	Halle P.
	143 002	DR	Bo-Bo	1984	M	DBM. Halle P.
	143 005	DR	Bo-Bo	1984	M	DBM. Halle P.
-	143 007	DR	Bo-Bo	1984	M	Weimar.
-	143 117	DR	Bo-Bo	1986	M	TEV Weimar. Painted as 243 001.
-	143 806	DR	Bo-Bo	1988	MS	Falkenberg/Elster
E44 001	144 001	DB	Bo-Bo	1930	M	DBM. Nürnberg
E44 002	144 002	DB	Bo-Bo	1933	MS	DBM. Koblenz.
E44 044	244 044	DR	Bo-Bo	1936	M	Dessau Works.
E44 045	244 045	DR	Bo-Bo	1936	M	SEM. Chemnitz Hilbersdorf.
E44 046	244 046	DR	Bo-Bo	1936	M	Leipzig Hbf.
E44 049	244 049	DR	Bo-Bo	1936	M	Falkenberg/Elster.
E44 051	244 051	DR	Bo-Bo	1936	M	Lokwelt Freilassing.
E44 059	144 059	DB	Bo-Bo	1937	MS	DBM/Pflazbahn, Worms.
E44 084	144 084	DB	Bo-Bo	1938	M	DBM/ Eisenbahn Erlebniswelt, Horb.
E44 103	244 103	DR	Bo-Bo	1940	M	Weimar.
E44 105	244 105	DR	Bo-Bo	1940	M	Weimar.
E44 108	244 108	DR	Bo-Bo	1939	M	DBM. Halle P.
E44 119	144 119	DB	Bo-Bo	1941	MS	DBM. Lichtenfels.
E44 131	244 131	DR	Bo-Bo	1942	M	DTM. Berlin.
E44 137	244 137	DR	Bo-Bo	1942	MS	SEH Heilbronn
E44 139	244 139	DR	Bo-Bo	1942	M	ETM. Prora.
E44 143	244 143	DR	Bo-Bo	1942	M	Weimar.
E44 148	244 148	DR	Bo-Bo	1942	M	Hermeskeil.
E44 150	144 150	DB	Bo-Bo	1942	M	DGEG. Neustadt (Weinstr).
E44 502	144 502	DB	Bo-Bo	1933	P	Freilassing.
E44 507	144 507	DB	Bo-Bo	1934	M	Weimar.
E44 508	144 508	DB	Bo-Bo	1934	M	Lokwelt, Freilassing.
E44 1170	145 170	DB	Bo-Bo	1944	M	DBM, Seebrugg.
E44 1180	145 180	DB	Bo-Bo	1947	MS	DBM/Pfalzbahn, Worms.
E50 091	150 091	DB	Co-Co	1963	M	DBM. Koblenz Lützel.
150 186	150 186	DB	Co-Co	1972	M	DBM, Koblenz Lützel.
151 121	151 121	DB	Co-Co	1976	M	DBM, Koblenz Lützel.
E52 34	152 034	DB	2B-B2	1924	MS	DBM. Lichtenfels.
152 040	152 040ⁱ	DB	Bo-Bo	1998	P	DB, Dessau Works
E60 09	160 009	DB	1-C	1932	M	DME, Darmstadt Kranichstein.
E60 10	160 010	DB	1-C	1932	M	DBM. Koblenz.
E60 12	160 012	DB	1-C	1932	M	TM. Sinsheim.
E63 01	163 001	DB	C	1935	P	Bw Rosenstein (TS), Stuttgart.
E63 02	163 002	DB	C	1935	M	BEM, Nördlingen.
E63 05	163 005	DB	C	1936	M	Bahnpark Augsburg.
E63 08	163 008	DB	C	1938	M	DBM, SEH Heilbronn.
E69 01	-	DB	Bo	1905	M	Lokwelt Freilassing.
E69 02	169 002	DB	Bo	1909	M	DBM. Nürnberg
E69 03	169 003	DB	Bo	1922	M	DBM, Koblenz Lützel.
E69 04	169 004	DB	Bo	1922	P	Murnau.
E69 05	169 005	DB	Bo	1922	M	BLM. Landshut.
E71 19	-	DB	B-B	1921	M	DBM. Koblenz Lützel.
E71 28	-	DB	B-B	1922	M	DTM. Berlin.

E71 30	-	DR	B-B	1922	M	VMD. Dresden.
E75 09	175 009	DB	1B-B1	1928	MS	DBM. Meiningen Works
E77 10	-	DR	1B-B1	1925	MS	DBM. Dresden Altstadt
	180 014	DR	Bo-Bo	1991	M	TEV, Weimar.
E91 99	191 099	DB	C-C	1929	M	Bahnpark Augsburg.
E93 07	193 007	DB	Co-Co	1936	MS	DBM, Koblenz Lützel.
E93 08	193 008	DB	Co-Co	1936	P	AKW Neckarwestheim.
E93 12	193 012	DB	Co-Co	1936	M	DGEG. Neustadt (Weinstr).
E94 040	254 040	DR	Co-Co	1942	M	Hermeskeil.
E94 052	254 052	DR	Co-Co	1941	M	Lokwelt, Freilassing.
E94 056	254 056	DR	Co-Co	1942	MS	Leipzig Hbf.
E94 058	254 058	DR	Co-Co	1941	M	Falkenberg/Elster.
E94 059	254 059	DR	Co-Co	1942	M	SEM. Chemnitz Hilbersdorf.
E94 066	254 066	DR	Co-Co	1942	M	Hermeskeil.
E94 080	194 080	DB	Co-Co	1942	M	Stiftung Eisenbahnmuseum Bochum Dahlhausen.
E94 106	254 106	DR	Co-Co	1943	M	TEV, Weimar.
E94 110	254 110	DR	Co-Co	1943	M	Hermeskeil.
E94 135	1020 017	ÖBB	Co-Co	1945	MS	BEM. Nördlingen.
E94 158	194 158	DB	Co-Co	1944	A	Mönchengladbach.
E94 192	194 192	DB	Co-Co	1956	MA	BEM Nördlingen.
E94 279	194 579	DB	Co-Co	1955	MA	DBM. Kornwestheim.
E94 281	194 581	DB	Co-Co	1955	MS	Kornwestheim (Spares for E94 279).
E94 580	194 580	DB	Co-Co	1955	A	Back in traffic as "194 178".
E95 02	-	DR	1Co-Co1	1910	MS	Halle P.
E244 31	-	DB	Bo-Bo	1936	MS	HEM. Mannheim.
250 001	155 001	DR	Co-Co	1974	M	Halle P.
250 250	155 250	DR	Co-Co	1984	M	TEV, Weimar.
E251 001	171 001	DR	Co-Co	1964	MS	DBM, Blankenberg.
E251 002	171 002	DR	Co-Co	1964	MS	DBM, Blankenberg.
E251 012	171 012	DR	Co-Co	1965	M	Weimar.
E310 001	181 001	DB	Bo-Bo	1967	M	DBM. Koblenz Lützel.
	181 201	DB	Bo-Bo	1974	M	DBM. Koblenz Lützel.
E320 01	182 001	DB	Bo-Bo	1959	M	DBM. Koblenz Lützel.
E410 003	184 003	DB	Bo-Bo	1968	M	DBM. Koblenz Lützel.
E410 012	184 112	DB	Bo-Bo	1967	M	DTM. Berlin.

9.3. DIESEL LOCOMOTIVES

Old No.	Computer No.	Co.	Wheel	Built	Status	Location
V15 002	-	DB	B DM	1935	M	Göteborg, (S).
V15 005	-	DB	B DH	1943	M	Göteborg, (S).
V16 100	-	DB	B DM	1936	M	MEM Minden.
V20 022	-	DB	B DM	1942	M	Almstedt.
V20 035	270 035	DB	B DH	1943	M	BLME, Braunschweig.
V20 036	270 036	DB	B DH	1943	P	DBM. Glückstadt.
V20 039	270 039	DB	B DH	1943	M	VVM. Schonberger Strand.
V20 051	270 051	DB	B DH	1943	M	EKF. Bhf Sinsheim.
V20 058	-	DB	B DH	1943	M	BLME, Braunschweig.
V29 952	-	DB	B-B DH	1952	MA	Bruchhausen Vilsen.
V36 027	103 027	DR	C DH	1939	M	DBM, Schwerin.
V36 102	236 102	DB	C DH	1945	M	DME Darmstadt.
V36 107	236 107	DB	C DH	1940	M	DBM Koblenz Lützel.
V36 108	236 108	DB	C DH	1940	MS	DBM. Lichtenfels.
V36 114	236 114	DB	C DH	1945	M	Oberhausen.
V36 116	236 116	DB	C DH	1941	M	DGEG. Neustadt (Weinstr).
V36 119	236 119	DB	C DH	1940	MA	WTB. Blumberg.
V36 123	236 123	DB	C DH	1940	MA	Ebermannstadt.
V36 204	236 204	DB	C DH	1939	MA	WTB. Blumberg
V36 211	236 211	DB	C DH	1942	MA	BEM. Nördlingen.
V36 225	236 225	DB	C DH	1944	MA	BLME, Braunschweig.

V36 231	236 231	DB	C DH	1939	MA	Stiftung Eisenbahnmuseum Bochum Dahlhausen.
V36 237	236 237	DB	C DH	1947	M	Bruchhausen Vilsen.
V36 262	236 262	DB	C DH	1948	M	Bodenwerder.
V36 311	-	DB	C DM	1940	M	BLME. Braunschweig.
V36 314	-	DB	C DM	1941	M	MEM Minden.
V36 316	-	DB	C DM	1942	M	Dieringhausen.
V36 401	236 401	DB	C DH	1950	MA	DME. Darmstadt Kranichstein.
V36 405	236 405	DB	C DH	1950	MA	HE Frankfurt/M.
V36 406	236 406	DB	C DH	1950	M	HE Frankfurt/M.
V36 411	236 411	DB	C DH	1950	M	DME. Darmstadt Kranichstein.
V36 412	236 412	DB	C DH	1950	MR	ET. Lengerich.
V45 009	245 009	DB	B DH	1956	M	DDM. Neuenmarkt Wirsberg.
105 072	345 072	DR	D DH	1977	M	Wittenberge (On loan from MEG).
105 152	345 152	DR	D DH	1982	M	TEV, Weimar
V60 1001	-	DR	D DH	1959	M	SEM. Chemnitz Hilbersdorf.
V60 1067	346 067	DR	D DH	1962	M	Belzig.
V60 1068	346 068	DR	D DH	1962	M	Aschersleben.
V60 1078	346 078	DR	D DH	1963	M	Falkenberg/Elster.
V60 1095	346 095	DR	D DH	1963	M	Heilgenstadt Ost.
V60 1100	346 100	DR	D DH	1963	M	Arnstadt.
V60 1120	346 120	DR	D DH	1963	M	SEM Chemnitz.
106 182	346 182	DR	D DH	1981	M	Falkenberg/Elster.
106 521	346 521	DR	D DH	1968	M	Oelsnitz.
106 660	346 660	DR	D DH	1970	M	Falkenberg/Elster.
260 114	360 114	DB	C DH	1956	MA	DFS, Ebermannstadt.
260 303	360 303	DB	C DH	1957	M	DBM. Koblenz Lützel.
260 328	360 328	DB	C DH	1957	M	DBK Crailsheim
260 366	360 366	DB	C DH	1957	M	SEH, Heilbronn.
260 447	364 447	DB	C DH	1959	MA	MEC Losheim.
260 555	360 555	DB	C DH	1960	MA	MKO. Norden
260 583	360 583	DB	C DH	1960	M	DGEG, Bochum Dahlhausen.
260 588	360 588	DB	C DH	1960	M	Radewormwald-Dahlhausen
260 615	360 615	DB	C DH	1961	M	HEF, Hamm.
261 689	363 689	DB	C DH	1959	MA	SVG Stuttgart
261 715	365 715	DB	C DH	1960	M	Technoseum, Mannheim
260 786	364 786	DB	C DH	1960	M	Battenberg/Eder.
261 815	363 815	DB	C DH	1960	M	PEF, Passau.
261 838	365 838	DB	C DH	1960	M	Gelsenkirchen Bismarck
260 860	360 860	DB	C DH	1960	M	BEM, Nördlingen.
260 882	360 882	DB	C DH	1960	MS	DBM, EF Grenzland, Aachen
261 234	361 234	DB	C DH	1960	M	Vienenburg.
V60 761	362 761	DB	C DH	1960	M	Passau.
261 715	365 715	DB	C DH	1960	M	LTA, Mannheim.
261 138	365 138	DB	C DH	1963	MS	DBM, EF Grenzland, Aachen
V65 001	265 001	DB	D DH	1956	MA	Osnabrück.
V65 011	265 011	DB	D DH	1956	M	DBM, Koblenz Lützel.
V80 001	280 001	DB	B-B DH	1952	MR	Private, Frankfurt/M.
V80 005	280 005	DB	B-B DH	1952	MR	DBM, NN2.
V80 007	280 007	DB	B-B DH	1952	MR	Altenbeken.
V90 001	290 001	DB	B-B DH	1964	M	DBM, Koblenz Lützel.
V100 003	201 003	DR	B-B DH	1968	MA	Lutherstadt Wittenberg.
V100 019	201 019	DR	B-B DH	1967	MR	Brieske.
V100 025	201 025	DR	B-B DH	1967	M	SEM Chemnitz.
V100 068	201 068	DR	B-B DH	1968	P	Plau am See.
V100 093	201 093	DR	B-B DH	1968	MA	VSM Beekbergen, (NL).
V100 101	201 101	DR	B-B DH	1968	MA	Nossen.
V100 143	201 143	DR	B-B DH	1969	M	Schwerin.
110 228-4	201 228	DR	B-B DH	1970	M	Belzig.
110 380-3	201 380	DR	B-B DH	1970	MS	Zinnowitz.
DE 2500	202 002	DB	Co-Co DE	1971	P	Bombardier Transportation, Kassel.
-	202 003	DB	Bo-Bo DE	1973	M	DTM Berlin.
-	202 004	DB	Co-Co DE	1983	M	LTA. Mannheim.
110 331-6	202 331	DR	B-B DH	1971	M	Löbau.

110 457-9	202 457	DR	B-B DH	1972	M	Halle P.
110 516-2	202 516	DR	B-B DH	1973	M	VSE Schwarzenberg.
110 565-7	202 565	DR	B-B DH	1973	MA	PRESS, Espenhain.
110 792-9	201 792	DR	B-B DH	1975	MS	Zinnowitz.
110 885-1	202 885	DR	B-B DH	1978	M	SEM, Chemnitz Hilbersdorf.
114 774	204 774	DR	B-B DH	1975	M	Wittenberge (On loan from MEG).
V100 1042	211 042	DB	B-B DH	1962	P	Eschenau.
V100 1200	211 200	DB	B-B DH	1962	MA	DGEG Würzburg.
V100 1357	211 357	DB	B-B DH	1962	MA	GES Kornwestheim.
V100 2001	212 001	DB	B-B DH	1959	MS	DBM. Gelsenkirchen Bismarck.
V100 2007	212 007	DB	B-B DH	1962	M	DGEG. Bochum Dahlhausen.
V100 2062	212 062	DB	B-B DH	1963	MS	Wiesbaden.
V100 2077	212 077	DB	B-B DH	1964	MS	DBM, Osnabrück Piesberg.
V100 2084	212 084	DB	B-B DH	1964	M	DBM/DBK, Crailsheim.
V100 2372	212 372	DB	B-B DH	1965	M	DBM Koblenz Lützel.
V140 001	-	DB	1-C-1 DH	1935	M	Deutsches Museum, München.
	215 049	DB	B-B DH	1970	M	DBM Oberhausen.
	215 122	DB	B-B DH	1970	M	DBM, DBK Crailsheim
V160 003	216 003	DB	B-B DH	1960	MA	DBM Lübeck.
V160 067	216 067	DB	B-B DH	1966	M	DBM, Koblenz Lützel.
V160 221	216 221	DB	B-B DH	1968	M	DBM Lübeck
V162 001	217 001	DB	B-B DH	1965	M	Eisenbahn Erlebniswelt, Horb.
	217 014	DB	B-B DH	1968	M	DBM, Koblenz Lützel.
	218 128	DB	B-B DH	1971	MS	Euskirchen
	218 137	DB	B-B DH	1971	M	DBM, Koblenz Lützel.
	218 184	DB	B-B DH	1972	P	Bremen Works
	218 212	DB	B-B DH	1973	P	Erlebnisbahnhof Amorbach
	218 217	DB	B-B DH	1973	M	DBM, Koblenz Lützel.
	218 225	DB	B-B DH	1972	M	HE, Mannheim.
119 003-2	219 003	DR	B-B DH	1978	M	DBM/SEM. Chemnitz Hilbersdorf.
119 084-2	219 084	DR	B-B DH	1981	M	DBM/TEV, Weimar.
119 158-4	219-158	DR	B-B DH	1983	MS	DBM/RSB. Ilmenau.
	229 184	DB	B-B DH	1992	M	Gera (On loan from MEG)
	229 188	DB	B-B DH	1992	M	TEV, Weimar.
	229 199	DB	B-B DH	1993	M	TEV, Weimar.
V180 005	228 505	DR	B-B DH	1963	M	Arnstadt.
V180 048	228 548	DR	B-B DH	1964	MR	Prora.
V180 075	118 075	DR	B-B DH	1965	M	DTM. Berlin.
V180 078	228 578	DR	B-B DH	1965	M	TEV, Weimar.
V180 086	228 586	DR	B-B DH	1965	M	Stassfurt.
	228 585	DR	B-B DH	1965	P	ITL, Pirna
V180 118	228 118	DR	B-B DH	1965	M	Schwerin.
V180 141	228 141	DR	B-B DH	1965	M	SEM Chemnitz.
V240 001	228 202	DR	C-C DH	1971	M	Dresden Altstadt.
V180 078	228 578	DR	B-B DH	1965	M	TEV Weimar.
V180 217	228 617	DR	C-C DH	1967	M	Tuttlingen.
V180 256	228 656	DR	C-C DH	1967	P	Gadebusch
V180 283	228 683	DR	C-C DH	1968	M	Löbau.
V180 292	228 692	DR	C-C DH	1968	M	Wittenberge
V180 314	228 714	DR	C-C DH	1968	M	Rennsteigbahn, Ilmenau.
V180 331	228 731	DR	C-C DH	1968	M	TEV Weimar
V180 349	228 749	DR	C-C DH	1968	MA	Arnstadt.
V180 376	228 776	DR	C-C DH	1969	M	VSE Schwarzenberg.
V180 382	228 782	DR	C-C DH	1969	M	SEM Chemnitz.
V180 388	228 788	DR	C-C DH	1969	M	TEV, Weimar.
V180 402	228 802	DR	C-C DH	1970	M	Halle P.
130 002-9	230 002	DR	Co-Co DE	1971	M	Dresden.
130 101-9	754 101	DR	Co-Co DE	1973	M	DBM. Halle P.
131 001-0	231 001	DR	Co-Co DE	1973	M	DBM. Halle P.
131 060-6	231 060	DR	Co-Co DE	1973	M	SEM Chemnitz.
131 070-5	231 070	DR	Co-Co DE	1973	M	Falkenberg/Elster.
131 072-0	231 072	DR	Co-Co DE	1973	M	Arnstadt.
132 010-0	232 010	DR	Co-Co DE	1973	M	TEV, Weimar (On loan from MEG).
132 500	232 500	DR	Co-Co DE	1977	M	Wittenberge (On loan from MEG).

132 372-4	232 372	DR	Co-Co DE	1976	M	Schwerin.
232 304-6	234 304	DR	Co-Co DE	1976	M	Nossen.
V200 001	220 001	DB	B-B DH	1953	MR	FME. Nürnberg.
V200 007	220 007	DB	B-B DH	1956	MA	HE, Lübeck.
V200 009	220 009	DB	B-B DH	1956	M	TM. ETM Prora.
V200 017	220 017	DB	B-B DH	1957	S	DGEG. Bochum Dahlhausen
V200 018	220 018	DB	B-B DH	1957	M	DTM. Berlin.
V200 033	220 033	DB	B-B DH	1956	MA	HEF. Hamm.
V200 058	220 058	DB	B-B DH	1959	M	TM. Speyer.
V200 071	220 071	DB	B-B DH	1959	M	TM. Speyer.
V200 077	220 077	DB	B-B DH	1959	S	Düsseldorf (Classic Train Tours).
V200 001	220 001	DR	Co-Co DE	1966	M	Schwerin.
120 198-7	220 198	DR	Co-Co DE	1969	M	TEV, Weimar.
V200 269	220 269	DR	Co-Co DE	1969	M	SEM Chemnitz.
120 274-6	220 274	DR	Co-Co DE	1969	M	Arnstadt.
	120 338	DR	Co-Co DE	1973	M	VMD. Dresden Altstadt.
120 366-0	220 366	DR	Co-Co DE	1975	M	Stassfurt.
V200 101	221 101	DB	B-B DH	1962	M	SEH. Heilbronn.
V200 104	221 104	DB	B-B DH	1963	MS	EOB (Spares).
V200 116	221 116	DB	B-B DH	1963	MS	DBM. Lübeck.
V200 120	221 120	DB	B-B DH	1963	M	SEH. Heilbronn.
V320 001		DB	C-C DH	1962	P	Bombardier Transportation, Kassel.
	295 078	DB	B-B DH	1977	M	Passau.
Kö 0049	-	DR	B DM	1933	M	VSE Schwarzenberg.
Kö 0073	-	DB	B DM	1933	M	Dresden Altstadt.
Kö 0082	-	DB	B DM	1934	MS	Heiligenstadt.
Kö 0099	-	DB	B DM	1934	M	ETM Prora.
Kö 0107	-	DB	B DM	1935	M	DBB Mittenwalde Ost.
Kö 0110	-	DB	B DM	1935	MS	EF Kraichgau, Sinsheim.
Kö 0116	-	DB	B DM	1935	MA	BEM Nördlingen.
Kö 0128	-	DB	B DM	1934	MA	MKB Berlin Lichterfelde.

▲ Museumseisenbahn Hamm's V200 033, formerly DB 220 033, passes through Wiltingen with a special from Trier Hbf to Merzig on 1 May 2018. The special was one of several taking place in connection with the Dampfspektakel 2018, centred on Trier.   **Matthias Müller**

Kö 0181	-	DB	B DM	1935	M	Selb.
Kö 0186	311 186	DB	B DM	1936	M	Stadt Museum, Schörndorf.
Kö 0188	311 188	DB	B DM	1936	M	Siegen.
Kö 0203	-	DB	B DM	1936	M	RIM Köln.
Kö 0204	311 204	DB	B DM	1936	MS	RSWE, Regensburg.
Kö 0206		DB	B DM	1936	M	Herborn.
Kö 0210	100 010	DR	B DM	1936	MA	LDC Cottbus.
Kö 0211	311 211	DB	B DM	1936	MR	HE Mannheim.
Kö 0221	311 221	DB	B DM	1936	MA	Gerolstein (98 80 3311 221).
Kö 0225	311 225	DB	B DM	1936	MA	DBM. Bielefelder EF, Bielefeld.
Kö 0227	311 227	DB	B DM	1936	MS	Altenbeken.
Kö 0229	311 229	DB	B DM	1936	MA	DBM Koblenz Lützel.
Kö 0232	311 232	DB	B DM	1936	MR	HE Mannheim.
Kö 0237	-	DR	B DN	1936	M	OSE Löbau.
Kö 0242	100 042	DR	B DM	1936	MA	DLF, Berlin Schöneweide.
Kö 0245	100 045	DR	B DM	1936	MS	SEM Chemnitz Hilbersdorf.
Kö 0247	311 247	DB	B DM	1936	P	Modellbahnausstellung, Mölschow.
Kö 0255	311 255	DB	B DM	1936	M	Vienenburg.
Kö 0258	311 258	DB	B DM	1936	MS	IG Nebenbahn, Kassel.
Kö 0260	311 260	DB	B DM	1936	MA	BEF Basdorf (98 80 3311 260).
Kö 0262	311 262	DB	B DM	1936	P	Warthausen.
Kö 0265	311 265	DB	B DM	1936	M	Eisenbahn Museum Oderland, Wriezen.
Kö 0274	311 274	DB	B DM	1936	MS	Almstedt-Segeste VL 4.
Kö 0278	311 278	DB	B DM	1936	P	Neustadt/Aisch.
Kö 0281	311 281	DB	B DM	1936	MA	Hespertalbahn V 2, Essen-Kupferdreh.
Kö 0289	100 089	DR	B DM	1936	M	Falkenberg/Elster.
Kö 1002	-	DRG	B DM	1940	MA	DME Darmstadt.
Kö 4002	310 102	DR	B DM	1961	M	Tuttlingen.
Kö 4006	310 106	DR	B DN	1961	P	Bad Langensalza-Merxleben.
Kö 4007	310 107	DR	B DM	1961	P	Grossheringen
Kö 4009	310 109	DR	B DM	1940	M	Wismar.
Ks 4013	-	DB	Bo BE	1930	M	Stiftung Eisenbahnmuseum Bochum Dahlhausen.
Ks 4015	381 101	DB	Bo BE	1930	M	BEM Nördlingen.
Kö 4024	310 124	DR	B DM	1961	MS	Blumberg.
Kb 4026	310 126	DR	B DM	1962	MA	Glauchau.
Kö 4028	399 110	DR	B DM	1962	M	Georgenthal, (Thüringen).
Kb 4031	310 131	DR	B DM	1962	M	Hermeskeil.
Kb 4066	310 769	DR	B DM	1932	M	ETB Stassfurt.
Ks 4071	381 201	DB	Bo BE	1932	P	DBM Bhf. Limburg.
Kbe 4090	310 190	DR	Bo DE	1934	P	Tottleben.
Kbe 4096	310 196	DR	Bo DE	1934	M	Magdeburg.
Kb 4103	323 906	DB	B DH	1933	P	Oberthingau.
Kb 4117	310 217	DR	B DM	1933	M	Falkenberg/Elster.
Kb 4118	310 218	DR	B DM	1933	M	Falkenberg/Elster.
Kb 4140	323 004	DB	B DH	1934	M	MEM. Prussisch Oldendorf.
Kb 4146	322 128	DB	B DH	1934	MA	Hanau.
Kö 4150	322 174	DB	B DM	1934	P	Reichelshofen.
Kö 4175	310 275	DR	B DM	1933	MA	Worms.
Kö 4178	310 278	DR	B DM	1933	MA	Marnheim.
Kö 4180	310 280	DR	B DM	1933	P	Wetzlar-Garbenheim.
Kö 4181	310 281	DR	B DM	1933	P	Rostock Seehafen.
Kö 4201	310 201	DR	B DM	1933	P	Stadtwerke Mainz.
Kö 4202	322 656	DB	B DH	1933	MA	HEF, Hamm 98 80 3322 656-0 D-MEH.
Kö 4210	310 212	DR	B DM	1933	P	Weisswasser.
Kö 4211	310 211	DR	B DM	1934	M	SEM Chemnitz Hilbersdorf.
Kö 4228	310 228	DR	B DM	1934	M	Private, Stendal.
Kö 4270	323 903	DB	B DH	1933	M	OEF. Giessen.
Kö 4274	322 141	DB	B DM	1934	M	DBG. Loburg. (V21 04).
Kö 4280	323 605	DB	B DH	1934	MA	BEF. Basdorf (9880 3322 605-7 D-BEF).
Kö 4285	322 137	DB	B DH	1934	M	Hermeskeil.
Kö 4287	322 613	DB	B DH	1934	M	Fladungen.
Kö 4290	322 143	DB	B DH	1934	MA	DME Darmstadt.
Kö 4293	322 607	DB	B DH	1934	MA	NTB. Wiesbaden (9880 3322 607-3 D-PBE).

Kö 4294	322 635	DB	B DH	1934	MS	ZHL Reutlingen.
Kö 4309	310 309	DR	B DM	1934	M	Hermeskeil.
Kb 4323	322 636	DB	B DH	1934	M	DDM Neuenmarkt Wirsberg.
Kb 4324	310 324	DR	B DM	1934	P	Bad Segeberg - Fredesdorf.
Kb 4326	310 326	DR	B DM	1934	P	Bad Segeberg - Fredesdorf.
Kö 4350	322 628	DB	B DH	1934	M	Petite Roselle, (F).
Kö 4352	310 532	DR	B DM	1934	M	Rheinsberg.
Kö 4353	310 353	DR	B DM	1934	M	DBB Mittenwalde Ost.
Kö 4371	310 371	DR	B DM	1934	M	Falkenberg/Elster.
Kö 4375	322 106	DB	B DH	1934	M	Braunschweig.
Kö 4407	310 407	DR	B DM	1934	P	Annaberg Buchholz.
Kö 4412	310 412	DR	B DM	1934	P	Potsdam Rehbrücke.
Kö 4418	310 418	DR	B DM	1934	P	Berlin Tempelhof (Bosepark).
Kö 4430	310 430	DR	B DM	1934	M	ETM Prora.
Kö 4439	310 439	DR	B DM	1934	P	Mainz-Mombach.
Kö 4445	310 445	DR	B DM	1935	M	Eschwege.
Kö 4471	310 471	DR	B DM	1934	P	Lichtenau-Ottendorf.
Kö 4492	100 492	DR	B DM	1934	M	Meuselwitz.
Kö 4498	310 498	DR	B DM	1934	MA	Nossen.
Kö 4500	310 500	DR	B DM	1934	MA	Dresden - Glittersee.
Kö 4501	310 501	DR	B DM	1934	P	Parkeisenbahn, Cottbus.
Kö 4528	310 528	DR	B DM	1934	M	Falkenberg/Elster.
Kö 4537	310 537	DR	B DM	1935	MA	VSE Schwarzenberg.
Kö 4543	310 543	DR	B DM	1935	M	EF Grossheringen.
Kö 4547	310 547	DR	B DM	1935	M	Wittenberge.
Kö 4572	322 618	DB	B DH	1934	MS	Gerolstein.
Kö 4573	310 573	DR	B DM	1934	P	Hotel Alterbahnhof, Prerow.
Kö 4579	310 579	DR	B DM	1934	M	Walburg.
Kö 4594	310 594	DR	B DM	1934	P	Neumarkt (Sachs).
Kö 4604	310 604	DR	B DM	1934	MS	Eisenbahn Club, Aschersleben.
Kö 4607	322 660	DB	B DH	1934	MA	Blumberg.
Kö 4610	322 109	DB	B DH	1934	M	Krefeld.
Kö 4617	310 617	DR	B DM	1934	M	Stassfurt.
Kb 4630	310 630	DR	B DM	1934	MA	Löbau.
Kö 4632	100 632	DR	B DM	1934	P	Zughotel, Wolkenstein.
Kb 4634	100 634	DR	B DM	1934	MA	Buckow (9880 3310 634).
Kö 4638	X110.02	ÖBB	B DM	1934	MA	ÖGEG Ampflwang (A).
Kö 4642	X112.02	ÖBB	B DM	1935	M	TM Berlin.
Kö 4646	100 646	DR	B DM	1935	MA	Finsterwalde (Klein Bahren).
Kö 4667	323 016	DR	B DM	1935	MA	FME. Nürnberg.
Kö 4669	323 508	DB	B DH	1935	M	Mittenwalde Ost.
Kö 4696	323 510	DB	B DH	1934	M	Private, Remagen.
Kö 4701	310 701	DR	B DM	1934	P	Rostock Stadthafen.
Kö 4705	323 485	DR	B DM	1934	M	La Spezia, Italy. (Ex T 4570)
Kö 4706	323 922	DB	B DH	1934	P	Hofheim.
Kö 4714	322 602	DB	B DH	1934	MA	SEH Heilbronn.
Kö 4731	-	DRG	B DM	1934	M	Alter Bahnhof, Coesfeld Lette.
Kbf 4736	100 736	DR	B DM	1935	P	Sachsendorf.
Kö 4737	323 482	DB	B DH	1935	M	Stiftung Eisenbahnmuseum Bochum Dahlhausen (9880 3323 482).
Köe 4744	310 744	DR	B DM	1934	MA	Belzig.
Köe 4751	310 751	DR	B DM	1935	P	Bitterfeld.
Köe 4755	310 755	DR	B DM	1935	M	Stassfurt.
Kb 4757	310 757	DR	B DM	1935	M	Falkenberg/Elster.
Kö 4772	322 121	DB	B DH	1935	MA	Private, Frankfurt/M.
Kö 4796	310 796	DR	B DM	1935	MS	Vacha.
Kö 4798	310 798	DR	B DM	1935	M	Tuttlingen.
Kö 4800	310 700	DR	B DM	1935	M	Neuf Brisach, France.
Kö 4809	322 646	DB	B DM	1935	MS	Ingolstadt.
Köf 4822	310 722	DR	B DH	1936	M	Nossen.
Kö 4842	323 017	DB	B DH	1936	M	Hanau.
Kö 4853	310 773	DR	B DH	1937	M	Meuselwitz.
Kbf 4858	310 758	DR	B DM	1935	MA	Rostock Seehafen.
Kö 4872	310 774	DR	B DM	1936	MS	IG Altensteigerle e V. Nagold.

Kö 4879	323 484	DB	B DH	1936	P	Pommersfelden
Kö 4880	322 157	DB	B DH	1936	MA	BEM Nördlingen.
Kö 4900	310 703	DR	B DM	1936	M	Bad Segeburg- Fredesdorf.
Kö 4902	310 704	DR	B DM	1936	P	Berlin Bohnsdorf.
Ks 4909	381 011	DB	Bo BE	1937	MS	BEM Nördlingen.
Ks 4910	381 012	DB	Bo BE	1937	P	Dorfen.
Kö 4911	310 711	DR	B DM	1937	M	Mittenwalde Ost.
Kö 4915	323 448	DB	B DM	1938	M	EHEH, Hochdahl.
Kö 4923	322 009	DB	B DH	1938	P	School, Mönchengladbach-Hardt.
Kö 4934	310 735	DR	B DM	1938	MA	Belzig.
Kö 4936	310 738	DR	B DM	1937	MA	Oelsnitz.
Köf 4959	310 759	DR	B DM	1937	P	Erfurt Mittelhausen.
Köf 4962	310 765	DR	B DM	1938	MS	Adorf.
Kö 4963	310 763	DR	B DM	1938	MA	Hafenbahn Neustrelitz.
Köf 4966	310 769	DR	B DM	1933	M	Stassfurt
Ks 4969	310 709	DR	B DM	1938	MS	Belzig.
Ks 4972	310 782	DR	B DM	1938	M	Adorf.
Köf 4978	310 778	DR	B DM	1939	P	Lontzen, Belgium.
Ks 4986	381 013	DB	Bo DE	1938	MS	Rottau.
Köf 4999	310 789	DR	B DM	1942	M	Tuttlingen.
Köf 5009	310 809	DR	B DH	1941	M	Belzig.
Kö 5044	323 442	DB	B DH	1943	P	Merzen.
Köf 5046	310 846	DR	B DH	1937	MS	Cottbus.
Kö 5048	322 150	DB	B DH	1938	MS	Reutlingen.
Kö 5049	310 849	DR	B DH	1939	M	Gramzow.
Kbf 5057	323 036	DB	B DH	1943	M	STAR. Stadskanaal, (NL).
Kbf 5064	310 864	DR	B DH	1943	MA	Cloppenburg.
Kbf 5067	310 867	DR	B DH	1943	M	ETM Prora.
Kbf 5072	100 872	DR	B DH	1943	MS	Kalbe (Milde).
Kbf 5116	323 044	DB	B DH	1943	M	DTM Berlin.
Kb 5142	310 842	DR	B DH	1944	M	DBM Halle P.
Kb 5159	X111.04	ÖBB	B DH	1944	M	Strasshof, (A).
Köf 5182	310 882	DR	B DH	1941	P	Cottbus Works.
Kö 5186	324 043	DB	B DH	1938	M	Treysa.
Köf 5193	310 892	DR	B DH	1942	MA	BEM Nördlingen.
Köf 5226	100 826	DR	B DH	1944	M	Aschersleben.
Kbf 5231	323 049	DB	B DH	1944	M	Verden.
Kbf 5250	-	DB	B DH	1944	M	Private, Braunschweig.
Kbf 5261	310 881	DR	B DH	1944	M	Hermeskeil.
Kbf 5262	310 822	DR	B DH	1944	P	Erfurt.
Kbf 5266	100 886	DR	B DH	1944	MA	Weimar.
Kbf 5271	323 463	DB	B DH	1944	MS	Hamburg Wilhelmsburg.
Köf 5274	323 470	DB	B DH	1944	M	Siegen.
Köf 5712	310 912	DR	B DH	1942	MA	Frankfurt/M (9880 3310 0912).
Köf 5714	310 914	DR	B DH	1942	MA	Adorf.
Kö 5722	-	DR	B DH	1935	P	Wittenberge Works.
Köf 5727	310 927	DR	B DH	1936	P	Neukulen
Kö 5728	100 928	DR	B DH	1934	P	Leuben-Scheinitz
Kö 5729	310 929	DR	B DH	1939	S	Lübbenau.
Kö 5730	310 930	DR	B DH	1934	MS	Helbra.
Kö 5731	100 931	DR	B DH	1934	MA	Putlitz.
Köf 5736	100 936	DR	B DH	1939	M	ETM Prora.
Kö 5742	310 942	DR	B DH	1941	P	Espenhain.
Kö 5743	-	DR	B DH	1935	MA	Magdeburg.
Kö 5746	310 946	DR	B DH	1943	P	Landgasthof St. Moritz, Möllenbeck-Quadenschonfeld.
Kö 5752	310 952	DR	B DH	1938	M	Schwerin.
Köf 5753	310 953	DR	B DH	1943	P	Beierfeld.
Kö 5755	310 955	DR	B DH	1952	M	Weimar.
Köf 6007	322 609	DB	B DH	1937	MA	Bad Salzdetfurth.
Kö 6020	-	DB	B DH	1937	M	Dieringhausen.
Köe 6042	-	DB	Bo DE	1938	M	ETM, Prora.
Köf 6046	322 173	DB	B DH	1941	M	Treysa.
Köf 6119	324 044	DB	B DH	1951	MA	Oberhausen.

Köf 6120	323 071	DB	B DH	1951	M	DGEG, Neustadt (Weinstrasse).
Köf 6124	322 036	DB	B DH	1951	MS	DBM Lichtenfels
Köf 6136	322 039	DB	B DH	1952	M	Werra Fulda Bahn e.V, Schenklengsfeld.
Köf 6139	322 172	DB	B DH	1952	M	Hermeskeil.
Köf 6152	322 041	DB	B DH	1953	MA	Norden.
Köf 6157	323 440	DB	B DH	1953	MS	DB (current situation not known).
Köf 6158	322 147	DB	B DH	1953	P	Nürnberg Langwasser.
Köf 6159	323 942	DB	B DH	1953	MA	Marnheim (98 80 3323 942-3 D-PBE).
Köf 6168	323 525	DB	B DH	1954	MA	Oberhausen Osterfeld Süd.
Köf 6169	323 526	DB	B DH	1954	MA	GES. Kornwestheim.
Köf 6170	322 510	DB	B DH	1954	M	DGEG Neustadt/Weinstr.
Köf 6182	322 640	DB	B DH	1954	MR	HEF, Mannheim.
Köf 6183	323 958	DB	B DH	1954	MA	FME. Nürnberg (98 80 3323 958-9 D-FME).
Köf 6189	323 525	DB	B DH	1954	M	EOB
Köf 6190	322 614	DB	B DH	1954	M	FME. Nürnberg.
Köf 6196	323 083	DB	B DH	1955	MS	EOB
Köf 6203	322 043	DB	B DH	1954	M	Darmstadt.
Köf 6204	322 044	DB	B DH	1954	MA	DFS 5, Ebermannstadt.
Köf 6211	322 047	DB	B DH	1955	M	København, (DK).
Köf 6244	323 552	DB	B DH	1955	M	EF Passau
Köf 6265	323 582	DB	B DH	1956	M	Treysa.
Köf 6276	323 593	DB	B DH	1957	M	Haltingen.
Köf 6277	323 594	DB	B DH	1956	M	Rinteln
Köf 6280	323 597	DB	B DH	1957	M	Struer, (DK).
Köf 6286	323 602	DB	B DH	1957	M	NTB. Wiesbaden.
Köf 6291	323 674	DB	B DH	1957	M	Nene Valley Railway, (UK).
Köf 6306	323 617	DB	B DH	1957	M	H.E. Gelsenkirchen e.V, Gelsenkirchen.
Köf 6311	323 626	DB	B DH	1958	MA	Bahnpark, Augsburg (98 80 3323 626-2 D – DGM).
Köf 6322	323 634	DB	B DH	1958	M	Private, Konigstein
Köf 6325	323 637	DB	B DH	1958	M	BSW Oberhausen Osterfeld Süd.
Köf 6330	323-642	DB	B DH	1958	S	Drachten, (NL).
Köf 6334	323 646	DB	B DH	1958	M	RSWE, Regensburg.
Köf 6338	323 650	DB	B DH	1958	M	MEH, Hanau.
Köf 6349	323 655	DB	B DH	1958	M	Struer, (DK).
Köf 6359	322 058	DB	B DH	1959	MA	Neustadt/Weinstr.
Köf 6372	323 102	DB	B DH	1959	M	VVM, Schönberg Strand.
Köf 6383	322 521	DB	B DH	1959	P	Osnabrück, Hafen Strasse.
Köf 6406	323 119	DB	B DH	1959	M	DGEG, Neustadt (Weinstrasse).
Köf 6424	323 137	DB	B DH	1959	MS	IGN, Kassel Rothenditmold.
Köf 6436	323 149	DB	B DH	1959	MA	Linz/Rhein.
Köf 6449	323 156	DB	B DH	1960	M	Hermeskeil.
Köf 6454	323 210	DB	B DH	1960	M	Battenberg/Eder.
Köf 6470	323 225	DB	B DH	1969	MS	Oebisfelde.
Köf 6472	323 227	DB	B DH	1960	MA	Kassel.
Köf 6482	323 237	DB	B DH	1960	MA	Rahden.
Köf 6498	323 680	DB	B DH	1959	MA	BEM München (98 80 3323 680-9 D-BYB).
Köf 6499	323 681	DB	B DH	1959	M	Walburg.
Köf 6501	323 683	DB	B DH	1959	MA	BEM Nördlingen.
Köf 6510	323 710	DB	B DH	1960	M	Vienenburg.
Köf 6524	323 724	DB	B DH	1960	MS	GES Kornwestheim.
Köf 6525	323 725	DB	B DH	1960	MS	Crailsheim.
Köf 6526	323 726	DB	B DH	1960	M	MEC Losheim.
Köf 6528	323 728	DB	B DH	1960	M	Azpeitia, (SP).
Köf 6533	323 733	DB	B DH	1960	MA	FME. Nürnberg.
Köf 6541	323 741	DB	B DH	1960	M	Gedser, (DK).
Köf 6546	323 746	DB	B DH	1960	P	St. Engimar.
Köf 6547	323 747	DB	B DH	1960	M	Petite Roselle, (F).
Köf 6551	323 751	DB	B DH	1960	M	DEW Rinteln.
Köf 6557	323 757	DB	B DH	1960	MS	DBM. Lichtenfels.
Köf 6558	323 758	DB	B DH	1960	P	Kriegenbrunn
Köf 6571	323 771	DB	B DH	1960	MR	Schwaben Dampf, Neuoffingen.
Köf 6579	323 871	DB	B DH	1961	M	DDM, Neuenmarkt Wirsberg.
Köf 6580	323 872	DB	B DH	1961	M	Bahnpark, Augsburg.

Köf 6606	323 174	DB	B DH	1959	MA	Hamm.
Köf 6617	323 185	DB	B DH	1959	M	MEC, Losheim.
Köf 6638	323 264	DB	B DH	1960	MS	EOB
Köf 6642	323 268	DB	B DH	1960	M	ET Lengerich.
Köf 6648	323 274	DB	B DH	1960	MA	Oberhausen.
Köf 6705	323 703	DB	B DH	1959	MA	BEM. München.
Köf 6712	323 782	DB	B DH	1959	M	St. Sulpice, (CH).
Köf 6718	323 788	DB	B DH	1960	MA	Seebrugg.
Köf 6731	323 801	DB	B DH	1960	M	DGEG, Würzburg.
Köf 6732	323 802	DB	B DH	1960	P	Koltental-Helmishofen.
Köf 6741	323 811	DB	B DH	1960	M	EF Untermain, Aschaffenburg.
Köf 6772	323 842	DB	B DH	1960	MA	Westerwälder EF, Westerburg.
Köf 6782	323 852	DB	B DH	1960	M	DBM. Koblenz.
Köf 6791	323 861	DB	B DH	1960	M	Hermeskeil.
Köf 6796	323 866	DB	B DH	1960	P	Gerwisch, Magdeburg.
Köf 6797	323 867	DB	B DH	1960	P	Dronsfeld.
Köf 6803	323 323	DB	B DH	1965	MA	DEW Rinteln.
Köf 6808	323 328	DB	B DH	1965	M	Crailsheim.
Köf 6815	323 335	DB	B DH	1965	MA	Bösingfeld.
Köf 6816	323 336	DB	B DH	1965	M	Herborn.
Köf 6817	323 337	DB	B DH	1965	P	Bischofsmais.
Köf 6833	323 353	DB	B DH	1965	M	Braunschweig.
Köf 11 066	332 066	DB	B DH	1964	M	Frankische Thüringische Museumsbahn e.V. Fladungen.
Köf 11 098	332 098	DB	B DH	1964	MA	Schwarzenden (98 80 3332 098-3 D-AKO).
Köf 11 003	332 801	DB	B DH	1959	MA	Münsingen
Köf 11 114	332 114	DB	B DH	1964	MA	DGEG, Neustadt (Weinstrasse).
Köf 11 139	332 139	DB	B DH	1964	MA	ZLSM, Simpelveld, (NL). (332-06).
Köf 11 156	332 156	DB	B DH	1964	MA	Westerstede Ocholt.
Köf 11 187	332 187	DB	B DH	1964	MS	ZLSM, Simpelveld, (NL). (332-3).
Köf 11 204	332 204	DB	B DH	1964	P	Adlerwerke, Frankfurt/Main.
Köf 11 227	332 227	DB	B DH	1966	M	Treysa.
Köf 11 238	332 238	DB	B DH	1966	M	HE, Frankfurt/M.
Köf 11 239	332 245	DB	B DH	1966	M	DBM Koblenz Lützel.
Köf 11 262	332 262	DB	B DH	1966	M	DBM, Lichtelfels.
Köf 11 271	332 271	DB	B DH	1966	M	FME, Nürnberg.
Köf 11 298	332 298	DB	B DH	1965	P	Bogen
-	335 039	DB	B DH	1968	M	Schwarzenden.
-	335 059	DB	B DH	1969	M	Schwarzenden.
-	333 068	DB	B DH	1969	M	DBM. Koblenz.
-	335 200	DB	B DH	1976	P	DB Systems, Frankfurt/M.
V15 1001	-	DR	B DH	1959	MA	Dresden Altstadt.
V15 1002	-	DR	B DH	1959	M	Magdeburg.
V15 1018	-	DR	B DH	1960	M	Speyer.
V15 2020	311 020-2	DR	B DH	1961	M	Löbau.
V15 2035	311 705-8	DR	B DH	1961	M	Falkenberg/Elster.
V15 2065	311 681	DR	B DH	1961	M	SEM, Chemnitz Hilbersdorf.
V15 2082	311 559 9	DR	B DH	1962	M	BEF. Basdorf (98 80 3311 559-9 D-BEF).
V15 2232	311 544-1	DR	B DH	1962	M	Wittenberge.
V15 2299	311 535-9	DR	B DH	1963	MA	Wittenberge.
V23 001	312 001-1	DR	B DH	1967	M	DBM. Halle P.
V23 004	312 004	DR	B DH	1968	M	Lutherstadt Wittenberg.
V23 009	312 009-4	DR	B DH	1968	M	Falkenberg/Elster.
V23 072	312 072-2	DR	B DH	1968	M	Falkenberg/Elster.
102 125	312 125	DR	B DH	1970	M	Weimar.
102 131	312 131	DR	B DH	1970	M	VSE, Schwarzenberg.
102 140	312 140	DR	B DH	1970	M	SEM. Chemnitz Hilbersdorf.
102 153	312 153	DR	B DH	1970	M	Eisenbahnverein Bad Düben - Eilenburg.
102 172	312 172	DR	B DH	1970	MA	Stassfurt.
102 182	312 182	DR	B DH	1970	M	Glauchau.
102 187	312 187	DR	B DH	1970	M	SEM. Chemnitz Hilbersdorf.
102 188	312 188	DR	B DH	1970	MA	Dresden Altstadt. (98 80 3312 188-6 D-IGDA).

329 501-1	399 101	DB	C DH	1952	MA	Klütz
329 502-9	399 102	DB	C DH	1957	MS	Stiftung Deutsche Kleinbahnen, Schwichtenberg.
329 503-7	399 103	DB	C DH	1957	MS	Stiftung Deutsche Kleinbahnen, Schwichtenberg.
329 504-5	399 104	DB	B DH	1957	MS	Stiftung Deutsche Kleinbahnen, Schwichtenberg.
199 007-6	399 701	DR	C DH	1972	MA	Jöhstadt.
199 101-7	399 601	DR	C DM	1980	MA	Berlin Park Railway.
199 102-5	399 602	DR	C DM	1980	MA	Berlin Park Railway.
199 103-3	399 603	DR	C DM	1980	MA	Berlin Park Railway.
Kdl 91-0001		DB	B DM	1953	M	Gerolstein.
Kdl 91-0005		DB	B DM	1958	P	Hemmor.
Kdl 91-0006		DB	B DM	1958	M	DBM Koblenz Lützel.
Kdl 91-0012		DB	B DM	1958	M	Fredesdorf.
ASF 01		DR	Bo BE	1964	MA	SEM. Chemnitz Hilbersdorf.
ASF 2		DR	Bo BE	1983	MA	Weimar.
ASF 4		DR	Bo BE	1966	MA	Halle.
ASF 8		DR	Bo BE	1966	MA	SEM. Chemnitz Hilbersdorf.
ASF 24		DR	Bo BE	1969	M	Weimar.
ASF 32		DR	Bo BE	1969	M	Weimar.
ASF 45		DR	Bo BE	1971	M	Pasewalk.
ASF 59		DR	Bo BE	1973	M	Glauchau.
ASF 60		DR	Bo BE	1973	M	Bitterfeld.
ASF 75		DR	Bo BE	1974	MA	Arnstadt.
ASF 76		DR	Bo BE	1974	M	Weimar.
ASF 94II		DR	Bo BE	1979	M	Nossen.
ASF 114		DR	Bo BE	1981	M	SEM. Chemnitz Hilbersdorf.
ASF 115		DR	Bo BE	1981	M	Glauchau.
ASF 122I		DR	Bo BE	1977	M	Schwerin.
ASF 122II		DR	Bo BE	1983	M	SEM. Chemnitz Hilbersdorf.
ASF 139		DR	Bo BE	1987	M	Weimar.
ASF 144		DR	Bo BE	1987	M	Lutherstadt Wittenberg.
ASF 146		DR	Bo BE	1987	M	Aschersleben.
ASF 14271		DR	Bo BE	1974	M	Arnstadt.
ASF 17762	ASF 1	IND	Bo BE	1982	M	Arnstadt.

9.4. ELECTRIC MULTIPLE UNITS

Old No.	Computer No.	Co.	Wheel	Built	Status	Location
1624ab		DB	2-car	1927	M	VVM. Aumuhle.
ET 11 01		DB	2-car	1935	M	DGEG. Neustadt (Weinstr).
-	410 001	DB	Bo-Bo	1985	P	ST Minden.
745 002-6	410 002	DB	Bo-Bo	1985	M	Deutsches Verkehrsmuseum, München.
-	420 001	DB	3-car	1969	MA	S-Bahn München.
-	420 298	DB	3-car	1978	MS	OEF, Giessen
-	420 300	DB	3-car	1978	M	Eisenbahn Erlebniswelt, Horb.
-	420 416	DB	3-car		M	DBM Nürnberg
ET25 015	425 115	DB	2/3/4-car	1935	MR	Haltingen.
ET25 020	425 120	DB	2/3/4-car	1935	MA	Stuttgart.
ET26 002	426 002	DB	2-car	1941	M	Peenemünde.
ET27 005	427 105	DB	3-car	1965	MR	Stuttgart.
ET30 414	430 114	DB	1 of 3-car	1956	MS	DBM. Eisenbahn Erlebniswelt, Horb.
ET 32 201 a	432 201	DB	1 of 3-car	1936	M	Eisenbahn Erlebniswelt, Horb.
ET 65 005	465 005	DB	Bo-Bo	1933	MS	Stuttgart.
ET 65 006	465 006	DB	Bo-Bo	1933	MS	Eisenbahn Erlebniswelt, Horb.
ET85 07	485 007	DB	Bo-Bo	1927	M	Eisenbahn Erlebniswelt, Horb.
ET183 05	-	DB	1Ao-Ao1	1899	M	DTM. Berlin.
ET188 511	-	DR	Bo	1930	MS	Dresden Altstadt.
ET188 521	-	DR	Bo	1930	MS	Dresden Altstadt.
	470.128	DB	3-car	1969	MA	Historische S-Bahn Hamburg e.V.

-	470 136	DB	3-car	1969	M	Kulturbahnhof Schmilau.
ET171 044	471 144	DB	3-car	1942	M	LHB Salzgitter.
ET171 082	471 182	DB	2-car	1958	MR	Historische S-Bahn Hamburg e. V.
270 001-1	-	DR	2-car	1985	MS	HSB Berlin.
275 003-2	475 001	BVG	2-car	1929	P	B-Kleistpark (Bar).
275 031-3	475 003	BVG	2-car	1928	M	Stiftung Eisenbahnmuseum Bochum Dahlhausen.
275 045-3	475 005	BVG	2-car	1928	P	Technolgie Park, Köln
275 061-0	475 008	BVG	2-car	1928	P	Dresdener Tor on A4 road.
275 081-8	475 009	BVG	2-car	1928	P	Beelitz Süd.
275 085-9	475 011	BVG	2-car	1928	P	Herzhausen (34516).
275 109-7	475 013	BVG	2-car	1928	P	Gaststätte, Breitenbrunn.
275 169-1	475 017	BVG	2-car	1928	MS	Walburg (?).
275 247-5	475 024	BVG	2-car	1929	MS	Beelitz.
275 343-2	475 037	BVG	2-car	1929	P	Luckenwalde (Gottower Strasse).
275 319-2	475 601	BVG	2-car	1929	MS	Walburg (?).
275 407-5	475 049	BVG	2-car	1928	MS	Walburg (?).
275 411-7	475 050	BVG	2-car	1928	P	Dessau
275 417-4	475 053	BVG	2-car	1928	P	Dessau
275 429-9	475 057	BVG	2-car	1928	M	ETM. Prora.
275 517-1	475 075	BVG	2-car	1929	P	Gaststätte, Dabendorf.
275 519-7	475 076	BVG	2-car	1928	P	Hohenschonhausen Bhf.
275 625-2	475 161	BVG	2-car	1927	M	Deutsches Museum Verkehrszentrum, München.
275 641-9	475 605	BVG	2-car	1928	MA	S-Bahn Berlin.
2303	488 165	DR	2-car	1928	MA	HSB Berlin.
275 683-1	475 608	BVG	2-car	1928	MS	Essban Bisto, Stuttgart Flughafen
275 693-0	488 166	DR	2-car	1928	MA	S-Bahn Berlin.
275 701-1	475 612	BVG	2-car	1928	P	Berlin - Lübars.
275 737-5	475 162	DR	2-car	1928	M	DBM. Nürnberg.
275 747-4	488 167	BVG	2-car	1928	M	DTM Berlin.
275 783-0	488 168	DR	2-car	1928	MA	S-Bahn Berlin.
275 815-9	488 169	DR	2-car	1929	MA	S-Bahn Berlin.
275 959-5	475 126	DR	2-car	1932	MA	S-Bahn Berlin (As 488 167II).
276 035-3	-	DR	2-car	1949	MS	DTM Berlin.
276 069-2	-	DR	2-car	1938	M	HSB Berlin.
276 531	476 033	DR	2-car	1928	M	DME. Darmstadt.
276 301-9	476 352	DR	2-car	1930	MS	Private, Berlin-Modersohnbrücke.
276 347-2	476 372	DR	2-car	1930	P	Stadthalle, Kirchberg (55481).
276 415-7	476 396	DR	2-car	1928	P	Tiroler Stadl, Senftenberg.
276 513-9	476 002	DR	2-car	1928	P	HSB Berlin.
276 535-2	476 013	DR	2-car	1928	P	School, Berlin Spandau.
277 003-0	477 197	DR	2-car	1938	M	HSB Berlin.
277 087-3	477 206	DR	2-car	1939	M	HSB Berlin.
277 129-3	477 053	DR	2-car	1939	P	Töpchin.
277 195-4	477 085	DR	2-car	1940	M	Ziesar-Bucknitzer Eisenbahn.
277 263-0	477 117	DR	2-car	1943	P	Töpchin.
277 267-1	477 119	DR	2-car	1943	P	Berlin-Schönefeld (Bar).
	477 601	DR	2-car	1939	M	Horb.
277 405-7	477 602	DR	2-car	1940	M	HSB Berlin.
277 407-3	477 603	DR	2-car	1936	M	Ziesar-Bucknitzer Eisenbahn.
277 415-6II	477 606	DR	2-car	1936	P	Berlin school.
278 005-4	478 004	DR	2-car	1925	M	S-Bahn Berlin.
278 007-0	478 005	DR	2-car	1925	M	HSB Berlin.
278 107-8	-	DR	2-car	1928	MS	HSB Berlin
279 001-2	479 601	DR	Bo	1930	MS	Buckow.
279 003-8	479 602	DR	Bo	1930	MS	Buckow.
279 005-3	479 603	DR	Bo	1930	MS	Buckow.
ET91 01	491 001	DB	Bo-2	1936	M	Bahnpark Augsburg.
ETA150 011	515 011	DB	Bo BE	1955	M	BEM Nördlingen.
ETA150 556	515 556	DB	Bo BE	1960	M	Stiftung Eisenbahnmuseum Bochum Dahlhausen.
ETA176 001	517 001	DB	Bo-Bo BE	1956	MS	DBM. Lichtenfels.
AT 589/590	-	DR	2A-A2 DE	1927	MR	VMD. Gotha.

9.5. DIESEL MULTIPLE UNITS

Old No.	Computer No.	Co.	Wheel	Built	Status	Location
VT 4.12.01	173 001	DR	1A-A1dm	1964	MR	Hoyerswerda.
VT 4.12.02	173 002	DR	1A-A1dm	1964	MR	Dessau.
VT 06 104ab		DB	2-car	1938	M	LHB Salzgitter.
VT 06 106a		DB	1/3 3-car	1938	P	Lübeck Travemünde Hafen.
VT 06 106bc		DB	2/3 3-car	1938	P	Konstanz.
VT 137 856a	182 009	DR	2-car	1938	MS	Forderverein Diesel Schnelltriebwagen. Berlin
VT 137 856b	182 010	DR	2-car	1938	MS	Forderverein Diesel Schnelltriebwagen. Berlin
VT 08 520	613 620	DB	B-2 DH	1954	MS	DBM. Meiningen Works.
VT 11 5003	602 003	DB	B-2 GTH	1957	M	Eisenbahn Erlebniswelt, Horb.
VT 11 5006	601 006	DB	B-2 DH	1957	M	Bahnpark Augsburg (Restaurant train).
VT 11 5008	601 008	DB	B-2 DH	1957	M	Eisenbahn Erlebniswelt, Horb.
VT 11 5012	602 012	DB	B-2 GTH	1957	M	DBM. Eisenbahn Erlebniswelt, Horb.
VT 11 5013	601 013	DB	B-2 DH	1957	M	Bahnpark Augsburg.
VT 11 5014	601 014	DB	B-2 DH	1957	M	Eisenbahn Erlebniswelt, Horb.
VT 11 5015	601 015	DB	B-2 DH	1957	M	Bahnpark Augsburg (Restaurant train).
VT 11 5016	601 016	DB	B-2 DH	1957	S	Private, Solignano Nuovo, Italy.
VT 11 5018	601 018	DB	B-2 DH	1957	MS	SEH Heilbronn
VT 11 5019	601 019	DB	B-2 DH	1957	M	Bahnpark Augsburg.
VT 12 506	612 506	DB	B-2 DH	1957	MA	DBM Nürnberg.
VT 12 507	612 507	DB	B-2 DH	1957	MA	DBM Nürnberg.
614 005		DB	B-2 DH	1973	MS	DBM Nürnberg.
614 006		DB	B-2 DH	1973	MS	DBM Nürnberg.
VT 18.16.03a	175 005	DR	B-2 DH	1966	M	SEM, Chemnitz.
VT 18.16.03b	175 006	DR	B-2 DH	1966	M	SEM, Chemnitz.
VT 18.16.07b	175 014	DR	B-2 DH	1968	MS	DBM. Lichtenfels
VT 18.16.08a	175 015	DR	B-2 DH	1968	MS	Berlin Lichtenberg.
VT 18.16.08b	175 016	DR	B-2 DH	1968	MS	Berlin Lichtenberg.
VT 18.1610a	175 019	DR	B-2 DH	1968	MS	DBM. Lichtenfels
VT 60 531	723 003	DB	1A-2 DH	1940	MR	Osnabrück Piesberg.
VT 66 904	-	DB	1A-A1 DM	1927	MA	EBV. Zeven.
VT 66 906	-	DB	B-B DM	1928	MS	Freunde der Halle - Hettstedter Eisenbahn.
VT 70 919	-	DB	A-1 DM	1937	MA	Ebermannstadt.
VT 70 921	-	DB	A-1 DM	1937	MR	DME. Darmstadt.
VT 78 901	-	DB	A-1 DM	1932	M	Ebermannstadt.
VT 79 902	-	DB	A-1 DM	1932	M	DME, Darmstadt.
VT 88 902	-	DB	A-1 DM	1934	M	Prussisch Oldendorf.
VT 92 501	692 501	DB	B-2 DH	1932	MR	DBM. EVB Zeven.
701 065		DB	A-A DM	1962	MS	Deutsches Museum, Freilassing.
701 067		DB	A-A DM	1962	MS	DBM. Lichtenfels
701 095		DB	A-A DM	1964	MS	Deutsches Museum, Freilassing.
701 162		DB	A-A DM	1973	P	BBR Verkehrstechnik, Braunschweig.
VT 95 9122	795 122	DB	A-1 DM	1953	MR	HEF. Hamm.
VT 95 9144	795 144	DB	A-1 DM	1953	P	Wuppertal Cronenberg.
VT 95 9240	795 240	DB	A-1 DM	1952	MS	DBM, Lichtenfels
VT 95 9256	795 256	DB	A-1 DM	1952	MA	VEB, Gerolstein.
VT 95 9286	795 286	DB	A-1 DM	1955	A	HWB VT 53.
VT 95 9326	795 326	DB	A-1 DM	1957	P	Rehlingen (Saar). Tennis court clubhouse.
VT 95 9396	795 396	DB	A-1 DM	1954	MA	BEF, Basdorf.
VT 95 9414	795 414	DB	A-1 DM	1954	M	Dieringhausen.
VT 95 9445	795 445	DB	A-1 DM	1954	M	Wesseling.
VT 95 9465	795 465	DB	A-1 DM	1954	M	DTM. Berlin.
VT 95 9626	795 626	DB	A-1 DM	1955	M	VEB, Gerolstein.
VT 95 9627	795 627	DB	A-1 DM	1955	M	KBE VT 12, Wesseling.
VT 95 9662	795 662	DB	A-1 DM	1955	MA	CFV3V, Mariembourg, Belgium (As 551.662).
VT 95 9669	795 669	DB	A-1 DM	1955	MA	AMTF, Train 1900 Petange, Luxembourg.
VT 98 9597	796 597	DB	A-A DM	1956	MA	OEF, Giessen.
VT 98 9625	796 625	DB	A-A DM	1956	MR	EFZ. Rottweil.

VT 98 9680	796 680	DB	A-A DM	1960	MA	Goes, Netherlands.
VT 98 9683	796 683	DB	A-A DM	1960	M	DBM. EF Grenzland, Aachen
VT 98 9690	796 690	DB	A-A DM	1960	MR	VEB, Gerolstein.
VT 98 9699	796 699	DB	A-A DM	1960	MA	MAS, Westerstede-Ocholt
VT 98 9702	796 702	DB	A-A DM	1960	MA	Volkach.
VT 98 9710	796 710	DB	A-A DM	1960	MA	Volkach.
VT 98 9721	796 721	DB	A-A DM	1960	M	HE, Gelsenkirchen Bismarck
VT 98 0734	796 734	DB	A-A DM	1960	P	Old Folks Home, Dransfeld
VT 98 9739	796 739	DB	A-A DM	1960	MA	DDM. Neuenmarkt Wirsberg.
VT 98 9740	796 740	DB	A-A DM	1960	P	Old Folks Home, Dransfeld
VT 98 9744	796 744	DB	A-A DM	1960	MS	Schenklengsfeld.
VT 98 9745	796 745	DB	A-A DM	1960	M	OEF, Giessen.
VT 98 9761	796 761	DB	A-A DM	1960	MS	Kassel.
VT 98 9784	796 784	DB	A-A DM	1961	MA	Gerolstein.
VT 98 9790	796 790	DB	A-A DM	1961	S	Reutlingen.
VT 98 9792	796 792	DB	A-A DM	1961	M	HE, Gelsenkirchen Bismarck
VT 98 9796	796 796	DB	A-A DM	1961	MA	EVB Zeven (VT 167)
VT 98 9802	796 802	DB	A-A DM	1961	MR	VEB, Gerolstein.
VT 97 902	797 502	DB	A-A DM	1962	MR	ZHL Reutlingen.
VT 97 903	797 503	DB	A-A DM	1962	MR	ZHL Reutlingen.
VT 97 905	797 505	DB	A-A DM	1962	MR	ZHL Reutlingen.
VT 98 9514	798 514	DB	A-A DM	1955	MR	Werlte.
VT 98 9522	798 522	DB	A-A DM	1955	MA	BEM. Nördlingen.
VT 98 9554	798 554	DB	A-A DM	1955	MS	Krefeld.
VT 98 9585	798 585	DB	A-A DM	1956	MR	KBEF, Wesseling.
VT 98 9589	798 589	DB	A-A DM	1956	MA	OEF, Giessen.
VT 98 9598	798 598	DB	A-A DM	1956	MA	EVG. Linz/Rh.
VT 98 9622	798 622	DB	A-A DM	1956	MA	PEG, Frankenthal
VT 98 9623	798 623	DB	A-A DM	1956	M	Horb.
VT 98 9629	798 629	DB	A-A DM	1956	MA	HE, Frankfurt/M .
VT 98 9632	798 632	DB	A-A DM	1956	MS	Kalibahn Wathlingen, Niedersachsen.
VT 98 9643	798 643	DB	A-A DM	1956	MA	Goes, Netherlands (Via StLB VT 23).
VT 98 9645	798 645	DB	A-A DM	1956	P	Private, Frankfurt/M
VT 98 9647	798 647	DB	A-A DM	1956	MA	Simpelveld, Netherlands.
VT 98 9652	798 652	DB	A-A DM	1959	MS	Langeschemmen
VT 98 9653	798 653	DB	A-A DM	1959	MR	Chiemgau Bahn.
VT 98 9659	798 659	DB	A-A DM	1959	MS	MAS, Westerstede-Ocholt.
VT 98 9668	798 668	DB	A-A DM	1959	MR	ZLSM. Simpelveld, Netherlands.
VT 98 9670	798 670	DB	A-A DM	1959	MR	VEB, Gerolstein.
VT 98 9675	798 675	DB	A-A DM	1959	MS	Wilburgstetten.
VT 98 9677	798 677	DB	A-A DM	1959	MS	WEMEG, Wittenburg
VT 98 9706	798 706	DB	A-A DM	1960	MA	PEF, Passau.
VT 98 9726	798 726	DB	A-A DM	1960	P	Schiltach.
VT 98 9729	798 729	DB	A-A DM	1960	MA	EVG. Linz/Rh.
VT 98 9731	798 731	DB	A-A DM	1960	P	EF, Rodachtalbahn
VT 98 9752	798 752	DB	A-A DM	1960	MA	Gerolstein.
VT 98 9766	798 766	DB	A-A DM	1960	MS	EVG. Linz/Rh.
VT 98 9776	798 776	DB	A-A DM	1960	MR	PEF, Passau.
VT 98 9778	798 778	DB	A-A DM	1960	MR	Wilburgstetten.
VT 98 7979	798 794	DB	A-A DM	1961	MS	Seelze.
VT 98 9818	798 818	DB	A-A DM	1962	MS	Pfalzbahn, Worms.
VT 98 9823	798 823	DB	A-A DM	1962	MA	MRU. Rahden
VT 98 9829	798 829	DB	A-A DM	1962	MR	OEF, Giessen.
VT 133 522	187 001	DR	A-1 DM	1933	MA	Wernigerode HSB.
VT 135 054	186 257	DR	A-1 DM	1935	M	Stassfurt.
VT 135 057		DB	A-1 DM	1935	M	MEM. Minden.
VT 135 060		DB	A-1 DM	1935	M	MEM. Pr. Oldendorf.
VT 137 063	723 101	DR	2-Bo DE	1934	MR	Dessau.
VT 137 099	185 254	DR	2-Bo DE	1935	MS	DBM. Schwerin.
VT 137 110	786 258	DR	2-Bo DE	1935	MS	DBM. Halle P.
VT137 225ab	183 252	DR	2-car	1935	P	Leipzig Hbf.
VT 137 234	183 251	DR	2-car	1935	MR	SFW Delitzsch.
VT 137 322	-	DR	B-2 DM	1938	MS	Bertsdorf.
VT 137 527	185 256	DR	1A-A1 DM	1939	M	Gramzow.

VT 137 532	187 101	DR	1A-A1 DM	1939	MA	DEV. Bruchhausen Vilsen.
VT 137 566	187 025	DR	1A-A1 DM	1940	MA	HSB Wernigerode.
188 001-2	708 001	DR	A-1 DM	1956	M	Stassfurt.
188 005-3	708 005	DR	A-1 DM	1959	M	Finsterwalde.
188 006-1	708 006	DR	A-1 DM	1959	MA	DBM Halle.
188 201-8	708 201	DR	2-Bo DE	1968	MR	Weimar.
188 202-6	708 202	DR	2-Bo DE	1968	M	VMD. Dresden.
188 203-4	708 203	DR	2-Bo DE	1968	M	SEM. Chemnitz Hilbersdorf.
699 001-4	699 101	DB	B-2 DH	1933	MA	DEV. Bruchhausen Vilsen.
Köl 6204	701 018	DB	A-A DM	1955	MR	VEB, Gerolstein.
VT38 002	712 001	DB	Bo-2 DE	1936	MA	Stiftung Eisenbahnmuseum Bochum Dahlhausen.
VT2.09 003	771 003	DR	A-1 DM	1962	MA	Gramzow.
VT2.09 056	771 056	DR	A-1 DM	1964	MR	Ifersgrun.
VT2.09 101	772 101	DR	A-1 DM	1964	MA	Neustrelitz.
VT2.09.103	772 003	DR	A-1 DM	1965	MA	Stassfurt.
VT2.09 201	772 101	DR	A-1 DM	1965	P	Peckfitz.
	772 132	DR	A-1 DM	1968	MA	KSR. Chemnitz.
VT2.09 250	772 150	DR	A-1 DM	1968	P	Camping ground, Ifersgrun.
VT2.09 255	772 155	DR	A-1 DM	1968	MR	Wiesentalbahn, Muhltroff.
VT2.09 271	772 171	DR	A-1 DM	1968	MA	KSR. Chemnitz.
771 012	772 312	DR	A-1 DM	1963	MA	Ifersgrun.
171 032	772 332	DR	A-1 DM	1964	MA	LDC, Cottbus.
771 042	772 342	DR	A-1 DM	1964	MA	LDC, Cottbus.
771 067	772 367	DR	A-1 DM	1964	MR	Ifersgrun.
772 012	772 412	DR	A-1 DM	1965	MA	OSE. Löbau.
772 013	772 413	DR	A-1 DM	1965	MA	OSE. Löbau.
772 014	772 414	DR	A-1 DM	1965	MR	EF. Treysa.
SVT 877		DB	Part only	1932	M	DBM. Nürnberg.

▲ 217 014 stands next to Railpool RP-owned V160 002, on display as part of the "40 Jahre Vulkan-Express" celebrations at Brohl Gbf on 26 August 2017. **Matthias Müller**

APPENDIX I. BUILDERS

The following list of builder codes is not an exhaustive list of all builders of rolling stock shown in this book, but details only those builders for which an abbreviation is used.

ABB Henschel	ASEA/Brown Boveri Henschel, Kassel (to Adtranz).
Adtranz	ABB Daimler Benz Transportation, 2001 to Bombardier.
Alstom/LHB	Alstom/Linke Hofmann Busch, Salzgitter and Stendal.
AEG	Allgemeine Elektricitäts Gesellschaft Berlin-Hennigsdorf.
Bautzen	Waggon und Maschinenfabrik AG, (vorm Busch), Bautzen.
Beilhack	Martin Beilhack GmbH, Rosenheim.
Bergmann	Bergmann Elektricitäts Werke AG, Berlin.
BMAG	Berliner Maschinenfabrik AG, vormals Schwartzkopff, Berlin.
Bombardier	Bombardier Transportation. Various works but principally Kassel (locomotives), Hennigsdorf (dmu/emu).
Borsig	Borsig, Berlin Tegal.
Brown Boveri	Brown, Boveri & Cie (BBC), Mannheim. 1999 to Adtranz, 2001 to Bombardier.
Deutz	Motoren Fabrik Deutz AG Köln, later Klockner Humboldt Deutz AG.
Düewag	Düsseldorfer Waggonfabrik AG, Düsseldorf.
DWA	Deutsche Waggonbau AG works at Bautzen, Berlin, Görlitz, Halle Ammendorf, Nieksy, Vetschau. 2001 most to Bombardier.
DWM	Deutsche Waffen und Munitionsfabriken AG, Werk Posen, Poland.
Esslingen	Maschinenfabrik Esslingen, Esslingen am Neckar.
Floridsdorf	Wiener Lokomotivfabrik AG, Wien Floridsdorf, Austria.
Gmeinder	Gmeinder & Co GmbH, Mosbach, Baden.
Hanomag	Hannoversche Maschinenbau AG, Hannover-Linden.
Hartmann	Sächsiche Maschinenfabrik Rich. Hartmann AG, Chemnitz.
Henschel	Henschel & Sohn, Kassel.
Humboldt	Humboldt Lokomotivbau, Köln Kalk.
Jung	Arn.Jung Lokomotivfabrik Gmbh Jungenthal bei Kirchberg an der Sieg.
Krauss Maffei	Krauss Maffei AG München Allach, 1999 to Siemens-Krauss Maffei Lokomotiven GmbH now just Siemens.
Krupp	Friedrich Krupp AG Essen.
Karlsruhe	Maschinenbau Gesellschaft, Karlsruhe.
LEW	VEB Lokomotivbau Elektrotechnische Werke Hans Beimler, Hennigsdorf. (To Bombardier).
LHB	Linke Hofmann Busch, Salzgitter, 1994 to Alstom/LHB.
Linke Hofmann	Linke Hofmann Werke Breslau.
LKM	VEB Lokomotivbau Karl Marx, Babelberg (= O&K).
Maybach	Maybach Motorenbau Gmbh, Friedrichshafen.
MaK	Maschinenbau Kiel Gmbh, Kiel.
MAN	Maschinenfabrik Augsburg Nürnberg AG. 1999 to Adtranz.
MBA	Maschinenbau und Bahnbedarf AG, Berlin (= O&K).
MBB	Messerschmidt Bölkow Blohm GmbH, München and Donauwörth.
O&K	Orenstein & Koppel, Berlin Drewitz, Lübeck or Dortmund.
PESA	PESA Bydgoszcz S.A. Poland.
Plasser & Theurer	Plasser & Theurer, Linz Austria or Freilassing Germany.
Rathgeber	Waggonfabrik Josef Rathgeber AG, München.
SACM	Société Alsacienne de Constructions Mechaniques, France.
Schöma	Christoph Schöttler Maschinenfabrik GmbH, Diepholz.
SFT Krupp	Siemens Schienfahrzeugtechnik Krupp, Essen.
SGP	Simmering Graz Pauker, Granz and Wien, Austria.
Siemens	Siemens AG Berlin, Erlangen, Krefeld and München.
Skoda	Skoda Werke, Plzen, Czechoslovakia.
SSW	Siemens Schuckertwerke, Berlin und Erlangen.
Stadler	Stadler Fahrzeug AG, Bussnang (CH) and Berlin Pankow later Stadler Pankow GmbH.
Talbot	Waggonfabrik Talbot, Aachen (to Bombardier).
U23A	Uzinele 23 August, Bucuresti, Romania.
Uerdingen	Waggonfabrik Uerdingen AG, Krefeld, Uerdingen and Düsseldorf (now Siemens).
Voith	Voith Turbo Lokomotivetechnik GmbH & Co., Kiel.
Vulcan	Vulcan Werke, Stettin.
Wegmann	Wegmann & Co., Kassel-Rothenditmold.
Wismar	Triebwagen und Waggonfabrick AG, Wismar.
Westwaggon	Vereingte Westdeutsche Waggonfabriken AG Köln Deutz.

Wumag	Waggon und Maschinenbau AG Görlitz.
Waggon Union	Waggon Unionh, Berlin. 1996 to Adtranz, 2001 to Bombardier and later Stadler.
Windhoff	Rheiner Maschinenfabrik, Rheine, Windhoff AG Rheine.
WMD	Waggon und Maschinenbau GmbH, Donauwörth, to MBB.

APPENDIX II. VEHICLE TYPE CODES FOR RAILCARS & MULTIPLE UNITS

These are given in the European system with the British codes in parentheses.

(1) EUROPEAN SYSTEM:

A	1st Class.
B	2nd Class.
D	Luggage, i.e., vehicle with luggage space and guard's compartment.
R	Restaurant.
K	Buffet Kitchen.

Examples:

BD	Second Class with luggage/guard's compartment.
AB	Composite.

(2) BRITISH SYSTEM:

Coaching Stock codes are as used in the Platform 5 BR Pocket Books and "British railways Locomotives & Coaching Stock", e.g., F=first, S=second, C=composite, B=brake, O=open, K=side corridor with lavatory, so=semi-open.

Under 'accommodation' are shown the number of first and second class seats with tip-up seats in saloons in parentheses, followed by the number of toilets, e.g. 24/49(3) 1T indicates 24 first class seats, 49 second class seats, three additional tip-up seats and one toilet. TD indicates a toilet suitable for disabled people, W indicates a wheelchair space.

APPENDIX III. COMMON TERMS IN GERMAN AND ENGLISH

Lokomotive (Lok) – locomotive (loco).
Reisezugwagen – passenger coach.
Gleis – track.
die Fahrkarte – ticket.
Ausbesserungswerke (abbreviated to AW) – works.
Reichsbahnausbesserungswerke (abbreviated to RAW) – works (former DR).
Bahnbetriebswerke (abbreviated to Bw) – depot.
Bundesbahndirektion (abbreviated to BD) – division (DB).
Reichsbahndirektion (abbreviated to RBD) – division (former DR).
Baureihe – Class (as in "Class 110").
Speisewagen – restaurant car.
Klasse – Class (as in *Erste Klasse* – First Class).
Schlafwagen – sleeping car.
Bier – beer.
Liegewagen – couchette.
Verspätung – lateness.
Dampflok – steam loco.
Lokführer – driver.
Ellok – electric loco.
Zugführer – guard.
Diesellok – diesel loco.
Bahnsteig – platform.
Schienenbus – railbus.

Bahnhof (abbreviated to Bhf) – station.
Hauptbahnhof (abbreviated to Hbf) – main station.
Hauptguterbahnhof (abbreviated to Hgbf) – main goods depot.
Rangierbahnhof (abbreviated to Rbf) – marshalling yard.

APPENDIX IV. DB DEPOT CODES

Code	Sector	Depot name
AH1	F	Hamburg Eidelstedt including Hamburg Langenfelde.
AM	C	Maschen.
AK	R	Kiel.
ANB	F	Niebüll.
AOP	S	Hamburg Ohlsdorf.
BCS	R	Cottbus.
BFF	S	Berlin Friedrichsfelde.
BGA	S	Berlin Grunau.
BLO	R	Berlin Lichtenberg.
BOR	S	Oranienburg.
BRG	F	Berlin Rummelsburg.
BSE	C	Seddin.
BSN	C	Senftenberg.
BWS	S	Berlin Wannsee.
DA	R	Dresden Altstadt.
DBN	N	DB Netze (Netz/Fahrweg).
DC	R	Chemnitz Hbf.
DCX (Z)		Chemnitz Works.
DNDR (Z)		Niederau (storage site).
EDEF	N	Duisburg Wedau Entenfang.
EDO	R	Dortmund.
EE	R	Essen.
EHGV	C	Hagen Vorhalle.
EHM	N	Hamm.
EHM (Z)		Hamm (Storage site in yards).
EMST	R	Münster (Westf).
EOB	C	Oberhausen Osterfeld Süd.
FB	C	Bebra.
FF	S	Frankfurt/M Hbf.
FFU	N	Fulda.
FGM	F, R	Frankfurt/M Griesheim (two depots at same site).
FK	R	Kassel.
FL	R	Limburg.
FMB	C	Mainz Bischofsheim.
FSK	R	Schöllkrippen (Depot for Aschaffenburg).
HBH	C	Bremerhaven.
HBS	R	Braunschweig.
HE	C	Emden.
HHL	R	Hannover Leinhausen.
HO	C	Osnabrück.
HS	C	Seelze.
HWG	F	Wangerooge.
KA	R	Aachen Hbf.
KD	R	Düsseldorf Abstellbahnhof.
KG	C	Gremberg.
KK2	R	Köln Deutzerfeld.
KKN	F, S	Köln Nippes (Two separate depots).
LDLX		Delitzsch Works.
LH1	C	Halle G.
LH2	R	Halle P.
LHAD		Ammendorf Works (Private).
LL		Leipzig.
LMB	R	Magdeburg Buckau.
LMR	C	Magdeburg Rothensee.
MAOB	N	Augsburg Oberhausen.
MH1	F, R	München Hbf Süd (F), München Hbf West (R) (depots side by side).
MH2	R	München Pasing.
MH6	S	München Steinhausen.
MKP	R	Kempten.
MMF	R	Mühldorf.
MN	C	München Nord.
MTL (Z)		Treuchtlingen (Storage site).
NHO	R	Hof.
NN1	R	Nürnberg West.
NN2	C	Nürnberg Rbf.
NWH	R	Würzburg.
RF	R	Freiburg.
RHL	R	Haltingen.
RK	N	Karlsruhe.
RL	R	Ludwigshafen.
RM	C	Mannheim.
RO	C	Offenburg.
SKL	R	Kaiserslautern.
SSR	C	Saarbrücken Rbf.
STMI	N	System Technik Minden.
STMU	N	System Technik München.
STR	R	Trier.
TK	C	Kornwestheim.
TP	S	Plochingen.
TS	R	Stuttgart.
TT	R	Tübingen.
TU	R	Ulm.
UE	R	Erfurt.
UKF (Z)		Karsdorf (Storage site).
UMX		Meiningen Works.
.WHF	R	Heringsdorf.
WM (Z)		Mukran (Storage site).
WN	R	Neubrandenburg.
WR	R	Rostock Hbf.
WRS	C	Rostock Seehafen.

DBN: DB Netze includes DB Netz and DB Fahrweg. Some locomotives are shown with a particular depot but all are controlled nationally and maintained at any suitable depot when maintenance is due.

Stored locos are denoted by (Z) after the depot code. Z= *Zurückgestellt* ("put back"). There are now four major storage sites that are not depots; Hamm, Karsdorf, Mukran and Niederau are places where DB has stored a large number of locomotives, railcars and carriages pending sale or scrapping.

SECTOR CODES

C	DB Cargo.
F	DB Fernverkehr.
N	DB Netze.
R	DB Regio.
S	S-Bahn (Berlin, Frankfurt/Main, Hamburg, München, Stuttgart).

APPENDIX V. ABBREVIATIONS

AKW	Atom Kraftwerk.
AMTF	Association des Musées et Tourisme Ferroviaires.
AW	Ausbesserungwerk.
BEF	Berliner Eisenbahnfreunde.
BEM	Bayerische Eisenbahn Museum.
BLME	Braunschweigische Landes Museums Eisenbahn.
BLV	Bayerische Lokalbahn Verein.
Bww	Bahnbetriebeswagenwerke (wagon shop).
CD	České Dráhy (Czech Railways).
CFL	Chemins de Fer Luxembourgois (Luxembourg Railways).
CFV3V	Chemen de Fer Vapeur Trois Vallées.
CIR ELKE	Computerised Integrated Railroading – Erhöhung der Leistungsfähigkeit im Kernnetz.
DB	Deutsche Bundesbahn (former German Federal Railway) or Deutsche Bahn AG.
DBB	Draisinenbahn Berlin Brandenburg.
DBG	Dampfzug Betriebsgemeinschaft.
DBK	Damfbahn Kochertal.
DBM	DB Museum.
DDM	Deutsches Dampflok Museum.
DEV	Deutsche Eisenbahn Verein.
DEW	Dampf Eisenbahn Weserbergland.
DFS	Dampfbahn Fränkische Schweiz.
DGEG	Deutsche Gesellschaft für Eisenbahn Gesichte.
DKM	Dampf Kleinbahn Mühlenstroth.
DL	Dampflokfreunde (Berlin).
DME	Deutsche Museums Eisenbahn.
DR	Deutsche Reichsbahn (former East German State Railway).
DRG	Deutsche Reichsbahn Gesellschaft (German Railway Company - pre 1945).
DRM	Dampfbahn Rhein Main = Frankfurter Feldbahnmuseum.
DTM	Deutsches Technik Museum.
EBULA	Elektronischer Buchfahrplan & Langsamfahranweisung (Computer display of timetable and speed restrictions).
EF	Eisenbahn Freunde.
EFB	Eisenbahn Freunde Betzdorf (now dissolved).
EFZ	Eisenbahn Freunde Zollernbahn.
EHEH	Eisenbahn und Heimat Museum Erkrath – Hochdahl.
ET	Eisenbahn Tradition.
ETB	Eisenbahnfreunde Traditionsbahnbetriebswerk Stassfurt.
ETCS	European Train Control System.
ETM	Eisenbahn Technik Museum.
EVB	Eisenbahn und Verkehrs Betriebe Elbe-Weser Gmbh, Zeven.
EVG	Eifelbahn Verkehrs GmbH.
FME	Fränkische Museums Eisenbahn.
FS	Ferrovie dello Stato (Italian Railways).
GES	Gesellschaft zur Erhaltung von Schienenfahrzeuge e.V.
GPS	Global Positioning Satellite System.
GSM-R	Global System for Mobile Communications – Rail.
HE	Historische Eisenbahn.
HEM	Historische Eisenbahn Mannheim.
HSB	Harzer Schmalspur Bahn.
HWB	Hochwaldbahn.
IG	Interessengemeinschaft.

IGN	IG Nebenbahn Kassel.
INDUSI	Inductive Zugsicherung – signalling warning system.
KBE	Köln Bonner Eisenbahn.
KSR	Köstner Scienenbus Reisen, Chemnitz.
KWS	Konventionelle Wendezeusteuerung. (Original DB push-pull system – pre TDM).
LDC	Lausitzer Dampflok Club.
LTA	landesmuseum für Technik und Arbeit.
LZB	Linienzugbeeinflussung (cab signalling).
MBS	Museum Buurt Spoorweg.
MEC	Modell Eisenbahn Club.
MEG	Mitteldeutsche Eisenbahn Gesellschaft.
MEM	Museums Eisenbahn Minden.
MKO	Museumseisenbahn Küstenbahn Ostfriesland e.V. Norden.
MME	Märkische Museums Eisenbahn.
MRU	Museumseisenbahn Rahden – Uchte e.V.
NBS	Neubaustrecke (newly built line – in effect high speed lines).
NS	Nederlandse Spoorwegen (Dutch Railways).
NVR	Nene Valley Railway.
ÖBB	Österreichische Bundesbahnen (Austrian Federal Railways).
OEF	Oberhessiche Eisenbahnfreunde, Giessen.
ÖGEG	Österreichische Gesellschaft für Eisenbahngesichte.
OHLE	Overhead Line Equipment.
OSE	Ostsächsische Eisenbahnfreunde.
PRESS	Eisenbahn-Bau- und Betriebsgesellschaft Pressnitztalbahn mbH.
PZB	Punktförmige Zugbeeinflussung.
RBH	RBH Logistics GmbH.
RSB	Rennsteigbahn.
SBB	Schweizerische Bundesbahnen (Swiss Federal Railways).
SHE	Süddeutsche Eisenbahn Museum Heilbronn.
SEM	Sächsische Eisenbahn Museum.
SIFA	Sicherheitsfahrschalung (deadman's pedal).
SFW	Schienen Fahrzeuge Werk.
SNCB	Société Nationale des Chemins de Fer Belges (Belgian National Railways).
SNCF	Société Nationale des Chemins de Fer Français (French National Railways).
SSN	Stoom Stichting Nederlandse.
ST	Systems Technik.
STAR	Stadskanaal Rail.
SZ	Slovenske Železnice (Slovenian Railways).
TDM	Time Division Multiplex.
ThEV	Thüringer Eisenbahn Verein.
TM	Technik Museum.
UEF	Ulmer Eisenbahn Freunde.
VBV	Verein Braunschweiger Verkehrsfreunde.
VEB	Vulcan Eifel Bahn.
VMD	Verkehrs Museum Dresden.
VSE	Verein Sächsische Eisenbahnfreunde.
VSM	Veluwse Stoomtrein Maatschappij.
VSSB	Verin zur Förderung Sächsische Schmalspurbahnen.
VVM	Verein Verkehrsamateure und Museumseisenbahn.
WEMEG	West Mecklenburgische Eisenbahn Gesellschaft.
WFL	Wedler Franz Logistik GmbH & Co KG.
WL	Werklok.
WTB	Wuchtachtalbahn.
ZBF	Zugbahnfunk (train radio).
ZHL	Zahnradbahn Honau – Lichtenstein e.V.
ZLSM	Zuid Limburgse Stoomtrein Maatschappij.
ZWS	Zeitmultiplexe Wendezugsteuerung (time division multiplex push-pull control).